Political Islam

Political Islam

Essays from Middle East Report

EDITED BY
Joel Beinin and Joe Stork

Published in cooperation with
Middle East Research and Information Project

UNIVERSITY OF CALIFORNIA PRESS
Berkeley   Los Angeles

University of California Press
Berkeley and Los Angeles, California

Middle East Report is published by the
Middle East Research and Information Project
Suite 119, 1500 Massachusetts Avenue NW
Washington, DC 20005
Phone (202) 223-3677
Fax (202) 223-3604
E-mail merip@igc.apc.org

The following chapters of this book were published in earlier versions in *Middle East Report*:
chap. 3 (*MER* 183); chap. 4 (*MER* 179); chap. 5 (*MER* 183); chap. 6 (*MER* 183); chap. 7 (*MER*
183); chap. 9 (*MER* 153); chap. 14 (*MER* 172); chap. 16 (*MER* 173); chap. 17 (*MER* 164/5);
chap. 18 (*MER* 192); chap. 19 (*MER* 190); chap. 22 (*MER* 178); chap. 23 (*MER* 180); chap.
24 (*MER* 179); chap. 27 (*MER* 198); chap. 28 (*MER* 185); chap. 29 (*MER* 189); chap. 31 (*MER*
133); chap. 32 (*MER* 153).
Chapter 11 is translated from "Hezbollah: La nébuleuse," *Arabies* (Dec. 1992). Reprinted by
permission of *Arabies*.
Chapter 20 was published in an earlier version in *Review of African Political Economy* 54 (1992):
27–41. Reprinted by permission of ROAPE Publications Ltd.
Part of chapter 23 is adapted from "Finding a Place for Islam: Egyptian Television and the
National Interest," *Public Culture* 5, No. 3: 493–513. Reprinted by permission of the University
of Chicago Press.
Chapter 30 was published in an earlier version in *Race & Class* 37, no. 2: 65–80. Reprinted by
permission of the Institute of Race Relations.

Library of Congress Cataloging-in-Publication Data

Political Islam : Essays from *Middle East Report* / edited by Joel Beinin and Joe Stork.
   p.   cm.
   Includes bibliographic references (p.   ) and index.
   ISBN 0-520-20447-6 (alk. paper). — ISBN 0-520-20448-4 (pbk.: alk. paper)
   1. Islam and politics—Middle East. 2. Islam and politics—Africa, North. 3. Middle
East—Politics and government.—4. Africa, North—Politics and government.—I. Beinin,
Joel, 1948– . II. Stork, Joe. III. *Middle East Report.*
BP63.A4M5368 1997
322'.1'0956—dc20   95-39810

Manufactured in the United States of America

08   07   06   05   04   03   02
9 8 7 6 5 4 3

CONTENTS

ACKNOWLEDGMENTS

This book is a product of the long-standing collaborative effort known as MERIP (Middle East Research and Information Project) that has given both of us enormous satisfaction and sustenance over many years. First and foremost we owe our thanks to the authors who have contributed their work to these pages. Many of them have been Editors and Contributing Editors of *Middle East Report* or members of the Board of Directors of MERIP. The section introductions have been written by current or past editors of *Middle East Report*. Editors and Contributing Editors commented on drafts of the introduction and offered advice on various aspects of this project from its inception. This book could only have materialized through the combined efforts of all those who have been part of MERIP. We place a high value on the personal and political bonds and collective work of the editors and members of the board who provided the inspiration, intellectual engagement, and editorial dialogue that made it possible.

The intellectual production and political vision that comprise this book in the first instance have taken material form thanks to the skilled and dedicated work of the MERIP staff. Assistant Editors Maggy Zanger and Geoff Hartman, Publisher Peg Hutchison, Associate Publisher Esther Merves, and Administrative Assistants Ann Schaub and Kim Kahlhamer comprised this staff while this book was being produced. We would also like to give special mention to Martha Wenger and Michaelle Browers, who worked as Assistant Editor and Administrative Assistant respectively when much of the material presented here was first produced in magazine format. Several *Middle East Report* editors—Bruce Dunne, Ellen Fleischmann, Lisa Hajjar, and Barbara Harlow—assisted with the task of proofreading the manuscripts.

MERIP interns Mentwab Muhib, Deevy Holcomb, Leena Khan, Peter Ogram, and Laura Abrahams provided invaluable assistance with the important tasks of inputting text changes requested by the authors or by ourselves, proofreading the texts, and coordinating communications between ourselves and the authors.

Finally, we would like to thank Salim Nasr and Salim Tamari who, from Cairo and Ramallah respectively, urged us to make available in book form for classroom use some of the best of what has appeared in *Middle East Report*. And we thank our own companions and children—and those of our contributors—who supported and tolerated the attentions given to this book instead of to them.

Introduction

1

On the Modernity, Historical Specificity, and International Context of Political Islam

Joel Beinin and Joe Stork

Let us begin with the matter of terminology. Why is this book entitled "Political Islam" and not "Islamic fundamentalism"? Certainly the phenomena and processes examined here can be and have been meaningfully compared to politically activist, socially conservative movements mobilized by revivalist Christian, Jewish, and Hindu identities.[1] Nonetheless, "fundamentalism" is a problematic comparative term. It is inescapably rooted in a specific Protestant experience whose principal theological premise is that the Bible is the true word of God and should be understood literally. In this regard, it makes no sense to speak of fundamentalist Islam because one of the core elements of the creed of all believing Muslims is that the Qur'an is the literal (hence absolutely true) word of God as revealed to his Prophet Muhammad through the intermediacy of the angel Gabriel. The Islamic tradition has been very concerned with how Muslims should understand the Qur'an—which passages can be understood literally and which are so complex that they require allegorical or other forms of interpretation. But the divine origin of the text has never been a topic of legitimate debate.

There is another, more important, sense in which the term "fundamentalism" is inappropriate. "Fundamentalism" suggests the restoration of a pure, unsullied, and authentic form of the religion, cleansed of historical accretions, distortions, and modernist deviations. This is indeed how many Islamist leaders and ideologues present their ideas and the movements they lead. But it is a substantial error to conceptualize these movements as restoring an "original" form of Islam. Rather, they seek to revitalize and re-Islamize modern Muslim societies.

We term the movements examined in this volume "political Islam" because we regard their core concerns as temporal and political. They use

3

the Qur'an, the *hadiths* (reports about the words and deeds of Muhammad and his companions), and other canonical religious texts to justify their stances and actions. And they do so in all sincerity. But as many contributors to this volume suggest (especially the chapters of Sami Zubaida and Gudrun Krämer), today's Islamist thinkers and activists are creatively deploying selected elements of the Islamic tradition, combined with ideas, techniques, institutions, and commodities of the present and recent past, to cope with specifically modern predicaments: political, social, economic, and cultural issues that emerged in the Middle East as a result of the expansion of the world capitalist market, the colonization of important areas of the region by England and France, the formation of new territorial nation-states, the rise and decline of secular nationalist movements, the frustrations and failures of economic development, the reformation of gender relations, and the hybridization of culture and identity in the course of the wide range of contacts and interactions among Europeans and their cultures and the peoples of the Middle East.

Concepts like "Islamic republic" (in Iran), or the belief that post-1952 Egypt is a society of pre-Islamic ignorance (*jahiliyya*), simultaneously critique and accept the institution of the modern national state. And as Karen Pfeifer makes clear, variant forms of Islamic economics do not oppose the technology of modern capitalism. Islamists do not uncritically reject modernity; they are trying to reformulate it and regulate it, using the discursive terms of the Islamic heritage.

Many of the solutions political Islam offers have no specific historical precedent in Islamic tradition. The organizational and mobilizational forms of political Islam—high-speed international communications using faxes, cassette tapes, and posters—rely on modern technology. Specific movements are often funded by businesspeople or regimes whose wealth depends on petroleum markets and other international circuits of capital. Women activists in Islamist movements respond and offer an alternative to an egalitarian model of gender relations perceived as specifically Western.

Islamist movements have posed sharp challenges to postcolonial, nationalist regimes—in Algeria (see the chapters of Meriem Vergès and Susan Slyomovics), Egypt (see the chapters of Alexander Flores and Carrie Rosefsky Wickham and the interviews with Tal 'at Fu'ad Qasim and Nasr Hamid Abu Zayd), Tunisia (see François Burgat's interview with Hamid al-Nayfar), Sudan (see the chapters of Khalid Medani and Sondra Hale), Turkey (see the chapter of Ronnie Margulies and Ergin Yıldızoğlu), and Iran (see the chapter of Sami Zubaida). But by and large they accept the territorial and political framework of the existing states and their economic foundations, which have been shaped by the legacy of European interests in the Middle East.

THE SALAFIYYA ORIENTATION

The current upsurge of political Islam, which can be said to date from the early 1970s, is not the first Islamic movement to emerge in the modern era. Historians of the modern Middle East have established a widely known canon of leaders and influential texts.[2] This narrative, though misleadingly simple, usefully summarizes essential historical information, and we begin with it to lay the foundation for more complex alternatives.

In the Sunni tradition—the affiliation of the majority of Muslims who accept the legitimacy of the historical succession of the Caliphs who exercised political and military leadership of the Muslim community (*umma*) after the death of the Prophet Muhammad—the conventional genealogy of modern Islamic thought begins with Sayyid Jamal al-Din al-Afghani (1839–97). Sayyid Jamal al-Din was most likely a Shi'a, but presented himself as a Sunni.[3] His political career included activity in Egypt, Iran, and the Ottoman capital of Istanbul. The common theme linking his diverse activities was the need for all Muslims to unite to confront European, especially British, imperialism.

Muhammad 'Abduh (1849–1905) was a young associate of Sayyid Jamal al-Din in Egypt during the 1870s and 1880s. They spoke out against the foreign economic and political domination of Egypt that culminated in the British invasion and occupation in 1882. Exiled in Paris, they published a pan-Islamic journal (*Al-'Urwa al-Wuthqa*, The firmest link). When 'Abduh returned to Egypt, he partially reconciled himself to the British occupation and, with the approval of the British Consul General, Lord Cromer, eventually became chief *mufti* (jurisconsult) of Egypt. 'Abduh occupied himself with reforming the teaching of Arabic and the understanding of Islam, arguing that a proper understanding and implementation of the moral and ethical principles of Islam were compatible with the adoption of modern science and technology (noting, of course, that Muslims had inherited and developed Greek philosophy and science before transmitting it to the Western European Christians). 'Abduh argued that the early Muslims, the *salaf* (ancestors), practiced a pure and more correct form of Islam unsullied by medieval accretions and superstitions perpetuated by ignorance and unconsidered imitation.

Rashid Rida (1865–1935), who came to Egypt from Tripoli, Lebanon, was Muhammad 'Abduh's most influential student. He wrote a biography of 'Abduh, compiled the writings of his teacher, and publicized a conservative interpretation of 'Abduh's doctrine. Using the magazine *Al-Manar* (The lighthouse) as his mouthpiece, Rida promoted the *salafiyya* movement—a neotraditionalist orientation that restricted what was to be regarded as "correct" in Islam to the Qur'an and the *hadith* reports of the period of Muhammad's life and the reign of the first four "rightly guided" Caliphs in the Sunni tradition: Abu Bakr, 'Umar, 'Uthman, and 'Ali.

The *salafiyya* movement influenced many *'ulama'* (Muslim scholars) in the Sunni Arab world. It was a factor in the formation of the Association of Algerian 'Ulama' in 1931, an Islamist current that was largely absorbed into the National Liberation Front (FLN) and later became a source of inspiration for the Islamist opposition to the Algerian regime in the 1980s (see the chapter of Meriem Vergès and the interview with Rabia Bekkar). *Salafiyya* ideas also influenced the thinking of 'Izz al-Din al-Qassam, a Muslim religious functionary in Haifa who organized a short-lived Palestinian guerrilla movement against the British and the Zionists in 1935. The military units of Hamas (Harakat al-Muqawama al-Islamiyya), the 'Izz al-Din al-Qassam Brigades, are named after him (see Graham Usher's chapter and interview with Bassam Jarrar).

Hasan al-Banna (1906–49), an Egyptian schoolteacher working in Isma-'iliyya, the headquarters of the Suez Canal Company and a highly Europe-anized site, was one of those influenced by Rashid Rida and *Al-Manar*. In 1928 he established the Society of Muslim Brothers (Jam'iyyat al-Ikhwan al-Muslimin), which became the largest and most influential Islamist organization in the Sunni Arab world. After emerging as an important factor in Egyptian politics in the late 1930s, the Muslim Brothers established branches in Syria, Palestine, Jordan, and Sudan. As Hamid al-Nayfar explains in his interview, the Muslim Brothers were also a negative example for the Islamic Tendency Movement in Tunisia.

Many of the radical Islamist movements of the 1970s are inspired by the thinking of Sayyid Qutb, a Muslim Brother leader executed for allegedly planning to overthrow the Egyptian government in 1966. Qutb had argued that the regime of Gamal 'Abd al-Nasir, since it had tortured and imprisoned pious Muslims, was not a Muslim state but a regime of pre-Islamic ignorance (*jahiliyya*). Hence, it was legitimate to launch a *jihad* against such a regime.[4]

The Shi'a tradition—the minority orientation which regards the Prophet's cousin, 'Ali, as the first legitimate Caliph and believes that succession to the leadership of the Muslim community should have been confined to members of Muhammad's family—has an entirely different genealogy. It is geographically centered in Iran and southern Iraq, where the Shi'a form the large majority of Muslims. An important political focus of much of modern Shi'i thought is the struggle of the *'ulama'* (or *mullahs* in Persian) to assert the primacy of their authority against the Qajar and Pahlavi monarchies of Iran.

ISLAM AND MODERN POLITICS

The conventional narrative of the origins of modern Islamic thought easily lends itself to the erroneous thesis that political Islam is the result of the failure of modern Muslims to assimilate European liberal ideas such as the separation of church and state, the rule of positive law, citizenship, and secular nationalism.[5] In discussing political Islam, we must move beyond the explication of texts and the biographies of intellectual figures to examine the local circumstances and historical particularities of each movement, which often turn out to be more substantial than a simple conception of "Islam" in opposition to secular politics.

Al-Afghani's activities, for instance, contributed to the nationalist movements in both Shi'i Iran and Sunni Egypt. Muhammad 'Abduh was a religious reformer, a friend of Lord Cromer, and also the intellectual inspiration of many of the secular liberal Egyptian nationalists of the late nineteenth and early twentieth centuries. His circle included the leading secularist, Ahmad Lutfi al-Sayyid, the future leader of the Wafd, Sa'd Zaghlul, and the early proponent of women's rights, Qasim Amin. 'Abduh may actually have written part of Amin's widely discussed book, *The Liberation of Women*.[6] Rashid Rida's arguments for dismantling the Ottoman Empire—a regime headed by a sultan who also claimed to be the Sunni Caliph—on the grounds that it was despotic, contributed to the development of Arab nationalism.

The Muslim Brothers were among the first political groups to popularize the cause of Arab Palestine in Egypt, collecting financial contributions for the 1936–39 Arab Revolt and sending volunteers to fight in 1948. The Brothers also participated in the guerrilla attacks against the British base on the Suez Canal in 1951–52, an important component of the upsurge of the nationalist movement that ended the Egyptian monarchy. They were an early ally of Gamal 'Abd al-Nasir and the Free Officers, who came to power on July 23, 1952, but they later fell out with the new military regime. Many varieties of Arab nationalism in the 1956–67 era—Nasirism, the Ba'th, the Algerian FLN—easily appropriated Islamic themes and symbols into a predominantly secular ideological orientation.

There are certainly links among the various components of the Islamist movement. The Iranian religious opposition to the Pahlavi regime and the revolution of 1979 inspired and promoted a network of Shi'a activism, including Amal and Hizb Allah in Lebanon (see the chapters of Salim Nasr and Assaf Kfoury), elements of the Iraqi opposition to the Ba 'thist regime, and movements among the Shi 'a minorities in the Persian-Arab Gulf states. The success of the Iranian revolution inspired other political Islamist tendencies, including many Sunni groups. As noted earlier, the Muslim Brothers and the several Islamic groups (Gama'at Islamiyya) that emerged as their radical opposition in Egypt are organizationally and intellectually linked to movements in Algeria, Palestine (see Graham Usher's chapter), and Syria. Hamas was not only the Gaza branch of the Muslim Brothers; it was also promoted by Israel as an alternative to the PLO, which it subsequently emerged to challenge (see the chapters of Rema Hammami and Graham Usher and the interview with Bassam Jarrar).

All these movements draw strength from the widespread deficiencies of the postcolonial states in the Middle East: massive corruption, overreliance on coercion, and the failure of Arab socialism in Egypt, Syria, Iraq, and Algeria—and a comparable form of state-led development in Turkey—to produce sustained economic development (see Karen Pfeifer's chapter on Islamic economics). These failures have coincided with the collapse of various secularist, nationalist, and leftist political projects, leaving the field of opposition politics more or less open to Islamists.

PETRO-ISLAM?

The Islamist movement since the 1970s has been the object of investigation by many analysts who view it as either a politico-military-strategic threat or a civilizational conflict (see Yahya Sadowski's chapter). The interpretation offered in this book rejects the thesis of "petro-Islam"—a comprehensive explanation for the movement advanced by the neoconservative, pro-Israel "policy intellectual" Daniel Pipes in the US media and by the Egyptian progressive secularist Fu'ad Zakariyya in the Arab world, among many others.[7] According to this thesis, the defeat of secular Arab nationalism (Ba'thism in Syria and Nasirism in Egypt) in the Arab-Israeli war of 1967 strengthened the cultural and political weight of Saudi Arabia in the Middle East, especially after the sharp rise in oil prices following the 1973 Arab-Israeli war. The Saudis and/or Egyptians working in Saudi Arabia used their financial resources to fund the Muslim Brothers and other Islamist groups, who emerged as opponents of the regime of Anwar al-Sadat in Egypt: the first site of an important political opposition to a secular nationalist state and its ideology in the name of Islam in the post-1967 Arab world, followed shortly by Iran.

While superficially attractive in accounting for a certain historical conjuncture, this explanation is flawed because of the very partial set of factors it includes in its account. The Egyptian version of Fu'ad Zakariyya suggests that the source of a "backward" form of Islam is the culturally underdeveloped but materially rich Arabian Peninsula, which has been able to impose its values on "civilized" but materially poor Egypt. This approach ignores the prior history of political Islam in Egypt, where the Muslim Brothers clashed violently with the regime in 1948–49 and again in 1954, when they attempted to assassinate Gamal 'Abd al-Nasir.

As Richard P. Mitchell's classic study established,[8] the Brothers had a substantial popular base in the 1940s and 1950s. Their activists were largely educated, urban effendis—the same social stratum that provided the main body of organizers and activists for all the political movements of twentieth-century Egypt. The Nasir regime put an end to formal political democracy and sharply constricted the space of civil society by incorporating trade unions and professional associations into the apparatus of the state, heavily regulating other voluntary organizations, and banning all political parties except that of the regime. This was accompanied by a significant degree of repression directed primarily against the Marxists, but also against the regime's former allies, the Muslim Brothers.

In 1966, when Sayyid Qutb was "martyred" (in the terminology of the Islamist movement), Egypt was facing an economic crisis because of inability to increase simultaneously both investment (hence, long-term industrial and social development) and consumption (an important source of the regime's popular legitimacy). The 1967 war with Israel and its effects intensified the economic crisis and the repressive measures of the regime. It also created an opportunity for Islamist activists to argue that "the Jews" had won the war because they combined their religion and politics in the form of the State of Israel, whereas the Muslims had lost because of the secularism of 'Abd al-Nasir and the Ba'th. 'Abd al-Nasir died before he had to face the full consequences of the limits of his regime. His successor, Anwar al-Sadat, quickly moved to dismantle major elements of the Nasirist system and recruited Muslim Brothers and student Islamist activists in the battle against the remaining Nasirists and leftists who opposed him. Only after al-Sadat's autocratic tendencies were clearly manifested, the promises of economic prosperity failed to materialize, and the peace treaty with Israel was signed did the Islamist movement break with the Egyptian regime.

Khalid Medani's chapter on Sudan underlines the importance of specific trajectories of capital to the growth of that country's Islamic movement and the Islamist regime installed there in June 1989. Islamic movements in Algeria, Egypt, and Iran have also been associated with local mercantile and financial interests that have avoided the control of the state and established their own links to international capital. The Egyptian and Jordanian movements have benefited from the remittances of workers employed in the oil-producing states. These funding links certainly played a role in the regional success of political Islam.

Yet Islamic movements have demonstrated a high level of autonomy from their original patrons. Following the debt crisis of the 1980s, the decline of the price of oil, and the IMF-imposed economic restructuring projects that limited state expenditures, the efficacy of states has tended to become restricted to urban middle-class areas. States are unable to provide previously established levels of services or to insure adequate supplies of commodities to all sectors of their territory and population. The political and moral vacuum thus created has been occupied by the Islamists, who have established a social base by offering services that the various states have failed to provide (see the chapters of Carrie Rosefsky Wickham, Ronnie

Margulies and Ergin Yıldızoğlu, and Meriem Vergès). The mass support for political Islam throughout the Middle East is more substantial and sustained than would be possible if it had simply been bought by oil money. And it gained strength as a result of the combined failure and repression of liberal and left secular alternatives.

The case for "petro-Islam" in Iran is even weaker. Political activism of the Shi'a *mullahs* has been an integral part of modern Iranian politics since the Tobacco Protest of 1890–92 and the Constitutional movement of 1906–11. Despite this history of activism, the political positions of the *mullahs* have not been unified: some supported, and others opposed, adopting a constitution based on positive law, for example. Some of the Shi'a clerical hierarchy resisted the removal of the nationalist Mossadeq government and the restoration of Muhammad Reza Shah by a CIA-sponsored coup in 1953; others accepted funds from the United States to mobilize opposition to Mossadeq.[9] The regime of the Shah, a major regional ally of the United States with important links to Israel, benefited enormously from the explosion of oil prices in 1973–77. Widespread popular perceptions of governmental corruption, economic discontent resulting from oil boom-caused inflation, and a perceived relaxation of the regime's repressive apparatus after US President Jimmy Carter announced he would pursue a foreign policy of promoting "human rights" created an opening for the political activity that grew into a revolutionary movement.

The early stages of this movement were initiated by secular liberals, with the participation of Marxists and feminists. Only after January 1978 did Ayatollah Khomeini, who established a reputation of militant resistance to the Pahlavi regime as early as 1963, emerge as the titular leader of the revolutionary movement. After Khomeini returned to Iran in February 1979, pro-Khomeini clericalists fought a complex battle against secular political forces and religious forces with a different orientation. The local issues that generated support for the revolutionary movement may have had little to do with Islam, although Shi 'i ritual provided an important symbolic language and public space for staging the opposition to the Shah. And as Sami Zubaida suggests, the contest over what constitutes an "Islamic state" in Iran has produced some surprising outcomes.

POLITICAL ISLAM AND UNITED STATES POLICY

The most visible and prominent Islamist movements today are insurgent movements that represent challenges to existing regimes and to a political order that by and large has served Western interests well. This insurgent character, not their Islamic demeanor, underlies the generally adversarial relations between the United States and these movements. In one case, that of Iran, such a movement has seized and consolidated state power. Iran's revolution in 1979 marks the beginning of widespread American perceptions of an "Islamic threat." Subsequent developments elsewhere, most potently the kidnappings of Westerners in Lebanon in the mid-1980s, the targeting of Western tourists in Egypt in the early 1990s, and the rise of Palestinian Islamist groups resisting Israeli occupation in the 1990s, have sustained and amplified these perceptions of threat.

US policy spokespersons have recently taken great pains to stress that the United States has no inherent differences with Islam, or even with regimes that identify themselves as Islamic.[10] This is to a large extent true. US policy toward Islamists has been basically instrumentalist. The professedly Islamic regimes of Saudi Arabia and Pakistan have been key strategic allies of the United States in the Middle East, and Sudan's Islamist military regime moved decisively into the adversary column only after shifting from the Saudi to the Iranian orbit. Some American policy makers assert, in fact, that the United States does not oppose Islamists, only extremists.

From 1980 to 1989 in Afghanistan, though, the largest CIA covert aid program in US history financed and armed the most extreme of the *mujahidin* groups fighting the Afghan communist regime in Kabul and the Soviet interventionary force that tried to save it. This US support has been a factor of major importance in the growth and military capabilities of militant Islamist forces in Egypt and elsewhere[11] (see the interview with Tal'at Fu'ad Qasim).

Saudi funding for Islamist groups and institutions going back to the mid-1960s was benignly observed from Washington because such assistance worked against radical nationalism—the Ba'th in Syria and 'Abd al-Nasir in Egypt—and supported conservative figures like King Husayn in Jordan. Similarly, there was no hint of any US reproach in the 1970s when the Egyptian government of Anwar al-Sadat, then on its way to becoming the second largest recipient (after Israel) of US economic and military aid, encouraged the Muslim Brothers and its radical offshoots to organize against nationalists and leftists. French scholar Olivier Roy writes, with only a little exaggeration, that "[t]he notion of a radical opposition between fundamentalism and the West is typically French. . . . Americans have never seen Islamism as an ideological enemy. They have favored neoconservative fundamentalism . . . in order to take the wind out of the radicals' sails."[12]

The Iranian revolution marked the end of a phase of "benign neglect" on the part of the United States and its allies in the region. But even US hostility toward Islamist Iran has been tempered by instrumentalism, particularly in the service of the American *jihad* against Soviet communism. The multibillion dollar campaign in support of militant Islam in Afghanistan was more of a pattern than an exception. In 1983, for instance, the CIA passed to the Khomeini regime an extensive list of Iranian communists and leftists working in the Iranian government. As the official Tower Commission inquiry into the Iran-contra scandal dispassionately observed, "Using this information, the Khomeini government took measures, including mass executions, that virtually eliminated the pro-Soviet infrastructure in Iran."[13] Two years later, backing Iraq in its war against Iran but fearing that a collapse of the Iranian regime might benefit the Soviet Union, the Reagan administration teamed up with Israel to initiate the arms shipments that became the Iran-contra affair.

Iran's revolution marked a watershed in the evolution of American attitudes and policy toward political Islam for several reasons. First, it demolished the main US regional ally and military surrogate in the Persian Gulf. Coming only four years after the US defeat in Indochina, and after a series of apparently successful revolutions and national liberation struggles in Ethiopia, Angola, Mozambique, and elsewhere, Iran's revolution seemed to mark a decisive decline of American power. The US role in restoring the Shah to power in 1953 and sustaining his regime, moreover, infused the revolution from the beginning with a fiercely anti-American character. A polarization of popular as well as elite attitudes in both countries occurred with the November 1979 takeover of the US embassy (following Washington's decision to allow the Shah to enter the United States). President Jimmy Carter's public dismissal of the events of 1953 as "ancient history" captured this polarization on the American side.[14]

Second, events in Iran were followed by several deeply disturbing indications, from an American elite point of view, that Iran's revolution might not be contained within its borders. One was the November 1979 takeover of the grand mosque in Mecca by a group of radical Islamist opponents of the Saudi regime; that rebellion had to be put down with the help of Jordanian and French military advisors. The second was the Soviet military intervention in Afghanistan beginning in December 1979, which exacerbated an American and Western sense of vulnerability in the Persian Gulf region. A third development was the October 1981 assassination of Anwar al-Sadat by Islamist Egyptian army officers.

The third complex reason relates to overlapping perceptions of Cold War vulnerability and rivalry. Although the disruption of oil markets caused by the Iranian revolution was relatively brief, it was popularly associated with the oil embargo triggered by the October 1973 Arab-Israeli war and the enormous increase in oil prices that accompanied the embargo. That Iran was not an Arab country mattered little: it was a Muslim Middle Eastern country that had visibly profited from the increase in oil revenues. These perceptions were further complicated by the campaign of conservative American political forces to scuttle detente with the Soviet Union and increase US military spending. Part of this campaign involved portraying the United States and its one reliable ally in the region, Israel, as beset by an Arab-Soviet axis, the Arab component threatening Israel and gouging the wallets of ordinary Americans while the Soviet Union exploited detente to expand its global power.[15]

Iran's revolution unfolded within this perceptual framework. Seeing Iran in Cold War terms suited the agenda of the American right. The Islamic Revolution inserted a Muslim dimension into this familiar adversarial paradigm. This Muslim aspect, of course, came encumbered with its own perceptual freight: the European history of Christian-Muslim rivalry; the profile of American Black Muslim militancy in US race relations; and the very present and well-nurtured image of Muslim Arab hostility to Israel. All these elements were poured into the reductionist fray of American domestic politics and media representations.

LEBANON, ISRAEL, AND THE PLO

The perception of political Islam as militantly hostile to the United States (the West, Israel, etc.) intensified in the cauldron of the civil war which erupted in Lebanon in 1975. The conflict was commonly represented as pitting leftist Muslims, backed by the PLO, against rightist Christians, backed by Israel, though the reality was far more complex. The shifting alliances and complex regional ramifications of the civil war allowed the Iranian revolution to extend its influence into Lebanon. This was not because Shi'ism has an innate proclivity for political opposition, martyrdom, or terrorism, as many facile Western analyses proposed.[16] It was the result of the historic underrepresentation and marginalization of the Lebanese Shi'a (the largest single religious community in the country by the 1970s), the effects of the alliance between Israel and the Maronite Phalange in opposition to the PLO on the heavily Shi'i areas of south Lebanon, US support for Israel's invasion of Lebanon in 1982 and, subsequently, US military intervention as a party in the civil war.

The Iranian revolution further invigorated the already growing political mobilization of Lebanon's Shi'a community (see Salim Nasr's chapter). Simultaneously, Israel escalated its military efforts to eliminate the PLO as a political force. This climaxed with a full-scale invasion in June 1982, transparently backed by the Reagan administration, and a protracted military siege of Beirut over that summer.

When the Israeli siege of Beirut ended, US troops were brought in as part of a larger Western peacekeeping deployment. Over the following months, though, US forces became increasingly and openly engaged in supporting efforts of the Israeli-installed and Maronite-dominated government headed by Amin Gemayel to extend its power beyond the walls of the presidential palace. In April 1983, a suicide truck bomb attack by a Lebanese Shi'i group, Islamic Jihad, destroyed the US embassy, killing top CIA officials among many others. In August and September 1983, in support of the

Maronite-dominated Lebanese army, US battleships shelled positions of Druze and other opposition militias. In late October, another suicide truck bomb destroyed the US Marine Corps barracks, killing 241 US troops. By February 1984, the Reagan administration acknowledged that its military and political position in Lebanon was untenable and withdrew remaining US forces.

Following the US intervention in Lebanon, several Shi'i militias kidnapped and held hostage Americans and other Western civilians working in Beirut. Only at the beginning of the 1990s was the last of these hostages finally released. In the same period, largely Shi'a resistance forces launched many effective suicide attacks against Israeli troops in occupied south Lebanon.

The sequence of the Iranian revolution and the Lebanese Shi'i campaign against the United States and the Israeli presence in Lebanon, as filtered through Western media, generated images and attitudes that unproblematically equated Islamism with irrational, anti-Western, and anti-Israeli terrorism. (Sporadic attacks and counterattacks between the United States and Libya under Mua'mmar Qadhdhafi also fed this imagery, though Qadhdhafi's regime, in fact, opposed most Islamist currents.) The subsequent emergence of armed Islamist forces in Egypt, Algeria, and occupied Palestine, their military skills honed in the US- and Saudi-funded Afghanistan campaign, solidified and enlarged these images and attitudes.

POLITICAL ISLAM AND US POLICY AFTER THE COLD WAR

The mutually reinforcing relationship between these images and attitudes and US policy formation is complex. Perceptions of Iran and Lebanon altered Washington's historically largely instrumentalist approach to political Islam. The demise of the Soviet Union and the end of the Cold War further eroded the earlier pragmatism.

Over the past several years, as indicated above, the executive branch—the State Department, the National Security Council, and the Pentagon—has promoted a fairly consistent line, most prominently articulated by Assistant Secretary of State for Near Eastern Affairs, Robert Pelletreau, and his predecessor, Edward Djerejian. This approach rhetorically acknowledges the variety of Islamist political formations and distinguishes between those that, in Pelletreau's words, "choose to participate in their countries' electoral processes, hoping to affect change within existing political structures," and those that "have opted for the use of violence against existing governments, indigenous minorities, and foreigners."[17]

But US policy formulation is more than the words of high-level diplomats. Scanning the post–Cold War policy landscape, we find that the former focus of the instrumentalist approach, the Soviet Union, which served as a policy compass or gyroscope for three-quarters of a century, is no more. An instrumentalist orientation now must take its bearings from the impact of Islamist politics in particular societies and the consequences for US interests in those countries. This is especially the case where Islamist political forces have, as in Algeria, become components of a popular oppositional consensus.

The collapse of the Soviet Union as a policy touchstone has created a vacuum of sorts, a phenomenon abhorred by "policy intellectuals" and geostrategists as much as by nature. There seem to be few contenders for a replacement; issues like hunger and social equity will not sustain outsized military budgets. One nominee is "the unknown," an intrinsically unreliable policy guide.[18]

A somewhat more serviceable contender is "Islamic fundamentalism." The sophisticated pronouncements of the Assistant Secretary of State for Near Eastern Affairs notwithstanding, "Islamic fundamentalism" does resonate with popular perceptions of the encounters of the United States with Iran and Lebanon over a decade and a half and, more recently, with the fierce hostility to US policies that apparently lies behind events like the bombing of the World Trade Center in New York. Equally important, Washington has opted for a policy of confrontation with Iran in the Persian Gulf region. This is not primarily because Iran is "Islamic" or "fundamentalist," but because Iranian nationalism, and the experience of Iran's mass political mobilization, represent the strongest challenge to the present configuration of Western interests and client regimes there.

That this Iranian radical model is clothed in a supranational Islamist ideology is pertinent but secondary. The core problem for American policy is Iran, not Islam. Islamist ideology and discourse, though, extend beyond Iran to include Palestinians, Lebanese, Egyptians, Sudanese, Tunisians, Algerians, and others. Most Western representations stress the similarities—including a vociferous anti-imperialism and anti-Americanism—rather than the differences and rivalries among these different movements. Undeniably, factional struggles in Iran have resulted in provocative and sometimes murderous behavior by the Iranian government or its agents. This facilitates and encourages a displacement, both intentional and otherwise, of the policy problem: Iran is a threat because it is "fundamentalist"—with all the attributes of irrationality and fanaticism that this notion has acquired.

Does Iran have legitimate interests in the Persian Gulf region which US policy might better accommodate than deny? Is a conflict between Iranian and American interests intrinsic and unavoidable? These questions lie beyond the scope of this essay; our point here is that Iran's posture facilitates a policy of containment and confrontation that is only incidentally related to that country's Islamic character. One way to explore how this policy has emerged is to consider the differential impact of that confrontation/containment approach on policy elsewhere in the Middle East.

FROM TEHRAN TO ALGIERS

US rhetoric and policies with regard to Algeria, Tunisia, Egypt, Palestine, and Iran reveal some interesting contrasts and variations. The further away from the Persian Gulf and the Israeli-Palestinian arena—away, in other words, from core US economic and strategic concerns—the more nuanced and situationally specific are the articulations of policy.

In the case of Algeria, Assistant Secretary of State Pelletreau in November 1994 asserted that a solution to that country's political crisis "lies not in a strategy of repression, but one of inclusion and reconciliation," and expressed concern over "the growing influence of hardliners in the military leadership who reject compromise with the opposition and intend to step up efforts to crush the armed insurgency by force." The US government, he claimed, has "repeatedly stressed to Algerian leaders at the highest levels the need for concrete steps to establish dialogue with opposition elements—secular and Islamist—willing to work towards a non-violent solution."[19] Reports from Algiers and Paris as well as Washington suggest that these remarks fairly characterize Washington's current approach, though US policy has not gone so far as to oppose financial support for the regime via the International Monetary Fund, for instance.

And when the Algerian military intervened in January 1992 to cancel elections that almost surely would have brought the Islamic Salvation Front (FIS) to power, Washington's protests were lax. Former Secretary of State James Baker recently acknowledged that "[w]hen I was at the State Department, we pursued a policy of excluding the radical fundamentalists in Algeria, even though we recognized that this was somewhat at odds with our support of democracy."[20] It appears that Washington's current tack is largely a result of the failure of the earlier approach to stem the growing power of the Islamist forces.

The former US policy in Algeria is similar to the present policy toward other regimes where the balance of power between the state and the Islamist opponents has not shifted quite so dramatically. Speaking of Tunisia—where the regime of Zayn al-'Abidin Ben 'Ali has, for the moment, successfully repressed all Islamist and secular manifestations of political opposition—Pelletreau praised its participation in the Arab-Israeli "peace process" and its "GDP growth in excess of 5 percent per year for the past five years," with only the faintest plea for "a corresponding openness in the political system together with greater emphasis on human rights."[21]

Political Islam in Tunisia became a substantial factor under circumstances comparable to the Egyptian case. President Ben 'Ali has acknowledged that "to some extent fundamentalism was of our own making, and was at one time encouraged in order to combat the threat of communism. Such groups were fostered in the universities and elsewhere at that time in order to offset the communists and to strike a balance." He added, "My background in the military and security has provided me with a rich experience in understanding the problem."[22]

Pelletreau's comments regarding Egypt were similarly discreet. Algeria's "armed Islamist insurgency," he acknowledged, arose from "political exclusion, economic misery, and social injustice." The same list—rampant corruption might have been added—applies equally to Egypt. In November 1994, 'Abd al-Rahim Shihata, the governor of Giza province, which includes much of greater Cairo, said the violent clashes in the poor quarter of Imbaba were "the least that should have happened, given the living conditions we found there. Actually, there probably should have been more violence."[23]

The Clinton administration reportedly told Egyptian officials in private that, as one US official put it, "you can't repress your way out of this."[24] President Mubarak, for his part, has rebuked the US embassy for maintaining contacts with the Muslim Brothers.[25] But Washington's stake in the Mubarak regime's survival, and the apparent US assessment that the Islamist groups do not pose an immediate threat to the regime's hold on the levers of power, has led Pelletreau and others to confine themselves in public to platitudes about political pluralism and human rights. There are no signs that the Clinton administration has considered conditioning US military and economic aid to Egypt on respect for basic human and political rights.

In Algeria, Washington preaches conciliation and inclusion, but in Palestine-Israel the United States has unreservedly supported an Israeli policy of eradication. The US has never acknowledged the Israeli government's role in promoting the Palestinian Islamist forces as a counterweight to the secularist PLO (see Graham Usher's chapter), a cynical policy that has created something of a Frankenstein. Washington has not restrained, even rhetorically, Israel's subsequent efforts to wipe out those same Islamist forces. The label of terrorist, once reserved for the PLO, is now deployed against Hamas and Hizb Allah, even when they target not civilians but troops and armored patrols. In the protracted Israeli-PLO negotiations following the September 1993 Declaration of Principles between the two sides, Washington unreservedly backed Israel's insistence that the priority task of Yasir 'Arafat's new Palestinian National Authority in Gaza and Jericho was to suppress Hamas.

Israeli strategists, in search of a rationale for a post-Soviet "strategic relationship," have been quick to cast their repression of Hamas as part of the battle for Western civilization. In December 1992, days after Israel expelled some 415 alleged Hamas activists across the Lebanese border, Prime Minister Yitzhak Rabin told the Knesset that Israel was "stand[ing] first today in the line of fire against extremist Islam."[26] In the weeks and months that followed, Israeli and pro-Israeli US "terrorism experts" peppered US media with provocative but typically unverifiable sketches of Hamas funding networks and "command centers" in the United States, inferring that Israel's policies of expulsion, mass arrests, house demolitions, and extrajudicial killings were also defending America.[27]

Palestinian Islamists alone hardly warrant the over $3 billion in military and "economic security" aid Israel receives from the United States each year. In any event, between the "Oslo II" agreement of September 1995 and January 1996, Israel changed tack and facilitated negotiations between 'Arafat and Hamas over participation in upcoming elections and ending armed attacks against Israeli targets. Iran's nasty reputation as an enemy of the "peace process" still rests largely on its support for Hamas, though in fact most of Hamas's outside funding has come from US allies Saudi Arabia and Kuwait. Israel has actively promoted the notion of the Iranian threat. In early December 1992 Thomas Dine, then executive director of AIPAC (American-Israel Public Affairs Committee, the premier pro-Israel lobby organization), declared that his "most pressing" priority would be "moving Iran to the top of the US Mideast agenda," and predicted that the many reports of an Iranian military buildup—not a few of which originated with Israeli "experts"—would make Iran "one of the top five" foreign policy concerns of the incoming Clinton administration.[28] Israeli Prime Minister Rabin, embarking on his first visit to the Clinton White House, told an Israeli reporter that Iran was on a "megalomaniacal" quest "to be a Middle East empire, by using all the varieties of fundamentalist Islam to shake Arab regimes."[29] Immediately after Rabin's visit, a spate of unattributed "terrorism expert" stories appeared in the *Washington Post, New York Times,* and *Los Angeles Times* warning, as the *New York Times* headline put it, "Iran-Backed Terrorists Are Growing More Aggressive."[30]

In fact, the Clinton administration seems to have paid little heed to the claims of the Egyptian and Algerian governments that the Islamist insurgencies they confront are inspired and sustained by Iran.[31] But this reasonable position is not public policy. More typical is Secretary of State Christopher's insistence, on his March 1995 visit to Tel Aviv, that "[w]herever you look, you will find the evil hand of Iran in this region."[32]

While Israel and its US partisans have loudly promoted the view that Iran is US enemy number one, this mutually self-serving and self-reinforcing exercise in threat construction finds many influential proponents in US policy circles as well. The February 1993 Joint Chiefs of Staff report on "Roles, Missions and Functions of the Armed Forces of the US," for instance, observes that "[i]n the Middle East and Southwest Asia radical political Islam and a politically and militarily resurgent Iran threaten regional stability and directly challenge a number of US interests, including access to Gulf oil, political reform, democratic development and settlement of the Arab-Israeli dispute."[33] The domestic source of this orientation is the US concern to preserve the institutions, privileges, and circuits of capital of military Keynesianism that marked the Cold War era. For the powerful US interests advocating high military spending, Iran thus serves as the new "evil empire"—an Islamist Comintern. In addition, hostility to Iran resonates with a pervasive American sense of betrayal that Iran dared to have its revolution. Iran's image as a trouble-making revolutionary regime obviates examining the behavior of US allies such as Israel or Egypt. Most importantly, in promoting the Iranian threat Washington justifies its growing military presence in the Persian Gulf.

CLASH OF CIVILIZATIONS?

The ideological scaffolding for this project is spelled out in Samuel Huntington's "Clash of Civilizations" thesis presented in *Foreign Affairs*. The operative threat, Huntington proposes, is what he calls the Confucian-Islamic connection. "In the post–Cold War world the primary objective of arms control is to prevent the development by non-Western societies of military capabilities that could threaten Western interests. . . . The flow of weapons and weapons technology is generally from East Asia to the Middle East."[34] This is complete nonsense: readily available US government data document that the United States in 1993 accounted for 61 percent of all arms transfers to Third World countries, with three-quarters of this—worth more than $11 billion per year to American military contractors—going to the Middle East.[35]

But then, it is precisely to justify such sales, and a Pentagon budget that has shrunk so very little from the Cold War era, that Huntington constructs his fantasy. Against such a profound "Confucian-Islamic" threat, moreover, there is no need to pursue what the Clinton administration characterizes as its policy of "democratic enlargement." US national security strategists have never keenly favored too much democracy for the Middle East. Yahya Sadowski's chapter in this volume cites former Secretary of Defense and CIA chief James Schlesinger's rhetorical question: do "we seriously desire to prescribe democracy as the proper form of government for other societies[?] Perhaps the issue is most clearly posed in the Islamic world. Do we seriously want to change the institutions in Saudi Arabia?" Schlesinger heads off any potential affirmative, allowing nothing to chance: "The brief answer is no: over the years we have sought to preserve those institutions, sometimes in preference to more democratic forces coursing throughout the region." This line of reasoning explains why the United States does not complain too much about systematic human rights abuses by Saudis, Turks, Egyptians, or Israelis.

Another serious deficiency of the "clash of civilizations" thesis advanced by Huntington, and in a different version by Bernard Lewis, is that the boundaries it draws between civilizations can be arbitrary, ignoring important cleavages within national states and regional blocs.[36] This culturalist analysis (or neo-Orientalism, as Sadowski calls it) is easily assimilated to the racist stereotyping of Arabs, Iranians, and Muslims so widespread in American popular culture. It promotes a metaphysical concept of cultural unity and an ahistorical notion of fixed civilizational blocs. Such a vision cannot be plausibly sustained against recent scholarship offering a nuanced account of the interaction among the Christian, Muslim, and Jewish traditions in the Mediterranean basin contact zone.[37] It cannot even explain the important alliances between the United States and Muslim states such as Saudi Arabia, Kuwait, Pahlavi Iran, Egypt, Turkey, Pakistan, and the *mujahidin* of Afghanistan. "Civilization" is not an adequate analytical tool to explain the difference between "our" Muslims and the "fanatics" allegedly now ranged against Western civilization.

GENDER RELATIONS

One of the most salient public aspects of political Islam has been its association with a code of conduct for women that includes some form of veiling (*hijab*) or "modest" dress and a reaffirmation of the patriarchal family. The popular view is that political Islam is opposed to women's political and legal rights, education, participation in the wage labor force, and family planning in the name of restoring "traditional" Islamic gender relations. There has been a sharp contest over the comportment of women in public space in Algeria, Egypt, Iran, Palestine, and Sudan (see the chapters of Susan Slyomovics, Sami Zubaida, Rema Hammami, Sondra Hale, and the interview with Rabia Bekkar). Deniz Kandiyoti notes that after World War I some newly independent Muslim states adopted a form of "state feminism" as an integral part of their nationalist and state-building projects. But the nationalist project did not challenge male domination in the sphere of the family. As Suad Joseph argues, the public political space of the nation and its citizens was gendered male.

State-endorsed feminism resulted in some significant gains for women in the areas of legal and political rights, education, and labor force participation, especially in Egypt, Iran, Tunisia, and Turkey. But these achievements disproportionately benefited urban middle-class and elite women, who were mobilized by the state in the name of the national project, not the autonomous interests of women as a whole. A modernist image of middle-class women became part of the approved nationalist representation of a proper citizenry, as Lila Abu Lughod's discussion of Egyptian television serials notes.

Women's bodies and lives have become an important symbolic battle-ground in the contest between political Islam and existing regimes. In Algeria, some of the most zealous Islamist militants have specifically targeted women for deadly attacks, making the battle physical as well as symbolic. Susan Slyomovics cites the testimony of a young woman factory manager in Tlemcen who has reluctantly acceded to the advice of her family: "Wear the veil and stay alive. This will pass."

When Islamist forces have come to power, as in Iran, they have found it difficult to impose a dogmatically patriarchal agenda. The regime in Tehran has felt compelled to support, on pragmatic grounds, certain rights for women. This is especially apparent in the debates around issues of family planning. Homa Hoodfar notes, for instance, legislation passed in December 1992 providing wages for housework which must be paid upon divorce or upon a woman's demand. It has been difficult to enforce, to be sure, and it stands alongside a number of contradictory and ambivalent policies, but it does indicate a degree of responsiveness to women's demands.

In Iran, Algeria, Egypt, and elsewhere, the ascendance of Islamist forces has not succeeded in closing off struggles over gender relations. In several circumstances, Islamist movements have expanded the public space open to women by providing them with socially acceptable work situations and a morally approved framework for political action. Some Islamist women have begun to call for interpreting the *shari'a* in ways that will empower women.[38] They do not use and may even explicitly reject the discourse of Western feminism. But there seem to be forms of gender consciousness and activism emerging within several Islamist movements that challenge both the patriarchal agendas of male leaderships and Western notions of what constitutes women's emancipation.

DEMOCRACY AND CIVIL SOCIETY

It is not a new theme in Western circles to argue that "Islam" is somehow inimical to democracy and civil society (see Yahya Sadowski's chapter). This is a subset of the larger assertion that Muslim societies "lack" this or that attribute of Western societies or that they are otherwise "not like us." Like the "clash of civilizations" thesis, it invokes an essentialist, ahistorical cul-turalism. But Islam, like all cultural systems, is a contested field of meaning. There are understandable reasons why both ruling regimes and secular leftist parties have been losing the contest for meaning.

The vast majority of the people of the Middle East never ceased to consider themselves Muslim, even in the heyday of secularist Arab, Turkish, and Iranian nationalism. But before the 1970s most Muslims willingly ac-cepted rather different notions of Islam than are prevalent today. Since the 1970s there has been a lively debate over what "Islam" requires (see the chapters of Sami Zubaida, Gudrun Krämer, and Alexander Flores), involving competing currents of both Islamist and secularist thinking.

Political Islamists often do have intolerant attitudes toward non-Muslims, women, and foreigners. Many Islamist movements are not unequivocally committed to democratic forms of government, and some are expressly authoritarian. But the states engaged in the most brutal repression of political Islam have not been particularly democratic themselves, even where they maintain the formal apparatus of elections, parliaments, and parties. In the contest between political Islam and highly repressive national states, neither the governments nor the most prominent Islamist movements speak persuasively for democracy, human rights, and social justice.

This volume challenges many popular ideas about the economic, social, political, and cultural content of contemporary Islamist movements, their relationship to the West, and to the United States in particular. We especially intend to challenge the notion of a uniform and unchanging Islam confronting "moderate" regimes allied with a singularly liberal and democratic "West." The authors in this volume are not all of one opinion, but they do all argue that attention to historical specificity and to the nuances of difference and similarity among and within Islamist movements is essential to a useful understanding of these phenomena.

To argue for understanding, and for a spirit of dialogic engagement, is not in any way to endorse or favor the trends of Islamist politics. We acknowledge that our personal and collective bonds have been with political forces and individuals in the region who have promoted secularist and universalist approaches to the rights of women and minorities, to egalitarian social and economic development, and to issues of democracy and civil rights. We believe that these are the questions that define broad political agendas in the Middle East today, and will continue to do so in the period ahead. We are proud of the historic association of the Middle East Research and Information Project and *Middle East Report* with this intellectual and political tradition. In that light, we intend this volume to be in solidarity with all those, secularists and Islamists, who struggle for human and political rights against authoritarian and chauvinist states or movements of whatever stripe or complexion.

NOTES

1. Martin E. Marty and R. Scott Appleby (eds.), *The Fundamentalisms Project: A Study Conducted by the American Academy of Arts and Sciences*, 3 vols. published to date (Chicago: University of Chicago Press, 1991–). For a critique of this project, see Saba Mahmood, "Islamism and Fundamentalism," *Middle East Report*, no. 191 (November–December 1994): 29–30; Richard T. Antoun and Mary Hegland (eds.), *Religious*

Resurgence: Contemporary Cases in Islam, Christianity, and Judaism (Syracuse: Syracuse University Press, 1987).

2. One classic account is Albert Hourani, *Arabic Thought in the Liberal Age, 1798–1939* (Oxford: Oxford University Press, 1962).

3. Sayyid Jamal al-Din was born in Asadabad in Iran, probably as a Shi'a. He adopted the eponym "al-Afghani," suggesting he was from Afghanistan and, therefore, more likely to be a Sunni.

4. In the West, *jihad* is often narrowly construed as "holy war." In the Muslim tradition it can mean any effort for a religiously approved purpose. Many Islamists interpret Sayyid Qutb as advocating an armed struggle against the Nasirist regime, though this is not explicitly stated in his most influential text on the question, *Ma'alim fi al-tariq* (Signposts).

5. This is more or less the argument of Nadav Safran, *Egypt in Search of Political Community* (Cambridge, Mass.: Harvard University Press, 1961) and P. J. Vatikiotis, *The History of Egypt*, 3d ed. (Baltimore: Johns Hopkins University Press, 1986); and it is present in many of Bernard Lewis's writings.

6. Qasim Amin, *The Liberation of Women* (Cairo: American University in Cairo Press, 1992); Leila Ahmed, *Women and Gender in Islam: Historical Roots of a Modern Debate* (New Haven: Yale University Press, 1992), pp. 144–68.

7. Daniel Pipes, *In the Path of God: Islam and Political Power* (New York: Basic Books, 1983), pp. 281 ff. For a discussion and adaptation of Fu'ad Zakariyya's views, see Richard U. Moensch, "Oil, Ideology and State Autonomy in Egypt," *Arab Studies Quarterly* 10, no. 2 (spring 1988): 176–92. Fouad Ajami affirmed Ali Mazrui's observation that "the 'barrel of oil' and the 'crescent of Islam' were linked and the October 1973 war represented a resurrection of Islam." Fouad Ajami, *The Arab Predicament* (Cambridge: Cambridge University Press, 1981), p. 173. For an early critique of these views, see Richard P. Mitchell, "The Islamic Movement: Its Current Condition and Future Prospects," in Barbara Freyer Stowasser (ed.), *The Islamic Impulse* (London: Croom Helm, 1987), pp. 75–86.

8. Richard P. Mitchell, *The Society of the Muslim Brothers* (Oxford: Oxford University Press, 1969).

9. See Mark Gasioworski, "The 1953 Coup d'Etat in Iran," *International Journal of Middle East Studies* 19, no. 3 (August 1987): 261–86.

10. Anthony Lake, "Confronting Backlash States," *Foreign Affairs* (spring 1994): 52; idem, "The Middle East Moment," *Washington Post*, July 24, 1994.

11. For a somewhat sensationalist though generally forthright approach to this issue, see Tim Weiner, "Blowback from the Afghan Battlefield," *New York Times Magazine*, March 13, 1994, pp. 52–55.

12. Olivier Roy, *The Failure of Political Islam* (Cambridge, Mass.: Harvard University Press, 1994), p. 130.

13. *Report of the President's Special Review Board* (Washington, D.C.: Government Printing Office, February 26, 1987), p. B-2.

14. "Transcript of the President's News Conference on Foreign and Domestic Matters," *New York Times*, February 14, 1980.

15. Fred Halliday, *The Making of the Second Cold War* (London: Verso, 1983); idem, "The Arc of Crisis and the New Cold War," *MERIP Reports*, no. 100/101 (October–December 1981): 14–25.

16. For a particularly overwrought example, see Ayla Hammond Schbley, "Resurgent Religious Terrorism: A Study of Some of the Lebanese Shi'a Contemporary Terrorism," *Terrorism* 12, no. 4 (1989): 213–47.

17. Robert H. Pelletreau, "Islam and United States Policy: Remarks to the Middle East Policy Council," Washington, D.C., May 26, 1994, p. 3.

18. "Prepared Statement of Gen. Colin L. Powell," Fiscal Year 1993 Defense Budget, Hearing before the Committee on the Budget, House of Representatives, 102 Congress, Second Session, February 5, 1992 (Washington, D.C.: US Government Printing Office, 1992), pp. 105–6.

19. Robert H. Pelletreau, "US Policy and Political Developments in North Africa: Remarks to the North Atlantic Assembly," Washington, D.C., November 15, 1994, pp. 3–4.

20. James Baker, interview in *Middle East Quarterly*, cited in *Middle East International*, March 3, 1994, p. 17.

21. Pelletreau, "US Policy and Political Developments in North Africa," pp. 4–5.

22. Roger Matthews interview with Ben 'Ali, *Financial Times*, July 27, 1994.

23. Chris Hedges, "Cairo Journal: In the Slums, A Tug-of-War for Hearts and Minds," *New York Times*, November 29, 1994, p. A4.

24. Thomas W. Lippman, "Arab States Battling Militants Counter U.S. Stance on Rights," *Washington Post*, May 30, 1993, p. A41.

25. Mary Anne Weaver, "The Novelist and the Sheikh," *New Yorker*, January 30, 1995, p. 69.

26. David Hoffman, "Rabin Tried to Keep Expulsions Secret to Avoid Court Trial," *Wasington Post*, December 22, 1992, p. A16.

27. Ehud Ya'ari, *New York Times*, January 27, 1993, recapitulated the essential arguments of an Israeli Television documentary he hosted, relying heavily on Israeli military sources.

28. *Jewish Bulletin*, December 11, 1992.

29. *Davar*, quoted in David Hoffman, "Israel Seeking to Convince U.S. that West Is Threatened by Islam; Jewish Leaders Say Only Washington is Capable of Restraining Tehran," *Washington Post*, March 13, 1993, p. A14.

30. Douglas Jehl, *New York Times*, March 17, 18, 1993, p. A8.

31. Concerning the frequently heard charge that Iran is arming the Algerian insurgency, US sources have only verified that "at least one arms shipment has transited via Sudan." Philip Wilcox, the US State Department coordinator for terrorism, has stated, "there is little hard evidence of a coordinated international network or command and control apparatus among these groups." Robin Wright, "World View: Islam in the '90s: A Study of Diversity; Despite Pervasive Stereotypes, Major Islamist Groups Differ Widely in Tactics and Tenets," *Los Angeles Times*, February 7, 1995, p. 1.

32. Elaine Sciolino, "Condemning Iranian Oil Deal, U.S. May Tighten Trade Ban," *New York Times*, March 10, 1995, p. A2.

33. David Isenberg, "Desert Storm Redux?" *Middle East Journal* 47, no. 3 (summer 1993): 437.

34. Samuel P. Huntington, "The Clash of Civilizations?" *Foreign Affairs* (summer 1993): 46–47.

35. Richard F. Grimmett, *Conventional Arms Transfers to the Third World, 1987–1994* (Washington, D.C.: Congressional Research Service Report, August 1995), p. 51; US Arms Control and Disarmament Agency, *World Military Expenditures and Arms Transfers, 1991–1992* (Washington, D.C.: US Government Printing Office, March 1994).

36. For Bernard Lewis's version, see "The Roots of Muslim Rage," *The Atlantic Monthly* 266 (September 1990): 60.

37. See S. D. Goitein, *A Mediterranean Society: The Jewish Communities of the Arab World as Portrayed in the Documents of the Cairo Geniza,* 6 vols. (Berkeley: University of California Press, 1967–93). Amitav Ghosh extends the spirit of Goiten's analysis to South Asia in his wonderfully readable *In an Antique Land* (New York: Alfred A. Knopf, 1993).

38. See, for example, "It is time to launch a new women's liberation movement—an Islamic one." An interview with Heba Ra'uf Ezzat, *Middle East Report,* no. 191 (November–December 1994): 26–27.

PART ONE

Islam, Democracy, and Civil Society

2

Introduction to Part One

Sheila Carapico

The end of the Cold War brought with it a temporary euphoria about prospects for a worldwide "third wave" of democratization to sweep the globe. If civil society had triumphed in the former Soviet bloc, perhaps political liberalism would spread elsewhere. No sooner had the sweet taste of victory over communism subsided, however, than Western observers turned their attention to another, allegedly uniquely, antidemocratic current—Islam—whose civilizational values seem to clash with Western liberalism even more fundamentally than Marxism. Whereas people in other parts of the world crave civil society, so the argument goes, political openings in the Muslim world have only fanned the flames of religious extremism. This argument finds much support in Orientalist literature, scholarship, and journalism.

Orientalist is here used in the sense established by the Palestinian-American literary critic Edward W. Said's well-known book, *Orientalism*, to mean those who study, seek, and depict the Middle East. Said argued that Western literary treatment of the world of Islam and Arabs was based on an inversion of idealized images of European culture. He later expanded on this thesis to show how the American news media "covers" (a very deliberate pun) Islam and the question of Palestine.[1]

Orientalism can also be found in the social sciences. For instance, Max Weber, an important European sociologist, used an inversion to define his ideal-typical concept of (European) legal-rationality, contrasting it with what he called "kadi-justice," or the personalized application of Islamic law (*shari'a*). Weber tells his readers that Muslim justice is the antonym of modern Western practice.

In Orientalist depictions, Islam is often seen as the antithesis of tolerance, social justice, individualism, and legal-rationality. *Jihad* (often erroneously

understood solely as "holy war") appears more central to this great mono-
theistic religion than prayer or charity. It is frequently repeated that "there
is no separation of religion and politics in Islam," again substituting the
inversion of a Western ideal for understanding the complex relationship of
Islamic law to religious practice and political regimes.

The Orientalist mind-set attributes political struggles in the Middle East
to culture, not social, economic, or individual factors. For instance, while
lynchings, hate crimes, and family violence in America are but individual
exceptions to a sound social ethic, "Islam*ic* terrorism" is portrayed as if it
were a religious expression. Most social scientists look to the humiliations
of Versailles and the deprivations of the Great Depression to explain the
"escape from freedom" into a violent, chauvinistic, exclusivist, right-wing
European movement—fascism—in the 1930s. But how often do we look to
military defeat and economic crisis to explain Middle Eastern extremism?
Rarely, although these factors are clearly present. Instead (at least when
comparing the West to the Orient), Westerners typically view Western
experiences with slavery, fascism, and individual brutality as cultural anom-
alies in a tolerant, humane, egalitarian Judeo-Christian civilization. Yet
comparable phenomena in the Muslim world, widely "covered," appear to
be indicators of a civilization that valorizes violence, book-burning, capital
punishment, and chauvinism. Most of us do not believe right-wing Zionists
or Christians who claim to speak for God, but we tend unquestioningly to
accept that clenched-fisted Islamists waving green flags are the voice of the
Muslim Allah.

This view holds that cultural impediments to pluralist politics, peaceful
expression of dissent, and the rights of citizens are greater in the Islamic
world than almost anywhere else. Civil society, the sphere of autonomous
civic groups and activities that protect the private sphere from the state, is
critical for modern democracy. Islam, the argument goes, has no such civil
society.

The following essays help us to transcend the Orientalist myopia and then
to look at Islamist[2] political movements, in particular, on their own terms.
Yahya Sadowski's thickly-argued critical analysis of "neo-Orientalism" attempts to deconstruct scholarly arguments about the presumed nature of
Islamic civilization. Two prominent Orientalist scholars derive central
themes of traits they say characterize Arab culture today from their historical
studies of one medieval Egyptian "slave" dynasty. Based on complex ex-
trapolations from this rather exceptional historical example, they argue that
the modern Muslim world cannot develop civil society.

The arguments Sadowski confronts are more subtle, nuanced, and sophisticated than a simple inversion. While a consensus reigns among the
neo-Orientalists that the Middle East can never achieve the ideal of democracy, they differ about whether the obstacle is the state or society.

Sadowski notes that in the Middle East, as in Europe, major political movements are not likely to be explained by enduring cultural "essences." In the twentieth century North Africa and western Asia have seen nationalist, revolutionary, and Arab socialist movements, as well as sectarian violence; and important elements of the Muslim Brothers have opposed the use of violence. Some formerly Marxist or nationalist radicals are now radical Islamists. The politicization of a socially conservative, "fundamentalist" interpretation of the Qur'an into the most powerful current in the Middle East in the 1980s and 1990s must be explained in terms of its social, political, and economic context—not medieval history.

What of the potential for civil society and democracy in Middle Eastern countries other than Israel, often unproblematically regarded as the lone Western-style democracy? Is Islam antithetical to democracy? If so, would we go so far as to say, "Their culture is violent and antidemocratic, so that's okay for them"? Sami Zubaida, Suad Joseph, Gudrun Krämer, and Alexander Flores each present something rare in English—insight into ongoing debates among Muslim scholars, jurists, and political thinkers.

What strikes many Western readers of these articles is the extent to which Muslims do explicitly confront, and differ on, constitutional issues of law, governance, and citizenship. Even though Islamists claim to be "authentic" representatives of the "true" Islam, there are debates among scholars and differences between countries and contexts. "The debate," as Krämer points out, "is how the *shari'a* (Islamic law) is to be defined—as a comprehensive set of norms and values regulating human life down to the minutest detail, or as a set of general rules of good life and moral behavior."

This theme of defining the *shari'a* and its relationship to modern law and social policy, discussed on a theoretical level in this group of essays, carries over to the empirical case studies in the sections that follow. Zubaida and Flores guide readers through the transition from theory to on-the-ground issues. Zubaida shows that the contest in Egypt is not simply between reactionary Islamists and enlightened liberal democrats, but one that involves secular human rights activists and Islamists in a struggle with a government trying to contain them both. In this struggle, as Flores explains, the Egyptian regime initially encouraged the religious conservatives in order to combat the left; later, progressives found themselves in strategic political alliances with the Islamists against the government. These politics are dynamic and fluid.

We do not have to accept right-wing zealots' claim to speak for all Muslims. Nor does understanding the Islamist current in its own terms and in a dynamic social, political, and economic context mean condoning either the totalizing aims or the violent methods of the religious right. All five of these essays are clear about this. Particularly moving is Joe Stork's interview with Suad Joseph, an Arab woman who, like many Arab women, grapples with the multiple ways in which women's political space is constricted—by dehumanizing Orientalist stereotypes as well as by Middle Eastern patriarchal structures of class, community, and nation. Both imperialism and Arab politics limit her full citizenship and her exercise of basic rights.

NOTES

1. Edward W. Said, *Orientalism* (New York: Pantheon, 1978); *The Question of Palestine* (New York: Times Books, 1979); *Covering Islam* (New York: Pantheon, 1981).

2. Note the distinction between Islam*ic* and Muslim, which refer to the religion based on the Qur'an and the teachings of the Prophet Muhammad; and Islam*ist*, referring to the twentieth-century political movements claiming the Qur'an is their constitution.

3

The New Orientalism
and the Democracy Debate

Yahya Sadowski

The "collapse of communism" in 1989 and the victory over Iraq in 1991 sparked a wave of triumphal declarations by Western pundits and analysts who believed that all "viable systemic alternatives to Western liberalism" had now been exhausted and discredited. Some then tried to sketch a foreign policy appropriate to the "new world order."[1] A consistent theme of this "new thinking" was that the peoples of the developing countries must now acknowledge that liberal democracy is the only plausible form of governance in the modern world. Accordingly, support for democratization should henceforth be a central objective of US diplomacy and foreign assistance.[2]

This trend was not welcomed by all. Autocrats in the Arab world, particularly the rulers of the Gulf states, were appalled at the thought that Washington might soon be fanning the flames of republican sentiment. "The prevailing democratic system in the world is not suitable for us in this region, for our peoples' composition and traits are different from the traits of that world," declared King Fahd of Saudi Arabia in March 1992.[3] The king's stance suits many US policy makers just fine. Former Secretary of Defense and CIA chief James Schlesinger spoke for more than himself recently when he asked "whether we seriously desire to prescribe democracy as the proper form of government for other societies. Perhaps the issue is most clearly posed in the Islamic world. Do we seriously want to change the institutions in Saudi Arabia? The brief answer is no: over the years we have sought to preserve those institutions, sometimes in preference to more democratic forces coursing throughout the region."[4] Schlesinger went on to cite the king's views as endorsement of his own.

For their part, some partisans of Israel feared that US endorsement of democratic trends in the Arab world might abet the rise to power of "Islamic fundamentalist" regimes. (They may also privately worry that Arab democratization might erode Israel's claim to US support as "the only democracy in the Middle East.")

Those who oppose democratization initiatives in the Middle East could, moreover, turn for support to Western academic "experts." "[A]mong Islamic countries, particularly those in the Middle East," wrote Samuel Huntington in a typical dismissal, "the prospects for democratic development seem low."[5] The thesis that Middle Eastern societies are resistant to democratization had been a standard tenet of Orientalist thought for decades, but in the 1980s a new generation of Orientalists inverted some of the old assumptions and employed a new vocabulary which allowed them to link their work to a wider, international debate about the relationship between "civil society" and democratization. These updated arguments sought to prove not only—as neo-Orientalist Daniel Pipes put it—that "Muslim countries have the most terrorists and the fewest democracies in the world," but that they always would.[6]

STRONG STATE, WEAK SOCIETY

There are dozens of theories about what factors promote democracy. A country may be more likely to become democratic if it becomes richer, or redistributes its wealth in an egalitarian manner, or specializes in manufacturing consumer durables, or rapidly converts its peasantry into proletarians, or switches to a nuclear family structure, or gets colonized by England, or converts *en masse* to Protestantism.[7] Scholars quibble endlessly about which recipes are most effective, but generally concur that democracy thrives in those countries that possess a "civil society."

The term civil society has been bandied about recently with an enthusiasm that has not made its meaning any clearer.[8] For most scholars, civil society refers to the collection of autonomous social organizations that resist arbitrary exercises of state power. This conception goes back to the eighteenth century, when thinkers like Montesquieu and Thomas Paine argued that the despotic tendencies of Europe's absolute monarchs could be checked if "intermediate powers" such as the nobility, the bourgeoisie, the churches, and the press united to assert their independence.[9] Today corporations, labor unions, chambers of commerce, professional syndicates, public action groups, local governments, lay religious fraternities, voluntary associations, and assorted collectivities would all be considered elements of civil society inasmuch as they help to curb the powers of the state.

Groups are common enough in all human societies, but those with a level of internal organization and assertiveness that enables them to challenge state power are rare. For several centuries the consensus of Western scholars was that such groups were missing in the Orient. This lack of civil society, they contended, was the primary reason why governments in the region were so prone to despotism.[10]

Until recently, Western experts argued that in Islamic societies groups were

> strikingly different from their supposed counterparts in Western history. Their leaders were spokesmen, not directors. Entry into such groups was seldom marked by any formal observance, or datable from any specific moment. Men belonged to such groups because they identified themselves and others as belonging to certain accepted categories such as "merchant" or "scholar"; and, in general, they rallied to such groups only when the categories with which they identified were threatened.[11]

Weakly organized and lacking strong corporate identities, social associations in the Middle East tended to be "informal, personalistic, and relatively inefficient as a means of winning support and extracting resources from the populace."[12] They were too feeble to challenge the power of the state and constitute a civil society.[13]

Rather than challenging the ruler's authority, the argument went, groups in Islamic societies tended to be vehicles of supplication and collaboration. The most common form of political organization was the clientage network, whose members traded their loyalty for the patronage and protection of some notable.[14] In this setting, apparently modern organizations such as unions, peasant associations, and professional syndicates only provide a patina that disguises the continuing struggle of atomized clients to secure the sponsorship of elite patrons.[15]

Why were groups in the Middle East so weak? Western experts offered several distinct answers, but the prevailing one was that proffered by the Orientalists: Islam accounted for this weakness in Middle Eastern society, just as it explained the region's other peculiarities.[16] Despotism was implicit in the very core of Islam. After all, the very name Islam came from the Arabic word for "submission." The image that Islamic doctrine presented of the pious believer—fatalistic, prostrate before God, obeying His every whim—served as a trope for discussing not only religious but also political behavior in societies where rulers acted as "the shadow of God upon earth."[17] In the words of the definitive Orientalist cliché, Islam was not just a religion but a total way of life. The totalistic character of the faith seemed to imply that only a totalitarian state could put its dogmas into practice.[18] Islam, moreover, discouraged the formation of groups that might have resisted despotism, since "Islamic law knows no corporate legal persons; Islamic history shows no councils or communes, no synods or parliaments, nor any other kind of elective or representative assembly. It is interesting that the jurists never accepted the principle of majority decision—there was no point, since the need for a procedure of corporate collective decision never arose."[19]

Thus, groups such as the *'ulama'* (Islamic jurists), the military, and the provincial notables, who might have shared an interest in restraining the authority of the sultan, lacked any practical foundation for organizing to do so. As a result, "the political experience of the Middle East under the caliphs and sultans was one of almost unrelieved autocracy, in which obedience to the sovereign was a religious as well as a political obligation, and disobedience a sin as well as a crime."[20]

The classical Orientalists argued that orthodox Islam promoted political quietism. Supposedly the great medieval Islamic thinkers, horrified by the periodic rebellions and civil wars that wracked their community, decreed that obedience to any ruler—even an unworthy or despotic one—was a religious duty. "As the great divine Ghazali (d. 1111) declared: 'The tyranny of a sultan for a hundred years causes less damage than one year's tyranny exerted by the subjects against each other.'"[21] As a result of this blanket prohibition of all dissent, "there could be no question of representative bodies being set up to carry on a dialogue between ruler and subject; neither could there be institutions of local self-government in town or countryside; nor could craft or professional associations flourish unhindered, since they would always be suspected of limiting the sway of the government over its subjects."[22] The upshot of the suppression of such groups was a despotic regime in which "the state is stronger than society."[23]

Among Western experts, the idea that in the Middle East the weakness of society assured the dominion of the state persisted until quite recently, although there had always been a handful of unorthodox scholars who argued that the prevailing consensus underestimated the real strength of society. They insisted that groups, solidarities, and classes had been historically influential and that their collective action remained a critical force.[24] The size of this minority grew as political scientists found studies of clientage networks increasingly unsatisfying and began to identify authentic interest groups in Islamic societies.[25] Historians began to question the idea that the state had always been dominant. Ervand Abrahamian noted, for example, that although a late eighteenth-century Qajar Shah could execute anyone who attended his court, he probably enjoyed less real control over the countryside surrounding his capital than did a contemporary French monarch.[26]

The popularity of these dissident ideas exploded after the Iranian revolution of 1979. Until then, most students of Iran shared the Orientalist assumption that Islam had the effect of promoting despotic authority and claimed that Twelver Shi'ism was, if anything, an even more quietistic faith than Sunni Islam.[27] After the revolution Western experts quickly reversed their views, and now portrayed Iran as a country where society had traditionally been strong and the state weak. The Iranian clergy and its supporters among the traditional bourgeoisie of the bazaar and the new urban middle classes formed a genuine civil society capable not only of challenging the state but of toppling it. Shi'ism, with its cult of martyrs and delegitimation of secular authority, was now an ideal revolutionary ideology that had a long history of encouraging insurrections.[28]

This revisionism was not confined to Iranian studies. During the 1980s, three new trends were discernible in Middle Eastern studies. First, as Islamic or Islamist movements grew more potent and challenged the ruling authorities, a host of studies of "radical Islam" appeared to reveal how Islamic doctrine disposed believers to form militant groups and contest the authority of the state. Second, as oil prices declined and government revenues dried up, scholars came to appreciate that states in the region were less powerful than they had once appeared.[29] Finally, as the intellectual foundations for the idea of "weak" Middle Eastern societies collapsed, there was a slow growth of interest in studies of mafias, mobs, interest groups, solidarities, and classes that *might* act as the equivalents of "civil society" in the region.[30]

In 1987, the Social Science Research Council launched a major program to fund research on the now-trendy theme of "Retreating States and Expanding Societies" in the Middle East. There was already a sense that the growing weakness of states would create opportunities for civil society to assert its independence in the region.[31] Today most scholars confidently affirm that both intermediate powers and autonomous social groups exist in the Middle East. Both Harvard and New York University have sponsored large-scale research projects on these questions.[32] An articulate minority of scholars are even prepared to argue that civil society is sufficiently well grounded to serve as a platform for the development of democracy in the Middle East.[33]

STRONG SOCIETY, WEAK STATE

Many Western Middle East experts, though, remained skeptical about the democratic potential of the region, and found intellectual comfort in a new trend, which began even before the Iranian revolution, to reform and update Orientalism. This new generation of Orientalists was uncomfortable with its predecessors' claim that Islam promoted political submission—though it shared the latters' conviction that Islam was incompatible with democracy.

Patricia Crone is probably the most persuasive and rigorous of these younger Orientalists.[34] One of her central themes is that Islamic civilization is unique in the way that it forcefully refuses to legitimize political authority. She traces this characteristic back to the eighth century when the 'Abbasid dynasty seized power from the Umayyads and the *shari'a* (Islamic law) was first codified. The *'ulama'* of this period were men of tribal origin, she argues, and the law they drafted reflected their "profound hostility to settled states."[35]

> the *'ulama'* defined God's law as *haqq al-'arab*, the law of the Arabs, just as they identified his language as the *lisan al-'arab*, the normative language of the bedouins, the consensus being that where God had not explicitly modified tribal law, he had endorsed it. The result was a tribal vision of sacred politics. . . . Kings were rejected as Pharaohs and priests as golden calfs, while God's community was envisaged as an egalitarian one unencumbered by profane or religious structures of power below the caliph, who was himself assigned the duty of minimal government.[36]

The *'ulama'* portrayed all secular rulers as prone to corruption and despotism and volunteered to act as guardians against these excesses. They won enough support for these ideals from the mass of Muslims, urban and tribal alike, to prevent any dynasty from legitimating its empire.[37]

Conforming to this critique of political power, ordinary Muslims offered only tepid and intermittent support for their rulers. Unable to raise sufficient troops from among their subjects, Muslim rulers were forced to import military slaves, *mamluks*, to staff their armies. These slaves edged aside civilian dynasties before being replaced themselves by other warrior factions. "[B]etween foreign slaves and alienated secretaries," Crone writes, "politics degenerated into mere intrigues and bickerings for the proceeds of a state apparatus which neither party could permanently control, both parties squandering resources on an impressive scale while few indeed were reinvested in the state."[38]

Crone writes mainly about early Islamic history, but another of the young Orientalists—Daniel Pipes—has boldly spelled out the contemporary implications of this research in medieval politics. When Pipes was writing his own doctoral dissertation, also about the *mamluks*, he read Crone's thesis and concurred with her general argument.[39] He claimed that the *mamluk* institution was a phenomenon unique to Muslim societies which reflected the pernicious influence of the *'ulama'* and of Islamic doctrine. "While all religions postulate ideals that human beings cannot consistently maintain," he writes, "Islam alone of the universalist religions makes *detailed political* [italics in original] ideals part of its basic code, the Shari'a."[40] By establishing ideals that are impossible to fulfill, Islam ensures that Muslims will view any form of government, sooner or later, as illegitimate.[41] Sincere Muslims consequently tend to withdraw support from their rulers. Since Muslims declined to serve in armies, slave soldiers had to be recruited. This bred both political instability and weakness. This political infirmity of Islamic civilization would eventually allow European civilization to outstrip it.

Pipes's analysis of the contemporary Islamic resurgence argues that the medieval failure to develop a stable political system continues to be one of the "difficulties Muslims face in modernizing."[42] This view has proved congenial to the framers of elite opinion in the United States, and Pipes has been able to purvey his ideas about "Muslim anomie" to an ever widening audience—as a consultant to the State Department, as a director of the right-wing Foreign Policy Institute in Philadelphia (and editor of its journal, *Orbis*) and as a contributor to the *Wall Street Journal, The New Republic, Foreign Affairs,* and other outlets.[43]

While Pipes has had the highest public profile among propagators of neo-Orientalist ideas, others have labored to spread them within the academic community. Patricia Crone is closely associated with a group of neo-Weberian scholars that includes some of the hottest young talents in several disciplines—J. G. Merquior (political philosophy), Michael Mann (political sociology), and John Hall (political science).[44] These colleagues propagated Crone's ideas among the wider scholarly community and enriched them by weaving them into a broader argument about the evolution of societies.

John Hall in particular deserves credit for drawing out the implications of Crone's work for contemporary Islamic societies. In Hall's apt phrase, Crone has shown that, as a religion, Islam was essentially "monotheism with a tribal face."[45] Islamic history was the story of a strong society that consistently withheld its support from political authority. "Government thus has very slim roots in society," he wrote, "and stability came to depend upon such solidarity as the rulers of society could themselves achieve, as is true of most conquest societies."[46] Hall argues that the strength of society in Islamic civilizations not only made the state unstable; it also obstructed the development of true "civil society" and democracy. Precisely because society remained aloof from the state, and because dynasties tended to be very unstable, no "organic state" could emerge in the Middle East. Europe alone possessed an

> organic state, a *stronger* state, in place over long periods of time, and forced to provide infrastructural services for society, both because of the pre-existence of a civil society and because of the need to raise revenue to compete in war with other similarly stable states. In Islam such stable states did not exist. The fear of tribesmen meant that urban strata could not rule themselves, and a premium was accordingly placed upon military power. The states that resulted were transient and predatory.[47]

"Transient and predatory" states, lacking the cooperation of society, cannot be good candidates for democratization. The development of capitalism and democracy ultimately depends upon a pattern of *collaboration* between state and society.

Hall derived this vision of the origins of democracy from the work of his mentor, Ernest Gellner. The impact of Gellner's vision of history is evident in many aspects of neo-Orientalism and particularly in the idea that the cooperation of the state and society is crucial to development.[48] Gellner has argued that in most agrarian societies the commercial elite was doomed as soon as it began to grow wealthy and powerful enough to tinker with the social order.[49] Either the ruling military elite reacted to the danger of the rising commercial class by exterminating it, or the commercial elite triumphed and turned itself into a landed aristocracy. Either way, the tendency toward capitalism found among merchants usually snuffed itself out. The Protestant ethic, however, made the rising capitalist elite of Europe in the sixteenth to eighteenth centuries different. "For peculiar ideological reasons, this set of producers continued to be such even when grown rich enough to become powerful and to enjoy the fruits of their previous accumulation. They turned profits neither into swords nor into pleasure nor into ritual display. They had an inner compulsion to carry on, and the modern world was the byproduct of their obsessional drive."[50]

European capitalists were not inclined to abandon commerce and demand entry into the aristocracy. And, equally important, this class "did not oblige the encompassing state to control and dominate it in sheer self-defence. It did not create a political dilemma in which the new commercial class either had to eat or be eaten by the old power-holders."[51] This permitted the state and the emerging economic powers to not merely tolerate one another but increasingly to collaborate.

Gellner's argument mobilizes Weber's old (and somewhat discredited) Protestant ethic thesis for a new purpose: to explain the origins of the modern state rather than the rise of the modern economy.[52] This subtle shift has dramatic implications. It suggests that the success of development in the West was a result not of aggressive-assertive societies, but of passive-quiescent ones. It implies that capitalist development was most likely not where society constrained the state but where society avoided antagonizing authority. Gellner's argument stands the old ideas about civil society on their head. He portrays "civil" society not as a raucous band of solidarities that check the state's tendency toward despotism, but as a "civilized" assemblage of groups that expand production without threatening state power.[53]

Gellner's revisionist ideas about Protestantism in the Baroque Era had been prompted by his observations of England in his own time: an epoch of high inflation, stagnant economic growth, and growing political uncertainty. Gellner, like many other scholars, blamed these ills on the excessive growth of demands by special interests: farmers seeking crop subsidies, businessmen seeking tariff protections, and—above all—labor unions demanding wage and benefit increases. These demands triggered stagflation and arrested economic growth, and their increasingly desperate competition for a larger share of a diminishing social surplus was leading to a crisis of "governability."[54]

This anxiety about economic and political paralysis triggered a reassessment of the virtues of democracy. Some scholars claimed that it was precisely because authoritarian regimes (such as Japan and Germany) had suppressed the autonomy of social groups that they seemed especially likely to enjoy economic growth.[55] While few argued that the West would be better off abandoning democracy, many sought to dampen demands and help the state to resist such pressures.[56] Students of Germany, Switzerland, and other economically successful states wrote warmly of their "corporatist" pattern of organization in which a handful of large industrial cartels and labor federations represented business and labor. By focusing and amalgamating the demands of their constituents, these corporatist bodies could negotiate industrial compromises that neutralized the peril of inflation.[57] Students of Austria and the Low Countries admired their model of "consociational" democracy, in which strong regional or religious loyalties limited the degree to which parties could compete for broad public support. Under consociation, because no single party could hope for an outright majority in elections, most parties are forced to enter into broad coalitions that dilute special interests and promote corporatist negotiating patterns.[58]

This broad intellectual shift, which emphasized the virtues—even the necessity—of curbing the autonomy of social groups and the growth of their demands on the state, created a receptive audience for the neo-Orientalists. Their argument, that tribes, *mullahs*, and *mamluks* had demanded too much autonomy and created a crisis of governability in Islamic societies, sounded plausible because Westerners could discern a trend toward the same ills in their own society.

The irony of this conjuncture needs to be savored. When the consensus of social scientists held that democracy and development depended upon the actions of strong, assertive social groups, Orientalists held that such associations were absent in Islam. When the consensus evolved and social scientists thought a quiescent, undemanding society was essential to progress, the neo-Orientalists portrayed Islam as beaming with pushy, anarchic solidarities. Middle Eastern Muslims, it seems, were doomed to be eternally out of step with intellectual fashion.

STRONG SOCIETY OR STRONG STATE

Today there is a broad empirical consensus among Western and Middle Eastern scholars about political conditions in the Middle East. They agree that states are weak and, as their economic crises grow worse, getting weaker. They concur that the weakness of the state partly reflects and partly encourages greater assertiveness by social groups: while the states are paralyzed, movements like the Islamists appear to have seized the initiative. Some think the growing energy of social groups can be harnessed to help forge democracies in the region. The neo-Orientalists, in contrast, assert that the proliferation of social movements will discourage any trend toward power sharing and greater tolerance in the region, if it does not breed civil war and anarchy.

It is clear that the neo-Orientalist argument is seriously flawed. Crone, Pipes, and Gellner have retained exactly those ideas that vitiated classical Orientalism. They too portray Islam as a social entity whose "essential" core is immune to change by historical influences. Crone describes how the *'ulama'* wrote their tribal biases into the structure of Islamic doctrine—and claims that this bias continued long after the Arabs settled down, the *'ulama'* grew sedentary, and Muslim society became largely detribalized. Like the classical Orientalists before them, the neo-Orientalists portray Islam (the religion) as a kind of family curse that lives on, crippling the lives of innocent generations after the original sin that created it. They claim that Muslim efforts to build durable states—from Ibn Khaldun's radical insights in the fourteenth century to Ottoman tax reformers in the seventeenth century or Islamist revolutionaries today—have not, and never can, bring about a change in the essential antistate and therefore antimodern core of Islamic dogma.[59]

As a corollary to this essentialism, the neo-Orientalists also (like the classical Orientalists) downplay the importance of imperialism. A fairly consistent refrain in Orientalist analyses is that "in the Middle East the impact of European imperialism was late, brief, and for the most part indirect."[60] For Orientalists of all varieties, there is no point in dwelling on the fact that half the populations of Libya and Algeria died during the course of their colonial occupation. The fact that the Ottoman and Qajar empires were effectively deindustrialized when European imports wiped out their protoindustrial manufactures during the nineteenth-century era of "free trade" is irrelevant to issues of economic development.[61] According any weight to these events would tend to undermine the claim that the obstacles to development are overwhelmingly internal and have not changed during the fourteen hundred years of Islamic history. Essentialism and the dismissal of Western colonialism and imperialism are commonly paired together, since each makes the other more plausible.[62]

Neo-Orientalist analyses do not prove that states in the Middle East must be weak, any more than classical Orientalism proved that states had to be strong. But does this mean that the alternative proposition—that the strong societies of the Middle East provide a groundwork for democratization—is correct? The fact is that both traditional and neo-Orientalist analyses of civil society are deeply flawed. Both claim that the key to building effective states and successful democracies lies in the proper balance of power between state and society. They disagree only over what the proper balance is, over how strong society should be. The traditionalists claim that society must not be too weak; the neo-Orientalists claim it must not be too strong. Perhaps there is a narrow range where society is neither too strong nor too weak but "just right."

How can we determine whether the strength of civil society is "just right"? Studies of state-society relations almost invariably issue sweeping judgments: "In the Arab homeland, the state means everything and it monopolizes almost all facilities, while the society means very little."[63] Some critics suggest that there is no way to determine the optimum strength of civil society because there is no fixed balance of power between state and society. Albert Hirschman has argued that there is a cyclical pattern in which the public and private sectors alternate in strength.[64] Periods of expanding state authority are followed by correcting periods of liberalization. (The evolution of the concept of civil society may even reflect these cycles: successive generations tend to emphasize either the independence or the civility of society.)[65]

The relationship between state and society may be more complex than the classic models allow. Not only may the relationship evolve over time but the state and society may be antagonistic and collaborative in distinct areas simultaneously. "The British fiscal-military state," noted John Brewer in a brilliant study of the role of taxation in British state formation,

> as it emerged from the political and military battles that marked the struggle with Louis XIV, lacked many of the features we normally associate with a "strong state," yet therein lay its effectiveness. The constraints on power meant that when it was exercised, it was exercised fully. As long as the fiscal-military state did not cross the bulwarks erected to protect civil society from militarization it was given its due. Yet it was watched with perpetual vigilance by those who, no matter how much they lauded its effectiveness against foreign foes, were deeply afraid of its intrusion into civil society.[66]

Perhaps the key to combining state building with democratization is not the Goldilocks solution of finding the balance that is "just right," but the more subtle question of finding an optimal "division of labor" between state and society.[67]

Students of the Middle East can be forgiven for not having easy answers to these questions. After all, they study a region where practical experience with democracy is rare. But they should not be excused from attending to these questions. The fact that democracy has not flourished in the Middle East does not mean its development is impossible. If Middle East experts look for models of how to study democratization in the region, they will find some admirable ones without much trouble. It is long past time for serious scholars to abandon the quest for the mysterious "essences" that prevent democratization in the Middle East and turn to the matter-of-fact itemization of the forces that promote or retard this process.[68]

NOTES

1. Francis Fukuyama, "The End of History?" *National Interest* (summer 1989): 3.

2. See Larry Diamond, *An American Foreign Policy for Democracy* (Washington, D.C.: Progressive Policy Institute, 1990); and Joshua Muravchik, *Exporting Democracy: Fulfilling America's Destiny* (Washington, D.C.: American Enterprise Institute Press, 1992).

3. *Foreign Broadcast Information Service,* March 30, 1992. See also A. H. Fahad, "The Arabs and the Just Despot," *Wall Street Journal,* October 9, 1990.

4. James Schlesinger, "The Quest for a Post–Cold War Foreign Policy," *Foreign Affairs* 72, no. 1 (winter 1993): 20.

5. Samuel P. Huntington, "Will More Countries Become Democratic?" *Political Science Quarterly* 99 (summer 1984): 216. A survey of the prospects for democracy published volumes on Asia, Africa, and Latin America but did not include any studies of the Middle East because "with the exception perhaps of Egypt, Lebanon, and certainly Turkey (which appears in our Asia volume), the Islamic countries of the Middle East and North Africa generally lack much previous democratic experience, and most appear to have little prospect of transition even to semidemocracy." (Larry Diamond, Juan J. Linz, and Seymour Martin Lipset, eds., *Democracy in Developing Countries,* vol. 2, *Africa* (Boulder: Lynne Rienner, 1988), p. xx.

6. Daniel Pipes, "The Muslims are Coming! The Muslims are Coming!" *National Review* 42 (November 19, 1990): 29.

7. For a tongue-in-cheek list, see Samuel P. Huntington, *The Third Wave: Democratization in the Late Twentieth Century* (Norman: University of Oklahoma Press, 1991), pp. 37–38.

8. The growing popularity of the concept of civil society is analyzed in John Keane, *Democracy and Civil Society* (London: Verso, 1988). Adam B. Seligman describes its use as a kind of shibboleth in Eastern Europe in *The Idea of Civil Society* (New York: Free Press, 1992). The increasing reliance on this concept in analyses of developing countries is described in Atul Kohli, *India's Democracy: An Analysis of Changing State-Society Relations* (Princeton: Princeton University Press, 1988). Its spread among Arab intellectuals is also evident; see the special issue on civil society of *Al-Mustaqbal al-'Arabi,* no. 158 (April 1992); *Al-Mujtama' al-madani fi al-watan al-'arabi wa-dawruhu fi tahqiq al-dimuqratiyya* (Beirut: Markaz Dirasat al-Wahda al-'Arabiyya, 1993); and the Ibn Khaldun Center's *Al-Mujtama' al-madani wa'l-tahawwul al-dimuqrati fi al-watan al-'arabi* (Cairo: Dar Su'ad al-Sabah, 1992).

9. John Keane provides an excellent history of the evolution of the concept in "Despotism and Democracy: The Origins and Development of the Distinction between Civil Society and the State," in John Keane (ed.), *Civil Society and the State* (London: Verso, 1988), though Keane slights Montesquieu, who contributed both to the conceptualization of civil society and to the foundation of Orientalism. De Tocqueville did not employ the term "civil society," but his *Democracy in America* (New York: Vintage Books, 1945), especially pp. 198–206, may have influenced thinking about how civic associations affect political power more than any other study.

10. The early development of the idea that civil society does not exist in the Orient is brilliantly analyzed in Patricia Springborg, *Western Republicanism and the*

Oriental Prince (Austin: University of Texas Press, 1992). Also see Bryan Turner, "Orientalism and the Problem of Civil Society," in Assaf Hussein (ed.), *Orientalism, Islam and Islamists* (Brattelboro: Amana Press, 1984), pp. 23–42.

11. Roy Mottahedeh, *Loyalty and Leadership in an Early Islamic Society* (Princeton: Princeton University Press, 1980), p. 4.

12. Robert Springborg, "Patterns of Association in the Egyptian Political Elite," in George Lenczowski (ed.), *Political Elites in the Middle East* (Washington, D.C.: American Enterprise Institute Press, 1975), p. 87.

13. An unusually intelligent summary of this thesis is Şerif Mardin, "Power, Civil Society and Culture in the Ottoman Empire," *Comparative Studies in Society and History* 2 (June 1969): 258–81.

14. Clement Henry Moore, "Authoritarian Politics in Unincorporated Society: The Case of Nasser's Egypt," *Comparative Politics* 6 (1974): 207.

15. Two of the classic studies in this tradition are Clement Henry Moore, *Tunisia since Independence: The Dynamics of One-Party Government* (Berkeley: University of California Press, 1965); and John Waterbury, *The Commander of the Faithful: The Moroccan Political Elite, A Study in Segmented Politics* (New York: Columbia University Press, 1970). Both Moore and Waterbury later grew disenchanted with the classical Orientalist vision of civil society and undertook studies that gave greater emphasis to the independence of social forces; see Clement Henry Moore, "Clientelist Ideology and Political Change: Fictitious Networks in Egypt and Tunisia," in Ernest Gellner and John Waterbury (eds.), *Patrons and Clients in Mediterranean Societies* (London: Duckworth, 1977), pp. 255–73; and John Waterbury, *The Egypt of Nasser and Sadat: The Political Economy of Two Regimes* (Princeton: Princeton University Press, 1983).

16. Another popular explanation was the theory of hydraulic despotism, which attributed the state's power over society to its organization of essential irrigation works. The *locus classicus* of this concept is Karl Wittfogel, *Oriental Despotism: A Comparative Study of Total Power* (New Haven: Yale University Press, 1957). For a history of this concept, see "The 'Asiatic Mode of Production'" in Perry Anderson, *Lineages of the Absolutist State* (London: Verso, 1974), pp. 462–550.

17. This became, literally, the textbook description of Islamic political culture; see James A. Bill and Robert Springborg, *Politics in the Middle East,* 3d ed. (New York: Harper Collins, 1990), pp. 156–57.

18. The idea that Islam requires a totalitarian state is accepted by *some* modern Muslims, particularly those associated with al-Mawdudi, but even some Orientalists recognized that this is a historical novelty, appealing only to a minority, rather than something inherent in Islam. See W. M. Watt, *Islamic Political Thought* (Edinburgh: Edinburgh University Press, 1968), pp. 120–23.

19. Bernard Lewis, *The Middle East and the West* (New York: Harper Torchbooks, 1964), p. 48.

20. Ibid.

21. For a concise statement of the traditional Orientalist position, see Elie Kedourie, *Democracy and Arab Political Culture* (Washington, D.C.: Washington Institute for Near East Policy, 1992), p. 4.

22. Ibid., p. 8.

23. Ibid. See also P. J. Vatikiotis, *Islam and the State* (London: Croom Helm, 1987); and Bernard Lewis, *The Political Language of Islam* (Chicago: University of Chicago Press, 1988).

24. To mention only two of the most prominent, see the essays collected in Claude Cahen, *Les peuples musulmans dans l'histoire médiéval* (Damascus: Institut Français de Damas, 1977) (which, unfortunately, does not include his pioneering "Mouvements populaires et autonisme urbain dans l'Asie Musulmane du Moyen Age," *Arabica* 4–5 [1958–59]); and S. D. Goitein, *Studies in Islamic History and Institutions* (Leiden: E.J. Brill, 1966).

25. Clement Henry Moore, "Islamic Banks: Financial and Political Intermediation in Arab Countries," *Orient* 29 (1988):45–57.

26. Ervand Abrahamian, "Oriental Despotism: The Case of Qajar Iran," *International Journal of Middle East Studies* 5 (1974):3–31; and idem, "European Feudalism and Middle Eastern Despotisms," *Science and Society* 39 (summer 1975):129–56. An unusually large number of students of Iran were early supporters of the dissident tradition that emphasized the potency of social forces in the Middle East. See, for example, Ervand Abrahamian, "The Crowd in the Persian Revolution," *Iranian Studies* 2 (autumn 1969):128–50; Hamid Algar, *Religion and State in Iran, 1785–1906* (Berkeley: University of California Press, 1969); and Nikki R. Keddie, *Iran: Religion, Politics and Society* (London: Frank Cass, 1980).

27. For example, Leonard Binder, while acknowledging the participation of Shi'i religious leaders in insurrections such as the Tobacco Revolt and the Iranian revolution of 1905, dismissed such activism: "while some *'ulama'* were prominent in these actions against the Qajar dynasty, they never acted alone nor did they press for unfettered political power on the basis of a religious theory of political legitimacy." See his *Iran: Political Development in a Changing Society* (Berkeley: University of California Press, 1962), p. 74.

28. See Juan R. I. Cole and Nikki R. Keddie, eds., *Shi'ism and Social Protest* (New Haven: Yale University Press, 1986); Martin Kramer (ed.), *Shi'ism, Resistance, and Revolution* (Boulder: Westview Press, 1987).

29. For example, John Waterbury, "The 'Soft State' and the Open Door: Egypt's Experience with Economic Liberalization, 1974–1984," *Comparative Politics* 18 (October 1985):65–83; and Joel S. Migdal, *Strong Societies and Weak States: State-Society Relations and State Capabilities in the Third World* (Princeton: Princeton University Press, 1988). For related studies on other developing countries, see Alfred Stepan, *The State and Society: Peru in Comparative Perspective* (Princeton: Princeton University Press, 1978); Thomas M. Callaghy, *The State-Society Struggle: Zaire in Comparative Perspective* (New York: Columbia University Press, 1984); and Vivien Shue, *The Reach of the State: Sketches of the Chinese Body Politic* (Stanford: Stanford University Press, 1988).

30. A growing number of works tried to apply the American tradition of "interest group analysis." See Robert Bianchi, *Interest Groups and Political Development in Turkey* (Princeton: Princeton University Press, 1984); and Samia Sa'id, *Man yamluk misr?* (Cairo: Dar al-Mustaqbal al-'Arabi, 1986). Although Arab authors developed a growing interest in the influence of social groups, they tended to concur with the classical Orientalists that these groups lacked the necessary power to press for democratization of the Arab world; see Sa'd al-Din Ibrahim, *Al-Mujtama' wa 'l-dawla fi al-watan*

al-'arabi (Beirut: Markaz Dirasat al-Wahda al-'Arabiyya, 1988); and Mustapha K. Al-Sayyid, "Slow Thaw in the Arab World," *World Policy Journal* 8 (fall 1991):711–38. For an exception to this generalization, see Rachad Antonius and Qussai Samak, "A Civil Society at the Pan-Arab Level? The Role of Non-Governmental Organizations," in Hani Faris (ed.), *Arab Nationalism and the Future of the Arab World* (Belmont, Mass.: Association of Arab-American University Graduates, 1986), pp. 81–93.

31. See the think piece written for the project: Peter von Sivers, "Retreating States and Expanding Societies: The State Autonomy/Informal Civil Society Dialectic in the Middle East and North Africa" (unpublished mimeograph, 1987). Similar conclusions are evident in another paper written for the SSRC project: Emmanuel Sivan, "The Islamic Resurgence: Civil Society Strikes Back," *Journal of Contemporary History* 25 (1990): 353–64.

32. The three-year NYU-based Civil Society in the Middle East Project, under the direction of Augustus Richard Norton and Farhad Kazemi, published a two-volume set of case studies on civil society, a primer, and a monthly newsletter. Augustus Richard Norton (ed.), *Civil Society in the Middle East*, vol. 1 (Leiden: E.J. Brill, 1994); vol. 2 (Leiden: E.J. Brill, 1996); Jillian Schwedler (ed.), *Toward Civil Society in the Middle East? A Primer* (Boulder, Colo.: Lynne Rienner, 1995).

33. Asad Abu Khalil, "A Viable Partnership: Islam, Democracy and the Arab World," *Harvard International Review* 15 (winter 1992/93): 22–23, 65; Muhammad Muslih and Augustus Richard Norton, "The Need for Arab Democracy," *Foreign Policy*, no. 83 (summer 1991): 3–19; and Michael C. Hudson, "After the Gulf War: Prospects for Democratization in the Arab World," *Middle East Journal* 45 (summer 1991): 407–26.

34. Crone's first book, *Hagarism: The Making of the Islamic World* (Cambridge: Cambridge University Press, 1977), argues that originally Islam was a Judaic heresy dedicated to reclaiming Palestine for the Arabs and that Muhammad was not its major prophet but just a messenger who announced the appearance of the Messiah ('Umar ibn al-Khattab). This controversial thesis did not win wide acceptance, but it did gain respect for her erudition and lucid analysis. Crone's more recent writings have won much wider support; see R. Steven Humphreys, *Islamic History: A Framework for Inquiry* (Princeton: Princeton University Press, 1991), pp. 84–85.

35. Patricia Crone, *Slaves on Horses: The Evolution of the Islamic Polity* (Cambridge: Cambridge University Press, 1980), p. 62.

36. Ibid., pp. 62–63.

37. For a chronology of these events, see Patricia Crone and Martin Hinds, *God's Caliph: Religious Authority in the First Centuries of Islam* (Cambridge: Cambridge University Press, 1986).

38. Crone, *Slaves on Horses*, p. 84.

39. For criticism of "mamlukism," the idea that the medieval *mamluk* institution can be hypostatized to serve as a model for contemporary Arab politics, see Haim Gerber, *The Social Origins of the Modern Middle East* (Boulder, Colo.: Lynne Rienner, 1987), pp. 149–61; and Jean-Claude Garcin, "The Mamluk Military System and the Blocking of Medieval Muslim Society," in Jean Baechler, John A. Hall, and Michael Mann (eds.), *Europe and the Rise of Capitalism* (Oxford: Basil Blackwell, 1988), pp. 113–30.

40. Daniel Pipes, *Slave Soldiers and Islam: The Genesis of a Military System* (New Haven: Yale University Press, 1981), p. 62.

41. Ibid., p. 70. The notion that the gap between ideals and realities was particularly acute in Islam was already a well-established theme in Orientalist literature, although Pipes deduced new implications from it; see Gustave E. von Grunebaum, "The Body Politic: Law and the State," in *Medieval Islam* (Chicago: University of Chicago Press, 1965), pp. 142–69.

42. Daniel Pipes, *In the Path of God: Islam and Political Power* (New York: Basic Books, 1983), pp. 187–88. For a critical response, see Edward W. Said, "Orientalism Reconsidered," in Francis Barker et al. (eds.), *Literature, Politics and Theory* (London: Methuen, 1986), pp. 210–29.

43. See, for example, Pipes's "Fundamental Questions About Muslims," *Wall Street Journal,* October 30, 1992; "Why America Can't Save the Kurds," *Wall Street Journal,* April 11, 1991; and "Why Arabs Aren't Rioting," *Wall Street Journal,* January 22, 1991. Pipes also serves as editor of *Middle East Quarterly,* which he started in 1991 as a "journal [that] promotes American interests in the Middle East."

44. See J. G. Merquior, *Foucault* (Berkeley: University of California Press, 1985); Michael Mann, *The Sources of Social Power,* vol. 1 (Cambridge: Cambridge University Press, 1986); and John A. Hall, *Powers and Liberties: The Causes and Consequences of the Rise of the West* (Harmondsworth: Penguin, 1985). These scholars shared several sources of inspiration in common, including the works of Ernest Gellner (see note 48 below) and E. L. Jones, *The European Miracle: Environments, Economies and Geopolitics in the History of Europe and Asia* (Cambridge: Cambridge University Press, 1981).

45. Hall, *Powers and Liberties,* p. 89.

46. Ibid.

47. Ibid., p. 102.

48. Gellner's direct contributions to Middle East studies include his classic anthropological study *Saints of the High Atlas* (Chicago: University of Chicago Press, 1969) and his brilliant resurrection of Ibn Khaldun's sociology, *Muslim Society* (Cambridge: Cambridge University Press, 1981). Gellner has also been a major voice in analytic philosophy, philosophy of science, and East European studies. For a critique, see Sami Zubaida, "Is There a Muslim Society? Ernest Gellner's Sociology of Islam," *Economy and Society* 24, no. 2 (May 1995): 151–88.

49. For an instance of this argument set against the wider background of Gellner's philosophy of history, see his *Plough, Sword, and Book: The Structure of Human History* (Chicago: University of Chicago Press, 1988).

50. Ernest Gellner, "A Social Contract in Search of an Idiom: The Demise of the Danegeld State," in *Spectacles and Predicaments: Essays in Social Theory* (Cambridge: Cambridge University Press, 1980), p. 286.

51. Ibid., p. 287.

52. For the classic critiques of Weber's Protestant ethic thesis, see Kurt Samuelsson, *Religion and Economic Action* (New York: Harper Torchbooks, 1957); and Maxime Rodinson, *Islam and Capitalism* (New York: Pantheon, 1973).

53. Hegel was similarly skeptical of claims that political assertiveness by social groups produced national progress; see Manfred Riedel, *Between Revolution and*

Tradition: The Hegelian Transformation of Political Philosophy (Cambridge: Cambridge University Press, 1984), pp. 129–58.

54. Richard Rose, "Overloaded Government: The Problem Outlined," *European Studies Newsletter* 5 (1975): 13–18; Samuel Brittan, "The Economic Contradictions of Democracy," *British Journal of Political Science* 5 (1975): 129–59; James Douglas, "Review Article: The Overloaded Crown," *British Journal of Political Science* 6 (1976): 498–500; and Philippe C. Schmitter, "Interest Intermediation and Regime Governability in Contemporary Western Europe and North America," in Suzanne D. Berger (ed.), *Organizing Interests in Western Europe* (Cambridge: Cambridge University Press, 1981), pp. 285–327.

55. Mancur Olson, *The Rise and Decline of Nations* (New Haven: Yale University Press, 1982), pp. 75–76. During the 1970s and 1980s, the continued economic growth of Japan, South Korea, Taiwan, and Singapore bred a growing respect—not just in the West, but also in communist China and the Soviet Union—for the virtues of strong effective states. For the idea that the economic effectiveness of the state in these societies rested on a "soft authoritarianism" which insulated policy makers from the demands of workers, consumers, and other cranky groups, see Chalmers Johnson, *MITI and the Japanese Miracle* (Stanford: Stanford University Press, 1982).

56. See Michel Crozier, Samuel Huntington, and Joji Watanuki, *The Crisis of Democracy: Report on the Governability of Democracies to the Trilateral Commission* (New York: New York University Press, 1975); James M. Buchanan and Richard E. Wagner, *Democracy in Deficit: The Political Legacy of Lord Keynes* (New York: Academic Press, 1977); and Olson, *Rise and Decline*. This type of analysis helped to provide the intellectual rationale for the neoconservatism of Reagan and Thatcher. For more critical studies of the politics of inflation, see Fred Hirsch and John H. Goldthorpe (eds.), *The Political Economy of Inflation* (Cambridge, Mass.: Harvard University Press, 1978); and Leon Lindberg and Charles S. Maier (eds.), *The Politics of Inflation and Economic Stagnation* (Washington, D.C.: Brookings Institution, 1985).

57. Philippe C. Schmitter, "Still a Century of Corporatism?" *Review of Politics* 36 (January 1974): 85–121; and Peter Katzenstein, *Small States in World Markets: Industrial Policy in Europe* (Ithaca: Cornell University Press, 1985). For an attempt to apply the concept of corporatism to the Middle East, see Robert Bianchi, *Unruly Corporatism: Associational Life in Twentieth Century Egypt* (Oxford: Oxford University Press, 1989).

58. See Arend Lijphart, "Consociational Democracy," *World Politics* 21 (1969): 207–25; Hans Daalder, "On Building Consociational Nations: The Cases of the Netherlands and Switzerland," *International Social Science Journal* 23 (1971): 355–70; and Gerhard Lembruch, "Consociational Democracy, Class Conflict and the New Corporatism," in Philippe C. Schmitter and Gerhard Lembruch (eds.), *Trends Toward Corporatist Intermediation* (Beverly Hills: Sage, 1980), pp. 53–61.

59. For Ibn Khaldun, see Yves Lacoste, *Ibn Khaldun: The Birth of History and the Past of the Third World* (London: Verso, 1984), pp. 92–131. For the Ottoman attempt to confront fiscal crisis and build an absolutist monarchy, see Rifa'at 'Ali Abou-El-Haj, *Formation of the Modern State: The Ottoman Empire Sixteenth to Eighteenth Centuries* (Albany: State University of New York Press, 1991); and Jack A. Goldstone, "East and West in the Seventeenth Century: Political Crises in Stuart England, Ottoman

Turkey, and Ming China," *Comparative Studies in Society and History* 30 (1988):103–42. Islamists are producing some of the most original thinking on state-society relations in the contemporary world; see, for example, Hasan Turabi, "Islam, Democracy, the State and the West," *Middle East Policy* 1 (1992): 49–61; and Sami Zubaida, "Religion, the State, and Democracy: Contrasting Conceptions of Society in Egypt," in this volume.

60. Bernard Lewis, *The Middle East and the West*, p. 31. Lewis has recently expanded on this idea, arguing that, since Muslims have no "real" reasons to complain about Western imperialism, their resentment of the West must be rooted in irrational feelings of "humiliation—a growing awareness, among the heirs of an old, proud, and long dominant civilization, of having been overtaken, overborne and overwhelmed by those whom they regarded as their inferiors." See his "The Roots of Muslim Rage," *The Atlantic Monthly* 266 (September 1990): 59. For a neo-Orientalist version of this argument, blaming Muslim radicalism on childish feelings of envy and magical thinking, see Daniel Pipes, "Dealing with Middle Eastern Conspiracy Theories," *Orbis* 36 (winter 1992): 41–46.

61. For casualty figures, see Mahfoud Bennoune, *The Making of Contemporary Algeria, 1830–1987* (Cambridge: Cambridge University Press, 1988), pp. 35–43; Lisa Anderson, *The State and Social Transformation in Tunisia and Libya, 1830–1980* (Princeton: Princeton University Press, 1986), pp. 201, 215. For the economic impact of imperialism, the best single work is Roger Owen, *The Middle East in the World Economy, 1800–1914* (London: Methuen, 1981). See also Huri Islamoğlu-Inan (ed.), *The Ottoman Empire and the World Economy* (Cambridge: Cambridge University Press, 1987).

62. Gyan Prakash has defined Orientalism as the "fabrication of the Orient in terms of founding essences invulnerable to historical change," in "Writing Post-Orientalist Histories of the Third World: Perspectives from Indian Historiography," *Comparative Studies in Society and History* 32 (April 1990): 384. Imperialism is one of the most important mechanisms of historical change that Orientalists must discount.

63. Bassam Tibi, "Political Freedom in Arab Societies," *Arab Studies Quarterly* 6 (summer 1984): 225.

64. Albert Hirschman, *Shifting Involvements: Private Interest and Public Action* (Princeton: Princeton University Press, 1982).

65. Keane, "Despotism and Democracy."

66. John Brewer, *The Sinews of Power: War, Money and the English State 1688–1783* (New York: Alfred A. Knopf, 1989), p. xx.

67. Measuring the strength or responsibilities of state and society is bound to be made more difficult by a lack of agreement over how to distinguish between the two; see the debate provoked by Timothy Mitchell, "The Limits of the State: Beyond Statist Approaches and Their Critics," *American Political Science Review* 85 (March 1991): 77–96.

68. See Dietrich Rueschemeyer, Evelyne Huber Stephens, and John D. Stephens, *Capitalist Development and Democracy* (Chicago: University of Chicago Press, 1992); and Nicos P. Mouzelis, *Politics in the Semi-Periphery: Early Parliamentarism and Late Industrialization in the Balkans and Latin America* (New York: St. Martin's Press, 1986).

4

Religion, the State, and Democracy: Contrasting Conceptions of Society in Egypt

Sami Zubaida

The quest for democratization and human rights in the Middle East has prominently featured the term "civil society." Oppression and corruption, it is argued, have followed from an overintrusive state and its bureaucracies. Democratization must include a withdrawal of the state to allow free spheres of social autonomy and initiative, whether economic or associational. These are the spheres of civil society.

"The state," though, is not a unified entity. It has many functions and facets. The conditions for the development of spheres of social autonomy are not only the "withdrawal" of the state, but also an active state intervention of another kind: clear legislation and institutional mechanisms which provide the framework of rights and obligations for these spheres. In the economic arena, for instance, the state must provide a clear and comprehensive framework of legislation on contract, labor, market standards, banking and finance, and so on. Similarly, trade unions and professional associations need enabling legislation as well as clear protection of individual members' rights.

Fragmentary and ambiguous legislation in these spheres, resulting from ad hoc liberalization measures such as those of Egypt's *infitah* (economic opening), lead to situations in which the new spheres of activity are burdened with ambiguous regulation, or operate on the margins of the law. As the case of Egypt's Islamic investment companies in the 1980s illustrates, individuals and enterprises are at the mercy of administrative interpretations and applications, and can only succeed through the informal facilitation and evasions of bureaucratic functionaries. They are not autonomous from the state, but depend on another of its facets: the corrupt bureaucracies.

TWO CONCEPTIONS

Egyptian intellectuals currently engaged in debates on liberalization and democratization have utilized two contrasting concepts of civil society. Saad Eddin Ibrahim, the well-known sociologist and writer, argues that reinforcement of civil society is the condition for building up democratic sentiments and institutions in the Arab world.[1] He opts for a definition in terms of voluntary associations. This is in contradistinction to the spheres of the state on the one hand, and of "primordial organizations" of kinship, tribe, village, or religious community on the other.

Both the state and "primordial associations" are spheres of authority and coercion which can oppress the individual and trample over human rights. Voluntary associations, by contrast, are areas which foster individual autonomy and provide experience in the exercise of social and political rights and responsibilities. The main examples of such associations are trade unions, professional associations, voluntary societies and clubs, pressure groups, and political parties. These can act as conduits for the expression and organization of members' rights and demands vis-à-vis the state and the wider society. They also protect their members from arbitrary administrative and political measures by state agencies. Interestingly, Ibrahim does not mention the spheres of private property and business enterprise as elements of civil society, although these are central to conceptions of civil society in classical social and political theory.

Ibrahim's ideas are widely shared by liberal and leftist Egyptian intellectuals and inform much of the human rights campaigning in that country. One such campaign is directed against Law 32 of 1964, which seriously impedes the formation and functioning of voluntary associations. This underlines my argument that civil society in the form of voluntary associations is essentially dependent on the "law-state."

To what extent is the Egyptian state a "law-state"? In theory, it is a constitutional state, and the agencies of the state are governed and regulated by the provisions of the constitution. In practice, though, the president has sweeping powers of rule by decree. Over the years, these decrees and emergency regulations, notably Anwar al-Sadat's emergency laws of 1981 which are still in operation, have abolished or suspended many of the rights guaranteed by the constitution. State ministries and bureaucracies have, in effect, wide administrative regulatory powers which do not derive from the constitution.

The strategy of human rights campaigns is to challenge some of these provisions as incompatible with the constitution. In line with this approach, the Constitutional Court has made a number of crucial judgments in recent years against government decisions, especially regarding licenses for the formation of political parties and on electoral procedures. On a few occasions lower courts have also ruled in favor of challenges to government regulations, such as that forbidding strikes, on the grounds that they are incompatible with international conventions to which Egypt is a signatory. Lawyers defending striking railway workers in 1986 used this argument successfully, but the court's judgment did not end the interdiction on strikes.

To sum up, in most respects the Egyptian government has wide administrative and legal powers which give its organs almost unlimited sway. The exercise of these powers is limited to a small extent by a few independent legal judgments, but to a much greater extent by sensitivity to local and international public opinion, especially in the United States and Europe. President Husni Mubarak's government is trying to project a moderate liberal-democratic image to its own intellectuals and to the Western world. This project is constrained by two factors: the inertia of its own entrenched bureaucracy, and the pressures against liberalism from the increasingly strident Islamic current.

A different conception of civil society comes from Tariq al-Bishri, a prominent historian and intellectual, previously Marxist but now sympathetic to the Islamic current, who views civil society as an informal network of relationships. The context of his argument is a qualified defense of the Islamic investment companies, which were threatened in the late 1980s with government regulation and control. Al-Bishri argues in terms of authenticity, as well as Islamic legitimacy.[2] The companies deal directly with investors, bypassing the financial network of official banks. Largely unregulated by government, the companies are, according to al-Bishri, an extension of traditional practices in the Egyptian countryside and provinces, where, rather than entrust his savings to a bank, a man would turn to a local merchant or landowner to whom he was connected by personal networks. The latter would invest them in his enterprises and give the lender a portion of the yield. This is precisely what the Islamic companies were doing, albeit on a much larger and more impersonal scale. To impose government and central bank regulation on such companies would be to make them part of the official financial establishment, thereby ruining this authentic traditional relationship. It would discourage small savers from investing their wealth in the development of Egypt through native enterprise.

Liberal commentators, such as the Wafd newspaper, also defend the Islamic companies against regulation in the name of the *sahwa* (renaissance) of civil society, which ought not to be stifled by the dead hand of bureaucracy. Civil society, in this conception, lies essentially outside the government, whose regulation would contaminate its authenticity. Informal networks and social relations of reciprocity or dependence are the essence of civil society. The focus of its activity is property and business (in contrast to Ibrahim, who leaves these elements out of his definition of civil society).

Behind Ibrahim's and al-Bishri's concepts lie two contrasting world-views—one secular-liberal, the other Islamic-communal.[3] One of the important political articulations of the first view is the campaign for human rights and democratic institutions, directed primarily at the government and the law, but increasingly also against the illiberal demands of the second, Islamist, worldview. This is not to say that all Islamist worldviews (and there are many) are necessarily or essentially illiberal. We are discussing here the specific case of the dominant "Islamic current" in Egypt.

VOLUNTARY ASSOCIATIONS AND THE LAW

In 1984, a group of Egyptian intellectuals, including lawyers, applied to the government to license two human rights associations: one Arab and the other, a branch of the first, Egyptian. Licenses were refused on security grounds. The two associations were nevertheless formed and function without licenses but with a high public profile. This illustrates the contradictions within the regime: an authoritarian bureaucratic rigidity, but also a sensitivity to international public opinion, before which Egypt must appear liberal and moderate. The law under which licenses are granted or withheld to civil associations is Law 32 of 1964, itself the object of a human rights campaign.[4]

Law 32 regulates only voluntary associations, not trade unions, professional associations, or political parties, to which other laws apply. Examples of voluntary associations include community development associations, village associations, educational and medical charities, women's societies, sporting clubs, art and music societies, and political pressure groups, such as the human rights associations.

Before 1952, the Egyptian civil code featured carefully drafted items on the licensing and operation of voluntary associations. The law, generally liberal, distinguished between three types of associations: politico-military societies, which were forbidden; nonprofit civil associations directed to any other purpose, which were constituted as legal persons and as such enjoyed full rights under the law; and charities, to which different and specific regulations applied. Infringements of the law by any of these societies could only be established and punished by the courts. Judgments against societies entailed financial penalties, but not the dissolution of the society or punishment of its officers. In the first half of the century, civil associations, alongside newspapers and universities, played a vital part in the renaissance of the intellectual, cultural, political, and sporting life of Egyptian society. Cairo University (then Fu'ad University) was established by precisely such an association. Some associations, newspapers, trade unions, and political parties suffered occasional police interference and oppression, but most survived.

In 1956, a Republican decree annulled items 54 through 80 of the civil law dealing with associations. All such associations, as well as political parties and charities, were dissolved and forced to reapply for licenses. Without the empowering legal codes, relicensing was at the whim of administrative regulation and discretion. In 1964, Law 32, rather than remedying this situation, explicitly gave sweeping powers to the Ministry of Social Affairs, local government, and their officials to license, regulate, monitor, and dissolve associations.

Under Law 32, prospective societies apply to the Ministry of Social Affairs for a license. This ministry must then send copies of the application to the directorate of security, the Arab Socialist Union (the sole recognized political organization in 1964) and those sections of the ministries in whose areas of competence the proposed society operates. Each of these bodies has to approve the application or express an opinion on its suitability. One clause of the law states that "if a society is constituted which proves to be contrary to public order or morality or if its objectives are illegal or contrary to the safety of the Republic or its social system, then that society is annulled."

Another clause forbids members of trade unions and professional associations to form any association to pursue activities appropriate to that union or profession. This is aimed at interest groups, mutual funds, and cooperatives formed among workers and colleagues. That is to say, the government-controlled unions are given complete monopoly over their members. Other arbitrary powers include the right to refuse the formation of a society because there is no need for it or because an existing society fulfills the same functions.

The Minister of Social Affairs can dissolve the board of management of a society and appoint his own nominees for a maximum period of three years. His appointee (usually an official of the ministry) has control over the society's funds. The minister also has the power to dissolve a society or amalgamate it with another which he judges to have similar objectives. In such cases, the board of the society must hand over to the ministry all the records and documents as well as the funds of the society. The minister can annul any resolution passed by the association if he judges it contrary to public order. The minister can also appoint officials or representatives of his ministry to the management board of any society, up to a half of its membership, for an unlimited period.

STATE DISCRETION

All these powers are administrative. The ministry need never resort to a court or a judge. Members of a dissolved association may take the matter to court, but they have to do so while all their records, documents, and funds are held in the ministry.

A 1972 directive from the Ministry of Social Affairs (No. 754) adds that members of the management boards of private societies and institutions have to obtain permission from the minister at least one month before traveling abroad to meetings or conferences where they represent their societies. Their requests have to be approved by the Ministry of Foreign Affairs and any other relevant authority. On their return, they also have to report on the conference to the General Directorate of Societies at the ministry. Local governments at the provincial level have similar sweeping powers over private societies.

A notable victim of this law is the Arab Women's Solidarity Association (AWSA), incorporated in Egypt and led by the well-known feminist writer and activist, Nawal El-Saadawi.[5] The AWSA was dissolved in June 1991 by the deputy governor of Cairo because of alleged financial irregularities, and its funds transferred to an Islamic women's organization. Informal favoritism toward Islamic associations by ministry functionaries is a regular occurrence. The dissolution of the AWSA was challenged by human rights campaigners in the Administrative Court in May 1992, but the case was eventually lost.

The powers of the Ministry of Social Affairs are not only regulative and disciplinary; they include the means of dispensing patronage and favor. Certain associations can be placed in a privileged category of "general" or "public" interest. Organizations in this category cannot have their funds confiscated. A recent study found that a disproportionate number of societies in this category have an Islamic reference.[6]

Societies may receive donations from private or public sources, including foreign agencies, but at the discretion of the ministry. They can also collect funds from the public (with authorization from the ministry). They can generate income by selling goods and services. Foreign donors have been closely involved in financing various associations, mainly of a charitable and self-help nature, such as those operating dispensaries and nurseries, and providing professional training. Whether a society can receive foreign funding or not is determined by a clause written into its constitution at the discretion of ministry officials. This authorization can be withdrawn at will. (The recent involvement of foreign aid agencies in human rights campaigns and explicitly in the efforts to reinforce "civil society" is an interesting development, not confined to Egypt.)

Many religious voluntary associations and activities operate under the aegis of *awqaf* (pious foundations) or particular mosques, and as such are not subject to the provisions of Law 32. Some 27 percent of registered associations have an Islamic reference.[7] Their functions include organizing the pilgrimage, teaching the Qur'an, and delivering social and medical services.

Islamic societies apparently enjoy special favors and privileges with ministry officials. Reportedly, ministry officials are included on the boards of management of many of these societies and paid a salary. This arrangement appears to be legal under Law 32 and in some cases required. Islamic associations are said to be the most likely to obtain authorization to collect money from the public. These arrangements are consistent with rising Islamist sympathies among government functionaries. It is notable in this respect that Islamist political groups and their organs, vociferous in their demands on other constitutional matters, have been remarkably silent on Law 32.[8]

These apparently cozy relations between Islamic associations and government officials are pertinent to the contrast drawn above between the two images of civil society. Islamic associations here seem to have greater freedom of operation—not by virtue of empowering legislation, but thanks to informal or semiformal arrangements with ministry officials. Law 32 is highly inimical to civil society in the formal legal sense because it requires the state to facilitate its operation, and constitutes a perfect illustration of the authoritarian bureaucratic state directly impeding the free associations of civil society. The Islamic associations get around these impediments through informal arrangements and networks which include state officials.

UNIONS AND PROFESSIONAL ASSOCIATIONS

Trade unions and professional associations are a central pillar of Saad Eddin Ibrahim's conception of civil society. After 1952, trade unions were integrated into the Nasirist state. Until recent years, the post of Minister of Labor was reserved for the general secretary of the Trade Union Federation. These unions, primarily comprised of workers in the vast public sector, are conduits of formal representation on boards of companies and enterprises and for communications between workers, management, and government. They do not negotiate pay and work conditions, though they do bargain for bonuses and incentives at particular plants. Unions are also the conduits of social welfare benefits to their members, and avenues for education, training, and promotion. As such, they have developed patronage networks which ensure the election of "responsible" officials.

Recent liberalization measures have attempted to separate unions from government in order to make them more credible and less alienating to their members. Only the existing single union for each industry remains licensed; the formation of independent unions is forbidden. Strikes remain outlawed under emergency regulations. Important unofficial strikes in the 1980s and 1990s in steel, textiles, and railways were forcefully repressed by the police.

Elections for union officers and delegates in 1991 were reported to have been free. The Islamists and the left were both disappointed; the successful candidates were mostly apolitical.

The unions constitute a glimmer of hope for the fortification of civil society in Egypt. They remain at present firmly tied to government and the public sector, in spite of liberalization measures, but the leadership behind the unofficial strikes may have a chance to flourish legitimately if pressure for change in the strike laws and on the monopolies of the official unions is successful. Privatization of parts of the public sector, if it proceeds, may further union autonomy.

The professional associations are the most advanced sectors of public life in Egypt, enjoying high status and speaking with an autonomous and respected voice. The Bar Association has been at the forefront of the campaigns for human rights and the rule of law. (In September 1992, candidates backed by the Muslim Brothers won a majority of seats in the Bar Association election. See Carrie Rosefsky Wickham's chapter in this volume.)

In the 1980s, the medical and engineering associations were largely dominated by the Islamist current. They are, however, quite different from one another in their internal politics and alignments. The Engineers' Association raises many complex issues; let us therefore take the simpler example of the Medical Association.

An estimated 70 percent of Egyptian doctors are under 35 years of age.[9] Only 25 percent are in private practice; most of the rest are employees of the Ministry of Health. Large numbers of recent graduates have brought with them into the profession and the association the Islamist ideologies and commitments prevailing in the universities, and especially the faculties of medicine. The Islamic influence arose in response to corruption in the faculties—the high prices of photocopies of lectures and manuals, the need to buy private lessons from professors at high fees in order to pass exams, and the special privileges accorded the children of faculty members and senior doctors. Another factor is the increasing importance of medical services provided by hospitals and clinics attached to mosques and Islamic charities. These provide an important avenue of employment for young doctors, superior to that offered by the ministry, as well as a reinforcement of their religio-political commitments.

What does the Islamic dominance in the Medical Association imply for our argument? The associations are important pillars of civil society in Ibrahim's sense. They are democratic and voluntary associations of public interest and commitment. At the same time, and in that capacity, the Medical Association is becoming involved in the networks of the Islamic sector, the informal civil society that al-Bishri advocates. To survive as an autonomous and democratic body, the Medical Association requires enforceable legal guarantees provided by a law-state.

THE ECONOMIC SPHERE

The secure right to private property, freedom of contract, and a free market are essential elements of the classic conceptions of civil society, whether liberal, Hegelian, or Marxist. Security of private property and of contract are seen in this context as bases for multiple centers of social power which defy attempts by authoritarian and despotic rulers to monopolize power.

Anwar al-Sadat's *infitah* was meant to end state control of economic activity. State bureaucracies, however, in the form of the "public sector," remained firmly in control of the commanding heights of the economy. Private enterprise was at its most successful in partnership (official or unofficial) with or under the patronage of these bureaucracies and their personnel. Osman Ahmad Osman was the perfect example of *infitah* achievement in the Sadat era: a contractor-businessman with firm official and personal connections to the state bureaucracies and with family-cum-marriage connections to the president.

The Mubarak regime remains committed to economic liberalization, including the privatization of public sector enterprises. How much of this will be accomplished remains to be seen. An important element in the program of *infitah* and privatization is adequate legislation to facilitate the operation of enterprises: contracts, licenses, consumer protection, labor laws, and so on. Here again the law-state is an essential condition for civil society.

The Egyptian case is admirably summed up by Robert Springborg:

> Instead of undertaking basic structural reforms which would create an environment truly conducive to private investment, the government of Egypt has been preoccupied with tinkering with the legal superstructure. The tinkering has produced some more liberal conditions governing investment, but the gain is partially offset by uncertainty resulting from the tinkering itself. Moreover, even while seeking to entice private investment through special incentives, the Egyptian authorities have presided simultaneously over the further expansion of the state's role in the economy. Public revenue as a percentage of GDP climbed steadily during the *infitah*, rising from 34.4 percent in 1975 to 43 percent in 1984. The state, far from withdrawing from this arena in favor of private enterprise, has occupied a greater share of it.[10]

The resulting uncertainty, together with the corruption of large sectors of the bureaucracy, imposes constraints but also provides incentives for entrepreneurs to acquiesce in easy, bureaucracy-dependent moneymaking. This situation does not facilitate the formation of independent and organized business classes, one of the pillars of "civil society" in classical social theory. However, it does overwhelmingly favor the informal civil society of al-Bishri as against the social autonomies of Ibrahim. Civil society in this sense is not outside the state, but dependent—indeed, parasitic—upon it.

The Islamic investment companies illustrate this point very well.[11] Al-Bishri and others defend them in the name of social autonomy from the state: private enterprise outside the regulative dead hand of bureaucracy; Egyptians investing directly in their own economy. This is a myth. These companies only functioned freely because they recruited influential high-ranking officials, both retired and in office, to their boards of directors and consultancies at high fees. When the ruling politicians realized that they were losing control over the loyalty of their own bureaucracies, as well as risking public scandal, they clamped down firmly. And when the government acted, its control was arbitrary: there was no law or constitutional provision to qualify or temper the absolute power of the state to promulgate decrees. True, these companies were involved in all kinds of irregularities and dubious practices. The ultimate government response to them, however, is an example of arbitrary power which could have been employed against any target perceived as a threat.

THE ISLAMIC SECTOR

There is no organized, unitary Islamic sector. The investment companies do not seem to have strong links to political organizations. The *gama'at islamiyya* (Islamic groups) may be loosely connected among themselves. What they have in common, however, is a mode of operation through private social networks, communal powers, communal welfare provisions, and so on.[12] For instance, the *gama'at* are trying to establish their control over villages and in urban quarters in Cairo and elsewhere. Alain Roussillon puts forward the hypothesis that these groups are attempting to replace the traditional notables who controlled these units, establishing client networks, mediating with authorities, enforcing rules of morality and order at the local level, and settling disputes. The violence in the 'Ayn Shams quarter in the late 1980s can then be seen as a battle for control against local resistance, and possibly against rival groups.[13]

The "Islamic economy" is not a distinct or unitary sector. There is little evidence of a connection between Islamic banks and Islamic investment societies; the latter prefer Western banks. Neither are connected to medium and small Islamic enterprises. The Islamic welfare institutions also operate at different levels, from small clinics attached to private mosques to the grand, modern hospital in Muhandisin. What they have in common is that they provide a wide range of employment opportunities and welfare benefits (not free but affordable). The criteria for enjoying these opportunities and benefits are personal and particularistic: adherence to Islam (including the codes of social and family morality), but also networks of patronage and clientship, communal membership and loyalty, and possibly political allegiance.

What kind of civil society is this? It is outside the state, but not necessarily against the state: it fulfills an important function of social control. It could, under certain conditions, be mobilized against the state. But if the quest for civil society is one which seeks a framework for the exercise of human rights and social autonomy, then the model presented by the Islamic sector does not fulfill these requirements. It reproduces under modern conditions the authoritarian and patriarchal framework of the associations of kinship, village, and religious community at a time when such communities have been effectively loosened and dispersed by the socioeconomic processes of modernity.

"SOCIAL ISLAM" AS AN OBSTACLE

Egyptian human rights activists are concerned by the antidemocratic thrust of these kinds of arrangements. It is clear that the authoritarian impulse in Egypt, as elsewhere in the region, does not emanate solely from the state and its organs, but also from various Islamist quarters of authority and communal organization. Islamist sympathizers in ministries and among government functionaries often draw on both sources. Authoritative voices from al-Azhar, the voice of "official" Islam in Egypt, are raised increasingly against secularist and liberal opinion. They and their Islamist allies seem to have great influence over the media, from which they are able to exclude their opponents. Their call for the banning of books has been successful in many cases, notably that of 'Ala' Hamid's *A Distance in a Man's Mind*, condemned for blasphemy by an emergency court in 1991 and its author sentenced to eight years in jail. The attempt to ban Judge 'Ashmawi's critical books on law and government has so far failed. The assassination of prominent secularist writer and activist Farag Fuda by a Jihad militant is a tragic example of the campaign of intimidation of opposing voices. The "extremist" Jihad shares the objectives of the "moderate" Muslim Brothers and its state-backed Azhar allies.

Authoritarian inputs into Egyptian society also come from communal organizations, the "informal" model of civil society. The control of Islamist groups over some villages and urban quarters has replaced the traditional authority and control of local notables and bosses. Against the romantic view that this is some sort of grassroots, "authentic" popular expression, Muhammad al-Sayyid Sa'id has pointed out the authoritarian nature of the relationship of Islamist leaderships to the masses at the local levels.[14] The religious networks make no effort to recruit local leaders onto their councils of administration, which consist exclusively of their own members. Far from being popular organizations, the Islamic associations constitute the instrument by which the Islamist current controls and directs the masses. They do not encourage or foster autonomous popular organization or action, but treat the masses as objects of religious reform and control. The religious discourse does not give voice to the masses, but is directed at ethical pedagogy at the individual level and political organization at the national one. The levels between the individual and the state are covered by an unalterable *shari'a*.

One of the most disturbing elements of this kind of authoritarian communalism is the attacks on Coptic targets in the towns and villages of Upper Egypt, but also in Cairo, with loss of life as well as property. This is now one of the central problems for the Egyptian human rights organizations and activists. Baha' al-Din Hasan, when director of the Egyptian Human Rights Organization, campaigned in defense of the Christian inhabitants of Manshiyyat Nasr in the south. They have been subjected to violent attacks by the *gama'at* attempting to control the village by fanning communal tensions and intimidating Muslim inhabitants into taking sides. The police and the Ministry of the Interior have concentrated on protecting their own personnel and installations in the area, ignoring the plight of the inhabitants.[15]

The campaigns for human rights, freedom of expression and association, women's rights, and equality of religious minorities come up not only against the authoritarian state but also against religious authority and forms of authoritarian communal organization which derive legitimacy from the prevailing religious ambience. These illiberal forces are increasingly represented in government apparatuses, both formally, in the constitutional commitment to the *shari'a* enshrined by al-Sadat, and informally, in terms of networks and sympathies. Elements of the Islamic sector, such as *gama'at* violence in Upper Egypt, pose a threat to public order. On the other hand, much of the Islamic sector represents a force for social control by providing authoritative social and economic organization in sectors of society which could otherwise be disorderly.

In the current discourse, there is a ready identification of democracy with the ballot box. Free elections are, of course, an important element in democracy. For democracy to be an ongoing system rather than episodic elections, however, it must be instituted as a constitutional framework. Legal reforms, constitutional guarantees of rights, independence of the judiciary—in short, progress toward a law-state—are necessary preconditions for free elections. The constituencies in Egyptian society in favor of progress in these directions are important: the liberal intelligentsia occupy prominent positions in the state, education, the press, and some of the professional associations. They are aided by the desire of the top political leadership to project a favorable image of Egypt as a liberal and moderate country. Western governments may be cynical in their attitudes toward democracy and human rights, but public opinion and the media in the West can exert pressures for democratization. Some of the nongovernmental organizations have been active on this front. The obstacles faced by the liberal forces are enormous, but there are a few bright spots where progress is possible.

NOTES

1. Sa'd al-Din Ibrahim, *Al-mujtama' al-madani wa'l-tahawwul al-dimuqrati fi al-watan al-'arabi* (Cairo: Ibn Khaldun Research Center, 1991).

2. Tariq al-Bishri, *Al-Ahram al-Iqtisadi,* no. 1018, July 18, 1988, pp. 20–25.

3. In fairness, it should be noted that Tariq al-Bishri is explicitly in favor of democratic institutions and respect for human rights. What follows relates not to these explicit views but to the implications for these issues of his conception of social and economic "authenticity."

4. For a history of the law pertaining to associations, see Amir Salim, *Difa'an 'an takwin al-jam'iyyat* (Cairo: Center for Legal Research and Human Rights Information, 1991).

5. See Joel Beinin, "Egyptian Women and the Politics of Protest," *Middle East Report,* no. 176 (May–June 1992): 41–42.

6. Sarah Ben Nefissa-Paris," Le mouvement associatif égyptien et l'islam," *Monde Arabe: Maghreb/Machrek,* no. 135 (January–March 1992):19–36.

7. Ibid., p. 28.

8. Ibid., p. 32.

9. Alain Roussillon, "Entre al-Jihad et al-Rayyan: phénomonologie de l'islamisme égyptien," in *Modernisation et nouvelles formes de mobilisation sociale* (Cairo: Dossiers du CEDEJ, 1991), pp. 39–69.

10. Robert Springborg, "Egypt," in Tim Niblock and Emma Murphy, eds., *Economic and Political Liberalization in the Middle East* (London: I.B. Tauris, 1992), p. xx.

11. For accounts of these companies, see Alain Roussillon, *Sociétés islamiques de placement de fonds et "ouverture économique"* (Cairo: Dossiers du CEDEJ, 1988); and Sami Zubaida, "The Politics of the Islamic Investment Companies in Egypt," *Bulletin of the British Society for Middle East Studies* 17, no. 2 (1990).

12. This is not to say that all Islamist politics must necessarily take this form. In Egypt today there are many prominent Muslims, such as Husayn Ahmad Amin, Hasan Hanafi, and Muhammad 'Imara, who favor liberal democracy and are highly critical of the dominant Islamic current which is the subject of discussion here.

13. Roussillon, "Entre al-Jihad et al-Rayyan," p. 45.

14. Muhammad al-Sayyid Sa'id,"Métamorphose du champ sociétal à partir du renforcement des mouvements à référence religieuse," in *Modernisation et nouvelles formes de mobilisation sociale,* p. 79.

15. See the *Guardian* (London), May 27, 1992, p. 10.

5

Gender and Civil Society

Suad Joseph, interview with Joe Stork

What questions does the idea of civil society raise concerning gender?

The Western construct of the nation-state, which became the compulsory political form for the rest of the world, is based on citizens as detached from communities, as individuals. In fact—in the Arab world, the Third World, and much of the West—persons are deeply embedded in communities, in families, in ethnic or social groupings.

The Western construct of citizen—that of a contract-making individual— implies a degree of detachment and autonomy that is not universal. The capacity to make contracts emerges from the fact that this individualized self is conceived of as a property owner, first of all as owner of himself. I use "him" consciously here.

Why "himself"?

The Western liberal notion of citizen implies a masculinized construct. Males were the property owners. Carol Pateman argues that the contemporary state is in fact a fraternal patriarchy. In the discourse that established the philosophical basis of liberal bourgeois society, the idiom is one of brothers. The social contract is entered into by free men who constitute themselves as a civil fraternity. It's an association of autonomous, individualized, contract-making persons, and contract making is possible only if you are a property owner, if you own yourself. The series of assertions that underlie this philosophical base are assertions of exclusion. Women are not contract-making persons because they are not property owners. Civil society is a fraternity, not a sorority and not a family.

If we move beyond the gender-bound language of these paradigms, and if women become more equal as property owners to men, what keeps the state masculine? Is this still a problem?

In liberal feminist thought, with its goal of integrating women into and not challenging the basic structure of the state, the problem starts to get resolved. Marxist feminists argue that this only resolves the problem for elite women. Class, race, patriarchy, and other forms of exclusion are still operating.

But isn't that just saying that the integration is not inclusive enough? Is it a critique of the model of the state itself?

There's no way that you can have enough inclusion without transforming the class-based structure of society. The very existence of classes is a demarcation of exclusion. Ultimately what gets reorganized and restructured are class boundaries. If you're going to use inclusion as the avenue of resolving the problem, that can happen only if class itself is challenged.

It still strikes me as more Marxist than feminist, in that the locus of the problem is class. What's more difficult to reconcile—class or patriarchy?

There are feminists who would argue that class and patriarchy are dual systems that operate autonomously of each other; you have to fight them on different grounds. Others argue that they are woven into each other and your organizational strategy has to take account of the fact that class already has patriarchy built into it. There isn't a single feminist answer as to the primary source of oppression—gender, class, or race.

The question we want to examine is: What has the imposition of the nation-state, with its gendered concepts of citizenship and civil society, meant in those countries where it has been imposed?

There was patriarchy in the Arab world prior to colonization. What is interesting to investigate is the intersections of the precolonial and postcolonial patriarchy in the attempts to construct the contemporary nation-state. My sense is that there was much greater fluidity to the patriarchy that existed in the Arab world in the seventeenth, eighteenth, and nineteenth centuries. Judith Tucker's recent work on Nablus courts, dealing with issues such as custody and divorce and child support cases in the eighteenth and nineteenth centuries, indicates that women made use of the courts effectively and actively, and across class lines. Women were very assertive in claiming their rights within what might be considered a public domain in Palestine. There's interesting work from medieval Egypt up to the nineteenth century which shows that women were active property owners. Julia Clancy Smith's work on colonial Algeria indicates that women were active in religious movements, were looked up to, and sought out as saintly figures.

The point that comes out of all of this is that there was a lot more fluidity in the precolonial period than we had previously imagined in terms of gender hierarchy.

Contemporary representations of the Arab world often depict more rigid gender hierarchies—greater exclusion of women from public domains, to an extreme degree in some states. Hisham Sharabi argues that what he calls neopatriarchy is a postcolonial phenomenon: it's not that there wasn't patriarchy before, but contemporary patriarchy is a product of the intersection between the colonial and indigenous domains.

Is this in any way similar to what's happened in other societies?

There are some parallels—although we have to situate gender-state dynamics culturally and historically in each society. I'm particularly interested in comparing the Arab world to India and China, for a couple of reasons. One is that all three are areas with very long histories of state formation, followed by periods of colonial control and later of attempted "modernization." In all three societies, the literature seems to indicate regression for women in the contemporary period: increasing control by men, families, communities, and the state. There's evidence that the contemporary period in some ways has consolidated and created new controls over women that were much more fluid earlier.

Is this owing to the gender character of capitalism per se, or also to the reactions to capitalism?

Both, and I think it's also related to the particular construct of the nation-state that these societies have attempted to erect.

But it's also a class construct of citizen.

Absolutely. Recall here Edward Said's argument in *Orientalism* that the East is feminized in relationship to the West. Many scholars subsequently argued that not only is the Orient feminized, but that the oppressed, the subordinate, the minority are feminized. Hierarchy tends to genderize: those in the superordinate position are masculinized, and subordinates are feminized. So constructs of class and citizenship have been imbued with gendered meanings.

And this is peculiarly modern?

The individual citizen, as an autonomous, contract-making self, is a peculiarly modern and Western discourse, a discourse that's become hegemonic. It is important to look at what these notions of civil society and citizenship are based on in Western discourse, and the problems created by their uncritical application to Third World societies.

I was struck years ago by an article by Rola Sharara, a Lebanese feminist, in *Khamsin*, in which she argued that women in Lebanon, as in many Arab states, cannot feel the impact of the state in their lives. They feel the impact of their communities, and in particular the men of their communities. I think Lebanon was an extreme example of this, where citizenship was mainly experienced through communities. That is, ethnic, religious, kin-based communities exerted considerable authority and claimed the loyalties of their members. In some societies, that was competitive with state authority. Women may at times feel the oppression of the patriarchy of their communities more directly than that of the state. Elsewhere, perhaps Iraq is an example, the communities are experienced as a source of protection from a repressive state. Local women's movements will take different forms as a result. My political stance is one of critical support—to support local forms of resistance, but to engage in a critical dialogue based on the historical experiences of other countries. I do not think the control of women by communities is independent of state control.

That's part of the paradigm of modernization.
    That's what many of these states, notably Iraq and Syria, were attempting to do by undermining these communities in order to claim the control and the loyalties of their citizenry.

We have to be careful not to romanticize the control that does or did exist at the communal level.
    Yes, it's coercive, particularly for women. It's not a question of preserving these ethnic, religious, tribal communities, or of the state saving women from these communities. States and communities can be competitive or collaborative forms of domination.
    These communities are organized through patriarchal idioms, moralities, and structures of domination. For women, in those states where communities are the primary vehicle through which they experience their membership in contemporary societies, these relations are mediated through patriarchy. In societies in which the state is more keenly felt, state forms of patriarchy penetrate more effectively into local communities. There are new, complex, shifting forms of gender domination. Insofar as the state is experienced as more repressive than the communities, then women often secure themselves in their communities, where they receive some protection from a repressive state. But to gain that protection they must submit to the control of the men of their community.
    Western liberal philosophers have advanced civil society as the solution to the problem of state authoritarianism or despotism. If civil society consists of voluntary autonomous organizations capable of resisting arbitrary

exercises of state power, let's look at who or what these voluntary organizations are. In contemporary societies, they would be professional associations, unions, political action groups, chambers of commerce, even religious fraternities. All are in the "public domain." They are the kinds of associations nearly always associated with men. Civil society is already identified or defined as a site from which women are thought to be excluded—the public domain. And it's characterized by sets of associations that are linked with male activity. If you go back to how this came to be, the construct of civil society assumes from the very beginning a split between public and private domains. It's based on an assumed three-way distinction between that which is kin-based and nonvoluntary, that which is nonkin-based, public, and voluntary—civil society—and that which is nonkin-based, public, and semivoluntary—the state.

That definition of what constitutes civil society is based on a gendered distinction between the public and private domains. Men and male activity are associated with the public and women and female activity with the private. The civil society construct, a Western construct, is now being challenged in the West by feminists and people of color. Its uncritical application to Third World countries and the uncritical use of the relative existence of components of civil society as measures of "modernity" or progress are highly problematic.

What does this mean in terms of the Arab world?
The distinction between what is public and what is private, and therefore the dichotomy that the concept of civil society rests upon, is even more problematical in the Arab world than in the West. In many Third World countries, Arab ones included, kinship and community are crucial organizers of social life. I don't see state institutions or civil society operating independently of kin-based relations. A person in a position of power in a government office or a voluntary organization brings with him or her the obligations, networks, and rights of kin and community, and acts accordingly. Those claims of kin and community operate for people in those positions. The people themselves don't separate public and private.

The boundaries between this triangulation of state, civil society, and kinship or private domain are highly fluid. People's commitments remain grounded in kin and community, and they carry those commitments with them, whether in the civil or state spheres. Men in Lebanon are no less identified with kinship, and therefore with private communities and obligations, than are women.

But it's patriarchal.
What's crucial for understanding the gendering of these relationships is not the split between public and private, say, or between civil society and

state, or civil society and the domestic sphere, but how gender hierarchy operates. In Lebanon patriarchy privileges males and elders, including elder women. Numerous other variables affect the operation of patriarchy—class, ethnicity, region.

What does this mean for the stance we take on these questions of civil society and human rights?

Because men are very nested in familial and highly patriarchal communities, as nested as women, and insofar as states are often seen as repressive and external, it is in these communal-based relationships that both men and women find security. For many progressive Muslims in the Middle East, gender issues are secondary; familial bonds are seen as sources of support and security against what's perceived as an even greater source of oppression—the state. That isn't to say that there aren't women and movements in the Middle East who argue that gender oppression is as virulent as class or colonialism.

If one's rights are experienced as emerging from being part of these familial, ethnic, sectarian communities to a greater degree than emerging from being citizens of a state, then you can see the problem for women, because these communities are highly patriarchal. The control of these communities over women's lives has in fact been reinforced by the state in many Middle Eastern countries, with Tunisia and Turkey being partial exceptions.

When the state intervenes actively to provide alternative arenas, at least in legal or administrative domains, for women's participation in society, it creates space for maneuver and negotiation and, over the long run, for mobilization.

This sense of space is implicit in the argument for civil society. Some would argue that the components of civil society work as much to help the state exercise social control as to hinder it.

I agree. We have assumed that the hegemonic discourse in the West actually describes the empirical reality of the West. Then we say: what's wrong with these Third World societies is that they're not coming up to the standard that in fact is not the reality even in the West. We have assumed distinctions between state and civil society, between civil society and the private sphere, and between the state and the private sphere. In neither the West nor the Third World are they so separate. The problem of exclusion of women from the state has been accentuated by the attempt to separate these domains. The attempts to separate state, civil society, and kinship weds women to the private domain and excludes them from the sphere of civil society and from the state. Saudi Arabia may be an extreme example of that. But that's a modern phenomenon.

The whole argument about whether we have a weak state or a strong state, a weak society or a strong society, in a way is a specious argument, linked to an Orientalist perspective which sees other societies as seamless webs, whereas the West is articulated and differentiated. I don't see the West being as articulated and differentiated as the West presents itself as being.

But formerly colonized societies to some extent have bought into the nation-state as the mode and vehicle of liberation.

The contemporary exclusion of women is in part—but not exclusively— the outcome of this compulsory model of the nation-state, a model which has built into it the marginalization of females and female activity.

The point I'm leading to is that people do not perceive themselves as having rights as a result of their being citizens of a state. They perceive themselves as having rights because they are embedded in communities. And insofar as those communities are hierarchical and patriarchal, they will maneuver these rights around those hierarchical and patriarchal structures of domination. When we speak of human rights, we assume that we all know what we mean by that term. But we've universalized human rights by glossing over the diversity in the ways in which rights are understood. Our construct of rights is premised on the construct of the autonomous, detached, contract-making, individualized and masculinized person that emerged out of liberal bourgeois thought.

We don't want to dismiss human rights as bourgeois constructs, as if they don't matter.

What I'm struggling to develop is a construct of rights, personal rights, human rights, that is not embedded in a specific construct of personhood. I don't have the answer to that now. The problem of the construct of human rights is closely linked to this concept of the individualized citizen. If we have a construct of citizen that is wedded to a particular concept of self, it allows us to dismiss the rights of persons who don't share that sense of self. The way we construct the notion of civil society, and the way we construct the notion of a nation-state—when you break out of those constructs, it not only allows for the possibility of the inclusion of women and other excluded groups, but it shows us that the ways in which men and women operate, act out their lives, maneuver and negotiate are not so fundamentally different from each other. We constructed a difference, which insofar as it became compulsory, became internalized. Gender difference is historically and culturally constructed and reproduced through complex moralities, idioms, and structures of power. Feminist discourse attempts to destabilize the hegemony of these constructs and by so doing create space for experiments in alternate forms of relationships.

6

Islamist Notions of Democracy

Gudrun Krämer

Most observers, in attempting to explain why the movement toward pluralism, liberalism, and democracy has been relatively weak in the Arab
world, have concluded that it must have something to do with culture, and
more particularly with Islam.[1] And while there has been growing interest
and research on the subject, this has not shaken the widespread notion that
there is one single political doctrine of Islam, more or less identical with the
historical caliphate and incompatible with pluralist democracy as it first
developed in the West. Islam, it is said, has not been democratic in the past
and will be unable to become so in the future.

This is, of course, an ahistorical view, and one which focuses on what
Leonard Binder referred to as a "cluster of absences": the missing concept
of liberty, the lack of autonomous corporate institutions, the absence of a
self-confident middle class, and so forth.[2] Recent studies on militant Islam
reinforce the conclusion that it is only through emancipation from Islam
(passing through the stages of enlightenment and secularization) that Muslims can hope to advance on the road to liberty and democracy. Daniel
Lerner popularized this theme in his seminal work on modernization in the
Middle East. What Muslims were facing, he wrote, was the choice between
"Mecca or mechanization."[3]

The debate about Islam and democracy is by no means new. Since the
1980s, it has witnessed some fresh thinking and considerable movement on
the ground.[4] A growing number of Muslims, including a good many Islamist
activists, have called for pluralist democracy, or at least for some of its basic
elements: the rule of law and the protection of human rights, political
participation, government control, and accountability. The terms and concepts used are often rather vague or deliberately chosen so as to avoid
non-Islamic notions. Many speak of *shura*, the idealized Islamic concept of

participation-qua-consultation; others refer to "Islamic democracy," just as in the 1950s and 1960s they would have talked about "Arab" or "Islamic socialism"; still others do not hesitate to call for democracy.

The phenomenon raises serious questions, political as well as methodological. Are Islamist activists sincere when they declare their democratic convictions, or do they merely hope to gain popular support and reach power through democratic elections? In either case it is significant that they should think such pronouncements can help them. I have examined the question elsewhere.[5] Here I would like to focus on the theoretical aspects of the issue: Assuming that they are acting in good faith and that they have adopted democracy as their "strategic option," is there an Islamic path to a pluralist democratic society? And how can it be analyzed?

There is among Muslims an explicit debate on the subject which directly compares Islamic modes of political organization to Western-style pluralist democracy, usually with the intent of proving Islam's superiority to Western concepts in moral as well as practical terms, indeed of proving that Islam served as the source and model from which democratic essentials such as the rule of law or the concept of the social contract were taken by European thinkers of the Middle Ages and the Enlightenment.[6] There are in fact a sizable number of comparative studies looking at specific concepts such as sovereignty, the social contract, or the separation of powers "in Islam," in the West, and in contemporary Arab politics.[7]

The fact that such studies are so numerous suggests that there is considerable demand. Yet, while of considerable interest, their apologetic thrust reduces their value to an outside observer. More rewarding is a look at the large body of books, pamphlets, draft constitutions, published talks, and conference proceedings that discuss the relationship of Islam, the state, and politics without direct reference to the West. Do these reflect basic notions, institutions, and procedures characteristic of pluralist democracy? To what extent have they been integrated into Islamic political thinking and thus been authenticated and rendered acceptable to a Muslim, or more specifically, an Islamist audience?

One thing has to be said at the outset: Contrary to much of the literature on the subject, it is not possible to talk about Islam and democracy in general but only about Muslims living and theorizing under specific historical circumstances. This may sound evident enough, and yet it is all too often ignored, not least because many of the authors themselves present their views as "the position of Islam" on any given matter, democracy, liberty, and pluralism included. There are certainly essentials of the faith (al-'aqida) accepted by all who consider themselves to be Muslims and who are recognized as such by their coreligionists. But Muslims differ considerably over how an Islamic society should be organized. What is required, therefore, is specificity.

I base the following remarks on those authors and activists whom I consider to be voices of the Sunni Arab mainstream. Some of them are generally ranked as conservative, others as progressive or "enlightened" thinkers. They include members of the Egyptian and the Jordanian Muslim Brothers and the Tunisian Islamist movement led by Rashid al-Ghannoushi (formerly the Mouvement de la Tendance Islamique and Hizb al-Nahda) as well as individual authors committed to the so-called Islamic awakening (al-sahwa al-islamiyya) like Muhammad 'Imara, Muhammad Salim al-'Awwa, Fahmi Huwaydi, Fathi 'Uthman, and others.[8] They clearly speak only for certain segments of the broad Islamic movement, representing the male educated urban elite and scriptural rather than mystical or so-called popular Islam. But it is in these circles that the question of Islam, shura, and democracy is being discussed.

RELIGION AND STATE

There is general agreement among these authors that Islam is comprehensive or, as the commonly used modern formula has it, that it is religion and state (al-islam din wa-dawla) or religion and world (al-islam din wa-dunya). This formulation signals the rejection of secularism as it was advocated by the Egyptian scholar 'Ali 'Abd al-Raziq in his book Islam and the Roots of Government (Al-Islam wa-usul al-hukm), published in 1925, shortly after the abolition of the caliphate. Almost three generations later, his claims—that Muhammad was a prophet and not a statesman, that Islam is a religion and not a state, and that the caliphate was from the beginning based on force— still provoke outrage. For these authors there can be no doubt that Islam comprises faith, ethics, and law as it was set forth in the Qur'an, exemplified by the life of the Prophet Muhammad and his Companions (the sunna), and later developed by Muslim theologians and jurists (the 'ulama' and fuqaha') into the shari'a.

The vocal denunciation of secularism, however, does not imply that these authors make no distinction between the spheres of religion proper and of worldly affairs, between the eternal and the temporal. In fact, this very distinction is reflected in modern Islamic legal theory (fiqh), which distinguishes between the 'ibadat involving a person's relation with his or her creator (essentially the five pillars of Islam—the profession of faith, prayer, fasting, almsgiving, and the pilgrimage) and the mu'amalat, covering all other aspects of economic, political, and family life. While the 'ibadat are eternal and immutable, the mu'amalat can be adapted to the changing requirements of time and locality, provided the results conform to the word (nass) and spirit (maqasid) of the shari'a. What they envisage, then, are two differentiated spheres of human life and activity: one revolving around faith and worship and the other around worldly affairs, both subject to the precepts of Islam.

There is further agreement that the hallmark of the truly Islamic system (*al-nizam al-islami*) is the application of the *shari'a* and not any particular political order—the historical caliphate included. What matters are the purpose of the state and the principles upon which it rests. These principles are to be found in the Qur'an and *sunna,* and they include, most notably, justice (*'adl*), mutual consultation (*shura*), equality, freedom, and struggle in the path of God (*jihad*). The militants go even further, declaring that any Muslim who does not apply God's judgment and follow divine law (*man lam yahkum bima anzala allah*) is to be considered, and fought as, a sinner, a tyrant, and an infidel.[9]

Usually no sharp distinction is made between Islam and the *shari'a,* and as a rule both terms are used interchangeably. In accordance with what might be called the functional theory of government, which sees the *shari'a* as the cornerstone of an Islamic order and government as merely the executive of God's law, the debate has shifted to how the *shari'a* is to be defined—whether as a comprehensive set of norms and values regulating human life down to the most minute detail, or as a set of general rules of good life and moral behavior aiming at people's welfare on earth and their salvation in the hereafter (and still leaving room for human interpretation). There is general consensus that the *shari'a* is comprehensive but at the same time flexible and therefore suited, as the formula goes, to all times and places. That leads to the crucial distinction between an untouchable and immutable core (*al-asl* or, in modern usage, *al-thabit*) that has been decisively defined by God's word (*nass*), and flexible elements (*al-furu'* or, in modern terminology, *al-mutaghayyir*) derived by human reason from this core, following the rules of Islamic jurisprudence (*ijtihad*).

This distinction provides one of the criteria by which one may delineate conservatives, modernists, and progressives, and it is vital to the debate about Islam and the state. The aim of "enlightened" modernist reformers has of necessity been to define the scope of human interpretation as extensively as possible, an endeavor which was characterized somewhat uncharitably by Malcolm Kerr as the attempt to define the *shari'a* primarily by its "empty spaces."[10]

When it comes to politics, even Muslim Brothers and *'ulama'* who on the basis of their social views would qualify as conservatives, hold remarkably modern ideas: To apply the *shari'a* requires social organization and a state. But God in his wisdom left the details of political organization to the Muslim community to decide according to its needs and aspirations. Government and politics are part of the *mu'amalat* that are to be regulated so as to realize the common good (*al-maslaha al-'amma*) which, if properly understood, coincides with the purposes (*maqasid*) of the *shari'a*. The logic of this argument takes them quite close to the conclusions of 'Ali 'Abd al-Raziq, whose theoretical premises they so emphatically denounce. ('Abd al-Raziq was probably attempting to establish orthodox credentials for what might otherwise have been considered a dangerously modern approach.) For the Muslim Brothers, unlike for 'Abd al-Raziq, Islam is religion and state, and yet both agree that the precise form of government is left to human reason to define.

This line of argument results in an apparent paradox which has not gone unnoticed by thoughtful observers: While the state is considered to be central to having Islamic law enforced, its form and organization are declared to be secondary, a matter not of substance but of technique.[11] This has to be seen in relation to the common assertion that Muslims are not prohibited from adapting techniques and modes of organization of non-Islamic origin, provided they do not adopt any un-Islamic values. If government organization is a matter of convenience and mere technique, then the adoption of democracy, or of certain democratic elements, may be acceptable, recommended, or even mandatory—provided this does not lead to the neglect or violation of Islamic norms and values.

SOVEREIGNTY AND AUTHORITY

At the core of much contemporary writing are a number of shared assumptions: that all people are born equal, having been installed as God's viceregents on earth (*istikhlaf*); that government exists to ensure an Islamic life and enforce Islamic law; that sovereignty (*siyada, hakimiyya*) ultimately rests with God alone, who has made the law and defined good and evil (*al-ma'ruf wa'l-munkar*), the licit and the illicit (*al-halal wa'l-haram*); that the authority (*sulta*) to apply God's law has been transferred to the community as a whole, which is therefore the source of all powers (*asl al-sultat*); and that the head of the community or state, no matter whether he (and they specifically exclude women from that function) be called imam, caliph, or president, is the mere representative, agent, or employee of the community that elects, supervises, and, if necessary, deposes him, either directly or via its representatives.

This simplified scheme of government does not constitute a sharp break with classical Sunni doctrines which, in contrast to Shi'i positions, declared that the caliphate was based on the consensus of the Muslim community (*ijma'*), not on any preordained divine order. But compared even to the widely quoted treatises of Ibn Taymiyya (d. 1328), with their emphasis on the centrality of the *shari'a*, modern positions mark a definite shift of emphasis away from the person of the ruler and the duty of obedience and acquiescence for the sake of peace and order, even under unjust rule, to the authority of the community and the responsibility of every individual believer. This shift no doubt reflects the impact of modern political ideas as well as the decline and final abolition of the historical caliphate.

What emerges as a core concern of modern Muslims is the desire to check and limit arbitrary personal rule and to replace it with the rule of law. That had already been the preoccupation of nineteenth-century Arab and Ottoman constitutionalists, ranging from 'Abd al-Rahman al-Kawakibi and Khayr al-Din al-Tunisi to Namik Kemal. It is basic to the advocates of *hakimiyya*, God's sole sovereignty, who radically deny the capacity of men and women to distinguish, by the light of their intelligence, between right and wrong, licit and illicit. In an interesting twist, they frequently present their argument in democratic guise: given that all people are created equal and that consequently no one has the right to impose his or her will on others, and given that people are too weak to control their passions and desires (*hawa*), a higher authority is needed to keep them in check. This higher authority is divine law, binding on all—high and low, rich and poor. The submission to God's sovereignty as demonstrated in the strict and exclusive application of the *shari'a*, therefore, signifies not just the (only genuine) rule of law, but also the (only genuine) liberation of man from servitude to man (*'ubudiyyat al-insan*).

Seen from this perspective, Islam serves as a theology of liberation. And it is in this sense that the writings of Abu al-'Ala' al-Mawdudi, Sayyid Qutb, or Taqi al-Din al-Nabhani have been understood by men and women in search of justice and disillusioned with the signs of all-pervading despotism and corruption. For the critical observer, by contrast, the utopian character and very real authoritarian streak of this argument are all too obvious. For who is it, after all, who hears and applies God's law if not men and women ruled by their passions and subject to the limitations of their understanding? Law, it has been stated often enough, does not apply itself, but is applied by fallible human beings.[12] Still, for contemporary Islamists, both radical and reformist, tyranny is the main enemy, no matter whether it be defined in strictly secular terms (*istibdad*) or on religious grounds as the taking of other gods than God alone (*taghut*), and therefore as one form of polytheism and apostasy (*shirk, ridda, kufr*).

By this logic, it is no longer very important whether the ruler (*al-hakim*) be called caliph, imam, or simply head of state or president (*ra'is al-dawla*). While certain groups like the Islamic Liberation Party or leading Algerian Islamists still propagate the restoration of the caliphate, many Muslim Brothers will use the term caliphate for what in fact is nothing more than a modern presidency. The underlying conception is in all cases similar: The ruler is the agent and representative of the Muslim community, entrusted with executing God's law. He has no religious authority whatsoever, though some of his tasks, such as the implementation of the *shari'a* or the propagation of *jihad*, would by Western standards be classified as religious. Thus, while the state rests on a religious foundation, its leadership carries no religious sanction. It is to emphasize this distinction, which is not all that difficult to make but often neglected, that many Muslim authors insist on saying that the ideal Islamic state is not a theocracy, which would be ruled by men of religion or a ruler of divine grace, but that it is a civil or, to be more precise, a lay state (*dawla madaniyya*).

Compared to classical treatises, then, the role and function of the ruler have been reevaluated and distinctly devalued. At the same time, there is heavy emphasis on the need for strong leadership (*qiyada*), though this is usually justified in strictly secular terms. The preoccupation with forceful leadership, unity, strict loyalty, and obedience is mirrored in the organizational structure of virtually all Islamist movements, from the relatively moderate Muslim Brothers to the militant underground, which in their internal affairs do not adhere to democratic principles.[13]

THE CHALLENGE OF PLURALISM

Characteristic of much contemporary political writing is its activist bent and the attempt to translate general ethicoreligious duties into principles of individual political responsibility and participation. Three elements are basic to this effort: the Qur'anic injunction to enjoin the good and prohibit evil (*al-amr bi'l-ma'ruf wal-nahy'an al-munkar*), the Prophet's appeal to give counsel (*al-din al-nasiha*), and the duty to consult (*shura*) that is based on both the Qur'an and *sunna*. They are interpreted so as to make political commitment and participation the religious duty (*farida*) of every single individual as well as the entire community. As a result, politics is literally sacralized, and at the same time ethical and religious duties and injunctions are systematically politicized, extended, and institutionalized. In a process that clearly betrays the impact of modern (Western) political ideas, the transition is made from the limited involvement of the community in selecting the leader via *shura* and the oath of allegiance (*bay'a*) to a constitutional system involving continuous consultation and permanent control over the ruler and over government in general, which are now held responsible not only to God but also to the electorate.

Considerable thought has been given to the potential means and instruments of political control. Going beyond al-Mawardi's (d.1058) concept of a separation of functions via delegation from the ruler (*tafwid*), more and more authors are inclined to accept the need for a separation of powers in which the executive (the ruler) and the legislature (the *shura* council, or parliament) effectively keep each other in check. In accordance with the theory of divine sovereignty, though, they often add that in an Islamic context legislation (*tashri'*) is in actual fact confined to the mere "application" of the *shari'a* (*tatbiq al-shari'a*). The independence of the judiciary is generally acknowledged, and some writers suggest the institution of a higher constitutional court or council to guarantee the rule of law.

Much attention is given to the principle of *shura,* which in the early history and tradition of Islam meant nothing more than consultation in all matters private and public. It is now presented as the functional equivalent of Western parliamentary rule and as the basis of an authentic Islamic democracy. A wide range of questions remain controversial—whether consultation is a duty of the ruler, and whether he is bound by the decisions of those consulted; whether they should be men (there is in general little mention of women) of his own choice or the elected representatives of the community; whether they should be private individuals only or members of formal institutions such as political parties, religious specialists only or other experts and community leaders as well; whether they should decide by majority rule; and whether all matters of general import have to be subjected to consultation.

Most authors tend to regard *shura* as both required and binding (*wajiba* and *mulzima*), to accept the principle of majority decision, and to see it as a formal process and an institution—that is, a *shura* council made up of elected members, who ought to include specialists in Islamic law as well as in other fields. What they have in mind, then, is a council of experts deciding on the grounds of "objective" (Islamically valid) right and wrong, judging on the basis of the common good (*al-maslaha al-'amma*) only, and not a political assembly representing conflicting opinion and interest. The ideal amounts to an expertocracy headed by the Just Ruler.

The point is an important one, for it highlights the difficulties most Muslim authors have in envisaging consultation and participation as a genuinely political process involving interest representation, competition, and contestation. It reflects the continued prevalence of a moral rather than a political discourse, strictly speaking. The ideals of unity (*wahda*), consensus (*ijma*'), and a balanced harmony of groups and interests (*tawazun*), often associated with the theological concept of *tawhid* (the oneness of God), are still paramount. In the debate about pluralism, there is general recognition that God created people to be different, and that therefore differences of opinion (*ikhtilaf*) are natural, legitimate, and even beneficial to humankind and the Muslim community—provided they remain within the confines of the faith and of common decency. There is great reluctance to allow for unlimited freedom of speech and organization of those different opinions.[14]

Most authors would protest that Islam protects human rights, and that it fully guarantees freedom of thought and conscience ("no compulsion in religion," *la ikrah fi al-din*). They generally concede that it is legitimate and may even be necessary to organize opinion, consultation, and control so as to make them effective upon a strong executive, and that there are therefore grounds for legitimizing associations and political parties, on condition that they do not represent particular whims, passions, and interests—again within the framework of Islam only. The bottom line remains: There can be no toleration of, and no freedom for, the enemies of Islam—the hypocrite, the skeptic and the atheist, the libertarian and the subversive. As long as there is no certainty as to who defines the "framework of Islam," and where exactly power and interest come into play, pluralism remains severely restricted.

ADVANCES AND HESITATIONS

These positions are ambiguous and less clear than one would hope, but they are not as antagonistic to the values of equality, pluralism, and democracy as the statements of some of the most forceful advocates of radical political Islam, such as the Egyptian Sayyid Qutb or the Algerian 'Ali Ben Hadj, would suggest. Moderate, pragmatic Islamists and Muslim writers in general are remarkably flexible with respect to modes of political organization, providing for institutionalized checks on the ruler in the form of a separation of powers, parliamentary rule, and in some cases even multiple parties. They are more positive than is often acknowledged concerning the protection of human rights, which are generally founded on duties toward God but nevertheless widely seen as part of the common heritage of all humankind. Indeed, the protection of individual rights and civil liberties from government supervision and interference, repression and torture figures prominently on the Islamist agenda. But mainstream attitudes remain highly restrictive with regard to freedom of political, religious, and artistic expression, if that involves the right to freely express one's religious feelings, doubts included, and even to give up Islam altogether.[15]

Recent debates on the status of non-Muslims, emphasizing the shared rights and duties of all inhabitants of the land, suggest that a concept of citizenship may be gradually evolving.[16] It is possibly in the domain of gender relations that change is least perceptible. Mainstream Islamist positions on women continue to be strictly conservative. While they subscribe to the equality of men and women as human beings, they still consider women to be simultaneously threatening and vulnerable, in need of special protection, and ultimately inferior to men in terms of their mental strength and physical condition.[17] Whereas slavery is no longer an issue in contemporary debate, polygamy and divorce continue to be discussed on traditional lines.

People like Ben Hadj and Qutb have tended to set the tone for this discussion, amplified by Western media treatment and by the strategy of repression pursued by various Arab governments. In a number of cases, including Egypt, Jordan, Lebanon, and Yemen, more subtle strategies have been used by the ruling elites as well as their critics and opponents, Islamists included. It is at any rate important to listen to the moderate, pragmatic voices of political Islam as well as to the militants. The Muslim Brothers and similar movements, representing urban middle-class values, interests, and aspirations, are at least as important socially and politically as al-Jihad, and the moderate approach they represent will likely become more generalized. Doubts about the credibility of certain actors, while justified, should not invalidate efforts to discover what the larger groups as well as individual intellectuals think. Their writings are as relevant, though certainly not as rousing, as 'Abd al-Salam Faraj's *The Neglected Duty* or Qutb's *Milestones*.

Put briefly, the moderate, pragmatic Islamists, whom I consider to be the mainstream of the 1980s and the early 1990s, have come to accept crucial elements of political democracy: pluralism (within the framework of Islam), political participation, government accountability, rule of law, and protection of human rights. But they have not adopted liberalism, if that includes religious indifference. Change is more noticeable in the domain of political organization than of social and religious values. Having said this, it cannot be too strongly emphasized that what we are observing is thought in progress, responding to a considerable extent to societal conditions and government policies. It is to a large extent not abstract but political, even activist, mobilizing thought, shaped and influenced by a political environment that in virtually all cases is neither liberal nor genuinely pluralistic, let alone democratic.

NOTES

1. For a sophisticated approach which does not reflect common stereotypes, see John Waterbury, "Democracy without Democrats? The Potential for Political Liberalization in the Middle East," in Ghassan Salamé (ed.), *Democracy without Democrats? The Renewal of Politics in the Muslim World* (London: I.B. Tauris, 1994), pp. 23–47. For a brilliant attack on current "Orientalist" notions, see Yahya Sadowski, "The New Orientalism and the Democracy Debate," in this volume.

2. Leonard Binder, *Islamic Liberalism: A Critique of Development Ideologies* (Chicago: University of Chicago Press, 1988), p. 225.

3. Daniel Lerner, *The Passing of Traditional Society: Modernizing the Middle East* (New York: Free Press, 1958), p. 40.

4. See, e.g., John L. Esposito and James P. Piscatori, "Democratization and Islam," *Middle East Journal* 45, no. 3 (summer 1991): 427–40; Gudrun Krämer, "Liberalization and Democracy in the Arab World," *Middle East Report*, no. 174 (January–February 1992): 22–25, 35; and several contributions to *Annals: Journal of the American Association of Political Science*, no. 524 (November 1992), notably by Lahouari Addi and I. William Zartman.

5. Gudrun Krämer, "The Integration of the Integrists: A Comparative Study of Egypt, Jordan and Tunisia," in Salamé (ed.), *Democracy without Democrats?* pp. 200–26, and idem, "Cross-Links and Double Talk? Islamic Movements in the Political Process," in Laura Guazzone (ed.), *The Political Role of Islamist Movements in the Arab World* (forthcoming).

6. For an interesting example, see Fahmi Huwaydi, "Al-Islam wa'l-dimuqratiyya," *Al-Mustaqbal al-'arabi,* no.166 (December 1992): 5–37.

7. These are frequently published theses previously submitted to the faculties of law or *shari'a.* For example, Sulayman Muhammad al-Tamawi, *Al-Sultat al-thalath fi al-dasatir al-'arabiyya al-mu'asira wa-fi al-fikr al-siyasi al-islami: dirasa muqarana* (Cairo, 1967); Fathi 'Abd al-Karim, *Al-Dawla wa'l-siyada fi al-fiqh al-islami: dirasa muqarana* (Cairo, 1976); Ahmad Siddiq 'Abd al-Rahman, *Al-Bay'a fi al-nizam al-siyasi al-islami wa-tatbiqatuha fi al-hayat al-siyasiyya al-mu'asira* (Cairo, 1988).

8. Among the first category, see 'Abd al-Qadir 'Awda, *Al-Islam wa-awda'una al-siyasiyya* and *Al-Islam wa-awda'una al-qanuniyya* (both Cairo, no date); 'Ali Jarisha, *I'lan dusturi islami* (al-Mansura, 1985) and *Al-Mashru'iyya al-islamiyya al-'ulya,* 2d ed. (al-Mansura, 1986). Both of these are from the Egyptian Muslim Brothers. Rashid al-Ghannoushi, *Al-Hurriyyat al-'amma fi al-dawla al-islamiyya* (Beirut, 1993). See also a widely read article by the leader of the Sudanese National Islamic Front, Hasan al-Turabi, "Al-Shura wa'l dimuqratiyya: ishkalat al-mustalah wa'l-mafhum," *Al-Mustaqbal al-'arabi,* no. 75 (May 1985): 4–22. Among the second category, see Muhammad 'Imara, *Al-Dawla al-islamiyya bayna al-'almaniyya wa'l-sulta al-diniyya* (Cairo and Beirut, 1988); Muhammad Salim al-'Awwa, *Fi al-nizam al-siyasi li'l-dawla al-islamiyya,* new ed. (Cairo and Beirut, 1989 [1975]); Fahmi Huwaydi, *Al-Qur'an wa'l-sultan: humum islamiyya mu'asira* (Cairo, 1982); and *Al-Islam wa'l-dimuqratiyya* (Cairo, 1993); Muhammad Fathi 'Uthman, *Dawlat al-fikra,* 4th ed. (Jidda, 1985). The debates of "enlightened" (*mustanirun*) intellectuals are mainly to be found in a number of periodicals, notably *Al-Muslim al-mu'asir, Al-Ijtihad, Al-Hiwar,* and *Al-Mustaqbal al-'arabi* (all Beirut), *Al-Fikr* (Cairo), *15/21* (Tunis), and *Al-Insan* (Paris).

9. For a refutation of this claim, which is based on the Qur'an (5:43–46), see 'Imara, *Al-Dawla al-islamiyya,* pp. 31–82.

10. Malcolm H. Kerr, *Islamic Reform: The Political and Legal Theories of Muhammad 'Abduh and Rashid Rida* (Berkeley: University of California Press, 1966), pp. 210 ff.

11. See, e.g., Khalid Muhammad Khalid, *Difa' 'an al-dimuqratiyya* (Cairo: Dar Thabit, 1985), pp. 267 ff.

12. The best known but by no means only proponent of this criticism has been Muhammad Sa'id al-'Ashmawi; see, e.g., *Al-Islam al-siyasi* (Cairo, 1987); and *Al-Shari'a al-islamiyya wa'l-qanun al-misri* (Cairo, 1988). For similar reflections by a conservative Indian Muslim, see Kemal A. Faruki, *Islamic Jurisprudence* (New Delhi, 1988), pp. 12–19.

13. For a theoretical formulation of Islamist authoritarianism, see, e.g., Husayn Ibn Muhsin Ibn 'Ali Jabir, *Al-Tariq ila jama'at al-muslimin,* 3d ed. (al-Mansura: Dar al-Wafa', 1989); for a critique, see 'Abd Allah Fahd al-Nafisi (ed.), *Al-Haraka al-islamiyya: ru'ya mustaqbaliyya: awraq fi al-naqd al-dhati* (Cairo: Maktabat Madbuli, 1989).

14. For further details, see Gudrun Krämer, "Islam et pluralisme," in *Démocratie et démocratisations dans le monde arabe* (Cairo: Dossiers du CEDEJ, 1992), pp. 339–51.

15. Apostasy (*ridda*) is generally equated with high treason and is at least theoretically punishable by death.

16. For example, see *Al-Hiwar al-qawmi al-dini* (Beirut: Markaz Dirasat al-Wihda al-'Arabiyya, 1989), esp. pp. 137–65.

17. For critiques, see Fatima Mernissi, *La Peur—modernité: Le conflit islam et démocratie* (Paris: Editions Albin Michel, 1992); and Nazih Ayubi, *Political Islam: Religion and Politics in the Arab World* (London: Routledge, 1991), pp. 35–47.

7

Secularism, Integralism, and Political Islam: The Egyptian Debate

Alexander Flores

"The Shaikh al-Azhar should thank God profusely that the *shari'a* is not in force in Egypt, for if it were he would certainly be in for a good flogging in punishment for smearing virtuous people," wrote Farag Fuda in March 1988—thus contributing to a debate that had been raging since the beginning of that year.

> The Shaikh al-Azhar should thank God that nobody opposes him and nobody asks what his position has to do with a sound understanding of religion—of that splendid religion that doesn't know priesthood, doesn't place anybody between God and his servants and doesn't leave space for men of religion. . . . Oh Shaikh al-Azhar, thank God profusely for the backwardness of Muslims, for it alone preserves your job for you! But don't imagine for a moment that anybody will allow you to preside over inquisition courts, to accuse and to oppress, to threaten and to forbid![1]

What was the controversy all about? In 1987, Muhammad Sa'id al-'Ashmawi published *Political Islam* (in Arabic), in which he insisted that Islam was, from the beginning, an apolitical religion concerned solely with spiritual and ethical guidance. The form Islam has subsequently taken—as "religion and state"—for him was a deviation from and a perversion of that true conception. Fahmi Huwaydi, in a pair of critical articles, countered that the political and legislative character of Islam were its main distinctive feature.[2] Both al-'Ashmawi and Huwaydi supported their arguments with selective readings of the "basic" texts (Qur'an and *sunna*) and of early Islamic history. In its juxtaposition of two mutually exclusive views of Islam, the controversy remained unresolved.[3] In this, it was typical of quite a number of exchanges taking place in Egypt around the mid-1980s.

BASIC QUESTION

Those debates, which tackled a variety of questions from many different points of view, revolved around one key question: Can secularism be reconciled with Islam? Does Islam necessarily prescribe all actions and thoughts, even in worldly matters? Does it call for the institutional enforcement of such conduct and thought? Or does it leave to Muslims the freedom to regulate these things at their own discretion?

The integralist position traditionally taken toward this problem says that all aspects of human life should be ruled by God's will enshrined in the *shari'a*, the law developed by Islamic scholars out of God-given foundations. Yet this position was theoretical: it could not prevent a considerable amount of autonomy of certain realms—most notably politics—vis-à-vis that hegemony of religion. This autonomy characterizes most periods of Islamic history, especially in modern times. On the level of mass consciousness, though, most Muslims continued to believe in the ideal of religious hegemony over everyday life and politics. This integralist stand still reflects the position of the vast majority of Egyptian Muslims.

Today, the proponents of political Islam constitute the "hard core" of the integralist camp. They note the widening cleavage between ideal and reality and reassert the claim of religious hegemony. Political Islam poses as a continuation of the traditional position, although in many ways it constitutes a departure from it. The basic difference lies in the role ascribed to the state: in the traditional conception, the *shari'a* is a means of orientation which the believer follows (or does not follow) out of his or her own free will and which the state enforces only selectively. The Islamists want to see the *shari'a* codified as a set of state-enforced laws in the Western sense.

The view opposed to the integralist one calls for the autonomy of large domains of human life from any institutionalized hegemony of religion. This position is manifestly secularist, although many of its proponents shun the term. The Islamist "hard core" gives the integralist position a sharp political edge, but there is also a position that subscribes to the hegemony of Islam in principle while at the same time rejecting many of the Islamist demands. Regarding concrete problems of law and politics, proponents of this latter position may very well side with the secularists against the Islamists or their extremist wing. The borderlines between these positions are by no means clear-cut.

Two of the fundamental questions of the debate are whether secularism is necessary in Islamic societies and whether it is admissible. The integralists answer both of these questions in the negative. Secularism, they argue, was born in premodern Christian Europe out of the need to fight the crippling dominance of the church over the political realm and over intellectual life.

Islam, they say, has no ecclesiastic institution that could possibly claim similar dominance over the state, and has a much more positive relation to intellectual freedom and reason than Christianity. Secularism is not admissible in Islam because the separation of religion and politics runs counter to Islam's claim to regulate all aspects of human life. "Under the auspices of Islamic civilization," writes Muhammad 'Imara,

> the call for the reign of secularism is far more strange and abnormal than just being an imitation of the West . . . and borrowing from it a solution for a problem we don't in reality have! . . . This call becomes an assault against the Islamic religion which the scholars, Muslims and non-Muslims alike, say is creed and *shari'a,* religion and state at the same time, and that it is not just a spiritual mission. . . .
>
> And if the European renaissance was linked to secularism, after its decline had been tied to the hegemony of religion and church over state and society . . . then the march of our Arab-Islamic civilization was exactly the opposite. For the Arab-Islamic renaissance was intimately linked to the hegemony of the Islamic *shari'a* over a state that was civilian and Islamic at the same time, while the deviation from the Islamic character of the law was the beginning of the path of our nation into inertia and decline.[4]

The secularists reject the claim of the specificity of the European experience. Islam, says Fu'ad Zakariyya, never lacked ecclesiastic authority, obscurantism, and the limitation of intellectual freedom.

> The thesis that Islam does not and did not know a religious institution at all is greatly exaggerated. . . . That religious authority existed throughout Islamic history. Sometimes it used its position and influence for the defense of the true principles of religion, and that led to intense clashes with rulers, be they caliphs, sultans, or princes. At other times, they put themselves at the disposal of the ruler and issued statements and *fatwas* for him, giving legal support for his behavior even if it was unjust or reckless. . . .
>
> [T]he conditions of medieval Christianity were not fundamentally different from the conditions prevailing in Islam. Of course, there are many details in which the two beliefs differ . . . but they shared the general feature of comprehensiveness, and thus one of the reasons justifying the emergence of secularism in Europe can also be advanced under the conditions prevailing in the Islamic world. . . .
>
> The Middle Ages are not only a period in time but they are also a state of mind, capable of reemerging in many societies and at different times. . . . Many characteristics of this state of mind are present in our contemporary Islamic societies. . . . This means that the reasons that pushed Europe in the direction of secularism are cropping up in our present Islamic world, and it means too that the widespread idea that secularism is the result of specifically European conditions in a certain stage of its development is baseless.[5]

The other question—whether a secularist position is tenable in Islam—has been less often discussed. Zakariyya gave one possible answer, quite in

line with traditional Islamic reasoning although probably not very acceptable to integralists. Islam as such, he wrote, does not exist: "Islam is what
the Muslims make of it."[6]

Most of the debates took the form of newspaper articles and books, but
there also were some widely noted public debates between proponents and
opponents of secularism, like the one in the Cairo headquarters of the
Medical Association in July 1986 between Fu'ad Zakariyya (secularist) and
Yusuf al-Qaradawi and Muhammad al-Ghazali (integralists).[7] Another debate (in this case before an audience of allegedly 30,000 people!) took place
at the Cairo Book Fair in January 1992. Here, Farag Fuda and one of the
"shaikhs" of the left nationalist Tagammu' Party, Muhammad Ahmad
Khalaf Allah, represented secularism; Muhammad al-Ghazali, Muslim
Brother spokesman Ma'mun al-Hudaybi and the "neofundamentalist" Muhammad 'Imara stood against them.[8]

THE CAMPAIGN FOR *SHARI'A*

Since the early 1970s, the demand to reintroduce the *shari'a* has been the
common denominator of Egypt's Islamists. Most non-Islamist political figures and commentators have consented, mainly because it was quite unpopular not to do so. The government never took its own consent very
seriously. Even as recently as the late 1970s, only a few intellectuals dared
to call for caution.

As the debate continued in the 1980s, the opponents argued their
position in a much more consistent and systematic way. The *shari'a* may
well be based on God's word, the opponents conceded, but everything to
do with its development, codification, and application is done by men and
therefore subject to the same reservations as all man-made laws. The legal
force of the *shari'a* was quite limited throughout Islamic history, and great
parts of prevailing laws are incompatible with it. Traditional *fiqh* (Islamic
jurisprudence) is not applicable under present circumstances and cannot easily be adapted. The *hudud* (the core of Islamic criminal law) contradicts the contemporary conception of human rights. The rash introduction of the *shari'a* would facilitate the dictatorial tendencies of rulers and
might give the Islamists a grip on political power. Finally, it would reduce
the status and rights of non-Muslims, which in turn would harm national
unity.[9]

The most prominent of these authors are Muhammad Sa'id al-'Ashmawi,
Husayn Ahmad Amin, and Muhammad Nur Farahat.[10] Their initiatives
compelled the partisans of the *shari'a* to refine and restate their arguments.
These included hard-core Islamists, but also more moderate and flexible
authors like the renowned historian Tariq al-Bishri and the influential

journalist Fahmi Huwaydi.[11] "Insofar as our system relies upon Islamic legitimacy," wrote al-Bishri,

> and insofar as the *shari'a* is considered the source of that legitimacy and the basis of legal judgment, we follow a rule that is prescribed to us by religion . . . the application of the *shari'a* is an undeniable part of our belief. Furthermore, the roots of the *shari'a* provide a secure basis for the erection of a civilized, independent, dynamic, and just social system, a system that sticks to *ijtihad* (independent reasoning in Islamic jurisprudence) and renewal in order to strive for the common interest and to prevent evil under changing social circumstances.
>
> This system is superior to positivist legal systems, even from the purely earthly and pragmatic angle, for it combines the dimensions of belief and of moral conduct with the social values of justice, integrity, and charity, and it heals the rift between law and ethics, between the values governing social relations and the ones that steer individual conduct, between our past and our future. And in all this it gives us the feeling of belonging—to the community, to the motherland, the belief, and the system.[12]

For Muhammad Nur Farahat, though, this call for the application of the *shari'a*

> rests upon a simplistic view of thought and history. . . . It starts from the assumption that there is a single, stable, and immutable conception and content of what is conventionally called the *shari'a,* and that just because we are disobedient servants (in the best and most merciful of assumptions) we refuse to take hold of that clear conception and content and apply it to our crisis-ridden reality. [But] the matter is not that simple. The principles and rules of the *shari'a* are not instruments in themselves ready for governing any society at any time. They become so once the instruments of our reason come into play. . . . The *shari'a* consists of goals: the preservation of religion, of the mind, of honor, of property, and of the person. It consists of indubitable texts in the Qur'an and *sunna.* It consists of an *ijtihad* that treats these texts in detail. And finally the *shari'a* consists of the practical application of all this.
>
> While the *shari'a* was officially the law of the land, the matter was not so clear on the practical level. Public order was solely governed by the law of oppression, tyranny, might, and force. Private law—that is, the relations of lesser importance between the common people—was governed by principles of Islamic jurisprudence administered by Islamic judges, and even here the application of the *shari'a* was not quite generalized, and the competence of the Islamic judge to cover them was not comprehensive. . . .
>
> Consequently—and this is the important thing—the era that preceded the introduction of national laws with French roots was not a golden era of Egyptian society ruled by the *shari'a.* Not only was the era not golden, but the *shari'a* was not reigning either.[13]

Many authors warn against the immediate application of the *hudud* (e.g., the cutting off of a thief's hand) regardless of whether they are for or against the introduction of the *shari'a*. Some argue that, in light of the greatly changed circumstances, the *hudud* no longer fit into present society; others argue that the *hudud* should only be applied once the basic needs of all people are secured. "Those who call for the execution of the *hudud* now and immediately aim to preserve their riches that they have amassed by well-known methods," wrote Khalil 'Abd al-Karim.

> They are afraid that the hands of the hungry and miserable stretch out for them. . . . They feign respect for the *shari'a,* but the *shari'a* itself obliges them to secure a decent life for everybody before the *hudud* are executed, and if they don't do so they violate text and spirit of the *shari'a*.[14]

The argument over the *shari'a* is not purely legal. It has become more a symbol than anything else: For lack of any other acceptable shibboleth, its enforcement is considered the distinctive feature of an Islamic state. For its proponents, the struggle for *shari'a* may be more important than the goal itself, for it gives them an opportunity to clamor against the existing conditions and to load the public discourse with notions that change the terms of political struggle. This struggle brings them closer to power than would implementation of the *shari'a*. Their main point is the principle of the introduction of the *shari'a,* not the introduction as such. Opponents see that clearly, and thus some warn not only against the legal application of the *shari'a* but against the very principle of its introduction. In the final analysis, this is a political struggle, not a legal one.

ISLAMISM, SECULARISM, AND POLITICS

Around 1980, the Egyptian state moved to interrupt the march of the Islamists, who had been gaining considerable ground thanks to encouragement from the regime itself and to an intensification of the "Islamic atmosphere." Clashes between the radical Islamists and Copts or representatives of the state became more frequent, including the assassination of Anwar al-Sadat. The state took (and still takes) a two-pronged approach. On the one hand, it suppresses violent outbreaks, initiates periodic waves of arrests, and defers introduction of the *shari'a*. On the other hand, the government tries to reduce the Islamists' public appeal through widely publicized theological refutations of their basic tenets, and takes on itself an "Islamic" coloring in order to remove any pretext for opposition from that angle.[15]

The swift progress of the Islamist movement did slow down, yet the movement did not retreat. It dug in and prepared for a war of position. It remained quite active and retained a large audience. Its different components have improved their coordination and cooperation, and are striving to strengthen their influence over large segments of society and key mechanisms of influence. They managed to penetrate parliament in 1984, and broadened their presence there in 1987. They also dominate a considerable part of the media and have some influence in the government-controlled press.

Quite a few intellectuals have been alarmed by the headway the Islamist movement has made. The government, to counterbalance the Islamists' influence in the media, also provided these intellectuals with greater opportunities to voice their fears and their criticism. Characteristically, the debate seldom limited itself to political questions, expanding into the broader argument against any kind of institutionalized hegemony of religion—in other words, against integralism in general.

A good example is the debate on *shura* and democracy triggered by novelist Yusuf Idris in June 1985. One prominent proponent of reintroducing *shari'a* was the "secularist renegade" Khalid Muhammad Khalid. Idris, in an article in *Al-Ahram*, asked why Khalid busied himself with a relatively marginal issue like the *shari'a* while the Muslim world was suffering from so many bigger problems.[16] He then asked what kind of Islamic state Khalid wanted to see established, and which *shari'a* applied. Khalid responded that the Islamic creed necessarily entails an Islamic state and Islamic legislation. As for the form of government, he said it should be the *shura* (consultation), which he in turn defined as being equivalent to the modern conception of democracy. Khalid went on to insist that parliamentary opposition, a multiparty system, and a free press were essential to "the system of rule in Islam without distortion or defect."[17]

Farag Fuda enthusiastically hailed Khalid's liberal and tolerant conception and his defense of democracy, but warned against calling it an Islamic conception and making it legally binding as part of the *shari'a*. One should acknowledge, Fuda argued, that this form of government was conceived outside the realm of Islam but endorse it nevertheless as compatible with the Islamic spirit. Making it an obligatory feature of Islamic law and an Islamic state validates the principle of an Islamic state and thus gives a platform to less tolerant proponents of such a state.

Fu'ad Zakariyya pointed out that Khalid would never have been able to arrive at his conclusions from the basic Islamic texts alone:

> Would he have been able to define the *shura* as division of powers, free parliamentary representation, existence of an opposition capable of toppling the government, multiplicity of parties, and freedom of the press had he not been influenced by the thoughts of some weak mortals like John Locke, Montesquieu, Rousseau, and Thomas Jefferson, and had the experiences of the modern states that preceded us in the field of democracy not come to support the thoughts of those philosophers by way of practice? Would Khalid Muhammad Khalid have been able to explain the *shura* in this way if he were not himself a man who acquired democratic leanings through his readings,

his culture, and his acquaintance with the experiences of the modern peoples? And if it were said that he was able to arrive at such a definition by the study of the heritage alone, how was it that these principles were never discovered, nor applied, throughout the history of that heritage?[18]

OPPORTUNISM AND ACCOMMODATION

Many have said that all Egyptian parties—the ruling party as well as the opposition parties—take an opportunist stand on this question, siding with the Islamist camp because they think it is popular, forming alliances with it, or at least adapting to an atmosphere saturated with Islamist slogans. This is definitely true for the Socialist Labor Party and the Socialist Liberals, who formed an alliance with the Muslim Brothers for the parliamentary elections in 1987. To a certain extent, it is—or at least was—also true for the ruling National Democratic Party, which tries to assume a certain Islamic coloring, and for the Wafd which, rather secularist until then, formed an alliance with the Muslim Brothers for the elections of 1984, though relations have cooled off subsequently.[19]

The same charges have been leveled against the leftist Tagammu' Party.[20] Its traditional line is mainly directed against the regime, which it sees as representing the parasitic bourgeoisie and allied with the US and Israel.[21] The influence of the left within the universities suffered considerably from the upsurge of the Islamic groups (*gama'at*) during the 1970s. Later, parts of the left expressed sympathy for the radical Islamic groups fighting, as they were, against the regime. In the framework of the Committee for the Defense of Democracy, the left defended Islamist prisoners who were tortured in jail. Yet the left stands to lose at least as much from the destruction of a civil political structure in Egypt as any other secularist force. Torn between two options, the Tagammu' did not take a clear and consistent stand.

When Husayn Ahmad Amin late in 1984 criticized the left (as well as other parties) for retreating before the Islamists, the Tagammu' was not interested in discussing the problem openly.[22] When Amin tackled the problem of the veil, the reaction was negative. One author described the impact of Amin's articles inside the Tagammu' as an "uproar."[23]

The next occasion for the left to ponder the problem of political Islam was when the novelist and journalist 'Abd al-Rahman al-Sharqawi called for a national front—an alliance of all important forces of society, including the ruling party—against an enemy he portrayed as externally sponsored, clearly referring to the radical Islamist groups.[24] It appears that his call had the backing of the government, perhaps even of the president himself. Al-Sharqawi repeated his call in several consecutive articles, and asked for an answer from the left. Husayn 'Abd al-Raziq, the editor of the Tagammu' weekly, *Al-Ahali*, answered that a national salvation front should be directed against the "alliance of America, Israel, and the government of the parasites."[25] Compared with that set of enemies, Islamic extremism was a secondary danger that could only be dealt with by curing the main ills of Egyptian society. The Tagammu' leadership as well as that of the other opposition parties at this point clearly refused to side with the government's attacks against the Islamist groups.

The question arose again, before and after the elections of 1987. Some suggested an alliance of the left, the Wafd, and the ruling party against the "Islamic alliance" (Muslim Brothers, SLP, and Liberals), but this was rejected by a leading Tagammu' member, Mohamed Sid-Ahmed.[26] Fu'ad Zakariyya wrote that to pose it in either/or terms, "fight against the government and its alliances versus fight against the Islamist danger," was dangerously artificial. An Islamist takeover would only mean a different form of the same dependence upon, and alliance with, US imperialism and Israel. The difference would be that the Islamist variety of rule would destroy the conditions for any free political and intellectual struggle. Zakariyya presented the government and the Islamist groups as two evils, but for him the prospect of an Islamist takeover allows for only one conclusion: the fight against that possibility has absolute priority.

> The participation of the left in the effort to demystify the political campaign that takes its slogans from Islam doesn't mean at all that it forsakes its main fight against exploitation internally and imperialism externally. . . .
>
> Any struggle between political parties and tendencies in Egypt . . . remains a struggle between two human positions, whereas the Islamic tendency, if successful, would move this struggle to a completely different level. It would become a struggle between heaven and earth, between the party of God and the party of the devil. . . . Once the governing body comes to speak in the name of the *shari'a*, opposition turns to unbelief, any difference becomes an insolence in the face of God's law or an apostasy that has to be punished applying the appropriate *hadd* [Qur'anic punishment—in this case, death]. The conditions of political and social struggle will become much worse and much more difficult. I am not exaggerating if I say that the idea of the struggle itself will then be thoroughly uprooted.
>
> Therefore the interest of the left, and with it all nationalist forces, in maintaining the proper conditions for a legitimate political struggle imposes on all the duty to close ranks and stand against a tendency threatening to eradicate the principle of struggle itself.[27]

Of the eleven articles in *Al-Ahali* commenting on Zakariyya's position, six rejected his conclusion and five supported him. Only one, though, explicitly called for an inclusion of the ruling party in a possible alliance. For one author, the biggest part of the Islamist movement, the Muslim Brothers, represented the interests of the big bourgeoisie and consequently should be fought. Others saw the radical wing of the movement as a potential ally. One author argued that the struggle against Islamism should be left to the forces of enlightened Islam—the tendency that was originally envisaged as a basic component of the Tagammu' but never came into being.

> The administrative and police treatment of political Islam—by arrests, torture, blockade, and defamation—has transformed that tendency from a wide to a narrow horizon. . . . The removal of the artificial factors standing in the way of a real intellectual, social, and political struggle in Egyptian society will give each tendency its real scope. The majority vote for the ruling party is no less artificial than the influence of the Islamist groups—rather, they are two sides of the same coin. The factors guaranteeing this majority—arresting the real political struggle, obscuring the opinions of the other parties and tendencies, especially those on the left, limiting their influence, defaming their positions, and outlawing them—also benefit the groups of political Islam. They also benefit from the chaotic economy protected by the ruling party. The fight for real democracy will create a strong public opinion able to distinguish between the tendencies and to choose from among them according to its interest. . . .
>
> Confronting this [Islamist] tendency from a non-Islamic standpoint gives [the Islamists] a wonderful opportunity to win any battle over the correctness of its interpretation of Islam and its social slogans. . . . The ideological struggle against [the Islamists] must essentially be left to that nonexisting tendency that was originally stipulated by the conception of the Tagammu' as one of its constituent parts, namely the enlightened religious tendency. The continued ideological and organizational absence of that tendency is the most serious mistake of the left, and it is high time to correct it.[28]

One author drew a parallel between the present anti-Islamist struggle and that against fascism in pre–World War Europe. In both cases, he says, there was more determining the priority of that fight than class considerations, and in both cases it took the left much time to realize that and act accordingly.[29]

The debate showed that the priority of the fight against the government still dominated the conceptions of the Tagammu'. Yet the issue now had been taken up in a much more controversial way than in 1984 or 1985. In the summer of 1990 it was again raised by a panel of leading leftists, in quite a controversial manner.[30] Clearly political Islam was a much more persistent and a much less secondary phenomenon than the left had originally assumed.

LIMITS OF THE DEBATE

Contemporary Egyptian secularists justify their position by advancing arguments that boil down to the view that any institutionalized dominance of religion over human life poses problems and holds dangers. They try to prove the dangers of an integralist conception of Islam either by logic or by adducing practical experiences. The integralists counter that those problems and dangers are the result of an inconsistent or faulty application of Islam, and that they can be avoided by its "proper" enforcement.

Many questions could not be decided because of the absence of criteria accepted by both sides in this debate. Agreement on questions of principle was precluded by the vast gap between the respective intellectual frameworks. Both parties then tried to shift it onto the level that best suited them: the Islamists to that of reverential silence before a discourse perceived as religious; the secularists to that of a clearly political struggle fought in purely political terms. They argued, for example, that the Islamists were more concerned with power, influence, and money in this life than with salvation in the hereafter.[31]

This debate was most intense from 1984 to 1988. The arguments seem to have been elaborated and repeated to the point where they have lost their impact. The incompatibility of the positions has been demonstrated beyond reasonable doubt. To be sure, publications and public exchanges have continued, but essentially the contest has left the lofty arena of intellectual debate and become a struggle for power and influence, most notably concerning the state. In July 1990, the al-Azhar authorities successfully demanded that a book of Farag Fuda, one which reprinted his attack on the Shaikh al-Azhar cited at the beginning of this essay, be withdrawn from circulation. Early in 1992, emissaries from al-Azhar's "Islamic Studies Academy" confiscated five books of al-'Ashmawi from a stand at the Cairo Book Fair, though their attempt to enforce a ban on these books was thwarted by presidential decree.

On June 8, 1992, two emissaries of a different sort struck. They, too, had obviously run out of intellectual arguments against secularism. But they knew their target. They shot down and killed Farag Fuda, the most daring and in many ways the most eloquent opponent of political Islam in Egypt in this era.

NOTES

1. Farag Fuda, *Al-Ahali*, March 23, 1988.

2. Fahmi Huwaydi, "Hadith al-ifk," *Al-Ahram*, January 19, 1988; and Fahmi Huwaydi, "Al-islam al-siyahi," *Al-Ahram*, January 26, 1988.

3. Many other writers contributed to the debate; for an account, see David Sagiv, "Judge Ashmawi and Militant Islam in Egypt," *Middle Eastern Studies* 28, no. 3 (July 1992): 531–46.

4. Muhammad 'Imara, *Al-'Almaniya wa-nahdatuna al-haditha* (Cairo and Beirut, 1986), pp. 28ff.

5. Fu'ad Zakariyya, *Al-Sahwa al-islamiya fi mizan al-'aql* (Cairo, 1989), pp. 63–66, 71ff.

6. Ibid., p. 9.

7. For a rather sketchy account, see Nancy E. Gallagher, "Islam v. Secularism in Cairo: An Account of the Dar al-Hikma Debate," *Middle Eastern Studies* 25, no. 2 (April 1989): 208–15.

8. For the proceedings, see *Misr bayna al-dawla al-diniyya wa'l-madaniyya* (Nicosia, 1992).

9. A good summary of the debate is given by Rudolph Peters, "Divine Law or Man-Made Law? Egypt and the Application of the Shari'a," *Arab Law Quarterly* 3, no. 3 (August 1988): 231–53.

10. Muhammad Sa'id al-'Ashmawi, *Usul al-shari'a* (Cairo, n.d.); and Muhammad Sa'id al-'Ashmawi, *Hawla al-da'wa ila tatbiq al-shari'a al-islamiyya wa-dirasat islamiyya ukhra* (Beirut, 1985); Muhammad Nur Farahat, *Al-Mujtama' wa'l-shari'a wa'l-qanun* (Cairo, 1986).

11. See, e.g., Tawfiq al-Shawi, *Siyadat al-shari'a al-islamiyya fi misr* (Cairo, 1987); and Mustafa Farghali al-Shuqayri, *Fi wajh al-mu'amara 'ala tatbiq al-shari'a al-islamiyya* (al-Mansura, 1986).

12. Tariq al-Bishri, *Al-Sha'b,* July 7, 1987.

13. Farahat, *Al-Mujtama' wa'l-shari'a wa'l-qanun,* p. 95.

14. Khalil 'Abd al-Karim, *Li-tatbiq al-shari'a . . . la li'l-hukm!* (Cairo, 1987), p. 47.

15. For a criticism of the regime's tactics from a secularist point of view, see Farag Fuda, *Al-Nadhir* (Cairo, 1989).

16. Yusuf Idris, *Al-Ahram,* June 17, 1985.

17. Khalid Muhammad Khalid, ibid., June 24, 1985.

18. Fu'ad Zakariyya, ibid., August 8, 1985.

19. That was the main reason for Farag Fuda and some other prominent members leaving the Wafd. See Alexander Flores, "Egypt: A New Secularism?" *Middle East Report,* no. 153 (July–August 1988): 27–30.

20. E.g., by Fuda, *Hiwar hawla al-'almaniyya* (Cairo, n.d.); Husayn Ahmad Amin, "'An al-intihaziyya wa'l-ahzab al-siyasiyya," *Al-Ahali,* November 7, 1984; Salah Hafiz, "Fi ja'ib Iran!" *Akhbar al-Yawm,* October 18, 1986.

21. See the proceedings of the second party congress, *Al-Tariq li-inqadh misr min al-fasad wa'l-tufayliyya wa'l-taba'iyya* (Cairo, 1985).

22. Amin, "'An al-intihaziyya wa'l-ahzab al-siyasiyya."

23. See *Revue de la presse égyptienne,* no. 15 (March 1985): 40–63.

24. 'Abd al-Rahman al-Sharqawi, "La budda min al-jabha!" *Al-Ahram,* July 6, 1985.

25. Husayn 'Abd al-Raziq, *Al-Ahali,* August 28, 1985.

26. Mohamed Sid-Ahmed, ibid., April 5, 1987.

27. Zakariyya, "Al-yasar wa'l-tayyar al-islami," ibid., April 29, 1987.

28. Salah 'Isa, ibid., May 13, 1987.

29. Yunan Labib Rizq, ibid., May 27, 1987.

30. "Ru'yat al-yasar li-mawqi' al-usuliyyin al-islamiyyin 'ala al-kharita al-tabaqiyya wa'l-siyasiyya," *Al-Yasar* (August 1990): 43–58; and *Al-Yasar* (November 1990): 43–58.

31. This was a recurring theme in the writings of Farag Fuda. See, e.g., his booklet *Al-Mal'ub* (Cairo, 1988), exposing the "Islamic" investment societies.

PART TWO

The Contest for the State and the Political Economy

8

Introduction to Part Two

Robert Vitalis

In many Middle Eastern countries Islamist movements have set their sights squarely on the seizure of state power. Since its founding as a unified national state in 1932, the rulers of Saudi Arabia have claimed to govern according to the tenets of Islam. In 1979 a very different kind of Islamic political order—a theocracy—was imposed in Iran under the leadership of the Ayatollah Khomeini and other clerics. In the late 1980s and early 1990s, political movements with more avowedly populist or communitarian commitments—some would call these Islamist currents postmodernist—seized power in Sudan and, aided by an extensive CIA program, toppled the regime in Afghanistan. In the mid-1990s, underground cells of armed, militant Islamists are waging war in Egypt, Algeria, and the Palestinian state-in-formation.

At the start of the twentieth century, as American statesmen discovered their "mission" on behalf of "primitive" peoples in Africa, Asia, and the Middle East, militaristic conceptions of Islam proliferated. Many Americans depicted the "propagators" of "Mohammadanism" (as they called Islam) in Africa as a force arrayed against the (Christian) "standard of the Western nations" and the "White races of the West." "The distinctive feature of Islam is the Holy War," bent on conquest by force of arms, wrote George W. Ellis.[1]

Decades later, the theorists of the American national security state turned from Islam to portraying communism using nearly identical language, as an "international conspiracy...directed generally against...the Judeo-Christian code of morals on which our western civilization rests."[2] Since the collapse of the Soviet Union, many scholars, journalists, and policy makers have reached once more for these nineteenth-century doctrines, divining in the forces of political Islam an alien world in collision with our own.[3]

The authors of the following chapters write against this powerful Islamophobic current and remind us that these political movements take myriad forms, from bottom-up mobilization of students and other urban strata in Cairo to the elite pact between Sudanese army officers and leaders of the National Islamic Front in Khartoum. The array of strategies, doctrines, and sites within which power is pursued and contested suggests a more fragmented terrain than that depicted in the image of Islam marching against the West. The project of seizing power and building Islamic states is inextricably shaped by the territorial *national* states that have emerged in the postcolonial Middle East, and the specific *state* boundaries and national histories of each of the governing regimes frame the account of political Islam in Iran, Egypt, Syria, Algeria, Palestine, Lebanon, and elsewhere.

The distinctly recent processes of building national *states* and *economies* in the region may be the most important commonality among the various currents and movements of political Islam. The shared focus on state power seems to undermine the notion that an essentially fixed cultural system called Islam—with "primordial" attachments to tribe and family—resists "alien" forms of nation-state identities. As Sami Zubaida notes in his contribution to this section, Islamist movements "are not continuous with historical Islam but rather are modern constructions influenced by current conjunctures."

A careful dissection of these conjunctures finds a politics more related to the previous half-century wave of decolonization that swept the region than to the community-state of Muhammad in Madina forged nearly fourteen hundred years ago. The dilemma for would-be Islamist wielders of state power is to create a stable governing coalition from the disparate and contradictory social bases of political opposition. And the most basic source of discontent is broadly the same as that which fueled opposition to the various forms of colonial rule and shaped the initial stages of state formation: the highly uneven impact of development and increasing levels of economic interdependence within the global economy.

Hoisting a secular-nationalist ideological standard, a generation of post–World War II "modernizing" leaders and regimes—the Nasir government in Egypt, Boumedienne in Algeria, the Ba'th in Syria and Iraq, Muhammad Reza Shah Pahlavi in Iran—pursued forms of guns-and-butter mercantilism: building massive armies, ministries, and state-owned enterprises around which the regimes' middle- and working-class constituencies could be nurtured and at least some of its opponents bought off. Inefficiencies in these highly bureaucratized and politicized economies could be ignored during decades of Cold War clientalism, rising oil prices, heavy borrowing, and massive remittances from migrant labor. But the economic recession of the 1980s led to protracted conflicts over the course of economic "restructuring" and the values that should guide society.

The wrenching economic transformation, together with (and arguably exacerbated by) governments' attempts to hold on to power, goes a long way to explaining the growth of Islamic movements in the 1980s. The effects of state-led development models, piecemeal liberalization, and deepening interdependency are rarely far from view in the chapters that follow. In Iran the national state—through its land reform decrees and its expanding armed presence in the countryside—and the global economy—through the ebb and flow of the price of oil—rent the fabric of village life.[4] In Khalid Medani's account of the political economy of the Islamist state in Sudan, remittances and investment capital from the Arab Gulf, generated by the 1970s oil boom, are central to the shifting fortunes of the independence-era parties and to the rise to power there of the Muslim Brothers.

Virtually everywhere in the region the consequences of mercantilism, which its architects often promoted as "indigenous" forms of socialism, and the barely disguised patronage circuits that buttressed the postcolonial regimes, left the government and its privileged clients open to attack as hopelessly corrupt captives of alien ideas or, in the more conspiratorial version, of foreign forces and agents. The strength of the secularist forces of the left—workers' unions, women's groups, minorities, professionals, and intellectuals—varies from country to country. Everywhere in the region, though, these embattled segments of society and their icons, such as Gamal 'Abd al-Nasir, are today seen as part of the problem rather than potential solutions to the social crisis.

The difference with Latin America, where the comparable 1960s revolutionary and populist currents have reversed course to embrace "liberalizing" development models and agendas, is striking. In the Middle East, Islamists keep populist hopes alive. Karen Pfeifer's "Is There an Islamic Economics?" looks for signs of laissez-faire or social-market ideas informing contemporary economic debates. These currents, she argues, are "no throwback to the social system of the Middle Ages."

They do, however, seem to echo the strands of romantic anticapitalism that have marked successive waves of populist "antisystemic movements" in the world economy over the past century. The promise of pioneering a "third way" between capitalism and socialism has been part of the ideology of all national-populist regimes inside the region, including Atatürk in Turkey and Nasir in Egypt—and outside it, as exemplified by Cardenas in Mexico or Peron in Argentina. Khomeini in Iran is only a recent entry, and in this respect there is not much that is unusual about the Islamic Republic or that cannot be comprehended using concepts applied to study of non-Islamic regimes. The most important difference is that clerics in Iran have come to form a distinct corporate group, much like army officers do in numerous other states.

In Egypt, which, along with Algeria, faces escalating violence as Islamists struggle for power, President Husni Mubarak prefers to emphasize shadowy foreign conspiracies and influences centered in Iran and Sudan rather than the continued deterioration of urban life in explaining the currents that appear to threaten his rule.[5] In contrast, Carrie Rosefsky Wickham's "Islamic Mobilization and Political Change: The Islamist Trend in Egypt's Professional Associations" identifies the economic and political failures of the postcolonial regime as the reason that tens of thousands of highly educated and alienated young Egyptians—engineers, doctors, lawyers, pharmacists—join the "Islamic trend." Her finely etched analysis subverts media stereotypes of the doctrines, practices, and the social groups that give political Islam resonance in the contemporary era.

On university campuses across the United States, young adults, worried about their future prospects, fret over the rituals of law school applications and medical school admissions tests that they hope will gain them security and prosperity. In 1990s Egypt, a professional education offers less than American students' worst nightmare—moonlighting at McDonald's—and no hope of escape from the psychological violence of living ten-to-a-room in deteriorating housing stock in neglected neighborhoods. By choosing to confront and undermine Islamic institution building and the Islamists' slow accretion of power from the bottom up, the Mubarak regime channels disaffection into more direct and violent forms of counterconfrontation.

Wickham also warns us not to mistake Islamic institution building for an incipient liberalization or democratization project. Pfeifer makes a similar point for those prone to see in Islamic economics a vindication of free market fundamentalism or a blueprint for surmounting Egypt's current crisis.[6]

Until recently, Egyptians took pride in a society generally unscarred by the sectarianism and violence endemic to the postindependence politics of Iraq, Syria, Sudan, and Lebanon—the latter two wracked by long and bloody civil wars. The consolidation of the post–World War II regimes in all these cases followed a pattern similar to other ethnically heterogeneous societies across Africa and Asia, where the power and resources of the state were monopolized by narrow confessional or regional groups.

In Syria in 1982, the regime of Hafiz al-'Asad faced Muslim militants who mounted an armed uprising in the north-central city of Hama. Al-'Asad's notoriously dictatorial regime is rooted in the 'Alawi community (considered heretical by Sunni Muslims) centered in northern Syria. Hanna Batatu argues that the Muslim Brothers' opposition was supported by urban merchants in Damascus and other cities whose fortunes declined in tandem with the 'Alawis' rise. The activists who took up arms against al-'Asad's regime comprised, as in Egypt and elsewhere, "university students, school teachers, engineers, physicians, and the like."[7] The timing of the Hama uprising itself may have been triggered by the regime's interventions in the economy on behalf of favored constituencies.[8]

The longevity of al-'Asad's rule, the cult that surrounds him, and the ruthlessness displayed in the confrontation with the Muslim Brothers project images of a strong state in Syria, in marked contrast to the visibly more fragile orders that govern postcolonial Sudan and Lebanon. As Khalid Medani shows, the military junta that seized power in Sudan in June 1989 turned to the Muslim Brothers and their political party, the National Islamic Front, in an alliance of convenience. The consolidation of political Islam as a governing force in Sudan is by no means assured, though the NIF has done a remarkable job of establishing its hegemony over the state apparatus. However, the NIF appears incapable of restructuring the forms of patron-clientalism that contribute to the economic crisis there and throughout sub-Saharan Africa.

The future of political Islam is even cloudier in Lebanon, where the central state rules Beirut and its environs at the sufferance of Syria and rules in name only in the south. There Hizb Allah's forces continue to challenge Israel's occupation, and there are strict limits to the tacit alliance that Assaf Kfoury's insider account describes between the southern Hizb Allah militia and the government in Beirut. With all Lebanese political parties and religious communities committed to ending the violence after more than a decade of civil war, Hizb Allah faces formidable obstacles to its project of transforming Lebanon into an Iranian-style Islamic state. As Kfoury shows, not all Shi'a support Hizb Allah. It is difficult, moreover, to imagine the Sunni and Shi'a Muslim communities coalescing around a common Islamic project. Kfoury demonstrates that, in the circumstances of a fragile parliamentary order, Hizb Allah has had to acknowledge the implausibility of a second revolutionary Shi'a state in the region and has opted instead to play the role of a contesting party in the struggle for resources and leverage.

Turkey is often contrasted with Algeria and Egypt as having "successfully" reformed a grossly inefficient state sector and public-owned industry. Yet such reform is apparently no guarantee of broad-based prosperity, unless perhaps in the very long term. In the short term, reform has been as potent a catalyst for real economic pain as failed mercantilist experiments.

The electoral regime in place since the end of "emergency" military rule in 1983 has provided significant space for an Islamist grouping, the Refah (Welfare) Party, to emerge in the 1990s as a leading opposition force in local and national politics. As Ronnie Margulies and Ergin Yıldızoğlu show, Welfare's carefully crafted campaign strategy, rhetorically emphasizing social justice, reflects the deepening splits over Turkey's adherence to IMF-style austerity programs. More generally, the party's rise is a response to the effects of the twenty-year-old strategy of economic reintegration with

Western capital, labor, technology and products markets on Turkey's disadvantaged regions and economic sectors. Turkish democrats, secularists, and free marketeers are all pinning their hopes on membership in the European Union, a course which Refah's leaders denounce, and on the army, which entered the political arena to smash the populist currents of the 1970s.

The readings in this section remind us once again that we should check the disposition of many Americans and other Westerners to regard political Islam in monolithic and transnational terms, and instead pay careful attention to political and economic conjunctures, national particularities, and local histories.

NOTES

1. George W. Ellis, "Islam as a Factor in West African Culture," *Journal of Race Development* 2, no. 2 (October 1911): 113; See also G. Stanley Hall, "Mission Pedagogy," *Journal of Race Development* 1, no. 2 (October 1910): 127–46.

2. NSC-17, "The Internal Security of the United States" (June 28, 1948) quoted in David Campbell, *Writing Security: United States Foreign Policy and the Politics of Identity* (Minneapolis: University of Minnesota Press, 1992), p. 29.

3. Samuel P. Huntington, "The Clash of Civilizations?" *Foreign Affairs* (summer 1993): 22–49; and Judith Miller, "The Islamic Wave," *New York Times Magazine,* November 21, 1993, pp. 62–65.

4. See, for example, Mary Hoogland, "Religious Ritual and Political Struggle in an Iranian Village," *MERIP Reports,* no. 102 (January 1982): 10–17.

5. See Mary Anne Weaver, "The Novelist and the Sheikh," *New Yorker,* January 30, 1995, pp. 52–69.

6. For a particularly harsh judgment on Islamic economics, see Simon Bromley, *Rethinking Middle East Politics* (Austin: University of Texas Press, 1994), pp. 180–83.

7. Hanna Batatu, "Syria's Muslim Brethren," *MERIP Reports,* no. 110 (November–December 1982): 12–20.

8. Fred Lawson, "Social Bases for the Hamah Revolt," *MERIP Reports,* no. 110 (November–December 1982): 24–28.

9

Is Iran an Islamic State?

Sami Zubaida

How applicable are the classic concepts of "state" and "politics" to the world of Islam? The current prominence of Islamic politics and the establishment of an Islamic Republic in Iran poses this question anew.

On this point there is convergence between the adherents of the Islamist movements and Westerners writing in the Orientalist tradition. Each postulates a cultural essence which underlies and unifies Islamic history and distinguishes it from an equally reductionist notion of the West. They see the territorial nation-state as an alien graft, imposed by the West but remaining "external" to Muslim society, the game of intellectuals and politicians. In Islamic societies, both Islamists and Orientalists argue, the global unit of solidarity is the Islamic community of the faithful, the *umma;* the territorial nation-state is incompatible with this higher unity. Western writers would add that alongside this global solidarity there is the more immediate solidarity of primary communities based on tribe, region, or sect, equally incompatible with the nation-state but played out within its alien political field under modern ideological labels like "nationalism" and "socialism."

The traditional form of the Islamic polity, the *dawla* of a dynasty or a clique, is compatible with both the *umma* and the primary community. The *dawla* enjoys absolute and arbitrary powers over peoples and resources. Though subservient clerics legitimize this rule as Islamic, it is scarcely limited by Islamic law. Writers in the Orientalist tradition see many Middle Eastern states as modern extensions of traditional Islamic absolute rulers, "neopatrimonial" states ruling by coercion and extensive patronage networks.

Contemporary Islamists judge this type of modern state as alien to Islamic principles, a creature of imperialism, even when it pretends to Islam. They seek a "truly Islamic" state, applying the *shari'a* and unifying the fragmented *umma* under a revived caliphate, thus providing for justice and the sovereignty of God. The primary model for such a state is contained in the "sacred history" of the community-state embodied in the Arabian city of Madina in the time of Muhammad.

These essentialist positions contrast with the view of modern states as products of social and cultural transformations accompanying the uneven expansion of a global capitalist economy. Broadly speaking, the region has experienced a breakdown of local self-contained socioeconomic units as they have been integrated into wider systems which are in turn linked up to an international economy. Aspects of this process include transport, migration, urbanization, conscript armed forces, education and literacy, as well as print and other communications media.

Nation-states are clearly of European origin, but their diffusion to other parts of the world (including much of Europe itself) did not create replicas of the British or the French political systems. In particular, political representation and legal constraints on the exercise of power have been weak or nonexistent in many Third World political systems, including those of the Middle East. A political sociology of particular countries explains these factors.

At the same time, the nation-state has itself structured political processes and ideas in the region, and dominated the assumptions and forms of underlying political activity there. Even for those who would transcend the nation-state into pan-Arabism or pan-Islamism, the nation-state represents an elemental political fact and constraint. In fact, the assumptions and concepts of the nation-state underlie, implicitly or explicitly, most modern Islamist ideologies. In this and many other respects, they are not continuous with historical Islam but rather are modern constructions influenced by current conjunctures.

EXISTING ISLAMIC STATES

This becomes clear when we examine the nature of the Islamic state in Iran. If the nation-state is an imported concept unsuitable for Islamic cultural and social conditions, then can the Islamic state escape its alien trappings in favor of a more authentic and harmonious form?

Of the existing Islamic states, Iran is the most appropriate case to consider. Saudi Arabia emerged out of tribal polities and is sustained in its present form by vast oil revenues. In Zia ul-Haq's Pakistan, as in present-day Sudan, Islam was imposed by a military regime in an effort to engender some legitimacy and reinforce control. Iran is the only example of an Islamic state installed through a popular revolution which engages all aspects of the question.

There is a dualism in Iran of nation-state concepts intermingled with Islamic forms. These forms are not revivals of continuities with historical instances but quite novel creations. Khomeini's doctrine of *vilayet-i faqih* (the jurisconsult's trusteeship, or rule by the leading *faqih*), for instance, as applied to government, is a major departure from historical Islamic political thought and practice, including Shi'ism. The duality is indicated in the very title of Islamic "republic" (*jomhuri*). "Republic" represents a link with the French revolution and all the revolutions of the twentieth century, in the region and outside, which have toppled a monarchy. It has a written constitution, drafted after wide-ranging and heated debates by an elected Assembly of Experts (on the model of a constitutional assembly), then amended in 1989 amid further political struggles. It also has an elected president and a parliament (Majlis, the same term used for parliament in the defunct monarchical regime, as well as in most countries of the region).[1]

The project of the Islamic Republic is to Islamize state, society, and culture. In what follows, I shall examine what is involved in this project. We shall see that the basic processes of modernity in the socioeconomic and cultural fields, as well as in government, subvert and subordinate Islamization. The Islamic authorities are often forced to adapt their policies and discourses to practical considerations. "Secularization" has not been reversed, but disguised behind imposed symbols and empty rhetoric.

THE PRINCIPLE OF NATIONALITY

The rhetoric of the Islamic Republic is internationalist, declaring the unity and brotherhood of all Muslims in one *umma*. Yet the Iranian constitution and state practice enshrine Iranian nationality as a condition for full citizenship in the Republic. Article 115 states that the president must be Iranian both by origin and nationality, and have a "convinced belief in the . . . official school of thought in the country," that is, he must be Shi'i. Jalaloddin Farsi, a longtime disciple of Khomeini, was prevented from standing in the presidential elections of 1980 because his mother was Afghan. At the same time, Iranian Christians, Jews, and Zoroastrians are accorded full citizenship rights, short of assuming positions of leadership in the Republic.

Iranian Islam, being Shi'i, reinforces Iranian nationalism, confronting as it does a predominantly Sunni Arab world and Turkey. Wahhabi Saudi Arabia, for instance, is deeply hostile to Shi'ism at the religious level, and to Iran at the geostrategic level. Iranian pilgrims to Mecca have always been regarded with suspicion and subjected to petty humiliations, an antagonism only sharpened by the revolution and the subsequent militant stance of Iranian pilgrims.

The war with Iraq (1980–88) sharpened the national identity of the revolution as Iranian and Shi'i, against a hostile Arab Sunni world. Khomeini and the other Islamic leaders spoke more frequently of the Muslim nation of Iran. While not abandoning its theoretical internationalist commitment to the Islamic *umma,* or to the *mostazefin,* the oppressed of the world, the emphasis was more clearly on the Iranian nation as the vanguard of the Islamic revolution.

LOCATIONS OF SOVEREIGNTY

It is important to note that the Constitution of the Islamic Republic is not the Islamic *shari'a.* It privileges the *shari'a* as a source of legislation, but this is only one of its many provisions. There is a dualism in the Iranian constitution between the sovereignty of the people (derived from the dominant political discourses of modernity) and the sovereignty of God, through the principle of *vilayet-i faqih.*

Article 6 of the constitution states that "the affairs of the country must be administered on the basis of public opinion expressed by means of elections." An elected parliament (Majlis) debates and enacts legislation (within stipulated limits, as we shall see). Government is responsible to parliament, which can scrutinize the actions and policies of the executive. Legislation must not depart from the basic tenets of Muslim law, but this, for the most part, exists not in a codified form but in the books of opinion and interpretation written by the jurists. It was a committee of jurists, in the form of the Council of Guardians, which was entrusted by the constitution with the task of ensuring that parliamentary legislation conformed with the *shari'a.*[2]

The religious element of the constitution emanates from the principle of *vilayet-i faqih* written into it. The Spiritual Leader (Guardian Jurisconsult, or *faqih*) combines legislative and executive functions. As the supreme *mujtahid* (jurisconsult), he has the ultimate powers of interpretation of the canonical sources, and therefore of the approval of legislation. As head of the executive, he has the prerogative of appointment and dismissal of the chief of general staff, the other chiefs of the defense forces, and the head of the Revolutionary Guards. The president, after being elected by popular vote, has to be appointed by the Leader, who can also dismiss him. These powers appeared appropriate for Khomeini, and that section of the constitution was therefore written with him in mind as the charismatic leader of the revolution. Since his death in 1989, constitutional amendments and political developments have diminished the power of the Leader, as we shall see.

The Leader appoints six of the twelve members of the Council of Guardians, the other six being appointed by the Majlis from a list approved by the Supreme Judicial Council, itself composed of high-ranking clerics. In effect, the Council of Guardians is composed of Muslim jurists with wide powers to scrutinize and censor legislation. They are charged with ensuring that legislation agrees with the "tenets of Islam." Given that these are not written in a codified form, the Council has unlimited areas and powers of intervention.

In practice, throughout the 1980s the Council used these powers to veto legislation which interfered with rights of private property, such as land reform and nationalization of foreign trade. They consistently ruled that such measures were incompatible with the basic principles of *shari'a*. These rulings were widely perceived to be political. In the context of debates between conservatives and radicals on economic policy, the Council of Guardians consistently favored the conservatives. It should be noted that these judgments were not inevitable: other jurists, also proceeding from the sacred sources, reached more radical conclusions. The stance of the Council was considered obstructive of government policy, and in 1988 pressure mounted on Khomeini to stop this intervention.

That year, in response to a Friday sermon by President Khamene'i (now Leader) which seemed to declare the principles of *shari'a* to be binding on the Islamic government, Khomeini issued a stern refutation. He declared that the Islamic government, acting in the general interests of the Muslim nation, can, if necessary, abrogate *shari'a* principles. It can, for instance, forbid even the most basic pillars of the faith such as prayer, fasting, and *hajj* (pilgrimage to Mecca). This declaration was widely read as an empowerment of government and parliament against the obstruction of the Council of Guardians in the name of *shari'a*. This weakening of the Council was institutionalized soon after with the founding of another body, the Council for the Identification of [the Republic's] Interest (also known as the Expediency Council), which included the members of the Council of Guardians but diluted their clout with a larger number of members drawn from government and parliament. In case of a deadlock between government and Council of Guardians, the new body would adjudicate and decide by majority vote.

This far-reaching ruling gives the government and the Leader the competence to decide when the provisions of Muslim law, however interpreted, are or are not binding. Given that the "tenets of Islam" are the ultimate constitutional limit on legislation and government power, their effective removal gives the government and parliament unlimited powers.

These changes were incorporated into the constitutional amendments of 1989. The main effect of these amendments was to create a presidential system: the post of prime minister was abolished in favor of the president, who would select the ministers. While the ministers would be subject to parliament's approval, the president, being directly elected, would not. At the same time, the position of Leader was downgraded, also in favor of the president. The Leader no longer needed the high religious rank of *marja'-ye taqlid* (source of imitation), and he no longer needed to be "acceptable to the majority of the electorate": he was simply chosen by the (popularly elected) Assembly of Experts. These amendments came into effect with the election of Hashemi Rafsanjani as president, and the appointment of 'Ali Khamene'i as Leader. Khamene'i was a relatively junior cleric, with the rank of *hojatolislam,* not even an *ayatollah.* His appointment was strongly contested by the "radicals" in parliament and government, who saw it, quite correctly, as a fundamental weakening of *vilayet-i faqih,* the founding principle of the revolution. Since his appointment, however, Khamene'i has been maneuvering with the aid of political allies to boost his religious standing and rank and to exercise his powers and authority as against the president. While Khomeini as Leader stood above factional strife (and manipulated it), Khamene'i leads one faction against others. The effect is to make the Leader just another politician and thus to denude the position of *faqih* of its sanctity and charisma.

THE LAW OF THE ISLAMIC REPUBLIC

The application of the *shari'a* is the central pillar of Islamist advocacy all over the world. How does the Islamic government of Iran fare in this respect? We have seen that the constitution does not coincide with the *shari'a,* and that most of its provisions accord with modern precepts of politics and statecraft. One of its provisions is that the *shari'a* is the basis of legislation. The empowerment of parliament to enact legislation amounts to a tacit recognition that the *shari'a* is not, or cannot be, a ready-made divine law to be applied. Indeed, the *shari'a* is not, for the most part, codified law. Its application in premodern Iran was in the hands of independent judges and *mujtahids,* each entitled to his own interpretation, without an overriding centralized authority. The "tenets of Islam" are so wide and indeterminate a frame of reference that they give the Council of Guardians unlimited powers of censorship over legislation. What, then, is the law applied in practice in the Islamic Republic?

In fact, the laws currently in force are derived from many sources. The Civil Code of the previous regime has been largely retained: the main alteration has been simply to delete items authorizing or recognizing dealings in interest. Nothing was substituted for the deleted items, which leaves these areas uncovered. In practice, interest is disguised. For example, bank deposits attract appropriate cash "prizes." Regarding criminal law, the Qur'anic penal code prescribing amputations and executions for theft, adultery, murder, and so on, was introduced in 1981. This code, however, was selectively used, often with political objectives. Special "revolutionary courts" have dealt with offenses against the revolution—that is, political offenses. These have drawn on a variety of sources including the *shari'a* to justify their political and mostly repressive verdicts. These were in the main associated with the imprisonment, torture, and execution of political opponents. These verdicts, so prevalent in the 1980s and now diminished but not ended, could accelerate if the political situation were to change. The post of Revolutionary Prosecutor, with his own staff of investigators, remains an important one in the judicial system, dealing with political offenses as well as those to do with conformity to Islamic ethics and correct comportment.

The most politically and socially significant area of the law has been personal and family law. This area is symbolic of the *shari'a*, one which arouses the highest passions for and against. It is also the area in which the *shari'a* is clearest and at its most systematically codified form. Most Muslim countries, including those which are relatively "secular" such as Egypt and Algeria, have included *shari'a* provisions for the areas of marriage, divorce, inheritance, custody of children, and so on. Only Turkey and Tunisia legislated on these areas independently of *shari'a* provisions. Under the monarchy in Iran, some *shari'a* provisions, especially on divorce, were amended in more "liberal" directions. The civil courts under the Islamic Republic have never fully abandoned these reforms. Although policies on women and the family have been, in many obvious respects, highly repressive for women, there have also been, paradoxically, major innovative departures in legislation and policy which have favored women's rights, as I discuss below.

GOVERNMENT AND POLITICS

The government of the Islamic Republic is organized in the form of a modern state, with functional ministries incorporating modern bureaucracies that work, for the most part, in accordance with rules and procedures not dissimilar to those of the *ancien regime*. Even in their mode of dress, most high-ranking male functionaries, politicians, and diplomats who are not mullahs wear a particular adaptation of Western dress: trousers and jackets, but collarless shirts and no ties. Many sport neat beards, although this trend is waning. The military wear modern uniforms.

What are the Islamic elements in this government? First, it is Islamic in personnel. From the first years of the revolution, ministries and public institutions, such as education, were purged and the personnel replaced by mullahs and their protégés. The other important Islamic elements were to be found in the multitude of revolutionary organizations at all levels of government, society, and the armed forces. Some of these parallel state organizations and intervene in their operations as revolutionary monitors and censors, if not rivals. The most important of these are the Pasdaran, or Revolutionary Guards, first started as a revolutionary militia with police and internal defense functions. The war with Iraq added general military functions parallel to the regular armed forces, partly to keep these latter forces in check. Eventually the Pasdaran became major rivals to the regular forces, organizationally complex and well-equipped in all three services and with a special ministry to handle their affairs.

Unlike the Pasdaran, revolutionary committees in government departments and public enterprises do not perform parallel functions. Rather they watch over the revolutionary purity of the relevant organizations (interpreted in relation to current political factions and struggles, with occasional purges of supporters of one side in favor of another). They also watch over the Islamic morals and comportment of the employees—rituals (prayers and fasting) and correct forms of dress, particularly as regards women. More important, in factories and other enterprises employing workers, they maintain industrial and ideological discipline and counter subversive radical but non-Islamic notions of trade unionism. Other Islamic committees and organizations control urban quarters, performing police and security functions; yet others administer charitable distributions to the poor, building up patronage networks in the process.

This proliferation of revolutionary committees and councils is highly reminiscent of the situations following other popular revolutions, such as the French or Russian: citizens' or workers' committees watching over the revolutionary purity of government and society and in the process engaging in factional struggles. Their Iranian equivalents are different in the content of their ideology and, crucially, in the fact that they are not elected but appointed from above. The "routinization" of revolutions typically includes the suppression or incorporation of zealous censors. In Iran this process has proceeded unevenly.

We might expect that the routinization of the revolution would have led to the absorption of these revolutionary organizations into regular state and security functions. Indeed, the Pasdaran became a regular force alongside other armed forces, fulfilling defense and internal security functions, such as quelling riots. Yet they retained their separate identity and command structure. Urban *komitehs* have been absorbed into the police forces, which retain their separate identities. Many workplaces now have Islamic workers' associations, with functions of discipline and control. Other extragovernmental organizations have come into existence in the context of the war with Iraq, most notably those of *basij-e mostazefin*. These were the volunteer forces of youths from poor families who were so prominent as cannon fodder in the war with Iraq. Now they are used by their mullah patrons as "enforcers" of Islamic morality as well as shock troops against demonstrations of political dissent. As we shall see, the continuing political factionalism within the Islamic state has sustained organizations and institutions which rival regular state departments.

If these revolutionary forces can be said to have been routinized in institutions, then these institutions have carried over the duality or the plurality of principles and forces of the revolution. This multiplicity of principles and forces has been perpetuated by factions of clergy and their supporters controlling different institutions and resources, the most important being the duality between the president and the spiritual leader.

The political arena of the Islamic Republic is Islamized in a number of respects. Religion enters prominently into political discourse: rival justifications, denunciations, and claims to legitimacy are made with appeal to religious formulae. Religious rhetoric and exhortation, and the stories and symbols of martyrdom of Shi'i heroes, have been important ideological resources for political and military mobilization, especially in the war with Iraq. Every city has an *imam jomeh* (Friday prayer leader and preacher) appointed by the government, and the Friday sermons are occasions for political exhortation and advocacy.

All those who stand for public office, primarily Majlis elections, have to demonstrate their "practical commitment to Islam and to the Islamic government."[3] The election law requires a candidate to be a believer in God and a loyal supporter of the Islamic regime, the constitution, and the Leader. The Council of Guardians is entrusted with the task of vetting each candidate for these qualifications. In the 1992 Majlis elections, nearly one-third of all candidates were ruled "unfit." Given that the Council does not have to give reasons for rejecting candidates, it is wide open to claims of political bias in the context of factional conflicts.

The approved parameters of correct Islamic politics exclude many devout Muslims who openly oppose basic elements of the Republic's constitution or the government's repressive political stances. One notable example is the Freedom Movement, led by Mehdi Bazargan, the first prime minister of the Republic, until his death in 1995. This party of Muslim liberals, after participation in the first Majlis, was suppressed and its members rejected as parliamentary candidates; some were imprisoned and tortured. High-ranking clerics opposed to *vilayet-i faqih* or to the regime's repressive policies are also excluded. Ayatollah Shariat-Madari, a senior cleric, who in the early months of the revolution opposed Khomeini's *vilayet-i faqih* in favor of a liberal republic, was in 1982 stripped of his religious rank (an unprecedented step in Shi'i history) and put under house arrest on charges of conspiracy. The criterion of Islamic rectitude, then, is one which seeks to verify political reliability and loyalty rather than faith and piety.

The approved arena of Islamic politics has featured a continuous struggle between different factions of political clerics and their supporters. The factions can be identified in the following terms:

- *Radicals,* who try to carry on the revolutionary momentum of populism, social justice, and anti-imperialism. In domestic policy they favor state control over the economy, with redistributive functions in favor of the poor, such as land reform and labor rights. In foreign policy they advocate an active export of the revolution to other countries in the region and uncompromising opposition to the United States and to Western influence. In short, they follow a Third Worldist line of anti-imperialism and national statist economic policy, much like Egyptian Nasirism in the 1960s, but without anything like Egypt's special relation to the Soviet Union.

- *Conservatives* consist, for the most part, of clerics who supported the revolution because of the power it gave them over society. They use clerical rule to reinforce what they see as the Islamic values of order, property, and hierarchy, with a strong emphasis on enforcing religious morality, observance, and conduct, including censorship of art, culture, and the media. They also favor private property and enterprise and oppose state controls. Khamene'i, as Leader, seems to be working primarily through this faction.
- *Pragmatists* try to rebuild the war-torn economy, favoring market reforms, selective privatization, and opening up to foreign investment and cooperation. Their priorities imply a conciliatory attitude to the West. Socially, they favor liberalization of controls on women, family and social mores, and a relaxed cultural policy. These latter measures have the objective of reassuring the educated middle classes, the depository of skills and expertise necessary for economic revival, and attracting such persons in exile back to Iran. President Rafsanjani is considered the leader of this tendency.

The pragmatists and the radicals are currently organized in rival clergy associations: the Society of Combatant Clerics of Tehran, known as "Ruhaniyat," for Rafsanjani's pragmatists; and the Association of Combatant Clergy of Tehran, or "Ruhaniyun," for the radicals. Conservatives are not so organized, but various of them support one or another of the groups, depending on the issues. It is important to point out that while some leading politicians are clearly identified with one or other faction, most current Majlis members have no definite allegiances. Those elected in 1992 tend to favor pragmatist or conservative lines, but this is the result of a manipulated election.

Following the death of Khomeini in 1989, the dilution of *vilayet-i faqih* in constitutional amendments and the appointment of Khamene'i to the diminished position of Leader were bitterly opposed by the radical faction in the Majlis and the cabinet, who favor continuity of the revolutionary process and of Khomeini's heritage. Prior to 1992 the Majlis had a majority of radicals, who contested and hindered many of Rafsanjani's efforts at reform and opening to the West. In the 1992 Majlis elections, Rafsanjani and his supporters tried to weaken these critics. Some well-known radicals, including a former minister of industry, were disqualified by the Council of Guardians, dominated by conservative clerics, from standing for elections. (The mood of the electorate at that time probably did not favor the continued agitation and upheaval implied by radical policies.)

The election results at first appeared to be highly favorable to Rafsanjani, whose supposed supporters secured an absolute majority. Conservatives, however, hold the balance of Majlis votes, and "Rafsanjani supporters" are not held to their allegiance by any organized party line. There is a certain fluidity in factional loyalties, which can shift in relation to success or failure of policy and the fortunes of political power. The effect of these processes is that the fourth Majlis, elected in 1992, has been no more favorable to Rafsanjani's reforms than its predecessor, only this time it is the conservatives who oppose him—sometimes and, depending on the issue, with the support of some radicals. Ministers appointed by the president have been censored and some forced to resign—notably the president's brother, who was a liberal Minister for Broadcasting, and a similarly liberal Minister of Culture.

The power of clerics who lead the different factions obtains not only from institutional positions in ministries, foundations, and the office of Leader, but also from material resources based on the control of foundations. Most of these foundations derive their wealth from the postrevolutionary take-over of abandoned properties, enterprises, and foundations of the *ancien regime* and rich families associated with it. Bonyad-i Mostazefin, the largest of these foundations, comprises many large enterprises with considerable revenues, including publishing houses and newspapers. Mullahs in control of these bodies, and their appointed managers are hardly accountable, and run them as personal fiefs. Widely publicized corruption scandals and investigation by the Majlis led to the resignation of certain clerics in charge in late 1994 and early 1995. But the foundations are still widely believed to foster nepotism and patronage, which adds to their political clout.

We see from the foregoing that the form of government organization in the Islamic Republic resembles in most basic respects that of other modern nation-states, and that the political field of contest, though Islamic in its discourse, is animated by much the same sort of factors of interest and ideology as prevail elsewhere. There are, of course, elements, including discourse and personnel, which make Iranian government and politics specific and unique.

WOMEN, FAMILY, AND SOCIAL POLICY

We shall now turn to an area of official policy and politics which above all others has symbolized the Islamic Republic—that of women and the family—to show how Islamic dogma is being subverted by political pressure and pragmatic socioeconomic considerations.

The compulsory veiling of women has been, to international public opinion, the hallmark of the Iranian revolution. The paradox of veiled women holding up machine guns, while widely remarked on and much photographed, has not brought home to most observers the contradictory implications of the revolution for women. In mobilizing and politicizing women, the revolution gave them sources of ideological and political powers which have prevented their complete subjugation. The social conservatives, who predominate among the mullahs and their supporters, while successful in imposing the veil, have not been able to impose fully their ideas of correct Islamic comportment and confinement of women within the family. Their success with the veil has obscured the fact that they are fighting a losing battle against the basic social processes of modernity and of the liberationist aspirations unleashed by the revolution, which they cannot turn back.

A central element of the Islamic oppositional discourse against the previous regime was the question of women and the family. The imposition of Western styles and norms, it was argued, debases women by making them frivolous sex objects and victims of capitalist consumerism, and in the process destroys family values, cohesion, and dignity. Islam would restore all these desirable values. This rhetoric, though, contradicted *shari'a* provisions for marriage and divorce which the mullahs attempted to restore after the revolution. These provisions allowed the man unilateral powers of renunciation, with women and their children helpless in the face of male whims. Women, by contrast, had very few grounds for initiating divorce. Muslim women activists and their supporters were able to proclaim the injustice and contradictions of this threatened situation, and to put pressure on mullahs, politicians, and legislators to live up to the promise of the revolution and provide safeguards for women and the family.[4]

The full rigors of the *shari'a*, as it prevailed in traditional Iranian religio-legal practice, were never seriously implemented under the revolutionary government. Khomeini was committed to repealing the Shah's Family Protection Law of 1967 and 1976, which he denounced at the time as contrary to Islam. Divorces obtained in accordance with this law, he declared, were not valid, and the subsequent marriages of parties so divorced were no more than adulterous relations to be punished as such. These laws had made unilateral divorce difficult and only obtainable by court order with provisions and protection for the wife. They empowered the wife to initiate divorce and left the custody of children for the court to decide according to circumstances.

These provisions, despite rhetorical denunciations, were never fully abandoned in the legal practice of the revolutionary regime. The Special Civil Courts (really *shari'a* courts in terms of personnel), instituted in 1979 and charged with implementing family law, continued with some of the previous procedures. In 1982, new marriage contracts were introduced which contained provisions enabling women to initiate divorce on a wide range of grounds, including the husband's maltreatment, delinquency, addiction, and contracting a second marriage without the consent of the wife.[5] These contracts also stipulate that a woman divorced through no fault of her own is entitled to claim a portion of the husband's wealth acquired over the period of marriage. Inserting clauses of this kind into the marriage contract is allowed in Muslim law. The Islamic government wrote these provisions into the standard contract. For these to be valid, however, the man must sign each clause. In practice, the courts seem to observe these provisions, with the exception of the claim on the husband's wealth, whether signed by the husband or not.[6]

It would seem, then, that despite the denunciations of the Shah's family law, the Islamic government has adopted most of its provisions. However, in a number of respects which also affected the previous legislation, some basic disadvantages to women remain, in that men have the ultimate right to unilateral divorce as well as the right to custody (boys at age two, girls at age seven) and to polygyny.

This last is not a widespread problem, as polygynous marriages constitute a tiny fraction of all marriages. The social stigma attached to such marriage and the conflicts and bitterness it engenders seems to have deterred most men from exercising this right—again, a triumph of expediency in relation to modern conditions against religious principle. The disabilities of women under the law, however, are matters of continuing and effective campaigning. This culminated in 1992, when the Majlis passed new legislation on divorce, this time enabling women, if unjustly divorced, to claim "wages" for housework performed in the husband's home. This legislation was initially rejected by the Council of Guardians as contrary to the *shari'a*, but ultimately affirmed by the president using the Interests or Expediency Council to overrule the Guardians. In practice this law appears to be difficult to implement, which has led to fresh campaigns from women and judges for further elaboration to make it more effective.

The campaigning for legislation and procedures to empower women, successful thus far, continues, and its objectives include the issues of unilateral divorce, custody, and polygyny. It is difficult to foresee how far these efforts can go, however, especially now that there is a conservative reaction in the government and the country.

The campaigns for women's rights and for family welfare are waged by prominent women in parliament, in the professions, and the media. Two women's magazines—*Zan-i ruz* (Today's woman), dating from the previous regime and taken over and Islamized by Muslim women under the revolution, and *Zanan* (Women), which started in 1992 as an intellectual and political forum for women's rights—have been at the forefront of these campaigns. The latter carries regular articles by a Qum *mujtahid* advocating modifications of the law in favor of women and the exercise of *ijtihad* to develop new ideas and principles. In the Arab world, Pakistan, and Bangladesh, those calling for the modernization of the *shari'a* through *ijtihad* have been vociferously denounced by the Islamists and their *'ulama'* supporters as subversive apostates, and some have faced consequent threats and intimidation. Under the Islamic Republic in Iran, though, such calls, if they emanate from the appropriate quarters, seem to be regarded as legitimate debate.

The ability of women to enter the political field as an active constituency is, in large part, the consequence of their almost full political enfranchisement. The constitution gives women full voting rights and the right to stand for public office, such as Majlis deputies, but not for the office of president. They can be appointed to many government positions, but not as judges. This is currently an issue of debate and agitation.

We should first note the startling innovation of enfranchising women, a step which would be unthinkable in traditional Islamic contexts, including Saudi Arabia. One of the issues of Khomeini's opposition to the Shah in the 1960s was over the vote for women. The inclusion of women in politics has not stopped at the vote. An important aspect of the liberationist rhetoric of the Iranian revolution was the insistence that Islam was the surest path to women's liberation. Islamist women came to the fore to elaborate and develop this idea. Behind the protection of the veil and female modesty, they have argued, Islam empowers women to participate in all fields of endeavor, including politics, and to work at all levels of society. While accepting the importance of women in their domestic roles, they have steadfastly refused to accept women's confinement to these roles.

The question of women and the family remains a contentious one. On one side are conservative forces, led by many mullahs, who wanted to limit women to the domestic sphere and to impose traditional interpretations of *shari'a* provisions on marriage, divorce, and conjugal relations. On the other are Islamist women activists and their liberal supporters, leading a vocal constituency of women and exploiting the ambivalence of government ideology to push their own definitions of the appropriate "Islamic" roles for women. In this conflict, socioeconomic forces have been on the side of the liberationists.

In spite of the declared intention of leading mullahs, the percentage of women in most spheres of work has continued to grow. Initially, many women government employees lost their jobs or resigned under pressure, as part of the declared aim of the mullahs to send women back to their homes. However, their employment in the private sector has risen, a trend furthered by employment needs stemming from the departure of many men to fight in the war with Iraq. Subsequently, it would seem, female employment in the state sector has resumed. In the mid-1980s it was estimated that the percentage of women in government employment slightly exceeded the prerevolutionary level. Now nearly 30 percent of all government employees are believed to be women. Women have also been prominent in higher education, where they constitute an estimated 40 percent of all graduates. The ban imposed on female entry into particular professions such as engineering and agriculture has now been lifted. Women are particularly prominent in medicine and are thought to constitute more than half of all practitioners.

As Homa Hoodfar's essay in this volume demonstrates, it is in the field of birth control and family planning that we witness the most spectacular retreat of ideology in favor of pragmatic considerations. At first the Islamic government shunned the idea of family planning as a Western conspiracy to limit the number of Muslims (following, in this respect, in the footsteps of early Maoist ideology in China). It dismantled the family planning provisions and organizations of the previous regime. Other pronatal measures included lowering the legal age of marriage to fifteen for boys and thirteen for girls, thereby encouraging family and fertility. By the mid-1980s, the effects of these policies in terms of high levels of population growth (3.9 percent in 1983, double the world average) were noted by the country's more astute political leaders, who contrived an about-face in population policy by launching a family planning campaign.

The example of birth control, abortion, and family planning illustrates very well the pragmatic attitude of policy makers in the Islamic Republic and the flexibility of religious doctrine in following these pragmatic objectives. This subordination of doctrine to utility can only facilitate a secularized attitude to religion and society.

The picture presented so far is one of a regime susceptible to pressures toward political and legal changes favoring women's rights. It is important to emphasize, however, that these changes occur in a society and government which start from a low point in disfavoring and oppressing women. The imposition of the veil, in itself an oppressive measure, leads to further opportunities for routine harassment of women in public places by various police and vigilante forces on the lookout for "*bad hijabi*" (inadequate veiling). This issue has come to the fore in recent years as part of the conservative reaction to limited measures of liberalization.

Some women, of course, have always worn the veil. Others favor it as allowing women wider freedom in work and participation in public affairs with unquestioned modesty and virtue. There are, however, many women who resent the imposition, and who were encouraged by the more liberal atmosphere of Rafsanjani's presidency to relax their observance of the dress code. They wore brighter and patterned clothes, allowed more hair to protrude from under the *hijab,* and used makeup. In the 1980s such liberties would have invited flogging and imprisonment, but in the 1990s they elicited no more than a reprimand and a fine.

A conservative reaction came in 1992, signaled by the Majlis censor and subsequent resignation of the liberal Minister of Culture. This was followed by a campaign by prominent mullahs, supported by Leader (*faqih*) Khamene'i, for the rigorous observance of Islamic morality. The mullahs denounced Western-inspired laxity and corruption, including the resistance to strict veiling, characterized as *"bad hijabi."*[7] These exhortations unleashed physical attacks on "badly veiled" women by various vigilantes and zealots, prompting calls for restraint from Khamene'i and others, who advised that laxity be corrected by guidance and reference to the courts, not by violence.

This conservative reaction has included the media and the arts. Stricter vigilance is maintained against corrupting Western influences. Satellite dishes were banned in late 1994 in legislation narrowly passed by the Majlis. Few believe this ban will be enforceable.

Unless the hard-liners succeed in reverting to a regime of violent repression, which is not impossible, mounting resistance in the social and cultural fields will continue. The basic secular trends of social development can only be suppressed by violence, and Islamic totalitarianism is no more popular than any other kind. Crucially, the social strata most resistant to sociocultural impositions are precisely the educated middle classes the regime needs for economic regeneration. Rafsanjani's awareness of this factor accounts for his attempts at liberalization as part of efforts to rebuild the war-torn and badly battered economy. On all these fronts his pragmatism is opposed by powerful conservative and radical interests.

CONCLUSION

What is the outcome of the project to Islamize government and society in Iran? To sum up, the government is Islamic in its personnel. The clerics are in control of the highest echelons of state, government, and public life (though there are signs that this numerical preponderance of clerics is now declining: the number of clerics elected to the Majlis dropped from 81 out of 270 in the third Majlis to 66 in the fourth).[8] Their political discourse is couched in religious terms, and their conflicts often conducted with religious rhetoric.

Beyond that, the form of organization of the state and its institutions have no particularly Islamic features, and it is difficult to see what such features would be like. There are no Islamic models for modern government and administration. As for the law, we saw that elements of *shari'a* enter the legislation of the Islamic Republic, but constitute only one element among many. The 1989 amendments to the constitution, sanctioned by Khomeini before his death, allow the government to disregard *shari'a* provisions in legislation and policy "in the interests of the Islamic community." In the field of family law and population policy, we saw the retreat of traditional interpretations of the *shari'a* in favor of new principles in line with political pressures and socioeconomic expediency. Economic policy and foreign relations issues are contested by the factions, just as similar issues animate the politics of secular nation-states.

An important difference between Islamic Iran and its Middle Eastern neighbors has been the continuing struggle, waged in the Majlis and in public arenas, between rival centers of power within the government and outside it in politico-religious institutions and foundations. Part of this phenomenon is embodied in the duality of power between the offices of president and Spiritual Leader. The negative consequences of these rivalries have been the paralysis of firm policy making, especially in the crucial economic sphere, a factor which is undermining Rafsanjani's rule and impeding economic reconstruction. On the positive side, it may be argued that this rivalry has prevented the monopolization of power by one center despite the totalitarian tendencies of the regime, and has allowed for a degree of pluralism in political and sociocultural ideas, and for some tentative movements in art and culture, particularly exemplified in a vital film industry.

NOTES

1. On the modernity of Khomeini's ideas and those underlying the Islamic Republic, see Sami Zubaida, *Islam, the People and the State,* 2d ed. (London: I.B. Tauris, 1993), pp. 1–37, 121–82.

2. For a study of the constitution of the Islamic Republic and its transformations since 1979, see Chibli Mallat, *The Renewal of Islamic Law* (Cambridge: Cambridge University Press, 1993), pp. 59–107.

3. Farzin Sarabi, "The Post-Khomeini Era in Iran: The Elections of the Fourth Islamic Majlis," *Middle East Journal* 48, no. 1 (winter 1994): 89–107, contains details of election procedures and discusses the conduct and outcome of the 1992 elections.

4. For information on women and family matters in Islamic Iran, I have drawn upon Ziba Mir-Hosseini, "Women, Marriage and the Law in Post-Revolutionary Iran," in Haleh Afshar (ed.), *Women in the Middle East* (London: Macmillan, 1993), pp. 59–84; Ziba Mir-Hosseini, "Powers of Negotiation and Limits of Interpretation: Shari'a and Feminism in Post-Khomeini Iran" (forthcoming, 1996); and Nesta Ramazani, "Women in Iran: The Revolutionary Ebb and Flow," *Middle East Journal* 47, no. 3 (summer 1993): 407–28.

5. Mir-Hosseini, "Women, Marriage and the Law in Post-Revolutionary Iran."

6. Ibid.

7. Ramazani, "Women in Iran," pp. 421–22.

8. Sarabi, "The Post-Khomeini Era in Iran," p. 104.

10

Islamic Mobilization and Political Change: The Islamist Trend in Egypt's Professional Associations

Carrie Rosefsky Wickham

On September 11, 1992, the Islamic Trend (*al-tayar al-islami*), as the Muslim Brothers' platform is often known, won control of the Egyptian Bar Association, defeating its rivals in free and competitive elections. The victory of the Islamic Trend in one of Egypt's last remaining strongholds of secular liberal and leftist opinion provoked shock and soul-searching among secular politicians and intellectuals. The election reveals little about the preferences of the majority of Egyptian lawyers, as only about 10 percent of the association's 140,000 members came out to vote. It does indicate, along with Islamic Trend victories in the professional associations of doctors, scientists, engineers, and others over the past decade, the growing alienation of the country's educated middle class from both the old guard ruling elites and their secular opposition, and the emergence of the Islamic Trend as the only credible political alternative to the regime.[1]

The victories of the Islamic Trend in the professional associations are part of a broader process of political change. Since the mid-1970s the Egyptian political system has shifted away from one-party rule toward a multiparty system embracing a range of legal opposition parties. Yet, despite elements of pluralism, the contest for state power remains tightly controlled from above. Through electoral laws denying Islamists and certain leftist forces party representation, government control over the electronic media, and restrictions on campaign practices, the regime limits the access of opposition forces to the public. Voter registration and turnout at elections are low, especially in the large cities. Recent surveys indicate that candidates are often selected more for their capacity to distribute services than for the political platform they represent.[2] Emphasizing services works to the advantage of the ruling National Democratic Party (NDP), which regularly captures a two-thirds majority of seats in parliament. Dominated by the

NDP, parliament serves as an instrument of state policy rather than a constraint upon it. In any case, real decision-making power rests with the president and military, as it has since the Free Officers seized power in 1952. Under Mubarak, the prerogatives of the executive have been further expanded by emergency laws passed after the assassination of Anwar al-Sadat and renewed since then on grounds of national security.

In light of the system's enduring authoritarian features, Egypt's movement toward liberalization and democratization should not be exaggerated. Yet important change has occurred outside the system of parliamentary politics, as forces denied the right to compete for state power directly have sought alternative channels to disseminate their views and establish links with critical sectors of Egyptian society. Pluralization of the polity in the Mubarak era has been largely the result of inadvertent state retrenchment rather than deliberate liberalizing reform. The exhaustion of Egypt's experiment in state-led development has diminished the government's distributive capacity, which has long substituted for participatory rights. The bloated and financially strapped state sector can no longer guarantee employment or basic services to strategic urban groups, while the NDP has failed to generate significant mass support for the regime. Fearful that a democratic opening will trigger social unrest, the Mubarak regime has maintained existing political controls while committing itself to an economic reform program that will, at least in the short term, exacerbate the economic hardships of middle- and lower-class groups. The Egyptian state has therefore shrunk—not in size, but in its capacity to incorporate (ideologically, politically, or materially) the masses in whose name it speaks.

In the space left by the state's retreat, pluralization has meant the mobilization of political energy at new sites of political power, the emergence of new forms of contestation and participation, and the articulation of new discourses of political legitimacy. The major force behind these changes is Egypt's Islamic movement, particularly the Society of Muslim Brothers and its affiliated groups. With liberal and leftist forces largely discredited and their organizations fragmented and in disarray, the Muslim Brothers are the only independent political force outside the state with broad-based mass support. Since the mid-1970s, when its leaders renounced the use of violence, the Muslim Brothers have been working toward Islamic reform through institution building, persuasion, and increased participation in legal, mainstream channels of public life. Support for the Brothers crosses class and generational lines, but its recruitment efforts have been particularly successful among recent secondary school and university graduates— doctors, engineers, pharmacists, lawyers, and other professionals—in large cities and provincial towns.

The Islamic Trend has attracted growing support among this younger generation of the educated middle class with a mobilization strategy involving: (1) efforts to replicate the logic of the Nasirist social contract by providing employment and services to unemployed or underemployed youth; (2) direct ideological outreach at the grassroots level; and (3) creating new models of political leadership and community which stand in sharp contrast to the policies and practices of state elites.

SERVING THE YOUNG PROFESSIONAL UNDERCLASS

Between the 1950s and the 1980s, the Egyptian government extended benefits to the urban middle and lower classes it regarded as a key constituency, including the promise of a government job to every graduate with a secondary school or university degree. Though Gamal 'Abd al-Nasir is most strongly identified with these and other populist commitments, it was in fact Anwar al-Sadat who promoted the greatest absolute expansion of higher education, opening the universities to an unprecedented number of students and extending the university system into the provinces. Between 1974 and 1978, seven new provincial universities (Tanta, Mansura, Zagazig, Helwan, Minya, Minufiyya, and the Suez Canal) were added to the existing four (Cairo, Alexandria, 'Ayn Shams, and Asyut), in addition to numerous four-year higher institutes and regional branches of established faculties.

The expansion in university enrollments, followed by a decade of prolonged economic recession, produced a large pool of graduates by the mid-1980s which the public sector of the economy could not absorb. By 1986, the waiting period for a public sector job extended to seven or eight years. While the exact number of unemployed graduates is notoriously difficult to establish, reliable estimates indicate that it is large and likely to increase in the immediate future. By 1994, there were roughly 1.4 million unemployed graduates of whom about 200,000 held university degrees.[3]

Not only does an unaccustomed burden of unemployment fall heavily on the educated; during the 1980s their earnings declined as well. Within the state sector, the purchasing power of civil service wages has declined at a faster rate than blue-collar wages, falling by 1987 to nearly half their 1973 value. Because of the small size of the Egyptian private sector, many graduates have resorted to temporary manual work in the service sector or petty trades—young accountants are waiting tables, civil engineers are installing refrigerators and in at least one instance I know of, lawyers are working the fields. With the modern sectors of Egypt's economy no longer able to absorb all the graduates produced by the universities each year, the professional middle class has split over the past decade into a small, predominantly older, upper stratum and a growing pool of young degree-holders with limited access to a middle-class income or lifestyle—a professional underclass or "lumpen elite."

The Islamic Trend has converted the social and economic grievances of this stratum to its political advantage. Islamic schools, health clinics, mosques, and community centers, which constitute the building blocks of a parallel society, have replaced the Egyptian state in providing basic services in many areas. They have begun to provide employment and income to young doctors, teachers, and other professionals, thereby reducing the share of their earnings derived from the state.

Concurrently, the professional associations under Islamic leadership have initiated projects to publicize and address the grievances of recent graduates. In December 1988, the Islamist-led Engineers' Association held a conference focused on the needs of the more than 20,000 predominantly young engineers without work. The Islamist leadership of the Medical Association conducted a survey of nearly 25,000 doctors in 12 governorates, in which two-thirds of those interviewed revealed that their salaries were not enough to cover their living costs. The executive boards of the Engineering and Medical Associations have initiated projects in the areas of housing, health care, and insurance, established training programs and pilot small business ventures for new graduates, and exerted pressure on the government to reduce university enrollments. Because of the limited financial resources of the professional associations relative to the number of graduates in need, the impact of Islamist initiatives on the living standards of new graduates remains slight. Yet they retain a symbolic value, particularly when contrasted to the pattern of neglect associated with the historic leadership of the professional associations.

The perceived empathy of Islamic Trend leaders is enhanced by their proximity to the majority of new graduates in age, class, and culture. As an elected Islamist official in the Medical Association explained, "We were youths much like them, and faced similar struggles."[4] The Islamist Assistant Secretary General of the Engineers' Association observed, "The old guard association leaders did not know what it was like to suffer from unemployment or no housing or riding the buses—but we are like the ordinary engineers, we have the same living standards, or even less. The younger members see that I can relate, that I understand their problems. Hence they feel less of a gap between the association's leaders and its members."[5] Residing in the same neighborhoods, speaking the same language, and familiar with the same deprivations as the audience to whom they appeal, Islamist activists leading some of Egypt's major professional associations have to a large extent managed to bridge the gap between elite and mass political culture.

THE ISLAMIST DA'WA

Islamist outreach also involves direct propagation of Islamist ideology, the *da'wa*, or call to God. There is no single *da'wa*, as a variety of legal and illegal Islamist groups with different outlooks and agendas promote competing versions of Islam. In theory, the *da'wa* is directed at all Muslims. In practice, most Islamist groups focus their outreach on youth. Through direct personal contact and communal activity at the grassroots level, reformist Islamist groups like the Muslim Brothers as well as more militant groups are working to reshape the political consciousness of educated youth, imbuing them with a new sense of civic obligation and a new perspective on their own capacity to effect social change. By indoctrinating youth with the idea that the reform of society is a religious duty incumbent on every Muslim, Islamist activists have begun to erode long-entrenched patterns of popular non-participation and to foster an activist subculture rooted in Islamic symbols and ideals.

The two major sites of Islamic mobilization are the neighborhood mosque and the university. Only 30,000 of the 170,000 mosques in Egypt are administered by the Ministry of Pious Endowments.[6] Beyond the control of the state, independent mosques are a key site where activists linked to the Muslim Brothers or more militant Islamist groups recruit new members.

In addition to prayer services, such mosques host a wide range of religious lessons for males and females, sponsor after-school programs and special events at Muslim holidays, and may serve as the organizational center for health clinics, kindergartens, charity distribution centers, and lending libraries for Islamic books and tapes. Particularly within newer lower-class neighborhoods with limited state-run services and no other networks of urban self-help, these Islamic institutions are functional substitutes for the welfare apparatus of the state and constitute a natural and familiar setting in which young activists can reach out to uncommitted peers. In private conversations, sermons, lectures, and religious lessons, as well as through pamphlets, books, and cassette tapes, activists joined in tight-knit groups introduce neighbors, friends, and family members to a new model of Islamist social commitment and activism. Islamist activists often say their work is far removed from the sphere of high politics, but their efforts to reform the consciences of young, educated Egyptians have direct political implications.

Because of the success of Islamic recruitment efforts, the Mubarak regime announced a new policy in December 1992 to incorporate activists' mosques into the Ministry of Pious Endowments network. Yet attempts to exert government control have been hindered by shortages of personnel and funds and by tacit cooperation between Islamists and state employees at the lower rungs of the bureaucracy. According to the Ministry of Pious

Endowments general director, to maintain a government mosque costs about £E 6,000 per year, and thus the government can only afford to incorporate 1,000 mosques each year, rather than the 10,000 it would incorporate were the funds available. In addition to budgetary constraints, he explained, the government already has a shortage of 40,000 *imams* (prayer leaders), as compared to some 5,000 Azhar graduates in 1992, of whom only 3,000 showed up for work.[7] In response to such incorporation efforts, Islamist activists have quietly shifted to smaller, less visible, outlets, such as basement prayer rooms (*zawiyas*), obtaining licenses from local municipal councils without informing the Ministry of Pious Endowments.

A second important site of Islamist mobilization is the university campus, where Islamic student associations (*gama'at*) have dominated the student unions of most faculties since the mid-1970s. Islamists are hegemonic in the elite technical faculties. In student union elections at Cairo University in 1990–91, for example, Islamists won 47 of 48 seats in the Faculty of Science, all 72 seats in the Faculty of Medicine, and all 60 seats in the Faculty of Engineering.

As in the professional associations, Islamist victories in student elections indicate the weakness of their rivals as much as their own success. Where leftist and liberal student groups maintain a presence, such as Cairo University's prestigious Faculty of Economics and Political Science, the Islamists gained only 13 of 48 contested seats. Yet in most faculties the main competitors of the dominant Islamist camp are rival Islamist groups who target the same constituency. While Muslim Brothers student leaders predominate in Cairo and Alexandria universities, more militant groups such as the Islamic Group (*al-gama'a al-islamiyya*) and Jihad appear to have the upper hand in several university faculties in Upper Egypt.

The formation of Islamist student cadres has had an impact far beyond the campuses. The activists who have led the Islamic Trend's entry into the professional associations emerged out of the student *gama'at,* which reached a peak of independent activity in the period 1976–79. These leaders gained valuable experience providing services, propagating Islamic ideology, countering alternative groups on campus, and negotiating with the regime. The professional associations offered them a channel to continue their political activity after graduation. Participation in the *gama'at* also shaped the political consciousness of a much broader circle of university students, thereby creating a constituency upon which Islamist candidates could draw, first in the student unions and subsequently in the professional associations. One leftist activist in the Engineers' Association explained, "You raise Muslim Brother students in the university, then five years later you have an electoral base for the professional associations. It's like planting seeds on a farm."[8]

THE CONTEST FOR THE PROFESSIONAL ASSOCIATIONS

In the mid-1970s the Muslim Brothers agreed to a limited rapprochement with the Sadat regime that lasted until 1979. This set the stage for its subsequent penetration of the social and political mainstream under Mubarak. Denied legal status and prohibited from forming their own party, the Brothers participated in parliamentary elections in alliance with legal opposition parties in 1984 and 1987. At the same time, under the banner of the Islamic Trend or the Islamic Voice, the Brothers put forward lists of candidates in professional association elections.[9] Whether inadvertently or as a deliberate attempt to open channels for dissent, beginning in the mid-1980s the Mubarak regime permitted moderate Islamist forces to compete openly against government and secular opposition candidates for control of the associations' executive boards. Though still subject to corporatist legislation and dependent on state funds, the associations became sites of political contestation by default.[10]

In 1984, the Muslim Brothers-affiliated Islamic Trend contested a professional association election as an organized bloc for the first time, offering a list of candidates in the Medical Association elections that year. Shortly thereafter, it ran candidates in the associations of engineers, dentists, scientists, agronomists, pharmacists, journalists, lawyers, and commercial employees. The gains scored by the Islamic Trend prompted the formation of counterblocs, involving alliances between secular leftist and liberal opposition candidates, and, in certain cases, progovernment candidates as well. At the same time, traditional electoral lists based on economic sector or workplace, often headed by an influential minister or other government candidate, remained a factor, as did candidates running as independents. As it has been just over a decade since the Islamic Trend first entered the associations, we must exercise some caution in identifying general patterns.[11] Yet it is clear that the Islamic Trend initially performed best in elite technical professions like medicine and engineering, scored significant but less decisive gains in the associations of lawyers and journalists, and barely penetrated the large associations of commerce, agriculture, and teaching.

In 1984 the Islamic Trend won 7 of the 25 seats on the Medical Association executive board.[12] By 1990 it occupied 20 of the seats, deliberately leaving the remaining five seats open for representatives of other groups. Coincident with the electoral rise of the Islamic Trend in the 1980s was a steady rise in voter turnout. While the number of registered doctors doubled from 1980 to 1988, the number of voters more than quadrupled during the same period. Over the past decade, voter participation has more than tripled, rising from 9 percent of total members in 1982 to about 30 percent in 1992. Assessing voter turnout on the basis of active membership (members who reside in the country, have paid their dues, and hence have the right to vote) yields even higher participation rates. Association records indicate that 45,500 doctors had the right to vote in 1990, and that 46 percent of all active members participated in that year's elections.[13] Such a turnout, Islamist association officials emphasize, is significantly higher than participation in parliamentary elections, which averaged about 20 percent of the eligible population nationally and only about 10–15 percent in urban areas.[14]

The Islamic Trend's rapid ascent in the Medical Association occurred against a backdrop of intense competition among three voting blocs— Islamists, left-liberals, and the progovernment list dominated by the Ministry of Health—in an association in which close to one-third of the members are Coptic Christians. The presence of multiple organized and competing interests may help explain the high voter participation and why, as this competition intensified from the mid-1980s, voter turnout increased over time. In this context of rising participation, the Islamic Trend captured a disproportionate share of new votes. Though they offer no hard proof, candidates and observers across the political spectrum concur that the bulk of these votes came from new graduates entering the association in the 1980s.

The Islamic Trend entered the Engineers' Association for the first time in 1985, with the blessing of its longtime president, construction industry magnate Osman Ahmad Osman.[15] The Trend won its first decisive victory in 1987, taking 45 of 61 seats on the executive board and defeating the association's most powerful occupational blocs in a bitterly contested election. Osman's close personal and business ties with the Muslim Brothers may explain his readiness to accommodate the Islamic Trend. But as the strength of the Islamic Trend grew, cooperative relations with Osman became strained. When Osman and his allies on the executive board were accused of financial improprieties, the Islamic Trend capitalized on his difficulties, juxtaposing its own clean credentials against the abuses associated with Osman. This exemplifies the Islamic Trend's willingness to ally with powerful statist interest blocs when expedient and to challenge them when circumstances change. By 1991 the Islamist Trend completed its takeover of the Engineers' Association by sweeping the elections for the executive boards of its occupational divisions, winning all 46 of the 50 seats it contested by margins of at least five to one over its closest competitors.[16]

Most members of the Engineers' Association, like most members of other associations, do not vote. In the 1991 elections, about 13 percent of total membership, or an estimated 20 percent of active members, participated in the elections. This rate is higher than in many other associations, yet still suggests that the Islamic Trend victories were the result of the support of a politicized minority amid widespread passivity and alienation. According to Assistant Secretary General and Islamist activist Abu al-'Ila Madi Abu al-'Ila, voting rates are higher in the provinces than in Cairo and are especially high among those under thirty-five. A large share of voters are youth, he noted, both because they constitute a large segment of the members and because they are most in need of the association's services to find work, secure housing, and generate enough savings to marry. As in the Medical Association, observers across partisan lines note that younger engineers vote at a higher rate for the Islamic Trend. According to Abu al-'Ila, who for several years has served as the association's election coordinator, of the roughly 4,000 engineers who voted in the Greater Cairo area in 1989, about 3,000 were under the age of thirty-five, and of these about 2,800 voted for the Islamic Trend.[17]

The Islamic Trend has yet to establish a foothold in the large professional associations of teachers, agronomists, and veterinary doctors, sectors characterized by low wages, poor working conditions, and low social status. Elementary and secondary schoolteachers, agricultural employees, and veterinary physicians fall near the bottom of Egypt's professional hierarchy. Yet rather than serving as vehicles for expressing political dissent, their associations have tended to function as arms of the state bureaucracy. The internal regulations of the 750,000-member teachers' union, for example, automatically designate the Minister of Education as president. Corporatist legal and institutional barriers help explain why sympathy for the Islamic Trend among rank-and-file members—which informed observers suggest is growing—has not translated into control of association boards. In addition, the vast majority of teachers, agricultural workers, and veterinary physicians are state employees. Satisfaction of their economic demands depends on the agreement of state authorities. The social and economic vulnerabilities of teachers and other state employees appear to have encouraged a focus on bread-and-butter issues favoring collaboration over confrontation with the state.[18]

In contrast, the associations of the elite free professions—medicine, engineering, journalism, and law—have traditionally exhibited greater political independence. In the 1970s, the journalists' and lawyers' associations were leading sites of opposition to Sadat's open door economic policy and rapprochement with Israel, while the engineering and medical associations were, with some exceptions, dominated by competing sectoral blocs and interest groups tied to the state. In the mid-1980s, however, the elite technical syndicates moved to the foreground of political activism under the leadership of the Islamic Trend. One reason that the elite professional associations have been so conducive to independent political expression is that, unlike the large associations of state employees, they encompass professionals working in all sectors of the economy. While most doctors work in public sector hospitals and clinics, a large proportion supplement their low public salaries through a second job in the private sector, which in many cases represents the majority of their income. Among the new sources of employment for young doctors are the Islamic-run clinics and hospitals which have multiplied in lower-middle-class neighborhoods over the past decade.

Members of the free professions also enjoy high prestige and visibility as the vanguard of the country's intelligentsia, independent of their employment or earning power. This has granted them a degree of immunity from state harassment. In addition, their socialization as an elite has fostered a collective sense of social responsibility as advocates for the "Egyptian people" (*al-sha'b*). This self-perception has fueled a tradition of political activism within the student unions, and more recently the professional associations. Structural and institutional factors such as enabling legislation, membership profiles, and political subtraditions may also explain why some associations offer a more conducive environment for Islamist activism than others. Yet the influence of such factors is not all-determining.

Perhaps the best evidence of the contingent nature of political space is the Islamic Trend's surprising victory in the Bar Association elections of September 1992. A large proportion of Bar Association members are state employees, which in other cases inhibited political activism. Moreover, the political climate within the association has long been dominated by secular liberal and leftist forces. The former earned respect for their outspoken defense of civil liberties, democracy, and the rule of law, while the latter gained stature through their staunch nationalist opposition to Sadat's economic and political opening to the West.

In the 1980s, intense political, professional, and legal disputes among rival political cliques diluted the syndicate's capacity to serve as a gadfly for liberal and national causes. By the early 1990s, chronic infighting between supporters of longtime president Ahmad Khawaga and those of his rivals paralyzed the executive board. Having gained exposure and credibility through their work in the association's committees on civil liberties and Islamic law, Islamist activists capitalized on the growing frustration and disgust felt by a growing number of lawyers toward the old guard leadership in the elections of 1992.

Leftist and liberal observers acknowledge the Islamists' superior election campaign organization, financing, and tactics, all of which enabled them to derive maximum leverage from the support of a politicized minority.[19] The Islamic Trend organized its candidates on a single, national list under the symbolic leadership of Sayf al-Islam al-Banna, son of the founder of the Society of Muslim Brothers. Prior to the elections, the Islamic Trend allegedly paid the back dues of up to three thousand of its supporters so they could vote. On election day it provided supporters with free transportation, food and, according to one account, "iced rosewater."

However, growing support for the Islamic Trend in the professional associations is not simply the result of a series of election day maneuvers. It is more fundamentally the result of the Islamic Trend leaders' cultivation of new forms of elite-mass linkages: (1) the social, cultural, and generational proximity of the Islamist leaders to their mass base; (2) the Islamic Trend's efforts to replicate the Nasirist social contract by initiating new programs and services targeted at younger members; (3) the appeal of an Islamic Trend platform deliberately short on programmatic detail and long on the call for a return to morals and accountability in public life; and (4) the development of more responsive and egalitarian models of political leadership and community which sharply contrast with the formalistic and hierarchical practices of state elites. After gaining control of the association executive boards, the Islamic Trend leadership has pointed to its record of service as proof that it can deliver something qualitatively different from the factional infighting and competition which long preoccupied old guard secular politicians. By initiating new programs to address the grievances of members, taking a public stand in support of democracy and human rights, and in some associations actively seeking the cooperation of secular opponents, the young Islamist leaders have attempted to portray themselves as representatives of a broad consensus for reform rather than a narrow set of political objectives.

A STATE WITHIN A STATE?

The image of the Islamic Trend as a servant of the public interest was reinforced in the days after the 1992 earthquake, when Medical Association volunteers arrived first on the scene in some of the most devastated areas, setting up tents, and distributing food, blankets, and medical care to the victims. Reacting to such initiatives, the Egyptian government complained, in the words of Minister of Interior Muhammad 'Abd al-Halim Musa, "What is this becoming, a state within a state?"[20] The words of the minister echo the Islamists' own conception of their mission. Rather than contesting state power directly, the Islamic Trend is self-consciously creating new models of political leadership and community on the ground. As Abu al-'Ila Madi Abu al-'Ila put it, "We are creating islands of democracy in a sea of dictatorship."[21]

One might dispute the claim that the community the Islamists are creating within the associations is democratic, at least in the liberal sense of the term. The model which inspires them might be better described as a political community in which ruler and ruled are united by faith and adherence to Islamic law. The key point is that intermediary associations formally attached to the state have become sites of political innovation, perhaps the Islamic equivalent of the parallel polis which emerged under communism in Central and Eastern Europe to contest official norms and practices well before the collapse of authoritarian rule.

The rise of the Islamic Trend in several of Egypt's professional associations is part of a broader process of evolutionary political change. By penetrating official intermediary institutions and creating new ones, the Muslim Brothers and affiliated groups have initiated a gradual appropriation of the public space from the bottom up. While the violent acts of armed Islamists have commanded greater media attention, it is the incremental, legal activities of Islamists in spheres like the professional associations which have had the greatest impact in reshaping public life.

The incorporation of Muslim Brothers activists within the formal political order reflects the broader restructuring of the relationship between regime and opposition forces which began in the mid-1970s and continues today. Initially, the participation of the Muslim Brothers in Egypt's professional associations suited both the regime and Islamist strategies. Opening limited channels for participation enabled the Mubarak government to incorporate moderate Islamist groups while preserving its monopoly on power. By giving Islamist reformers a partial stake in the system, the government wagered it could induce them to restrict their participation to activities like issuing statements and holding seminars, thereby limiting their access to the mass public. According to the unspoken bargain, the political autonomy of the professional associations would be respected while the regime remained in control of the street.

By penetrating the associations, Muslim Brothers activists gained an opportunity to hone their leadership skills, broaden their base of support, and present an alternative model of political life to a strategic middle-class audience. Though the capacity of Islamic-run syndicates to address the real-life problems of young professionals remains limited, the rhetorical emphasis on youth, backed in part by projects still in their infancy, has had a symbolic importance beyond the benefits actually distributed. In addition, juxtaposed against the seemingly out-of-touch military-bureaucratic state leadership, the Islamic Trend portrays itself as successor to a more humane and responsive political tradition which can be traced back to the exemplary rule of the four rightly guided caliphs of the first Islamic state.

In Egypt as elsewhere, the emergence of new zones of institutional autonomy may reshape the character of the polity, even in the absence of a change of regime. In contrast to the hegemonic control exercised by the state in the 1950s and 1960s, today we find the uneasy coexistence of multiple and competing legitimacy formulas, institutions, and practices. Such fragmentation of the polity is not an unambiguous movement toward the formation of civil society. As Mustafa Kamil al-Sayyid has noted, such movement would require, on the part both of the regime and the country's leading counterelites, "a tolerance for intellectual and political dissension as a legitimate right of minorities, however they are defined."[22]

Although the constitution of 1971 guarantees a broad range of civil and political liberties to Egyptian citizens, the regime continues to selectively limit or suspend many of these rights in practice, using emergency legislation to contain activities which appear to threaten its hold on power. As the leading opposition force in the country, the Islamic Trend has called repeatedly for the rule of law and greater respect for human rights and democracy, yet its own commitment to such principles has to be fully tested. While the changes wrought by Islamist executive boards of professional associations have heightened the morale of many rank and file members, they have also threatened to marginalize the Copts, liberals, and secular Muslim women and men who stand outside the Islamist consensus. The capacity of the Islamic Trend to encompass a broader following will depend on which elements within the movement assume control over its direction. While certain Islamic Trend activists are unwilling to compromise any piece of their agenda or cooperate with elements outside the fold, others have taken pains to reach out to other groups in pursuit of common goals.

THE REGIME STRIKES BACK

On February 16, 1993, a new law regulating professional associations was hastily proposed and passed in parliament by the ruling National Democratic Party majority.[23] It stipulates that unless 50 percent of all members vote in the first round of association elections or 33 percent in a subsequent round, the results will be voided and the association placed under the supervision of a panel of appointed judges. Backers of the law insist that requiring higher levels of participation in elections will prevent an organized minority from dominating the silent majority. Critics, including journalists, opposition leaders, and association officials across the political spectrum, have condemned the law as a transparent attempt to dislodge Islamic leaders and reimpose state control over the associations.

As the primary targets of the law, the Islamist-run executive boards of the Lawyers', Engineers', and Medical Associations have organized demonstrations and work stoppages, drafted petitions to the Speaker of Parliament, and sponsored special plenary sessions and joint conferences to mobilize protest against it. Perhaps most interesting are efforts by both the regime and the Islamists to appropriate the moral high ground. Each side claims to uphold democratic values and procedures against the antidemocratic tendencies of the other. Though antidemocratic in design and intent, the law has privileged such themes as representation, participation, and competition in public debates between the regime and mainstream Islamist forces. Even if the avowed democratic commitments of both the government and the Islamists are instrumental, this emphasis on rules and procedures could contain the seeds of a new form of contestation in which the struggle for power is transposed into a struggle for legitimate authority.

The dual process of state retreat and Islamic institution building does not fit neatly into existing paradigms of liberalization or democratization that imagine progress along a single trajectory toward a predetermined outcome. As an alternative to the present system of authoritarian rule, what the Islamic movement offers its supporters is not so much the restoration of individual rights against the state as the promise of a restored moral order, in which human impulses toward corruption, exploitation, and greed are restrained through enforcement of divine law.

Islamist mobilization alone cannot bring about the collapse of the authoritarian regime in Egypt. As elsewhere, factors such as the strategies of governing elites, the state's capacity for repression, and the role of external actors are all essential in determining whether popular mobilization becomes a serious challenge to military-bureaucratic rule. Yet to the extent that the preservation of authoritarian rule requires an acquiescent public, Islamist mobilization has begun to undermine it. The Mubarak regime may be able to contain the activity of armed Islamic groups through increased intimidation and repression, yet it is far less equipped to stem the Islamic Trend's social and ideological incorporation of new groups at the grassroots level. In private mosques, student dormitories, and even within organizations formally attached to the state, the Islamist movement is fostering a new ethic of participation among the younger members of Egypt's educated middle class, one which entails increasing disengagement from or confrontation with the present regime. In this way, it has begun to isolate the regime from a strategic sector of the public and provide the initial instances of organization and indoctrination upon which future attempts at mass mobilization can draw. Without the media attention reserved for stunning acts of violence, the Islamic Trend has begun to erode Egypt's authoritarian order from below.

NOTES

1. The Arabic word *niqaba* can designate either a professional association or a trade union. It is similar to the French *syndicat,* which has no easy English equivalent. To avoid locutions that unnecessarily exoticize the subject, *niqaba* is here rendered as association or union.

2. See Salwa Sha'rawi Gum'a, "Explaining Electoral Behavior: Comparative Study of the District of East Cairo and the Suez Governorate," in *People's Assembly Elections 1987: Study and Analysis* [Arabic] (Ahram Center for Political and Strategic Studies: Cairo, 1988); Ashraf Husayn, "Political Participation and Parliamentary Elections," and Ahmad 'Abd Allah, "Parliamentary Elections in Egypt: Which

Elections . . . Which Parliament . . . Which Egypt?" both in Ahmad 'Abd Allah (ed.), *Parliamentary Elections in Egypt: Analysis of the 1987 Elections* [Arabic] (Cairo: Center for Arab Research, Dar Sina', 1990).

3. Based on an early 1994 survey conducted by the Cabinet Information and Decision Support Center in conjunction with the Ministry of Manpower and Training, *Al-Ahram al-iqtisadi,* March 7, 1994. "Graduates" means holders of secondary school, two-year higher institute, and university degrees.

4. Interview with Dr. Hilm Gazzar, executive board member, Giza branch of the Medical Association, Giza, March 12, 1991.

5. Interview with the Assistant Secretary General and other executive board members, Engineers' Association headquarters, Cairo, December 17, 1990.

6. Middle East Watch, "Egypt: Human Rights Abuses Mount in 1993," *Memorandum* 5, no. 8, October 22, 1993.

7. *Akhir Sa'a,* December 2, 1992; and Middle East Watch, "Egypt: Human Rights Abuses Mount in 1993." On the privileged treatment of Islamists by some state employees, see Sarah Ben-Nefissa Paris, "Le mouvement associatif égyptien et l'Islam," *Monde Arabe: Maghreb/Machrek,* no. 125 (January–March 1992).

8. Interview, Ashraf Hilmi, engineer and leftist candidate in the February 1991 Engineers' Association elections, Cairo, June 24, 1991.

9. Technically, candidates in these elections run as independents. However, the campaign literature distributed by the Islamic Trend and other blocs identifies candidates as part of a list to indicate their affiliations.

10. The emergence of Egypt's professional syndicates as an outlet for opposition groups denied legal recognition, and particularly for the Islamists, has been noted by numerous Egyptian scholars and syndicate activists. See, for example, the section on professional syndicates in *Arab Strategic Report,* ed. Tariq al-Bishri (Cairo: Al-Ahram Center for Political and Strategic Studies), for 1987 through 1991.

11. A caveat about electoral data: Many studies derive election results from newspaper reports despite the fact that such reports often conflict. Coverage of professional association election results, particularly when they register large gains for opposition candidates, is conspicuously thin in the government press. Hence one must rely almost exclusively on opposition papers whose reporting may be colored by their political agendas. The associations themselves are the best source of information, yet their staff members are often unwilling or unable to provide an accurate chronology of election results across a span of several years. Moreover, their records generally identify winning candidates by name only, rather than by platform or list. Interpreting the results is further complicated by the fact that the political orientations of candidates are not always visible—Islamic candidates may run as independents, and lists may unite leftist or Islamic Trend candidates with government candidates without any declaration or statement of such an alliance reaching the public. When public association with an opposition platform may subject a candidate to various forms of harassment or hamper his career, affiliations are less visible than they would be in a less repressive environment.

12. Results are compiled from: "The Medical Association Elections Yesterday and Today," *Al-Atiba'* (the Medical Association journal), no. 11, August 1992/1413; *Al-Ahrar,* April 7, 1986; *Al-Ahram al-iqtisadi,* April 23, 1990; *Al-Nur,* May 2, 1990;

Amani Qandil, "The Islamic Trend in Interest Groups in Egypt"; idem, "Professional Associations in Egypt and the Process of Democratic Transformation" [Arabic]; and the section on syndicates in *The Umma in a Year: A Yearly Report on Egyptian Politics and Economic Affairs* [Arabic] (Mansura: Wafa' Publishers, 1991–92), p. 246. In cases of conflict, I preferred official association data.

13. *Al-Atiba'*, no. 11, August 1992/1413.

14. Voter participation in parliamentary elections is a contentious subject. Official figures indicate that 50.4 percent of registered voters participated in parliamentary elections in 1987. But only about half the number of citizens eligible to vote are registered: an effective participation rate of about 25 percent. Voter turnout is much higher in rural areas than in urban ones. Gum'a, "Explaining Electoral Behavior," studied electoral results in three urban areas in the 1987 elections yielding participation rates of 14.8 percent, 19.8 percent, and 22 percent; or roughly half these figures for all eligible voters. See also Husayn, "Political Participation and Parliamentary Elections."

15. In the Engineers' Association, the Islamic Trend is called the Islamic Voice (*al-Sawt al-islami*). Despite their different names, the Islamic blocs in the professional associations are part of one tendency of the broader Islamic movement. Consequently, I use the term Islamic Trend throughout.

16. Election results were provided to me by association officials. For 1987 results see *Arab Strategic Report, 1988* [Arabic], ed. Tariq al-Bishri (Cairo: Al-Ahram Center for Political and Strategic Studies, 1989), p. 499.

17. Association records and interviews with Abu al-'Ila Madi Abu-'Ila, Assistant Secretary General and chairman of the election steering committee, December–March, 1990–91.

18. Section on the Egyptian Teachers' Union in *Arab Strategic Report, 1987* [Arabic]; Amani Qandil, "Professional Associations in Egypt," pp. 6–7, unpublished paper presented at the conference on Democratic Challenges in the Arab World, Center for Political and International Development Studies, Cairo, September 1992.

19. Election commentary in *Al-Ahali*, September 23, 1992.

20. Chris Hedges, *New York Times*, October 21, 1992.

21. Interview, Engineers' Association headquarters, Cairo, December 17, 1990.

22. Mustapha K. al-Sayyid, "A Civil Society in Egypt?" *Middle East Journal* 47, no. 2 (spring 1993): 230.

23. The new law and responses to it are analyzed in *Al-Hayat*, February 15, 17, and 22; *Uktubur*, February 28, 1993; and in the opposition press during the spring of 1993. See also *Al-Mujtama' al-madani*, March 1993 (the Arabic edition of *Civil Society*), and the official association journals *Al-Atiba'*, April 1993, and *Al-Muhandisin*, May 1993.

11

Hizb Allah and the Lebanese State

Assaf Kfoury

Despite its overall victory in the Lebanese parliamentary elections in 1992, Hizb Allah is still looking for a starting place on the country's political game board. The party alternates between its original "Islamic revolutionary purity" and complete integration into the Lebanese political scene, which implies making certain concessions on its part. It sees the Israeli reluctance to leave South Lebanon as a means of avoiding decisive choices while continuing to play an important role at the intersection of local and international interests.

On more than one occasion since the spring of 1992, Iranian president 'Ali Akbar Hashemi Rafsanjani has made it clear to the leaders of Hizb Allah who have been to Tehran that their party is first and foremost Lebanese rather than pro-Iranian, and that it must integrate itself into Lebanese political life, like the other Lebanese political parties. He explicitly told them that, from his point of view, it is not a question of completely abandoning the ideology of Hizb Allah, but rather of transforming it from an ideology folded in upon itself, limited solely to its militant origins, into one that is open to the Lebanese state—land, people, institutions. This transformation, far from altering the principles, objectives, and revolutionary orientation of Hizb Allah, would instead give it new vigor. Rafsanjani thus encouraged the leaders he met to take part in the parliamentary elections, as this would be an opportunity for Hizb Allah to emerge from its isolation and to practice a policy of openness.

These initiatives by the Iranian president prompted a big debate among the leaders of Hizb Allah, as well as among its militants. Partisans of the pragmatic view, with the party secretary-general Hasan Nasr Allah at their head, decided to incorporate these directions into their policy for two reasons: first, because they emanated from the highest political authority in

Tehran, and second, because they answered a local, and more generally a Shi'i and Lebanese national, need. For their part, the extremists and their leader, Shaikh Subhi Tufayli (former secretary-general of the party), felt that these directions completely contradicted Hizb Allah's ideological bases and the choices it had made thus far. However, the pragmatists held sway over the hard-liners, and thus the party took part in the Lebanese parliamentary elections of August and September 1992. Hizb Allah achieved a brilliant victory, while the traditional feudal powers in the Shi'a community, represented by the Husayni family of Ba'albek, the Baydun family of Beirut, the Zayn family of Nabatiyya, and the 'Usayran family of Zahrani, found themselves marginalized. Even the Amal movement of Nabih Berri could not eclipse the performance of Hizb Allah.

This electoral victory is the fruit of an evolution brought about by a series of factors. What these are becomes clear from an examination of the historical context of the emergence and development of Hizb Allah in Lebanon.

WHERE IRAN AND SYRIA COME INTO PLAY

Hizb Allah has existed as a political movement in Lebanon since the early 1970s, but in a clandestine, unorganized form. At that time, a group of young people and religious dignitaries, who had come together around a number of religious and political ideas, began to influence certain popular and religious circles. The beginning of the Lebanese civil war in 1975 strengthened the links among the members of this group. But the determining factor in the emergence of Hizb Allah in Lebanon and its transition from an underground movement to an open one was the success of the Islamic revolution in Iran in 1979. Subsequently, the Israeli invasion of Lebanon in 1982 helped prepare the way for the development of fundamentalist Shi'i activism on the Lebanese scene. The invasion provoked a Syrian-Iranian accord that sent Iranian Revolutionary Guards (Pasdaran) into the Biqa' in order to help reinforce the anti-Israeli resistance. The cease-fire and disengagement of Syrian and Israeli forces at the entrances to the Biqa' led to a change in the mission of the Pasdaran. Instead of facing combat, they were put to work training Hizb Allah militants, and organizing its military forces and security apparatus.

In 1983, Hizb Allah suicide missions against Israeli troops and the multinational force focused attention on the organization and its influence in Lebanon. The subsequent strength of the military and security aspects of the party was effected by the combination of two factors: material support from Iran, in line with the Iranian strategy of exporting Islamic revolution and establishing Islamic republics whenever possible; and political support from Syria, in keeping with Syria's strategy of preventing an Israeli-Lebanese accord. The Syrian leadership had found in Hizb Allah a trump card it could substitute for the Palestinian card, which Israel's invasion had eliminated. For Syria, the Hizb Allah card was much stronger than the Palestinian card in that it represented Lebanese resistance to Israel, legally recognized at the international level.

While devoting itself to acts of resistance against Israeli forces, Hizb Allah was simultaneously distancing itself from everyday political life in Lebanon, and from political or security arrangements initiated by the Lebanese state. This did not prevent it from becoming a protagonist in Lebanon's internal conflict against the militia of the Lebanese Forces accused of being in alliance with Israel; against Amal which was vying with it for influence in the Shi'i zones; and against the Palestinians who were watching for an opportunity to regain their position, to the detriment of Hizb Allah, in South Lebanon. In another sphere, Hizb Allah had been linked with the kidnapping and imprisonment of foreigners in Lebanon, and with the bargaining which led to the liberation of these hostages.

In the fall of 1988, the leaders of Hizb Allah, meeting at a congress in Tehran, decided to gather the different groups active under the banner of their organization into a more cohesive partisan organization. This structure would include a political leadership with decision-making and executive power, and consultative and executive proceedings at all levels. At the head of this structure would be a secretary-general elected by the organization's *majlis al-shura* (consultative council). His term, like that of the *majlis,* would be for two years.

The transformation of Hizb Allah into a structured party constituted a qualitative leap forward, in the sense that political objectives took precedence over all others, whether military and security or religious and revolutionary ones. This explains how the slogans and principles to which different groups in Hizb Allah adhered became common to of all of them. Henceforth they were committed to work together to ensure the realization of these principles.

At the head of the list of aims was the establishment of an Islamic republic in Lebanon. But in view of the nature of the Lebanese scene, the establishment of such an authority presupposed the unification of the Shi'i regions under the banner of Hizb Allah. A violent struggle for control broke out in these regions between Hizb Allah and Amal. But even after more than two years of conflict, Hizb Allah was unable to swing the balance decisively in its favor. On the contrary, both these forces remained very much on the Shi'i scene. This constituted a reversal of Hizb Allah's plan for an Islamic republic. Hizb Allah could have subsequently tried to dominate inter-Shi'a relations had the Lebanese state not started in the spring of 1991 to enforce one of the key points of the Taif accord—ending the state of war in the country. The series of political measures taken by the state made Hizb

Allah's project more difficult, even impossible, given the new political context produced by the Taif accord.

PROVISIONAL ACCEPTANCE OF THE FAIT ACCOMPLI

Although Hizb Allah had explicitly rejected the Taif accord when it was signed in the fall of 1989, it ended up admitting the need to provisionally coexist with the "Republic of Taif." It felt obliged to do so especially because this "Republic" had managed to extend its authority over most of Lebanon, with the exception of the zone in South Lebanon controlled by the Israeli army and its auxiliaries in the South Lebanese Army of Antoine Lahad. This change in direction took place during the brief period when Shaikh 'Abbas Musawi was head of Hizb Allah and it continues today under Hasan Nasr Allah.

None of this would have been possible without a tacit arrangement—still valid—between Hizb Allah, then led by 'Abbas Musawi, and the "Republic of Taif." This arrangement endorsed and armed the anti-Israeli resistance, clearly contrary to the aim of the state to dissolve the militias and eventually to disarm their members. Preparations for the beginning of the Arab-Israeli peace talks paradoxically helped get this arrangement under way, as Syria did not wish to have to relinquish the Hizb Allah card so long as the prospects for negotiations remained unclear. These factors combined to allow the Shi'a to remain aloof from the official aim of putting an end to the state of war in Lebanon. Hizb Allah was also the only party to keep all its military equipment, and the only one to have a military and security role within the framework of Islamic resistance, though only in South Lebanon.

If Hizb Allah profited from this tacit arrangement, so too did the Lebanese state, which felt it had been protected by the leaders of Hizb Allah, unlike during the time of Subhi Tufayli when Hizb Allah had vilified the authorities on the least pretext. Even when the Lebanese authorities decided to take part in the peace talks with Israel, Hizb Allah was content to register its opposition in principle without accompanying this with street unrest, apart from some sporadic symbolic demonstrations. Along the same lines, when the Lebanese state decided to recover the properties and territories which the diverse militias had occupied, Hizb Allah immediately complied by restoring the Shaikh 'Abd Allah barracks to the Lebanese army. On more than one previous occasion, Hizb Allah had refused an army command to withdraw its militiamen from these barracks.

The scenario was similar when the government decided to hold the 1992 general election. Hizb Allah rose to the challenge and threw itself wholeheartedly into the electoral battle as no other party or candidate had ever done before. Once seated, the Hizb Allah deputies elaborated their plan of action in parliament. The party authorities agreed to carry out a census of their militants and sympathizers employed in public administration, in order to examine ways the party's deputies might help them in terms of advancement or change of post. On the larger political field, Hizb Allah had already come out in favor of suppressing political confessionalism in the institutions of state. From Hizb Allah's point of view, deconfessionalization of state institutions could put the project for an Islamic republic in Lebanon back on the agenda by making it possible for the president of the council, or even the president of the republic, to be an orthodox Muslim. In any case the leaders of Hizb Allah are aware that this project can only be carried out by taking into account the repercussions of the Taif accord on the Lebanese situation as a whole.

ELECTORAL TEST

The question of participation in the election stirred up great debate among cadres of Hizb Allah from top to bottom. One current was represented by Hasan Nasr Allah, the other by Subhi Tufayli. Secretary-general Nasr Allah's point of view prevailed. Three factors helped in this: the support of Iranian president Hashemi Rafsanjani; a correct evaluation of the balance of power in the *majlis al-shura*; and the fact that Muhammad Husayn Fadl Allah definitely favored participation. The results confirmed that Hasan Nasr Allah had made a good choice, despite his youth and relative lack of political experience, and thus strengthened his personal position in the party.

Determined to secure victory in these elections, Hizb Allah mobilized all its forces: free transport for voters; free sandwiches and refreshments; activists on permanent alert round the polling stations. Equipped with walkie-talkies, their brief was to transmit developments on the ground to the party's headquarters as they occurred, so that the leaders could deal with any problem that arose. Other young men went from one polling station to another, finding out from the Hizb Allah candidates' delegates what the turnout was as well as the political allegiance of the voters. They transmitted this information immediately to headquarters where a team worked constantly to sift through all the data received. On the women's side, party members wearing the *chador* acted as soon as similarly dressed women began appearing at the polling stations in order to make sure that they made the correct choice.

The factors that played a decisive role and allowed Hizb Allah to win the elections were mainly political. For example, in Ba'albek-Hermel, the principal list opposed to Hizb Allah was led by the outgoing president of the chamber, Husayn Husayni. This list carried no weight compared with that of Hizb Allah. The latter had, at the beginning of the campaign, committed itself to finding grounds for agreement with Husayni over a coalition list in which Hizb Allah would have had only two candidates. Husayni insisted that they should have only one. At that point Hizb Allah decided to form its own list and to throw itself into battle against Husayni, ready to lose the elections rather than find itself at his mercy. The results proved Hizb Allah right, even though they were a surprise to the candidates as well as to the party leadership.

In South Lebanon, Hizb Allah allied itself with Amal and its two candidates were elected. This did not happen in the West Biqa'-Rashaya constituency, where only one Shi'i seat was being contested and was won by the Amal candidate rather than by Hizb Allah. This person was on the strongest list, led by Sami al-Khatib, and voters in this ward belonged predominantly to the Sunni and Christian communities. In Beirut and in the Ba'abda constituency, two Hizb Allah candidates prevailed because no one stood against them. In Zahle, however, Muhsin Dallul was elected because he was on the strongest list and was opposed to the Hizb Allah candidate.

Other factors also played a role. According to the vice president of the political office of Hizb Allah, 'Ammar Musawi, the total commitment of party sympathizers to Hizb Allah candidates, as well as the desire of the electorate to see new blood in parliament, were decisive. "It is we, the Hizb Allah, who represent this change," affirmed Musawi.

As to the social services provided by Hizb Allah, they were the least important of the factors contributing to the election of party candidates, according to Musawi. "The main thing is that these services are not free." Because of this, "[t]hey could have played only a minor role in the victory of our candidates." He added, "Moreover, when Hizb Allah began to provide these services, it had no intention of exploiting them in parliamentary elections or any others, because our party considers itself to be of the people and feels the difficulties and problems of ordinary folk." Despite these denials, the social services of Hizb Allah did have a certain impact on the choice of electors not linked to the party and also on those who do not belong to the Shi'a community.

COMPENSATING FOR THE SHORTCOMINGS OF THE STATE

The difficulties of life during the war years and the powerlessness of the state to provide even the bare minimum in terms of services prompted Hizb Allah to turn its attention to the social sector, mainly in the areas where it was already established. It began with a step-by-step approach to the problems of daily life faced by the population in the predominantly Shi'i regions. Currently Hizb Allah provides medical care, hospital treatment, electricity, and water trucking. It sinks artesian wells in villages, paves roads, builds housing, manages sewage systems, and sets up gas stations, farms, and cooperatives where needed. Another area which Hizb Allah is tackling is education. It has created children's homes, nursery schools, nonreligious schools, and sports clubs. Few of these services are free: Hizb Allah does not distribute free food to the poor, nor does it waive school fees for children from impoverished families.

Social action on the part of Hizb Allah is provided by four bodies working independently of one another: the Department of Social Affairs within the executive of the party; the Campaign for Reconstruction; the Committee for Supplies; and the Martyrs' Foundation. The social office carries out projects nationally, by building hospitals, for example. Regionally, its offshoots in the predominantly Shi'i areas are involved in such things as setting up clinics or sinking artesian wells. This department charges for its services while the other three bodies provide them for free. The Campaign for Reconstruction, which principally repairs or constructs housing and roads, has a budget allocated to it by the Iranian minister for reconstruction. The Committee for Supplies, financed by the Khomeini Committee for Supplies in Tehran, provides material, food, and clothing to the needy. The Martyrs' Foundation also receives its funds from its counterpart in Iran.

Along with these more permanent social undertakings, Hizb Allah can sometimes act on an ad hoc basis according to circumstances, as it did during the particularly harsh winter of 1992 when numerous small towns in the Ba'albek-Hermel region were cut off by snow. When the Lebanese minister of the interior proved incapable of facing up to the consequences of the bad weather, Hizb Allah activists used their own means to get provisions and fuel to these places. The young men in the Shi'i village of Nabi Shayt, for example, used privately owned tractors to reach Khrayba after it was completely isolated by the snow. Fuel for the tractors was supplied by the local Hizb Allah branch in Nabi Shayt.

As regards hospitals, Hizb Allah is proud of the construction of two big projects, the Hospital of the Imam in Ba'albek and the Hospital of the Omnipotent Prophet in Beirut's southern suburbs. These well-equipped hospitals offer paid services and are able to call on specialists who are not part of their permanent staff. The fees of these practitioners are paid entirely out of hospital revenues. The hospital in Ba'albek charges relatively low prices; the one in the southern suburbs collects fees similar to those of other private hospitals in the capital. In addition, Hizb Allah runs several clinics scattered through the areas where it is well-established. These clinics are not more than ten kilometers apart, and thus provide at least minimal medical care for those living in these areas.

Parallel to its efforts in the field of health, Hizb Allah works to provide electricity and water, particularly drinking water, to many districts and towns. Hizb Allah takes charge of sinking artesian wells, while local inhabitants pool resources to cover the cost of the pump and piping. Hizb Allah sent whole tankers full of drinking water to the southern suburbs, notably in 1989 and 1990 during the battles initiated by General Michel Aoun. In order to deal with the incessant power outages, Hizb Allah set up generators in various districts and villages to provide electricity for inhabitants who wished for it, in return for payment. Hizb Allah also planned to install a powerful generator in the Bir al-'Abd district of the southern suburbs and surrounding areas.

Finally, regarding education, Hizb Allah has created a network of schools which it controls via the Shi'i clergy, following the example of schools run by Christian orders just about everywhere in Lebanon. These schools are being established gradually, class by class, up to the diploma stage at age fourteen. Currently Hizb Allah is studying the means of creating a pilot school which would take pupils from the elementary level through to the end of high school.

Financing for these activities comes from two different sources: one is internal, from the *khums* (a fifth) levied on the savings of Shi'i Muslims and from the *zakat* (donation of any amount offered by all Muslims); the other source is external, in the form of aid from the Khomeini Committee for Supplies in Iran. Represented in Syria and Lebanon by 'Isa Tabataba'i, this committee meets periodically in Tehran to decide on the amount of aid it can grant Hizb Allah and friendly governments or movements in countries such as Afghanistan, Pakistan, Sudan, and Syria.

In its next phase, Hizb Allah policy will probably continue to develop along two axes: provisional coexistence with the "Republic of Taif," with all that this implies regarding internal Lebanese politics, and anti-Israeli resistance in South Lebanon. It goes without saying that the leadership of the party will be in a firm position to administer the new political direction the organization is following. The continued existence of a tendency within the party opposed to Hasan Nasr Allah, active at the lower and middle levels of the organization, suggests that the present developments will lead to the control of Hizb Allah by the Lebanese government, and that the silence of Hizb Allah leaders over the Arab-Israeli peace process constitutes an abandonment of the basic principles of the party. Is Hizb Allah on the verge of a major schism, or will the Iranian leaders be able to put pressure on the opposition in the party to calm things down? It is possible that new cleavages and rivalries within the Iranian government itself will in the end have repercussions on Hizb Allah, leading to a reshuffle of the leadership.

Translated from the French by Margaret Owen.

12

The Resurgence of Islam
and the Welfare Party in Turkey

Ronnie Margulies and Ergin Yıldızoğlu

In nationwide local elections on March 27, 1994, the Islamist Welfare Party (Refah Partisi or RP) took over 19 percent of the popular vote and captured 26 of the 72 metropolitan municipalities in the country, including Istanbul and Ankara. In Istanbul the party's vote was just over 26 percent. Suddenly, Islam was on the verge of making a serious bid for power in a country regarded as a fortress of secularism in the Middle East.

Since the March elections, the secular, westernized, liberal sectors of society have been in a blind panic. All eyes have been fixed on the RP municipalities and all ears on the RP leaders' pronouncements. The non-Islamic press has been vigilantly on the lookout for any slipup on the part of the RP, any sign of corruption or wrongdoing, anything with which the Islamists can be hit over the head. Republic Day, on October 29, 1994, was turned into a celebration of Kemalism and secularism. An unofficial and nebulous "secular front" has brought together the most disparate elements in order to resist the further rise of the RP. But in national parliamentary elections in December 1995, Refah won 159 out of 550 contested seats and 21 percent of the vote, edging out the two main secularist parties.

The RP's success should have surprised no one. The party's popularity and grassroots support have shown steady growth in every general and local election since the early 1980s. From a historical perspective, in Turkey as elsewhere, religion has always emerged as a banner behind which the oppressed and the dispossessed have rallied in periods of economic and social hardship. After all, Marx did not only say that "religion is the opium of the people"; he added that it is "the heart of a heartless world, the sigh of the oppressed."

The widespread Western view of Islam as a religion conducive to mass revolutionary anti-Western mobilization is ahistorical and one-dimensional.

Islam has played both stabilizing and destabilizing roles; it has served as a banner for rebellion as well as oppression. Where it is the official state religion (formerly in the Ottoman Empire, today in Saudi Arabia, Pakistan, and Iran), Islam is a legitimating ideology for the ruling class and constitutes part of the state mechanism.

Unofficial Islam, on the other hand, has throughout history frequently expressed popular protest. Where the state generally claimed to represent orthodox Islam, unofficial Islam often assumed unorthodox, sectarian, or mystical (sufi) forms to challenge the center's religious and political legitimacy. Ottoman history abounds with examples of this. Bedreddin-i Simavni (1368–1420), a mystical philosopher, for instance, attracted a mass following with doctrines advocating equality and a fair distribution of wealth; he was attacked (and hanged) by the official religious establishment as a heretic. Similarly, the Celali revolts which shook Anatolia in the sixteenth and seventeenth centuries were started by a Safavid preacher who claimed to be the *mahdi* (messiah), and attracted a mass following of peasants and urban elements discontented with the high level of taxation. Both Bedreddin and Celal claimed religious authority in their bids to overthrow political authority.

SECULAR REPUBLIC, UNDERGROUND ISLAM

At the end of the nineteenth century, Sultan Abdülhamid II, Caliph of all Muslims, tried to pull his crumbling empire together by playing the pan-Islamic card, demonstrating a function official Islam was expected to fill. With the foundation of the republic in 1923, the Ottoman state's position as the world's leading Islamic power came to an end. The new Turkish state was secular: there was no official religion, and religiosity was distinctly frowned upon.

For the founders of the new state, the struggle against religion was part and parcel of their struggle against the *ancien regime*. The leading cadres of the new republic were veterans of a long struggle between the nascent Turkish bourgeoisie and the Ottoman ruling class. Their first measures amounted to a direct assault on the power of this old ruling class. They abolished the caliphate with its national and international religious function. They abolished the office of *şeyhülislam* and replaced the ministry of religious foundations with minor departments of religious affairs and religious foundations. They purged the Ottoman *ulema* class from the state apparatus and transferred the revenues from the properties of pious foundations (*vakif*) to the treasury, thus depriving the *ulema* of their source of income. They abolished *şeriat* courts and pensioned off their judges (*kadi*), thus eliminating the *ulema*'s judicial role. The abolition of the entire system of religious schools, sufi or dervish lodges (*tekke*), and cells (*zaviye*) helped sever the contact of the Ottoman ruling class with the populace. These measures did not aim chiefly to establish secularism, but to cripple the ability of the old ruling class to organize and fight back.

The nature of the new regime did not require it to create its own version of an official Islam. The historical conditions which forged the character of the Kemalist movement did not include a mass, popular movement of opposition to the *ancien regime.* Thus, the problem of establishing ideological hegemony over such a movement, for instance by putting forward an alternative official Islam, did not arise.[1] Rather, the Kemalists were attempting to create a Turkish national identity, which hardly existed in people's minds then. Islam, recognizing no national boundaries but the *umma,* stood in contradiction to a movement aimed at constructing a Turkish nation-state.

Following the establishment of the secular republic, Islamist movements continued to play a role in rallying popular discontent and opposition to the central state. Such movements now could argue that the center was godless and hostile to Islam. In the early years, when the Kemalist hold on power was still tenuous, several riots and uprisings occurred in which popular opposition took on an Islamic guise.[2] The state, for its part, could now condemn "opponents either as reactionaries if they came from the uneducated lower social strata or as subversive elements if they came from the intelligentsia."[3]

ISLAM IN THE MULTIPARTY ERA

The post–World War II period put the question of class co-optation squarely on the agenda of the Turkish state. Merchants, the dominant class in the country, had emerged from the war immensely richer in both urban and rural areas. Wishing to invest freely and circulate their accumulated capital, they chafed at the fetters imposed by the Kemalist bureaucracy and searched for alternatives to its etatism. In the consequent differentiation of the ruling class, this section found its political expression in the Democrat Party (DP).

At the same time, the shortages and hardships caused by the war, compounded by government policies and emergency measures, had alienated large sections of the peasantry. This was the situation as the transition to a multiparty regime in 1946 assigned "the electorate" an importance it had never previously enjoyed. The rural vote became all-important. The program of the newly formed DP was hardly distinguishable ideologically from that of the ruling Republican People's Party (RPP). One slight difference, however, was the new party's attitude toward religion. The DP program merely demanded greater respect for religion and less government intervention in religious affairs, but this proved sufficient to mobilize large segments of the population and incorporate many Islamic elements.

The DP's popularity forced the RPP to court the religious vote as well. In 1949, the government established official courses for prayer leaders and preachers. It introduced optional courses in religious education in elementary schools and approved the establishment of a faculty of theology later the same year.

In effect, the decade of DP rule (1950–60) saw the expansion and consolidation of Islam's place in the official political life of the country. Once again the call to prayer (*ezan*) could be read in Arabic (this had been banned under Atatürk). The radio regularly broadcast recitations of the Kuran. The government introduced courses on religion in secondary schools and established an Institute of Islamic Studies.[4] The list is neither long nor extreme. The atmosphere, however, had changed: Islam was no longer frowned upon. Sufi orders (*tarikat*) remained illegal, but were in fact tolerated and edged their way into the political scene. Saidi Nursi, leader of the Nurcu order, publicly stated that he would vote for the DP.

Until the end of the 1960s, Islam's profile in official politics continued to increase without assuming any decisive weight. One reason is that the DP and its successor, the Justice Party (JP), were able to implement economic policies which met the basic demands of the agrarian producers. Rising prices for cereals on the world market and several consecutive years of good harvests brought unprecedented prosperity to the countryside. Extensive state investment in infrastructural projects brought roads, electricity, and water to countless villages. Cheap credit and favorable prices enabled farmers to expand production; agricultural output increased dramatically throughout the 1950s. Domestic trade expanded correspondingly, much to the satisfaction of the provincial bourgeoisie of merchants, traders, and middlemen. The 1950s and 1960s were a prosperous time for the peasantry and the provincial middle classes, the two classes which would constitute the popular base of any Islamic resurgence.

THE NATIONAL SALVATION PARTY

In the late 1960s, the economic and political landscape of the country began to undergo dramatic changes. It was as if some time around 1968 history had speeded up. The rapid industrialization and rural-urban migration of the preceding decades now led to rising waves of workers' struggle. In the countryside, demonstrations and land occupation indicated growing peasant militancy. A part of the radical student movement transformed itself into urban guerrilla groups with little popular support but a high and violent profile.

The economic crisis of the late 1960s wrought a number of dislocations in the existing balance of class forces. The interests of big business, mostly based in Istanbul, organized in large holding companies and closely linked with foreign capital, began to clash with the interests of small and medium provincial capital. The Justice Party gradually assumed an identity as the party of big business and consequently lost the support of other constituencies, giving rise to a number of smaller parties. One of these, the National Order Party (later the National Salvation Party, or NSP), emerged as the first party in many decades openly to espouse an Islamist political philosophy. The party's first congress in 1970 echoed with cries of *"Allah-u ekber."*

The rise of the NSP signaled the return of Islam as a rallying cry for socioeconomic opposition to the central authority. The party's electoral base was among artisans, small traders, and others of low income from rural areas. These were the social groups hardest hit by the crisis and least able to defend themselves through existing political institutions. These groups felt not only their economic welfare but also their traditional institutions and values to be under threat. They saw the growing socialist movement as a threat to the family, and to religious and cultural values.

The NSP's propaganda stressed the importance of "morals and virtue," opposed secularism to the extent allowable under the law, and strongly attacked communism, freemasonry, and Zionism. Party leader Necmettin Erbakan became the champion of "independent industrial development." He opposed Turkey's entry into the European Economic Community, as this would further strengthen big business vis-à-vis smaller provincial businesses.[5] He branded the EEC a product of a "new crusader mentality."

In 1974, the NSP joined a coalition government led by the social-democratic Republican People's Party, breaking a historic barrier and lending the party and its policies a certain legitimacy. Through the 1970s, the NSP remained the third largest party in parliament, with around 11 percent of the popular vote. The party provided the urban poor and the provincial middle classes with a political organization and a national voice. In so doing, it invested the Islamist movement with the legitimacy of a national party platform. The very existence of the NSP forced all major parties to take the "Islamic" vote into account and to court it more explicitly.

While the NSP became the organized Islamist expression of popular discontent, an unofficial Islamist movement also grew alongside it. This movement spread far beyond the party, through unofficial Kuran courses, local associations, youth clubs, charitable associations formed around mosques, and a variety of journals. Various religious brotherhoods also flourished in this period. An Islamist youth movement (Akıncılar) linked to the NSP became increasingly active and militant, challenging both the left and the fascist right in armed street confrontations.

Significantly, the urban working class did not line up behind the Islamist banner: it had its own means of struggle—industrial action—and its own independent organizations—trade unions. An Islamist labor confederation (Hak-İş) remained marginal.

MILITARY TAKEOVER

The military coup of September 1980 had a twofold impact on the Islamist movement. On the one hand, the military leaders prosecuted the NSP leaders for violating article 163 of the penal code, which outlaws "the exploitation of religion for political purposes." On the other hand, the NSP's middle- and lower-tier cadres were quick to enter Prime Minister Turgut Özal's new party and organize within it as a distinct and influential faction. (Özal himself had been a parliamentary candidate on the NSP ticket in the 1970s.)

The antisocialist stance of the generals favored the religious right. With the physical elimination of the left and its organizations, socialism practically disappeared from the national arena as an oppositional movement. The right-wing opposition, by contrast, was able to obtain positions in parts of the state bureaucracy and the educational apparatus where the left had previously been influential.

These general effects of the coup combined with a number of developments to make the 1980s a fertile period for the growth of the Islamist movement. First, the socioeconomic conditions which gave rise to the movement in the 1970s continued and in some cases intensified after 1980. Clearly less important but nevertheless significant was the impact of the Iranian revolution and the Soviet occupation of Afghanistan. These two developments came together to present Islam as a world force, an alternative capable of fighting both capitalist imperialism and communism.

As a result of all this, the Islamist movement grew in strength. No one who spent even a few days in Turkey in the mid-1980s could fail to notice the larger crowds in mosques, the greater number of people wearing religious dress, the more observant atmosphere during the holy month of Ramadan. The religious orders, particularly the Süleymanci and the Nakşibendi, were involved in a range of activities.[6] Kuran courses brought in the very young; university entrance examination courses, where students received free tuition and lived in hostels run by the orders, attracted the educated youth of the future; recruitment among students of the military academies was aimed at gaining influence within the armed forces. Mosques and their attendant religious associations represented direct channels of neighborhood organization and recruitment. All the *tarikat*s were involved in these activities, often in competition with one other.

REFAH'S BID FOR POWER

All this lay behind the results of the local elections of March 1994. The Refah Party has come in from the cold. It is now one of the main parties in the country, on par with the two mainstream conservative parties, the True Path

Party (in government) and the Motherland Party (in opposition). All three have enjoyed levels of support of around 20 percent throughout 1994. When RP leaders confidently claimed that they would win the next general election, this was no longer seen as meaningless bravado but as a real possibility. This in itself gave the party further momentum: people could now vote for it as a real alternative, knowing that their vote would not be a wasted gesture of protest.

There are four basic reasons why RP is now a serious candidate for government. One is that RP voices the concerns of sections of the population in dire economic straits. The second is that no other party does so (certainly not the social democrats), thus enabling the RP to appear as the only radical alternative. The third is that international developments continue to highlight Islam as the most significant anti-imperialist force. Finally, the RP organizes on the ground in a way that no other party does.

The main thrust of Welfare Party propaganda does not concern Allah and His angels. It concerns privatization and the job losses this has caused. It concerns prices and public employees' salaries and workers' wages. RP posters are more frequently about "A Just Order" than they are about an Islamic state. This is powerful propaganda in a country where the government's privatization program is expected to cause the loss of between 500,000 and 600,000 jobs; an estimated 700,000 workers were made redundant in 1994; the annual rate of inflation is running at above 110 percent; and public employees are hardest hit by the government's spending cuts. In April 1994, the government announced a set of austerity measures which included a massive devaluation of the currency. Practically all prices doubled and the living standards of all but a small minority were halved within a matter of days.

One of the signatories to the austerity package and, indeed, to the new legislation on privatization later in the year, was the Social Democratic Peoples' Party (SDPP). The social democrats have been in government, as the minor party of the coalition, since 1991. They are therefore seen as part of the problem, rather than offering a solution.[7] This in itself would have been enough to eliminate them as an alternative radical channel for popular discontent. The party has additionally discredited itself by becoming embroiled in a number of scandals at the municipal level, and is now perceived to be as corrupt as any of the others.

In normal circumstances, the economic crisis and the havoc it has wreaked in people's lives might have been reflected in a shift in public opinion to the left, which would have benefited the social democrats.[8] With the SDPP in government, however, there is no left toward which to shift. The votes of those who want a change, who are disillusioned with the parties of the establishment and who seek a radical alternative, have thus gone to the RP, which carefully nurtures its radical, antiestablishment image.

International developments have also, for some years now, helped the RP project such an image. While Iran and Algeria gave Islamists hope, the Gulf war and the massacres of Muslims in Bosnia and Chechnya have made them angry and militant. The impression of a righteous Islamic community under attack on all sides by the forces of the Christian world is as strong in Turkey as anywhere in the Middle East. Islamist militants in Turkey may not share our Marxist understanding of imperialism, but it is not necessary to know the theory in order to recognize the phenomenon. Since the final collapse of Stalinism in 1989 and the disintegration of the Stalinist communist parties throughout the world, the banner of anti-imperialism in the Middle East now appears to be in the hands of the Islamic movements. This gives them great prestige in the eyes of those who are outraged at the sight on television of Cruise missiles exploding in Baghdad or Russian tanks battering Grozny.

Finally, the RP is the one parliamentary party with a local, grassroots organization which is active and militant. The party grows not through television debates and public relations stunts, but through old-fashioned community work. Its leaders claim an active membership of one million. Even allowing for wild exaggeration, there is no doubt that they have a large and growing number of local cadres. Given the endless opportunities for patronage and "jobs for the boys" afforded by control of twenty-six municipalities, this number will continue to grow. And these are activist cadres: tens of thousands can mobilize within hours and gather in Istanbul's main square, for instance, in response to rumors that napalm had been used against Bosnian Muslims.

AN ISLAMIC STATE?

All these factors are likely to remain operative for the foreseeable future. There is no short-term way out of the economic crisis. This will continue to erode support for the mainstream parties, regardless of whether the present coalition remains in power or not. Thus the rise of the Islamists to power is certainly a real possibility.

Many in Turkey hope (and expect) that this will be averted either by changes in electoral legislation (designed to make things more difficult for the RP) or by military intervention. This is to miss the point. While the RP can be stopped by such means, a mass movement of the dispossessed, rallying behind the banner of Islam, cannot.[9]

Two factors may stop such a movement. One is that the inner contradictions within the RP, and the Islamic movement more generally, may reduce its effectiveness and possibly split it even as support for it grows. Fundamentally, the party represents the interests of small provincial businessmen.[10] This is not inherently a radical constituency; it wants to see changes in government policies, but also longs for political and social stability. The party's base and mass support, on the other hand, is truly radical—the urban poor, the unemployed, youth with no prospect of employment. As it gains increasing support among the latter, as it must to bid for power, the contradictions will sharpen.[11]

A second factor which could stop the Islamist movement would be the emergence of a powerful and militant workers' movement which works to roll back the effects of the April austerity package and recoup the losses of the past fifteen years.[12] Such a movement would not be anti-Islamist, although the working class has remained very largely secular in its politics. It would be antigovernment, antiprivatization, antiausterity. It would change the atmosphere in the country from one of disillusionment, despair, and demoralization to one of hope and self-activity, thus diverting popular support away from the Islamic movement. An increasingly radical atmosphere in the country would also deepen the contradictions within the Islamic movement between its conservative and antiestablishment wings. It would, finally, enable the oppressed to fight back rather than sigh.

NOTES

Editors' note: This is an updated version of Ronnie Margulies and Ergin Yıldızoğlu, "The Political Uses of Islam in Turkey," *Middle East Report,* no. 153 (July–August 1988): 12–17.

1. Kemal gave short shrift to a proposal by southeast Asian Muslims that he assume the caliphate himself.

2. The Menemen incident in 1930 and the numerous Kurdish uprisings led by Şeyh Sait and others can be seen as examples of this phenomenon. The two official opposition parties which were allowed to be set up (the Progressive Republican Party in 1924 and the Free Republican Party in 1930) also unexpectedly turned into real opposition forces with strong religious elements. Both parties were closed down within their first year.

3. Kemal Karpat, "Recent Political Developments in Turkey and their Social Background," *International Affairs,* no. 28 (1962): 309.

4. Mehmet Yaşar Geyikdai, *Political Parties in Turkey: The Role of Islam* (New York: Praeger, 1984), p. 77.

5. Erbakan had previously been chairman of the Union of Chambers of Commerce and Industry, which largely represented (as it still does) the mass of small and medium Anatolian businesses.

6. On the religious orders (*tarikat*) in Turkey, see Erkan Akin and Ömer Karasapan, "Turkey's Tarikats," *Middle East Report,* no. 153 (July–August 1988): 16.

7. Many in the SDPP are, of course, aware of this; because of this there has been internal pressure to resign from the coalition since very early on. In failing to resign over the April 1994 austerity package, however, the party has effectively signed its own death warrant.

8. This is precisely what happened in the late 1970s, when Bülent Ecevit's party (the precursor of the SDPP) came to power, winning with the highest vote ever polled by social democrats in Turkey.

9. Events in Algeria since the military takeover demonstrate this. RP leader Necmettin Erbakan showed some awareness of this when he said to his opponents, on television: "We shall come to power. Whether this happens after bloodshed or bloodlessly is up to you."

10. Hence, most directly, its opposition to the European Community, membership in which would destroy businesses unable to compete, and to privatization, which benefits big business while depriving small businesses of state-subsidized inputs.

11. Already these contradictions are apparent within the party's leading ranks: there are those who favor breaking the law and those who do not, those who openly insult Kemal Atatürk and those who then apologize. (One leading member was expelled from the party for declaring that Atatürk's mother had been a prostitute.)

12. As we write, in January 1996, there has just been a general strike of public employees in Turkey, and the government has been compelled to withdraw a number of measures from its proposed 1996 budget.

13

Is There an Islamic Economics?

Karen Pfeifer

In response to the question, "What's different about Islamic economics?" one might well answer, "Somewhere between everything and nothing," depending on the relevant historical and institutional context. Islamic economic thinking is best understood through a socioeconomic approach. This approach sees economic behavior as embedded in social institutions, specific to a social system which evolves over time, and not as something given by nature, universal and unchanging. Whereas *"homo economicus"*—pursuing individual self-interest via "rational" utility-maximization—is the culturally approved behavior model for a capitalist market society based on private property and competition, other models were and still are appropriate for other sociocultural systems.[1]

In the socioeconomic view, an economy operates on the basis of shared cultural understandings regarding the proper ways of producing and distributing the necessities and luxuries of human life. The participants are trained as children to internalize and conform to certain rules which embody these culturally shared understandings. The rules may well encompass certain inequalities, by gender and class for example, which the parties effectively accept by means of their socialization, or by means of the negative sanctions that deviations from approved behavioral norms confront. In this view, individual choices are subject to social rules and constrained by an institutional framework, even in the free market economies in which individual consumption choices are posited to reign supreme (the "consumer sovereignty" taught in introductory economics courses).

As a society and its embedded economic relations evolve, so do the ideas held by its participants on how to explain the system and how to address economic problems which arise. Economic theory has evolved to reflect changing historical circumstances. Adam Smith's *Inquiry into the Nature and*

Causes of the Wealth of Nations appeared in the last quarter of the eighteenth century to explain free markets and competition and to address the problems of monopoly and constraints on the expansion of trade. Karl Marx's *Capital* appeared in the second half of the nineteenth century to explain the industrial revolution and to address the problems and historic role of the new wage-labor class. John Maynard Keynes's *The General Theory of Employment, Interest, and Money* appeared in the 1930s to explain the origins of capitalist depressions and to address the role of the government in a complex market system.

Far from being a throwback to the social system of the Middle Ages, Islamic economics is similarly a set of ideas evolving in the last decades of the twentieth century to explain and address the economic problems faced by the citizens of predominantly Muslim countries. Islamic economics responds to the achievements and failures of, first, state capitalism, and, second, the international capitalist system's antidote to state capitalism—economic liberalization.[2] It aims to recapture the original moral and political authority of the anticolonial movements that gave rise to state capitalism, but without the latter's domineering centralism and bureaucratic rigidities. It aims to provide scope for individual economic initiative and markets, just as proponents of economic liberalization do, but without the callous disregard for the evils of markets associated with unfettered capitalist systems in the West, such as extremes of poverty and wealth.

State capitalism was the institutional form which came to prevail in many Middle Eastern societies after independent nation-states were established. Examples include Turkey under Atatürk, Egypt under 'Abd al-Nasir, and Algeria under Boumedienne. Coming to power as part of anticolonial, national independence movements, these governments turned natural resources into public assets and promoted nationalist economic programs.

State capitalism had some significant successes, at least in the early years. Over time, problems arose which began to undermine economic growth and the promised rise in the standard of living, eroding public support for the state-capitalist model. Within the economy there appeared growing unemployment, inequities in the distribution of income and benefits (including corruption), inefficiency in many industries, and highly centralized authority in economic as well as political decision making.

Externally, these economies came to depend on export revenues to finance imports of essential industrial inputs, consumer goods, and even food. They turned to borrowing on international capital markets to finance purchases for which they did not have the cash in hand. When demand or prices for exports fell due to international factors beyond their control, they were unable to pay for imports or service debt and the regimes found themselves in crisis. Governments responded to the crisis by turning to the International Monetary Fund for help in debt management. With IMF guidance they liberalized and privatized, opening their economies wider to both domestic and foreign private capital, scaling back or even abandoning nationalist economic policies and central planning.

Economic liberalization programs across the Middle East have reduced or dismantled the major state capitalist institutions, and promise a return of economic growth and a rising standard of living in the long run as a result of private investment and free trade. As Turkey, Egypt, and Algeria illustrate, this path (or a pledge to follow this path, in Egypt's case) can provide significant short-run benefits, such as debt service relief, increased foreign aid, and growth in some sectors through the inflow of foreign capital and expansion of exports.

On the other hand, the short-run costs of liberalization are high and the long-run benefits are uncertain. The short-run costs exacerbate problems of unemployment and distributional inequity. Factory closings, reductions in real wages, cutbacks in government services, and reduction of price supports for consumer necessities lower the standard of living of many workers and small business operators. Furthermore, even after a long run of fourteen years in Turkey, where the policy has been most thoroughly applied, there is little evidence that a rising economic tide has lifted a majority of, much less all, boats.

An alternative development strategy would have to address directly the legacy of problems inherited from both state capitalism and economic liberalism.[3] The aim would be to encapsulate competition within a socially responsible institutional framework without losing the responsiveness of competitive markets and the price system to consumer demand and changing technology—in other words, a system which is neither laissez-faire nor centrally planned. Within the domestic economy, this would require a balance of competitive market activity among private firms and households with an active role for government in correcting market failures such as unemployment and monopoly power. In external economic relations, the strategy would require balanced, negotiated trade and investment relations with the international economic system in a framework of regional cooperation. The result would be a system of neither free trade nor autarchic protectionism but managed competition.

Proponents argue that Islamic economics, at least in theory, contributes to such an alternative economic development strategy.[4] They suggest that it is paradigmatically distinct from and ethically superior to pure market economics, on the one hand, and pure socialism (meaning public ownership of the means of production and central planning) on the other. Islamic economics may be interpreted to require that investment be undertaken for productive, socially beneficial purposes. This would constitute a social screen for resource deployment decisions, and could include criteria such as full employment, safe working conditions, and environmental protection. Islamic economics may also be interpreted to require that no interest be paid on borrowed capital, but rather that profits and losses be shared according to a precontracted formula by all contributors to the investment. Proponents argue that this would imply a more equitable income distribution, especially if workers were entitled to a share of profits as well as wages. Further, Islamic economics is a supranationalist philosophy. It could encourage cooperation among Muslim countries and enhance their bargaining power as a group within the world trading and financial system.

These ideas are not "fundamentalist" in the sense of harking back to an earlier era, but rather address modern economic problems. They are political, not theological. Just like the other economic theories mentioned above, Islamic economic ideas both reflect socioeconomic reality and in turn propose to change it through various policies. There is, thus, a dialectical relationship between reality and ideology. Furthermore, because Muslim countries have varied historical and cultural traditions, one should expect variation in country-to-country outcomes and further evolution, rather than a static, formulaic application of an Islamic economic gospel.

MAIN PRINCIPLES OF ISLAMIC ECONOMICS

Islamic economic thinkers range from the Islamist equivalent of social democrats to strong defenders of free markets and private enterprise. Some have adapted notions from the Marxian tradition for use in their critique of the Western capitalist system. For example, they may adhere to a simplified labor theory of value, which stresses that prices of commodities and returns to economic activity are tied to underlying contributions to production. Some utilize a theory of Western imperialism in which monopoly capitalism in Europe and the United States is seen as the root cause of European overseas expansion and colonialism.

Islamic economic thinkers, though, are generally hostile to socialism, for both its atheism and its stress on material (as opposed to spiritual) growth, much like capitalism. Most Islamic economic theorists present their ideas as variations on a "third way," distinct from capitalism on the one hand and from socialism on the other. This gives them room to approve of certain aspects of capitalism, including private ownership of the means of production, profit maximization as a motor force in economic behavior, and free-market competition in products, services, and labor.[5]

Unlike neoclassical economics, the ideological handmaiden of Western capitalism, Islamic economics stresses the social institutions framing economic activity which, its proponents claim, contribute to the difference and ethical superiority of Muslim society compared to Europe and its offshoots. There are three main differences.[6] First, and ideologically foremost, is the location of the individual in an Islamic social context. *Homo islamicus,* like his cousin *homo economicus,* may well aim to maximize utility, but he does so along two dimensions. He maximizes his own individual material utility, but this prosperity is hollow unless it is accompanied by the spiritual development that comes from serving others and the Muslim community (*umma*). Moral supervision of individual behavior by the community enjoins the entrepreneur to pay just wages and to charge just prices, for example.

Second, and practically the most important in the current sociopolitical context, is the prohibition on the payment or taking of interest on money loaned.[7] The ideological rationale is that interest represents a return to idle money balances, where no work or other contribution is forthcoming, and thus unjustly rewards passivity. Its practical importance in contemporary Muslim societies is that depositors in Islamic banks (or Islamic departments of ordinary commercial banks) become partners in the banks' investment decisions, sharing in the profits and losses from those decisions in proportion to their deposits. The banks in turn are partners with the firms in whose projects they invest, sharing profits and losses from those projects in proportion to their capital share. This, it is argued, draws more individuals into active investment and production, which are sorely needed in underdeveloped Islamic countries.

Related to the abolition of interest are the prohibitions against speculation and wasteful consumption, both believed to be associated with the excessive materialism of Western capitalism. Speculation, such as commodities futures markets, it is argued, diverts economic energy from production and rewards only the speedy turnover of exchange-based transactions. Wasteful consumer spending encourages price inflation more than increased production, and discourages the savings needed to fund investment for economic growth in developing societies.

A third feature is the principle of *zakat,* one of the five pillars of Islam. As interpreted by contemporary Islamic economics, *zakat* is a voluntary tax on wealth (i.e., productive assets) administered through the mosques, which generates a welfare fund to pay for various charitable and social projects (such as health care, education, and disaster relief). Islamic economists, who tend to be critical of the postcolonial secular states ruling in Muslim countries today, favor substituting this private, mosque-controlled network of benevolent societies for the inefficiently run, overly bureaucratic welfare-state institutions of their respective governments.

Related to *zakat* is the system of Islamic inheritance laws. Because these laws enjoin property owners to treat their sons equally, with each daughter receiving half the share of a son, property is less likely to be concentrated in the hands of a small number of people. While economic classes are not proscribed by Islamic economic thinkers, they do believe that the problem of severe inequality in income distribution will be obviated by the combination of this inheritance system and *zakat*. The exception to the inheritance law, the placing of undivided assets in a religious trust (*waqf*) is acceptable because control of the property is removed from the owner, the property is used for productive investment, and the income is dedicated to provide for some social good.

THREE KINDS OF CRITIQUES

Islamic economic thinking can be evaluated along theoretical, practical, and political dimensions.[8] On the theoretical plane, Western-trained economists often groan at what they perceive to be a lack of technical rigor in Islamic economic tracts. However, since the mid-1980s, there has been a spate of new work by Islamic economists who are themselves Western-trained.[9] Treatises replete with mathematical models and the technical lingo of the economics profession now deal with the labyrinths of macropolicy and microstructures of would-be and existing Islamic economies. There is a danger here that the one clear strength Islamic economic thinking had over Western neoclassical models, its explicit recognition of the embeddedness of economy in society, might get lost in a welter of "techspertise."

Perhaps a more serious theoretical deficiency is that, in rightly arguing that a social utility function cannot be simply constructed from individuals' functions, Islamic economic thinking goes straight to the social utility function of the *umma*, the Muslim community. This leaves unaddressed the question of where the preferences that determine this social utility function come from: From the rulers of the Islamic state? From the *imams* who lead the mosques? From Islamic economists themselves? While both free-marketeers and socialists recognize differences of interest among individuals or groups, these are left out of the agenda of Islamic economics on the unwarranted presumption of unanimity and harmony within the Islamic community.

A third theoretical problem is that certain kinds of economic decision making become awkward without an interest rate as the baseline measure of the cost of capital.[10] Even in centrally planned economies, a rate of return to invested capital is calculated, not as income to owners of capital but to indicate, for example, the rate of depreciation and replacement of the existing stock of physical capital and the investment fund needed to generate a larger stock to support economic growth and technical change. In market economies, banks make decisions about investment loans by ranking projects in terms of their riskiness and expected returns.[11] In fact, there is some evidence that existing Islamic banks use an implicit interest rate for the latter calculations. They compare their rate of return (the percentage of profit relative to capital invested for a given period of time) to the rate of return on lending portfolios in non-Islamic banks (or to other departments in traditional banks which have Islamic departments) to judge how well they are faring in the competitive race and to attract depositors.[12]

The interest rate in a capitalist economy is different from the social rate of return on invested capital (generically relevant to any society in which economic growth is a conscious goal) in that the former represents a contract for a fixed income transfer from the borrower to the lender over the period of the loan, with the amount set prior to the investment project. The consequence for lack of repayment with interest is foreclosure, in which the borrower is forced to render over his collateral property to the lender, or in which the lender has first claim to the proceeds as the bankrupt borrower's property is liquidated. In this sense, the risk of investment is not borne equally: those who invest their own capital are at greater risk than those who simply lend. This is unjust, in the Islamic economists' view.

Yet the elimination of this arrangement may create other injustices and social dangers. On a macro level, savings may be reduced because of the loss of low-risk repositories in which to place savings. Savers might then put their excess funds into luxury goods, such as carpets, gold, or real estate instead of banks. This would make fewer funds available for investment and thus reduce the potential rate of economic growth.

On the micro level, persons such as retirees living on fixed incomes from pensions or from their savings cannot generally afford the risk of profit sharing. They need a low-risk, dependable, predetermined rate of return on their savings—in other words, something like an interest rate. Similarly, firms need to hold their investment funds in secure, relatively inflation-proof forms at times when no new real investment is to be made. If an Islamic economic system is to work, it would have to invent low-risk savings accounts with dependable returns, functioning like US treasury bills or savings bonds or savings accounts, as an alternative to the profit-and-loss sharing arrangements of the higher-risk portions of banks' portfolios. It is hard to escape the concept, let alone the payment, of interest which in these cases would have to at least equal the rate of price inflation so as to keep the real value of such savings intact.[13]

A fourth theoretical issue involves the concept of "efficiency." In Western market-oriented economics, measures of efficiency refer to the maximum output per unit of input (in physical units) or the minimum average cost of a unit of output (in monetary terms). Islamic economic thinkers, in rejecting these purely material definitions, have so far not come up with alternative objective measures. Instead, they propose to subordinate efficiency to social goals (not unrelated to the social utility function issue above). This could mean that the rulers of an Islamic state would be able to avoid responsibility for poor economic performance, on the rationale that their material failures are more than compensated by the spiritual gains. This is an escape route even the current rulers of inefficient secular states could admire.

Beyond these theoretical questions lie the practical issues in implementing an Islamic economic system. First, there is no clear definition of "equity" or "justice," or of the means by which the members of the society would come to a consensus on these definitions. This leads to a tendency to revert to Islamic jurists' decisions instead of democratic processes, and to accept whatever the status quo level of inequality may be.

Second, the theory underestimates the size and complexity of contemporary Muslim societies. The presumption of harmony and unanimity of the *umma* is based on the time of the Qur'an and the *hadith* (reports of the words and deeds of Muhammad)—an era of small-scale agricultural communities with simple commodity production, linked through trade and personal or familial connections. In this respect, the Islamic economic vision is reminiscent of neoclassical free-market models. In contemporary societies, the need for objective information about trading and investment partners calls out for some form of social regulation.[14] The free-rider problem, curbed by social mechanisms in small-scale societies, is much more likely to appear in impersonal large-scale societies. Similarly, the existence of monopoly power or positive and negative factors external to complex modern economies requires either regulation at the level of the state or elaborate compensation rules enforceable by the courts.[15]

All modern societies based on competitive markets have social welfare programs to sustain the losers in the market competition game. If not, the society becomes politically unstable and conflict, most prominently in labor market relations, leads to unsustainable social costs. It is hard to believe that a voluntary *zakat* would be sufficient to sustain social stability, especially in times of economic recession when the donors' income falls. Modern societies require a system of mandatory income taxation, with a consensus on the degree of horizontal and vertical equity to be achieved in after-tax income distribution.

Third, monetary policy is essential to the governance of any modern society. Currency value must be stable both domestically and internationally in order to facilitate trade and investment and, in the Middle East and North Africa especially, the flow of remittances from émigré labor. Interest rate calculation is central to monetary policy, a higher interest rate serving to dampen investment and curb excessive—that is, inflationary—aggregate demand. A higher interest rate also serves to attract foreign capital and remittances and thus to redress deficits in the balance on current account. For domestic purposes, without an interest rate, monetary authorities would have to use far less subtle means of influencing the size of the money supply (changing the required reserve ratio, for example) and the volume of investment (setting ceilings on overall investment, targeting specific industries) or targeting the formulas for profit-sharing between firms and banks. These would entail as draconian a government intervention in private sector economic activity as ever was felt under state capitalist central planning.

Finally, fiscal policy will be more difficult to implement under an Islamic system. Since there is no plan to eliminate the business cycles, which are typical of all complex capitalist market economies, recessions will recur periodically. In order to cushion the economic impact of recessions, Western governments run deficits, with government spending rising and tax revenues falling during recessions, thus keeping aggregate demand from dipping as low as it would by relying on the private economy alone.[16] These deficits are financed by borrowing from the public via treasury bills which pay interest. Islamic systems would have to invent some other means for governments to borrow from the public but, since this borrowing is not profit making in the usual sense (the benefit being a widespread positive environment from a recession not becoming a depression), the returns to lenders could not be based on "profit sharing." Similarly, government revenues from the progressively structured income tax in Western capitalist countries automatically rise during expansions and fall during recessions, thus modulating the highs and lows of the business cycle. *Zakat*, being voluntary and calculated on the basis of wealth rather than income, could not serve this function and would have to be supplemented by other tax institutions.

Beneath the theoretical and practical problems of implementing Islamic economics lie the political questions of who would implement the system and whose interests it would serve. First, redressing the above-mentioned problems, for example around monetary and fiscal policy, implies that the Islamic forces control the state, and a big state at that. If anything useful is to be gleaned from the experience of the Western capitalist economies, and from the no less compelling lesson from the East Asian economies of Japan, South Korea, Malaysia, and Indonesia, it is that a modern economy requires a big state with appropriate social institutions to frame and support that economy, such as labor law, contract law, and regulation of monopolies and externalities like environmental pollution.[17]

Given the necessity of a large central government, one must ask who controls it. This is a modern question and, if anything is to be learned from the Marxian tradition, a question of class. It is no accident that the leadership and funding of the Islamic movements comes from the *bazaari* class (as it came to be called in Iran)—that is, the entrepreneurial class of merchants and bankers whose living comes from trade and the finance of trade and investment. Its political base, however, is composed mainly of the unemployed and disenfranchised young workers and bidonville (shantytown) dwellers rebelling against the status quo governments of the Middle

East unable to meet their basic material needs. The presence of these two social forces in the Islamic movements implies that if an Islamic movement came to power in, say, Egypt or Algeria, it would give rise to the same class struggles familiar to students of contemporary capitalist polities: struggles over the role of the state, the state's functions, and the distribution of the costs and benefits of economic development. But, as has occurred in Iran, these issues would be framed within an Islamic discourse.[18]

All this suggests that Islamic economics may well represent the contemporary equivalent in the Muslim world of the Protestant reformation. *Homo islamicus* is a modern incarnation of "the Protestant ethic": an entrepreneur who works hard for material gain and is spiritually pure will be rewarded here on earth in the form of shared profits and social recognition. Postcolonial state capitalism in the Middle East and North Africa served as the incubator of private capitalism. If its successor, economic liberalism, fails to restore growth with equity, while offending Muslim sensibilities with its Western materialist orientation, it may then be the historic role of Islamic economic regimes to break out of the nationalist shell and redefine the process of economic development. If Islamic economics were to resolve its theoretical and practical problems, its economic policies would be functionally equivalent to those in the capitalist West, but tailored to the sensibilities of Islamic culture and ready to replace the now-ineffective central governments held over from the state-capitalist era. Like the Japanese and East Asian forms of capitalism, Islamic economies could function as successfully and competitively as those of Europe and its offshoots, yet claim their own sociocultural distinctiveness based on "the Islamic ethic."

NOTES

Research for this chapter was assisted by a grant from the Joint Committee on the Near and Middle East of the Social Science Research Council and the American Council of Learned Societies with funds provided by the National Endowment for the Humanities and the Ford Foundation.

1. *Homo economicus* is viewed by neoclassical economics as a phenomenon of human nature, unchanging over time and place. Fine critiques of this point of view are offered by institutionalists such as Mark A. Lutz and Kenneth Lux, *Humanistic Economics* (New York: Bootstrap Press, 1988); and Amitai Etzioni, *The Moral Dimension: Toward a New Economics* (New York: Free Press, 1988).
2. Works placing Islamic economics in the context of a history of economic thought and serving as good introductions to its ideas are: Charles Issawi, "The Adaptation of Islam to Contemporary Economic Realities," in Yvonne Haddad et al. (eds.), *The Islamic Impact* (Syracuse, N.Y.: Syracuse University Press, 1984), pp. 27–45; Ibrahim A. Ragab, "Islam and Development," *World Development* 8 (1980):

513–21; Hamid Hosseini, "From *Homo Economicus* to *Homo Islamicus:* The Universality of Economic Science Reconsidered," in Cyrus Bina and Hamid Zanganeh, *Modern Capitalism and Islamic Ideology in Iran* (New York: St. Martin's Press, 1992), pp. 116 ff.

3. Economists in other parts of the Third World are tackling some of these same issues in a manner parallel to Islamist thinkers. See, for example, Cristovam Buarque, *The End of Economics? Ethics and the Disorder of Progress* (London: Zed Books, 1993).

4. For examples of this reasoning, see Mehmet Ozay, *Islamic Identity and Development: Studies of the Islamic Periphery* (New York: Routledge, 1990); and Abdul-Hamid Abu-Sulayman, "The Theory of the Economics of Islam"; Abdul Hadi Ghanameh, "The Interestless Economy"; and Muhammad Al-Nowaihi, "Fundamentals of Economic Justice in Islam," in *Contemporary Aspects of Economic Thinking in Islam: Proceedings of the Third East Coast Regional Conference of the Muslim Students' Association of the United States and Canada* (Indianapolis, Ind.: American Trust Publications, 1976).

5. Maxime Rodinson was the first to argue systematically and cogently that Islam is hospitable to a capitalist economic system in *Islam and Capitalism* (Austin, Tex.: University of Texas Press, 1978).

The most prominent theorist of Islamic economics in the Arab world (the Adam Smith of his time) was Muhammad Baqir al-Sadr, an Iraqi Shi'a *imam* who became well-known for his outspoken writings and activism in the 1950s and 1960s. See, for example, his *Islam and Schools of Economics* (Englewood, N.J.: Islamic Seminary, 1983). Al-Sadr overtly challenged 'Abd al-Karim Qasim's alliance with the communists in Iraq following the 1958 revolution. His outspoken criticism of Saddam Husayn earned him the enmity of the regime and led to his execution in 1980.

6. For a concise summary, see Frederic L. Pryor, "The Islamic Economic System," *Journal of Comparative Economics* 9 (1985): 197–223.

7. For an elaboration of this practice, see Ingo Karsten, "Islam and Financial Intermediation," *IMF Staff Papers* 29, no. 1 (March 1982): 108–142.

8. Useful critiques of the various aspects of Islamic economic thinking are provided by Sohrab Behdad, "Islamic Economics: A Utopian-Scholastic-Neoclassical-Keynesian Synthesis!" *Research in the History of Economic Thought and Methodology* 9 (September 1991): 221–32; idem, "Property Rights in Contemporary Islamic Economic Thought: A Critical Perspective," *Review of Social Economy* 47, no. 2 (1989): 185–211; Masudul Alam Choudhury, "Principles of Islamic Economics," *Middle Eastern Studies* 19, no. 1 (January 1983): 93–103; Timur Kuran, "On the Notion of Economic Justice in Contemporary Islamic Thought," *International Journal of Middle East Studies* 21, no. 2 (May 1989): 171–91; idem, "The Economic System in Contemporary Islamic Thought: Interpretation and Assessment," *International Journal of Middle East Studies* 18, no. 2 (May 1986): 135–64; Seyyed Vali Reza Nasr, "Islamic Economics: Novel Perspectives," *Middle Eastern Studies* 25, no. 4 (October 1989): 516–30.

9. For example, Mohsen S. Khan and Abbas Mirakhor (eds.), *Theoretical Studies in Islamic Banking and Finance* (Houston, Tex.: Institute for Research and Islamic Studies, 1987); and Masudul Alam Choudhury and Uzir Abdul Malik, *The Foundations of Islamic Political Economy* (New York: St. Martin's Press, 1992).

10. Explanations and critiques are offered by Izzud-Din Pal, "Pakistan and the Question of *Riba*," *Middle Eastern Studies* 30, no. 1 (January 1994): 64–78; and M. Siddieq Noorzoy, "Islamic Laws on *Riba* (Interest) and Their Economic Interpretations," *International Journal of Middle East Studies* 14, no. 1 (February 1982): 3–17.

11. From the firms' point of view, the interest rate is also an important variable in micro-decision making. In the Keynesian model, the volume of investment is expressed as an inverse function of the interest rate (all else held constant), meaning that firms will undertake only those investment projects which yield a rate of return greater than the cost of borrowed capital. The lower the interest rate, the greater the number of projects that will be perceived as profitable.

12. Confirmed by interviews with investment managers at the Egyptian-Saudi Finance Bank, Cairo, July 19 and August 10, 1994.

13. Both medieval and contemporary experience in the Muslim world show that interest reappears in disguised forms: a bank's "buying" a product, a car for example, for a client at one price and then "selling" it to him for a higher price with payment due in installments over an agreed-upon period of time.

14. The scandals of the Islamic investment companies in Egypt in the 1980s are evidence of this point.

15. This point was made in early Islamic history. Economic growth in Medina gave opportunities to monopolists to take advantage of their position. Consequently, price controls and other restrictions were imposed on these monopolists. See Timur Kuran, "The Economic System in Contemporary Islamic Thought: Interpretation and Assessment," *International Journal of Middle East Studies* 18, no. 2 (May 1986): 141–42.

16. The Keynesian expectation was that these deficits would be negated during business cycle expansions, when government spending fell and tax revenues rose because of increased income. The budget would be balanced over the business cycle (rather than in any given year). In current practice, budget deficits merely decrease during expansions; they do not turn into surpluses.

17. The articles of Choudhury and Nasr cited above both advocate an Islamic economic system. But whereas Choudhury sees a welfare state as inevitable in this era, Nasr worries about the intrusion of the state into civil society.

18. Class relations in Iran under the Islamic regime are described by Sohrab Behdad, "Winners and Losers of the Iranian Revolution: A Study in Income Distribution," *International Journal of Middle East Studies* 21, no. 3 (August 1989): 327–58; Sami Zubaida, "Is Iran an Islamic State?" in this volume; and Mehrdad Valibeigi, "Islamic Economics and Economic Policy Formation in Post-revolutionary Iran: A Critique," *Journal of Economic Issues* 27 (September 1993): 793–812. For evidence of comparable phenomena in Algeria, see Arun Kapil, "Les partis islamistes en Algérie: éléments de présentation," *Monde Arabe: Maghreb/Machrek*, no. 133 (July–September 1991): 103–11.

14

Funding Fundamentalism:
The Political Economy
of an Islamist State

Khalid Medani

While political Islam has become a major force in the Arab world in recent years, particularly in the countries of the Maghrib, Sudan is where the Islamist movement has realized its greatest ambition: controlling the levers of state power and setting itself up as a model for similarly oriented movements abroad. Islamist leaders in Sudan have actively supported groups elsewhere—reportedly helping to plan a recent failed military coup in Tunis and convening meetings with high officials of Algeria's Islamic Salvation Front (FIS) in Khartoum.[1]

Sudan's Muslim Brothers, through their political party, the National Islamic Front (NIF), were well placed to assume power, buttressed by a formidable economic base and supported by a particularly advantaged social group. The reasons underlying their success in Sudan can help us assess the prospects of other, similarly oriented movements elsewhere.

FUNDAMENTAL COUP

The members of the military junta that seized power on June 30, 1989 were practically unknown, but the timing of the coup pointed to a close alliance between the leaders of the "Revolution for National Salvation" (*thawrat al-inqadh al-watani*) and the NIF.

In December 1988, widespread strikes and demonstrations erupted in Khartoum, led by the newly revitalized workers' and tenants' unions and federations of professionals, civil servants, and artisans.[2] These were the social groups which in the 1950s and 1960s had supported the influential Sudanese Communist Party and were largely responsible for the downfall of the military regimes of Ibrahim 'Abbud (1958–64) and Ja'far Nimeiri (1969–85).[3] Once again these social groups took to the streets, calling themselves the "Modern Forces" (*al-quwat al-haditha*) in contrast to the traditional parties which have dominated Sudanese politics since independence.

Their actions stemmed from the frustration caused by the squabbling among the traditional Umma and Democratic Unionist parties, and the alliance of the NIF with the Umma Party to form a majority in parliament. The primary demands of the Modern Forces were a peaceful solution to the civil war between the government and the southern rebel movement, the Sudanese People's Liberation Army (SPLA), and the repeal of the *shari'a*-based laws of September 1983.[4] Two months later, in February 1989, a group of high-ranking military officers joined the Modern Forces' cause. They submitted a memorandum to the civilian government demanding that it seek an immediate solution to the war and stating their own refusal to pursue a military solution.

These events culminated in a National Memorandum for Peace, subsequently signed by all major parties except the NIF, which opted to leave the government and form an opposition front. This compelled the prime minister and Umma Party leader, Sadiq al-Mahdi, to form a new coalition incorporating members of the professional, trade, and workers' unions into the government. This coalition recommended peace talks based on an agreement signed in Addis Ababa in November 1988 by SPLA leader John Garang and Muhammad 'Usman al-Mirghani, head of the Democratic Unionist Party (DUP) and spiritual leader of the Khatmiyya sufi order (*tariqa*). The agreement called for repeal of the 1983 September Laws and postponement of *shari'a* law until a truly representative constitutional conference (*mu'tamar dusturi*) could be convened following a cease-fire.[5]

In mid-June 1989, the Mahdi government announced that a cabinet meeting on July 1 would formally repeal the September Laws, contingent upon the review of a legal committee comprising representatives from all political parties. On July 4, a government delegation and the SPLA were to meet to propose a permanent resolution to the civil war.[6] Twenty-four hours before the July 1 meeting, a group of mid-ranking officers took over the Republican Palace, the parliament, and the national broadcasting station, rounded up top party and union leaders throughout the capital and announced the Revolutionary Command Council under the leadership of Lt. Gen. 'Umar Hasan Ahmad al-Bashir.

It appears that the Muslim Brothers and the NIF greatly contributed to the success of the June 30 coup. The Brothers had been marginalized by widespread popular support for a swift resolution to the country's economic problems by way of ending the civil war. Their twofold aim was to preempt any peace agreement and reverse the ascendance of the largely secular forces newly incorporated into the government.[7] The junta targeted these forces for repression, dissolving all parties and structures of the constituent assembly and imprisoning a disproportionate number of members of work-ers' and professional unions. They banned all independent publications, forcibly retired over three hundred senior officers, and replaced hundreds of civil servants with NIF members and their sympathizers.[8]

SMALL TRADERS AND ISLAMIC BANKS

The greatest strength of the Muslim Brothers lies in two sectors of Sudanese society. The first, typical of Islamist movements in other countries, is the constituency of secondary school and university students, particularly in the capital. During the 1970s, a large number of the Brothers' supporters had become teachers in the western provinces, and consequently there has been major support for the movement there. When these students went on to universities in Khartoum, they came to dominate student politics.[9]

The second base is among small traders and industrialists, petit bourgeois entrepreneurs threatened by the traditionally powerful merchant families. Following the establishment of the Faisal Islamic Bank (FIB) in May 1978, under the initiative of the Muslim Brothers, "Islamic" banks have forcefully entered the Sudanese financial system and attracted these small traders and industrial entrepreneurs.[10]

The Nimeiri regime afforded them a special advantage over other com-mercial banks, exempting them from state control. In December 1983, three months after the *shari'a* decrees were instituted, a presidential com-mittee converted the entire banking system, including foreign banks, to an Islamic formula. Nimeiri timed this to outflank the traditional religious and political leaders and cultivate the allegiance of the Muslim Brothers, the only political group still supporting him.[11]

The Faisal Islamic Bank's paid-up capital had risen from 3.6 million Sudanese pounds (£S) in 1979 to as much as £S57.6 million in 1983. Over the same period FIB's net profits rose from £S1.1 million to £S24.7 million, while its assets, both at home and abroad, increased from £S31.1 million to £S441.3 million.[12] The FIB is not only the first of its kind but has also served as a model for similar banks which, taken together, have come to play an influential role in the country's financial sector. The FIB was founded in 1977 under the initiative of Prince Muhammad bin Faisal of Saudi Arabia. He and other private Saudi sources provide 40 percent of the bank's capital base. Sudanese citizens provide another 40 percent, while the remaining 20 percent comes from other foreign nationals, primarily from the Persian Gulf states.[13]

The FIB, like other Islamic banks in Sudan, has an office in Jiddah which accepts deposits from Saudi citizens and Sudanese expatriates living in the Gulf. Because most of these banks' capital is garnered from Arab sources, the success of this banking sector has paralleled the fortunes of the oil-exporting Arab countries. Sudan's Muslim Brothers found themselves well placed to dominate this system in Sudan.[14]

The investment pattern of these banks encouraged the growth of small- and medium-sized businesses (over 90 percent of their investments are allocated to export-import trade and only 4 percent to agriculture), and has effectively ensured support for the Muslim Brothers from the middle and lower strata of urban entrepreneurs. This has led to conflict with the traditional export-import merchants, mostly linked to the Khatmiyya order, who had previously dominated this sector and whose members have little access to Islamic bank financing. (These businessmen, as a result of the scarcity of hard currency and little access to commercial bank borrowing, have resorted to trading foreign currencies to maintain their own business operations. This partially explains the government's crackdown on "black market" currency traders, under the pretext of curbing inflation, in order to maintain the Islamic banks' monopoly on commercial lending.)

Islamic bank clients generally enter into a joint venture with the bank for a specific project. This usually takes the form of an equity participation agreement (*musharaka*) in which both parties agree on a profit-loss split based on the proportion of capital provided. If, for example, a trader buys and sells $10,000 worth of industrial spare parts, the bank (while not charging interest) takes 25 percent of the profits and the borrower the remaining 75 percent, assuming an equivalent proportion of capital provision.[15]

An aspiring businessman, to qualify for an Islamic bank loan, must provide a reliable reference from an already established businessman with a good record of support for the movement.[16] This has led to almost comic attempts on the part of many in the urban marketplace to assume the physical as well as religious and political guise of Islamists. The Brothers have also provided numerous philanthropic and social services to broaden their political base—for example, educational scholarships abroad to those who assume an ardent political posture on their behalf. They actively solicit employment for recent university graduates, an especially attractive service these days.[17]

The escalating national debt and lack of domestic savings have made Islamic banks one of the most important sources of finance. Prior to the Gulf war, the Brothers' close links with Saudi Arabia and the Gulf states meant there was almost no shortage of cash. In a country as poor as Sudan, it is not difficult to see why the Islamist movement grew dramatically from the late 1970s onward.

The conflict between this newly emerging small-scale trading and industrial bourgeoisie and the Khatmiyya order, which had managed, under colonial rule, to consolidate its power among the urban petty traders, has political ramifications as well. The leadership of the Democratic Unionist

Party comes from the Khatmiyya, which helps account for the National Islamic Front's alliance with the Umma Party. The Umma Party, deriving its economic fortunes primarily from agricultural schemes, poses much less of a threat to the Muslim Brothers. In response to the success of the Faisal Islamic Bank and others dominated by the Muslim Brothers, a number of wealthy Khatmiyya merchants established the Sudanese Islamic Bank in 1982, a clear bid to regain their monopoly of the country's retail trade and financial system.[18] (The Khatmiyya's spiritual leader, Muhammad 'Usman al-Mirghani, careful in the 1970s not to speak out against *shari'a*, in recent years has opposed its implementation on the grounds that it poses an obstacle to the peaceful resolution of the civil war.)

REMITTANCES IN SUITCASES

The oil price hikes of 1973 helped shape the political economy of Sudan primarily by privileging a specific social group which ingeniously translated economic opportunity into political clout. The "hidden" economy of remittance flows from the Gulf helped shape antagonistic economic relations which eventually found political expression of the most divisive and violent sort.

As late as 1985, formal remittances represented over 70 percent of the value of Sudan's exports and over 35 percent of imports (fig. 1). Labor is Sudan's primary export. The formal record vastly underrepresents the true magnitude of these external flows, since most are transacted illegally through the flourishing black market. The appropriate entry in the International Monetary Fund's (IMF) balance-of-payments statistics accounts for less than 15 percent of earnings reported by the migrant workers themselves.[19] Some estimate that the value of fixed and liquid assets reported by workers in the Gulf was close to $3 billion—most of it channeled through informal networks, the so-called "hidden economy."[20]

Sudanese social groups can be separated into those who profit from black market transactions and those whose survival depends on capturing as much hard currency as possible before it is absorbed by the hidden economy. The first group includes the workers themselves. Their remittances have produced the economic clout enjoyed by financial intermediaries known as *tujjar al-shanta* (suitcase merchants) who buy and sell hard currency on the black market. A broad spectrum of the Sudanese bourgeoisie engages in this type of transaction, but this "hidden industry" has been effectively monopolized by five powerful merchants.[21] The second group consists of the central bank and other government authorities responsible for official monetary policy. Their priority is to attract private foreign capital from nationals abroad. Commercial banks likewise depend on attracting this business.[22]

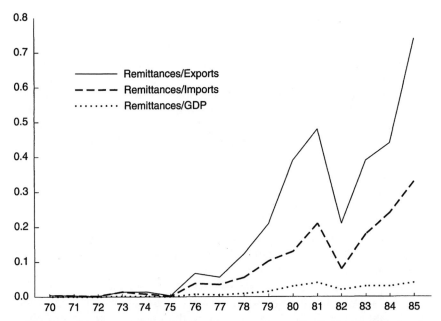

Figure 1. Remittances in Sudan's economy, 1970–1985. Source: *International Financial Statistics Yearbook* for selected years (Washington, D.C.: World Bank).

As formal sources of financing from the Gulf as well as from the West have declined, the economic weight of the governmental and commercial banks has shifted to that of *tujjar al-shanta* and the expatriates. At present, almost all the earnings of Sudanese living in the Gulf are remitted home via informal channels.[23] When the country's most powerful *tajir shanta*, Walid al-Jabil, was incarcerated for black marketeering, the National Bank of Sudan intervened on his behalf, reportedly because he had agreed to provide this primary financial institution with much needed capital from his own coffers.[24]

Remittances from the Gulf, in the context of Sudan's exceedingly bankrupt economy, have in recent years come to play an even more formidable role in privileging certain social groups and influencing political developments. A broad spectrum of Sudan's middle class has come to rely more and more on Gulf financing. Remitted earnings, by circumventing both the national banks and the Islamic banks, have contributed to an alliance between these former rivals, which are both losing the battle for hard currency. The recent crackdown on the black market represents an alliance between that faction of the Sudanese bourgeoisie dominating the commercial banks (organized under the banner of the NIF) and the state to try to capture a significant portion of the earnings of Sudanese working in the Arab countries of the Gulf.

This is not likely to curtail black market transactions. Many of the black marketeers were once themselves supporters of the Brothers. Important NIF bankers such as Shaikh 'Abd al-Basri and Tayyib al-Nus and the well-known currency dealer, Salah Karrar—all now members of the Revolutionary Command Council's Economic Commission—speculated in grain deals, monopolized export licenses, and hoarded commodities in their efforts to capture as much foreign exchange as possible. This is their profession.[25]

Having gained control of the state, the present regime considers it vital to marginalize rival factions of the bourgeoisie, while building an urban base among a new commercial class. When the junta executed several people accused of currency dealing in order to intimidate the big business families, though, they contributed to the virtual collapse of expatriate remittances from the Gulf. This was even before Iraq's invasion of Kuwait, which further exacerbated the state's financial woes.[26]

The appointment of 'Abd al-Rahim Hamdi, one of the most renowned of Sudan's "Islamic" financiers, as minister of finance and economy left little doubt about the NIF's overwhelming dominance of the state's chief financial institutions.[27] The only institution capable of maintaining some semblance of control over currency transactions and foreign trade had been the Central Bank. Under Hamdi, the authority of the state in economic matters became entirely subservient to the interests of the Muslim Brothers.

The political future of Sudan's Muslim Brothers to some extent depends on social groups with financial links with the Gulf states. Having sided with Saddam Husayn against the Gulf countries, the Bashir regime found itself in a precarious position. Threatened with the erosion of its own social base, it felt forced to make a number of overtures to the Gulf countries and the West.

But the regime's economic desperation also led it to alienate important sectors even further. In May 1991, concerned about the amount of local currency being kept outside the banking system to buy dollars on the black market, al-Bashir ordered the issuing of a new Sudanese currency.[28] Many Sudanese charge that Islamist businessmen were forewarned, affording them the opportunity to safeguard their assets while the rest of the population had to sell their money for one-fifth of its face value.[29]

ECONOMIC LIBERALIZATION OR ISLAMIZATION?

Just as previous regimes were beholden to a private sector dominated by the Muslim Brothers in the 1980s, the latter now find themselves in the position of competing with the rest of the population for rents generated by the parallel economy. The Brothers' drive to consolidate their power and marginalize the traditional merchant bourgeoisie was expressed in the battle over the capture of hard currency and the state's concern with stamping out the black market. This meant haphazard implementation of coercive regulatory mechanisms and promoting economic liberalization measures designed to revitalize the official, and particularly the commercial, sector of the economy.

After capturing state power, the Brothers declared "war" against informal economic activity, charging smugglers, hoarders, and black marketeers with "crimes against the state" and intimidating them with severe criminal penalties ranging from imprisonment to execution.[30] Sudanese expatriates working in the Arab Gulf states were ordered to declare their hard currency at Khartoum airport; local merchants were directed to post official price lists in their shops; and street vendors were imprisoned as part of the campaign to curb inflation and black market transactions. In response, merchants in the urban areas withdrew certain goods from the market, exacerbating scarcities and inducing hyperinflation.

The Muslim Brothers' preoccupation with the parallel sector was due to that sector's potential for capital accumulation. Members of the Islamist commercial class utilized this potential to great effect in promoting their economic and political fortunes during the 1980s. By 1992, however, the regime was still losing the battle to capture hard currency (particularly as the majority of expatriate workers continued to send their foreign exchange earnings through informal channels) and openly began to court the Western financial community for assistance. The Brothers-backed military junta accelerated its efforts to liberalize key sectors of the economy in order to lure much needed funds from the International Monetary Fund and other donors.

In February 1992, under the guidance of 'Abd al-Rahim Hamdi, the regime floated the Sudanese pound (causing a sixfold fall in its value), lifted key price controls, withdrew subsidies on a number of consumer goods, and embarked on an ambitious privatization program. Further, in response to declining remittance flows to the country, in June 1992 Hamdi abolished the mandatory declaration of hard currency holdings. The persistent desire to capture a share of the lucrative transfers of Sudanese working abroad eventually led the military government to decree compulsory money transfers ranging from $300 to $1,000, depending on estimated income, to be remitted annually through official channels. This measure was designed to halt the decline of official remittances from abroad, which dropped from $450 million at their peak to just $15 million in 1994.

Rather than reflecting an inherent Islamist affinity for free-market orthodoxy, the Brothers' structural adjustment reforms were consistent with the business interests of the Islamist bourgeoisie. The Islamization of the country's commercial and financial sectors is proceeding. The Islamist technocrats believe that economic liberalization will reduce the profit margins of the old commercial classes on black market transactions.

The IMF has continued to withhold assistance from Sudan, as have most of the Gulf countries, not least because of Khartoum's continued support of Islamist movements in the region. Sudan's relations with the IMF have been openly hostile since 1989. The IMF declared Sudan "non-cooperative" in 1990 because it owed $1.7 billion in arrears. In August 1993, citing Khartoum's "persistent failure" to meet its debt obligations, the IMF took the unprecedented step of suspending Sudan's voting rights and threatened the country with expulsion. In the same month the US State Department placed Sudan on its list of states that sponsor terrorism, cementing the country's political and financial isolation. To rescue itself from its pariah standing, Sudan looked to France to intervene on its behalf with other Western countries and the IMF. This was the meaning of the regime's cooperation with France in capturing Illich Ramirez Sanchez (Carlos the Jackal) in August 1994 and Hasan al-Turabi's effort to serve as mediator in the negotiations between the Algerian government and its Islamist opposition. These initiatives averted Sudan's expulsion from the IMF but did not immediately result in any new loans.

The regime's ouster in late 1993 of 'Abd al-Rahim Hamdi, a prominent advocate of neoliberal economic policy, reflected disenchantment among key leaders of the Muslim Brothers with a liberalization program that had failed to lure foreign assistance. However, Hamdi's removal was a cosmetic change initiated because of increasing social unrest resulting from the soaring cost of living accompanied by the liberalization program. Hamdi's successor as finance minister, 'Abd Allah Hasan Ahmad, a former manager of the Faisal Islamic Bank with strong ties to European-based Islamist financiers, continued the neoliberal reforms. With the appointment of Sabir Muhammad al-Hasan (an Islamist and former head of the Bank of Khartoum) as director of the central Bank of Sudan, the Brothers continued to dominate fiscal and monetary policy.

Muslim Brothers supporters have garnered economic benefits from preferential allocations of bank loans, customs exemptions, and foreign currency for imports. They have also greatly profited from a highly selective privatization program ranging from textiles and agribusiness to telecommunications and mineral rights, resulting in lucrative asset transfers for the most important Islamist businessmen.

Economic liberalization has also impoverished the majority of the Sudanese population, including civil servants and those engaged in the private sector but not affiliated with the Brothers. The budget deficit resulted in massive inflation; the government had to establish the Sudanese Printing Company to meet the country's requirements for banknotes. Only two sectors of society can meet the prohibitive cost of living: families receiving expatriate remittances and members of the NIF and their supporters.

In late 1993 fuel shortages and the high cost of food sparked riots in key towns, including Omdurman and Wad Medani, forcing the regime to reintroduce price controls on certain products as well as subsidies on basic commodities. On October 16, attempting to curb increasing domestic and external opposition, the Revolutionary Command Council dissolved itself. Its chairman 'Umar al-Bashir became President of the Republic, and power was formally transferred to the civilian, albeit Islamist dominated, Transitional National Assembly (TNA).

While the Muslim Brothers have demonstrated great willingness to liberalize practically every sector of the economy, they have singled out the financial sector—the basis of their support—for regulation. In December 1994, the TNA amended the Foreign Currency Dealing Act—a source of much debate among the Brothers' leaders.[31] The amended law reduced the penalty for currency violations and called for the confiscation of currency instead of previous punishments which ranged from twenty years' imprisonment to hanging and also recommended that a distinction be made between legitimate "possession" of and illicit "dealing" in foreign currency.[32]

The Brothers' appetite for self-aggrandizement through their "war" against black marketeers, selective privatization programs, and the monopolization of export-import trade has earned them the label of "market crocodiles" (*tamasih al-suq*) among the local population. Their overwhelming dominance of the state's financial institutions has not gone unnoticed. In February and April 1994, protest demonstrations led by students and members of the Modern Forces and sparked by a 2,000 percent inflation rate ransacked and burned a number of Islamic banks in the north and west of the country.

NOTES

1. "Islamic Front in Tunis, Algiers Disturbances," *Al-Wafd*, June 2, 1991, in *Foreign Broadcast Information Service* (FBIS), June 7, 1991, p. 7. According to Hazim Saghyia, Islamist groups in Tunisia and Algeria are increasingly looking to the experiment in Sudan as the model to emulate in their efforts at taking state control. "Al-Sudan wa-usuliyyu al-maghrib al-'arabi," *Al-Hayat*, June 6, 1991.

2. See "Bayyan min far' al-tadammun al-watani al-dimuqrati al-sudani bi-Washington," which is distributed by the Sudanese Opposition Front's Washington branch. I was also a witness to these events while in Sudan.

3. Tim Niblock, *Class and Power in Sudan* (Albany, N.Y.: State University of New York Press, 1987), p. 226.

4. "Bayyan min far' al-tadammun al-watani. . . ."

5. Ibid.

6. Ibid.

7. Interview with former Sudanese Minister of the Interior, Mubarak al-Fadl, in *Al-Hayat,* September 2–3, 1989.

8. "Bayyan min far' al-tadammun al-watani. . . ."

9. Charles Gurdon, *Sudan at the Crossroads* (London: Middle East and North African Studies Press, 1984), p. 68.

10. Ibid.

11. Bahman Roshan, "Sudan and the Faisal Islamic Bank," in *Arabia: The Islamic Worldview* (November 1985); and Arab Banking Cooperation, Occasional Paper Series No. 1, *Arab Banking Systems* (United Kingdom), January 1985, p. 41.

12. *Faisal Islamic Bank Annual Reports,* quoted in an untitled thesis-in-progress by Magdi Mutwakil Ahmed Amin (Princeton University).

13. Rodney Wilson, *Banking and Finance in the Arab Middle East* (London: St. Martin's Press, 1983), p. 85. The Faisal Islamic Bank was immediately successful and by the end of its second year had two branches in addition to its head office in Khartoum.

14. Ibid., p. 82.

15. Gurdon, *Sudan,* p. 69.

16. Interview with a prominent Sudanese journalist, June 17, 1990. Name withheld by request.

17. A student from the University of Khartoum recently rationalized his support for the Brothers in this manner: "I am not really interested in politics. In fact, that is why I support the Ikhwan [Brothers] in the student elections. I am much more concerned with being able to live in a comfortable house, eat, and hopefully find a reasonable job after I graduate. The fact is that the Ikhwan are the only ones who will help me accomplish that." Interview, June 15, 1989. Name withheld by request.

18. *IFDA Dossier* 75–76, January–April 1990, p. 36.

19. Nazli Choucri, "The Hidden Economy: A New View of Remittances in the Arab World," *World Development Report* 14, no. 6 (1986), p. 702.

20. Ibid., p. 709. See also "2 milliar dular tahwilat al-sudanin fi al-khalij," *Al-Majalla,* January 16–22, 1991, p. 49.

21. "Khamsa tujjar yusaytarun 'ala al-suq al-suda fi al-sudan," *Al-Majalla,* June 11–17, 1986, p. 31.

22. Choucri, "The Hidden Economy," p. 709.

23. Ibid.

24. "Khamsa tujjar yusaytarun," p. 30.

25. "Sudan: Fundamentalist Economies," *Africa Confidential,* January 25, 1991, p. 7.

26. Ibid.

27. "Islamic Banks Finally Bury the Sudanese National Economy," *Sudan Democratic Gazette,* September 1990, p. 3.

28. "Currency Change," *Africa Research Bulletin,* April 16–May 15, 1991, p. 10376B.

29. "Tabdil al-'umla fi al-sudan ijra' li-sahb al-siyula al-za'ida," *Al-Majalla,* June 4–5, 1991, p. 51.

30. "Sudan Regime Cracks Down on Merchants," *African Business,* September 1989, p. 58.

31. The Chairman of the Economic Committee of the TNA described the law on remittances as "the worst law made by this government" in "Iqtisad al-inqadh," *Al-Wasat,* April 26, 1994, p. 12.

32. "Foreign Currency Dealing Act Amended," *Horn of Africa Bulletin* (January 1994), p. 35. In 1994, the government continued to regulate foreign exchange transactions closely, instituting regulations prohibiting the acquisition of foreign currencies without official documents, but recommending that foreign exchange payable to the government (i.e., expatriate remittances deposited in state banks) be exempt from customs.

PART THREE

Political Islam and Gender Relations

15

Introduction to Part Three

Barbara Harlow

In December 1994 in Jericho, as the new Palestinian Authority was continuing to negotiate its own legitimacy with the Israeli government, a recently released Palestinian prisoner was about to celebrate his marriage to the woman he had been engaged to eight years previously, when he had been convicted and sentenced for the slaying of a collaborator. On the wedding night, however, the bride was shot and killed. Accusations were made against the collaborator's family who, it was claimed, in seeking revenge had missed their target, the bridegroom, and murdered his bride instead. Her funeral was a public event, attended by hundreds of mourners. A few days later, following further investigation, the bridegroom was himself in the custody of the Palestinian police, charged with the death of the woman. He had, it seems, discovered on their wedding night that his bride was not a virgin, and exacted his own revenge.

This incident, reported briefly in the Palestinian press, betrays in its tragically related two versions—the defense of the national honor and the punishment of a woman's dishonor—a larger narrative: the still contentious place and status of women within the historic gains and losses of modern Middle Eastern polities. Women have long figured large in Western constructions of the "Orient" throughout the confrontations—military, political, and cultural—that have engaged the two social orders for centuries, from the Crusades, through colonialism and decolonization, and now in the post–Cold War era. The contrasting narratives embedded in the account of the death of the Palestinian bride are emblematic of both the contemporary contradictions that disturb her own social order and its political aspirations, as well as the earlier histories of an Orient-Occident conflict, particularly as these have been scrutinized by Western observers. Islam, to be sure, remains the dominant motif, but the place of women within its theology, as in its applications—concealed as much as displayed by the markers of the "veil" and the "harem"—has consistently exercised the concern, patronage, indignations, and exploitative fantasies of Western encroachers onto eastern terrain. The issue of "political Islam and gender relations" has been and remains systemic to the cross-cultural misunderstandings that continue to make and unmake the conflictual interactions between "West" and "East."

As much out of prurience as from a patronizing benevolence, European colonizers identified among the cultural traditions of their colonized subjects particularly those customs specific to the female population as requiring redress. From a fascination with the isolation of women in the harem, or women's quarters, and the practice of veiling, to studied horror at "female circumcision" in some parts of the African and Islamic worlds or sati (widow-burning) in South Asia, these traditions were alleged to warrant intervention on the part of European representatives. Such intervention, which resulted variously in legislation, pious exclamation, or outright condemnation, has since been described by such critics as Gayatri Chakravorty Spivak as the irony of "white men saving brown women from brown men."

Indeed, in the course of national liberation struggles throughout the colonized world, these very practices were turned against the colonizer. As Frantz Fanon has described, for example, in his analyses of the Algerian revolution, the veil itself became not just a symbol of cultural identity but a weapon in the struggle, under which could be concealed both bombs destined for the French neighborhoods and the women who carried them. James Ngugi (now Ngugi wa Thiong'o), in his early novel *The River Between* about British colonialism in Kenya, has similarly located circumcision as a point of contestation between colonizer and colonized.

The women themselves, however, would not long defer the question of their own liberation, even in the purported interests of national liberation. More contentious still in the postindependence period of state building and nation formation, women's demands and the issues that they pose continue to generate not just critical debate but a persistent, even brutal, violence against women.

As Deniz Kandiyoti points out in "Women, Islam, and the State," much recent as well as past commentary on "gender and politics" in the Middle East has observed the age-old focus on Islam as central to the analysis. More recently still, Kandiyoti goes on, spokespersons of both feminist theory and developmentalism have argued the necessity of examining instead the influence of socioeconomic exigencies in determining the places and roles assigned to women in emergent states. Surveying the geopolitical examples of Turkey, Iran, the Arab world, and the South Asian subcontinent, she highlights the historical changes—from the early imperatives of cultural nationalism with women defined as the protectors of tradition, through the new sexual division of labor imposed by increasing demands for women's participation in the work force, to the sociopolitical requirements made by donors for the distribution of international aid—that have forced Islamist movements into compromises and conflicts with state-building processes.

If the conventional simplifications and rhetorical overgeneralizations of a monolithic Islam as explanatory device are to be avoided, material analyses and specific examples must be elicited from these same compromises and conflicts. The cases of Palestine, Iran, Sudan, and Algeria are precisely such cases in point.

Originally written in the first years of the Palestinian intifada which began in Gaza in December 1987 and soon spread throughout the Occupied Territories, Rema Hammami's "From Immodesty to Collaboration: Hamas, the Women's Movement, and National Identity in the Intifada" examines the reluctance of the Unified National Leadership of the Uprising (UNLU) to respond to Islamist assaults on Palestinian women. These assaults began with the demand that Gazan women observe "Islamic dress," in particular the veil, or *hijab,* and quickly escalated into efforts to curtail the movements and activities of women in and outside the home. Hammami, through examples and critical interpretation of the situation in Gaza in 1988 and 1989, addresses the combined issues of women, nationalism, and Islam as these developed at the time, and their problematic consequences for the eventual implementation of a Palestinian Authority in Gaza and Jericho following the signing of the 1993 Declaration of Principles between the PLO and the state of Israel.

The negative example of the fate of Algerian women following Algerian independence in 1962 has often been cited by Palestinian partisans of their own struggle for self-determination and statehood. The contemporary situation of women in Algeria during the more than three decades after decolonization is the focus of Susan Slyomovics's reading of "Women and Public Space in Algeria." Here the broken historical narrative, between resistance and state building, is determinative. Citing the instances of the many well-known heroines and their lesser-heard-of sisters from that classic resistance movement, the essay's title poses the dire outcome faced at the end of the century by its female protagonists: "Hassiba Ben Bouali, If You Could See Our Algeria. . . ." Identifying public space as the site of not only national struggle but gender struggle as well, Slyomovics looks at the school, the factory, and the mosque too, as places in which women have been variously defied, defined, defended, and delivered. Given the violence practiced now against Algerian women, on the part of government forces no less than by the Islamic Salvation Front (FIS), the last woman cited by Slyomovics, Khalida Messaoudi, maintains that the women will, once again and of necessity, have to take to the streets in a new offensive. Iran by contrast, according to Homa Hoodfar, is attempting to consolidate its state formation through a coherent family planning campaign. In her presentation of

"Population Policy and Gender Roles in the Islamic Republic," Hoodfar argues that the contest between "women-centered interpretations of Islam" and traditional structures of patriarchy is still a vital one. Through citation of historical precedent, scriptural justification, and education, the Iranian authorities—if not strictly responding to women's demands—have begun nonetheless to accede to the pressures of political and economic realities with policies designed to address the pressing concerns of overpopulation, the public interest, and women's health.

In the Sudan, too, women and the family remain practically as well as symbolically central to the government's decision-making processes. In her study of "The Women of Sudan's National Islamic Front" Sondra Hale traces the Islamization of Sudan, from then President Nimeiri's ideological shifts in the 1980s, through the coup that overthrew him, to the current NIF government. Unlike Iran's family planning campaign, the "authentic culture" campaign of the NIF maintains that women must, except—a powerful exception—in case of economic necessity, remain as protectors of the home and their children. In the case of Sudan, Hale argues, and as could be argued as well in the cases of Palestine, Algeria, and Iran, the question remains: "Are there social processes by which religions allow a society to realign itself when it seems at a 'tilt,' when structural changes are moving at a faster pace than cultural understandings?" And further, "Does Islam lend itself more easily than other religions to such 'realignment' strategies?"

As the Moroccan feminist Fatima Mernissi has long and decisively insisted, a crucial feature of the debate over "political Islam and gender relations" is located in the conflicting interpretations of Islam and its varied applications—emancipatory and oppressive alike—across historical periods and geopolitical contexts. Is Islam to be defended against women? Or women against Islam? And in the case of the Palestinian bride, was it for the sake of her honor, or to her nation's own dishonor, that she died? Or both?

16

Women, Islam, and the State

Deniz Kandiyoti

Most commentary on gender and politics in the Middle East assigns a central place to Islam, but there is little agreement about the analytic weight it carries in accounting for the subordination of women or the role it plays in relation to women's rights.[1] Conservatives have used the Qur'an, the *hadith,* and the lives of prominent women in the early period of Muslim history as sources to confirm that existing gender asymmetries are divinely ordained, while feminists have discerned possibilities for a more progressive politics of gender based on the egalitarian ideals of early Islam. These exegetical exercises mainly showed that, for both feminists and antifeminists, Islamic doctrine continued to provide the only legitimate discourse within which to debate women's rights.

Other analysts have renounced these treatments as essentialist, ahistorical, and lacking in class perspective.[2] These studies focus on the processes of socioeconomic transformation accompanying the region's incorporation into the world economy, as the concerns of Middle East scholars have begun to mirror those of Third World "women and development" specialists.[3] The influence of feminist theory has also made itself increasingly felt. Debates about the subordination of women now occur in a more complex theoretical field, in which the analytic primacy of Islam has temporarily been eclipsed.

The rise of Islamist movements has stimulated new interest in the relationship between religion and politics in the region, and the role of the state in expressing and implementing this relationship. The most immediate and visible targets in "Islamization" programs were the dress, mobility, and general status of women, putting the question of Islam and women's rights back on the agenda with a renewed urgency. For Moroccan sociologist Fatima Mernissi, Muslim fundamentalism is an assertion of identity in the face of rapid social changes threatening existing authority relations (especially between genders), and a response to the boundary problems created by the intrusions of colonialism, new technology, consumerism, and economic dependency.[4] I have argued elsewhere that socioeconomic transformation has aggravated social inequalities, dislocating local communities and producing massive migratory movements and the influx of women into the labor force. All this has dealt a severe blow to the material and normative underpinnings of patriarchy, increasing the attractions of compensatory, conservative ideologies.[5]

While such arguments may account for part of the popular appeal of Islamist ideologies, they cannot explain the differential incorporation of these ideologies into actual state policies. Significant variations in the condition of women in Muslim societies derive from, among other things, the different political projects of modern nation-states. The ways in which women are represented in political discourse, the degree of formal emancipation they have achieved, their forms of participation in economic life, and the nature of the social movements through which they express their demands are closely linked to state-building processes. Studies of women in Muslim societies have not always acknowledged the extent to which aspects of state practice define and mediate the place of Islam itself.

Relationships among Islam, the state, and the politics of gender comprise at least three distinct components: links between Islam and cultural nationalism; processes of state consolidation and the modes of control states establish over local kin-based, religious, and ethnic communities; and international pressures that influence priorities and policies.

CULTURAL NATIONALISM AND WOMEN'S RIGHTS

All Muslim societies have had to grapple with the problems of establishing modern nation-states and forging new notions of citizenship. Diverse processes of nation building have produced a spectrum of distinct, shifting, and actively contested syntheses between cultural nationalism and Islam. Women's rights were debated and legislated in the search for new ideologies to legitimize emerging forms of state power.

Turkey stands out with its early experience of secularism, as the multiethnic Ottoman empire dissolved and was replaced by an Anatolia-based nation-state. Mustafa Kemal Atatürk not only dismantled the central institutions of Ottoman Islam by abolishing the Caliphate, but took additional measures to heighten Turkey's "Turkish" national consciousness at the expense of a wider identification with the Muslim *umma*. The nationalist alliance that brought Mustafa Kemal to power included men of religion who resisted any changes in the position of women, but collaboration between the Ottoman Islamic establishment and Allied occupation forces after World War I had undermined their legitimacy. The abrogation of the *shari'a,* the adoption of a secular Civil Code in 1926, and the enfranchisement of women in 1934 became part of a broader struggle to liquidate the institutions of the Ottoman state and establish a republican notion of citizenship. Despite the growth of Islamist political platforms in recent years, the Turkish state has not, to date, acted to reverse the legislative reforms of the early republican era.

In Iran, Reza Shah openly claimed to derive inspiration from Mustafa Kemal's reforms. His ban on veiling in 1936 was certainly more drastic than Kemal's pedagogic and indirect approach. However, in terms of modern state building, Iran was a much more fragmented polity than the Ottoman empire. Reza Shah's regime, furthermore, was not the heir of a war of national liberation but a military-based monarchy, with a much shallower basis for legitimacy. While Reza Shah consolidated his rule by eliminating alternative sources of power, the Shi'i clergy was able to resist co-optation into the institutions of the Pahlavi state. Unlike the Ottoman clerical establishment, the clergy in Iran remained strong enough both economically and in its mass-based networks to re-enter the political arena after the 1960s.[6]

State-building projects in the Arab world have ranged from experiments with "Arab socialism" to continuing monarchic rule. Despite reforms permitting educational, juridical, and state institutions greater autonomy from religious authorities, *shari'a*-inspired legislation in family and personal status codes persists even where secular laws have been adopted in every other sphere. Equal citizenship rights of women guaranteed by national constitutions are circumscribed by personal laws granting men special privileges in the areas of marriage, divorce, custody, maintenance, and inheritance. Does this conservatism in the areas of women and the family derive from the centrality of Islam to Arab cultural nationalism and represent an attempt to preserve Arab cultural identity in the face of Western imperialism, as many Arab commentators maintain?[7] Samir al-Khalil takes issue with the notion that Arab nationalism, at least in its Ba'thist version, could ever embody a secular project. He argues that the demarcation of Arab national identity was made possible through arguments about the primacy of the Arabs within Islam, and that a particular version of Islam, Sunnism, was made coterminous with national identity.[8] The fact that Sunnism and Shi'ism can be mobilized as the respective markers of Arab and Iranian national identities was made amply evident and was fully exploited during the Iran-Iraq war.

The tensions and juxtapositions between Islam and national identity are clearest in the South Asian subcontinent. Pakistan emerged from partition as a state that claimed its separate identity and sovereignty on the grounds of religion; Islam was constitutive of nationhood in itself. Although Pakistan originated as a homeland for the Muslims of India rather than as an Islamic state, Islam was increasingly evoked as the legitimizing ideology of Pakistani unity. The "Islamization" package introduced by General Zia ul-Haq gave legal sanction to crude forms of sexual discrimination, which Pakistani women's organizations loudly protested.

This emphasis on control of women as a means of establishing Islamic credentials must be set in the historical context of pre-partition India. Ayesha Jalal argues that conservative entrenchment on issues pertaining to women and family life lay at the heart of Muslim cultural resistance to both Hinduism and British colonialism.[9] Many Bengalis, on the other hand, favored a linguistic and cultural nationalism in order to wrest their independence from their Pakistani coreligionists; Bangladesh emerged from the conflict of 1971 as a secular People's Republic. State secularism subsequently eroded under successive regimes until finally General Ershad declared Bangladesh an Islamic state in 1988. The Islamization policies of Bangladesh, though, have remained more tentative than those of Pakistan, continuing to express the contradictions of its nationalist history, of its varied internal constituencies, and of the conflicting agendas of various foreign aid donors.[10]

In India, the question of Muslim women's rights easily turns into a confrontation between minority (Muslim) and majority (Hindu) interests. As a result, any progressive attempt to redefine or expand these rights is thwarted by the logic of communal politics.[11]

STATE CONSOLIDATION AND FAMILY LEGISLATION

The fact that women represent the "inner sanctum" of diverse national collectivities and the focal point of kinship-based solidarities, as opposed to a more abstract and problematic allegiance to the state, has presented a dilemma for the "modernizing" states of the Muslim world. Modern states have had to confront and to some extent eradicate local particularisms in order to create new forms of civic consciousness and to liberate all available forces of development, including the labor potential of their female citizens. Depending on the nature of their political projects, states have variously challenged, accommodated, or abdicated to local or communal patriarchal interests, with important consequences for family legislation and more general policies affecting women.

Muslim modernists at the turn of the century put family reform high on their agendas. They denounced sex segregation, arranged marriages, repudiation, and polygamy and argued that the subjugation of women hinders national progress. Such views remained in the realm of polemic in societies with small urban populations, weak industrial bases, and vast rural or tribal hinterlands. The limited outreach of premodern states left many aspects of their citizens' lives untouched; regulation of marriage and family life remained under local kin control. Attempts at greater state penetration of society under Muhammad 'Ali in nineteenth-century Egypt and in the late Ottoman empire remained limited compared to the dramatic expansion of state power in this century.

The attempts of postindependence states to absorb and transform kin-based communities in order to expand their control had an important bearing on policies relating to women and the family. Mounira Charrad argues that variations in the balance of power between the national state and locally based communities in Tunisia, Morocco, and Algeria during accession to independence account for significant differences in family legislation.[12] In Iraq, the Ba'th had an interest both in recruiting women into the labor force in the context of a continuing labor shortage, and in wresting women's allegiances away from kin, family, or ethnic group to the state-party. Women were recruited into state-controlled agencies and put through public education, vocational training, and political indoctrination. The 1978 Personal Status Law, although limited in its objectives, aimed at reducing the control of extended families over women. In Lebanon, governments formally relinquished matters of family and personal status to the religious authorities of existing communities. This was part of the strategy of Lebanon's ruling elite to maintain the balance of sectarian power in the state.[13] The People's Democratic Republic of Yemen, by contrast, introduced the 1974 Family Law which, despite numerous concessions to Islamic laws and local customs, aimed to free women from traditional forms of kin control and create possibilities for their emergence as economic and political actors in the service of national development.[14]

Other considerations that have a bearing on state policies relating to women include the extent to which states are pressed to mobilize their internal resources.[15] Oil states, which until recently were able to recruit foreign migrant labor, were clearly less reliant on female labor than, say, Turkey or Egypt, though recent developments in the Gulf may force a partial redefinition of the existing sexual divisions of labor. Conversely, states whose foreign earnings are highly contingent on remittances from male international migrants may increasingly rely on female labor in their domestic economies. This is particularly true in countries that have shifted their industrial priorities from import-substitution to export-led strategies of development which stimulate the recruitment of low-paid female labor.

The interventionist measures of post-independence states, either through family legislation or education, employment, and population control policies, were primarily geared to national development. Their record with respect to the emancipation of women is quite mixed. Typically, authoritarian regimes did not encourage the creation of democratic civil societies in which women's gender interests could be autonomously represented. Women's attempts at independent organizations were considered divisive and actively discouraged. This was the case during the single-party regime in Turkey, under the Pahlavis in Iran, and under 'Abd al-Nasir in Egypt who, immediately after granting women suffrage in 1956, outlawed all feminist organizations.[16] Instead, state-sponsored women's organizations were set up which were generally the docile auxiliaries of the ruling state-party. Nonetheless, in regimes as diverse as those of Atatürk, Reza Shah, and 'Abd al-Nasir, an emphasis on national consolidation and unity and the creation of a modern, centralized bureaucracy were congruent with the mobilization of women to aid the expansion of new cadres and the creation of a uniform citizenry.

Some regimes have recently reversed what appeared to be the steady expansion of women's rights in the early stages of national consolidation. Others are experiencing legitimacy crises, the political outcomes of which may also encroach on women's rights. The expansion of women's citizenship rights coincided with the secularist thrust of nationalist state-building projects. The political and distributive failures of such projects in Pakistan and India, for example, have aggravated conflicts expressed in religious, ethnic, and regional terms. States have themselves used and exploited sectional rivalries in their patronage networks and distributive systems, exposing any initial universalist pretensions as shallow and fragile. Radical Islamist discourse typically identifies these failures not merely as political ones but as "moral" failures, requiring a complete overhaul of the world-views underpinning them. As religious and ethnic identities become increasingly politicized, they tend to sacrifice women's hard-won civil rights on the altar of a politics of identity that prioritizes control of women. Governments struggling to shore up their legitimacy may choose tactically to relinquish control of women to their immediate communities and families, thus depriving female citizens of full legal protection.[17]

In those cases where the state itself sponsors religious fundamentalism, as in Iran, Pakistan, or Saudi Arabia, the exercise of patriarchal authority extends to the clergy, the police, or even other unrelated men, who take it upon themselves to monitor the dress and conduct of women.[18] One of the deepest ironies behind this emphasis on the control of women is the fact that the ties of economic and political dependence in which most states are enmeshed restricts their autonomy quite severely in almost every other sphere. This brings us to a consideration of the international context in which state policies are formulated and implemented.

THE INTERNATIONAL CONTEXT

At the regional level, the cleavages between oil-rich and resource-poor countries had an important effect on the flow of migration, aid, and political influence in the Muslim world. Migrants went from poorer countries such as Egypt, Yemen, Bangladesh, Turkey, and Pakistan to the oil countries of the Gulf, while a reverse flow of cash and political influence strengthened the cultural and political prominence of local Islamist tendencies. This prompted diverse accommodations with Islam in aid-dependent countries. Internal Islamist constituencies either received a measure of acceptance and favor from ruling parties or governments, or created pressures pushing governments to declare their own commitment to religious orthodoxy as a means of upstaging more radical Islamist platforms.

Meanwhile, international monitoring of local economies reached unprecedented levels with the adoption of structural adjustment packages and stabilization measures imposed by the International Monetary Fund and diverse development projects sponsored by Western donor agencies. The shift from tight state control over the economy to private sector and foreign investment initiatives, and the adoption of export-led development strategies, had significant gender repercussions, notably a significant increase of the female labor force in the low-paid, casual, and nonunionized sectors of the economy.

Since the International Women's Year in 1975 and the United Nations Decade for Women (1975–85), the women-and-development lobby has exerted pressure on national governments to recognize the role of women in combating poverty, illiteracy, and high birth rates, and to eliminate all forms of legal discrimination based on sex. Since 1973, the Percy Amendment to the US Foreign Assistance Act has required that bilateral aid promote projects integrating women into development efforts. Monitoring bureaucracies were set up within the US Agency for International Development, the World Bank, and the foreign aid departments of the main European donor nations. Although these initiatives are still marginal to mainstream development funding, they indicate the success of international women's movements in placing gender issues on policy agendas. The "official" feminist rhetoric of modernizing, postindependence states has now been appropriated by supranational monitoring bodies, but with contradictory consequences at the local level.

Bangladesh, an impoverished country with a high level of dependence on foreign aid, offers interesting perspectives on the interaction between local politics and international influences. The declaration of the United Nations Decade for Women in 1975 coincided with the military coup that brought Zia ul-Rahman to power. Zia accumulated considerable political capital by championing the causes of the women-and-development lobby. However, he also needed the support of right-wing constituencies, including the army, to counter the opposition of the Awami League.

Oil-rich countries like Saudi Arabia, meanwhile, joined the ranks of major aid donors and increased their influence considerably. Zia embarked on an Islamization program which culminated in General Ershad's declaration of Bangladesh as an Islamic state in 1988. Both Zia's and later Ershad's strategies strove to balance the conflicting gender ideologies implicit in different aid packages: the development projects encouraged women's participation in the labor force and public life, while aid from wealthier Muslim countries strengthened religious education and the proreligious parties advocating stricter controls over women. The government, which supports attempts at population control funded by the United States, also funds Islamic organizations condemning them.[19]

Parallels may be found in other countries, where we see local machinery channeling development funds into projects designed to empower women against a background of increasingly conservative ideologies, and sometimes policies, concerning their appropriate roles. Donor governments and funding agencies aim to harness women directly to their vision of a more effective, though not necessarily more equitable, international economic order. The very manner in which the recipients of aid are integrated into this order encourages the rise of unstable and repressive regimes.

The development policies favored by such regimes have by and large led to more visible disparities in wealth, fueling widespread popular resentment and discontent, often in the absence of adequate democratic channels of expression. Islamist tendencies and movements enter this equation in ways specific to each context, which does not invite easy generalizations. A conclusion that does seem permissible is that when Islamist movements become a factor, tighter control over women and restrictions of their rights constitute the lowest common denominator of their policies.

NOTES

1. A debate indicative of these disagreements may be found in Mai Ghoussoub, "Feminism—or the Eternal Masculine—in the Arab World," *New Left Review*, no. 161 (January–February 1987): 3–13; Rema Hammami and Martina Rieker, "Feminist Orientalism and Orientalist Marxism," *New Left Review*, no. 170 (July–August 1988): 93–106.

2. Nikki R. Keddie, "Problems in the Study of Middle Eastern Women," *International Journal of Middle East Studies* 10 (1979): 225–40; Judith E. Tucker, "Problems in the Historiography of Women in the Middle East: The Case of Nineteenth Century Egypt," *International Journal of Middle East Studies* 15 (1983): 321–36.

3. These are the themes in "Women and Work in the Middle East," *MERIP Reports*, no. 95 (March–April 1981); "Women and Labor Migration," *MERIP Reports*, no. 124 (June 1984); and "Women and Politics," *MERIP Reports*, no. 138 (January–February 1986).

4. Fatima Mernissi, "Muslim Women and Fundamentalism," *Middle East Report*, no. 153 (July–August 1988): 8–11.

5. Deniz Kandiyoti, "Islam and Patriarchy: A Comparative Perspective," in Nikki R. Keddie and Beth Baron (eds.), *Women and Gender in Middle Eastern History: Shifting Boundaries* (New Haven: Yale University Press, 1991).

6. Afsaneh Najmabadi, "The Hazards of Modernity and Morality: Women, State and Ideology in Contemporary Iran," in Deniz Kandiyoti (ed.), *Women, Islam and the State* (London: Macmillan, and Philadelphia: Temple University Press, 1991).

7. Nadia Hijab, *Womanpower: The Arab Debate on Women and Work* (Cambridge: Cambridge University Press, 1988); Nawal El-Saadawi, "The Political Challenges Facing Arab Women at the End of the 20th Century," in Nahid Toubia (ed.), *Women in the Muslim World* (London: Zed Books, 1988); Leila Ahmed, "Early Feminist Movements in Turkey and Egypt," in Farida Hussain (ed.), *Muslim Women* (London: Croom Helm, 1984); Fatima Mernissi, *Beyond the Veil* (London: Al-Saqi Books, 1985).

8. Samir al-Khalil, *The Republic of Fear* (London: Hutchinson, 1989).

9. Ayesha Jalal, "The Convenience of Subservience: Women and the State of Pakistan," in Kandiyoti, *Women, Islam and the State.*

10. Naila Kabeer, "The Quest for National Identity: Women, Islam and the State of Bangladesh," in Kandiyoti, *Women, Islam and the State.*

11. Amrita Chhachhi, "Forced Identities: The State, Communalism, Fundamentalism and Women in India," in Kandiyoti, *Women, Islam and the State.*

12. Mounira Charrad, "State and Gender in the Maghrib," *Middle East Report,* no. 163 (March–April 1990): 19–24.

13. Suad Joseph, "Elite Strategies for State Building: Women, Family, Religion and the State in Iraq and Lebanon," in Kandiyoti, *Women, Islam and the State.*

14. Maxine Molyneux, "The Law, the State and Socialist Policies with Regard to Women: The Case of the PDRY 1967–1990," in Kandiyoti, *Women, Islam and the State.*

15. I am grateful to Suad Joseph for calling my attention to this consideration in her comments on an earlier paper.

16. For an extensive discussion of women's movements in Egypt, see Margot Badran, "Competing Agenda: Feminists, Islam and the State in 19th and 20th Century Egypt," in Kandiyoti, *Women, Islam and the State.*

17. This was the case in India, where Muslim women's access to secular law in matters of divorce was blocked by the Muslim Women's Act of 1986. Another significant but little noticed, and subsequently denied, development was the Iraqi government's announcement in March 1990 of a legal exemption for Iraqi men entitling them to kill female members of their family if they suspected adultery.

18. Chhachhi, "Forced Identities." See also Eleanor Abdella Doumato, "Women and the Stability of Saudi Arabia," *Middle East Report,* no. 171 (July–August 1991): 34–37.

19. Kabeer, "The Quest for National Identity."

17

From Immodesty to Collaboration: Hamas, the Women's Movement, and National Identity in the Intifada

Rema Hammami

In the summer of 1989, at the height of mass confrontations with the Israeli army, young boys in Gaza started to throw stones at women who were not wearing headscarves (*hijab*). At the time, much of the local population thoughtlessly accepted this as necessary social discipline to sustain the intifada, along the lines of leaflets of the Unified National Leadership of the Uprising (UNLU) which ordered workers not to go to their jobs in Israel, told merchants to observe general strike hours, and encouraged parents to organize substitute education for their children. The order to enforce the wearing of *hijab*, though, was of a completely different nature. It was the first time during the intifada that an issue once relegated to the arena of religious behavior had been mobilized as a nationalist issue. It was singularly aimed at women and was especially difficult to confront because it was never written as a command in a leaflet, and thus not open to public discourse or national debate. Instead, it was discussed among upper-level activists of Hamas (Harakat al-Muqawama al-Islamiyya) and then disseminated through their street cadre by word of mouth and localized graffiti. For at least a year women were left to confront a phantom—what seemed to be a generalized social impulse rather than a clear policy decision by a political faction.

The submerged political meaning of the *hijab* campaign did not evoke an appropriate political response from the nationalist movement. In retrospect, this was a transformative moment for the quietist Islamist group, al-Mujamma' al-Islami (the Islamic Center, a Gaza offshoot of the Society of Muslim Brothers), as it changed into the Islamic Resistance Movement, Hamas. Thereafter Hamas was able to conflate its social ideology with Palestinian nationalism and ultimately capture the direction and vision of the intifada.

Many local and international accounts have suggested that the intifada enabled Palestinian women to make great strides toward social and political liberation.[1] This is premised on the fact that women were mobilized to confront the occupation in large numbers and in qualitatively different ways than before.[2] While some positive developments have occurred, it is also true that the intifada became the context for a vicious campaign in Gaza to impose the *hijab* on all women there. The campaign included the threat and use of violence, and developed into a comprehensive social offensive. Social acquiescence, political inaction, family pressure, and a concurrent ideological transformation created a situation in which, one year into the intifada, only a few committed women in Gaza—women affiliated with the three leftist factions of the PLO—continued to not wear a headscarf. Although acting individually, they were all asserting, in the context of the uprising, the fundamental linkage between gender liberation and the possibility of a progressive and democratic future. Their struggle was not about the *hijab* as such, but about what the intifada would eventually lead to. However, the exigencies of national unity and the inability of the national movement to discern this same link meant that they received little support from either progressive men or the National Leadership, which waited a year and a half before addressing the question. Ultimately, these women's analyses were vindicated as Islamist victory over the *hijab* question led to more general social redefinitions positing women's behavior as the cornerstone of national integrity, hence the most vulnerable targets of the Israeli security apparatus. Female individualism came to be represented as a threat to the uprising rather than a means to sustain it.

THE HIJAB IN GAZA

Orientalists and Islamists alike generally assert a unitary interpretation of various forms of *hijab* as simply adherence to an Islamic textual injunction. Similarly they ascribe unitary meaning to the nonwearing of the *hijab* (for Orientalists, "modernity" or "westernization"; for Islamists, "westernization" or "nonbelieving"). Yet the meaning of various dress forms, female headcovering in particular, are much more complex. Even in the limited context of Gaza over the last forty years, changing social and political forces have been encoded in different forms of dress and headcovering with a fluidity of meaning.

Before the intifada, in Gaza as elsewhere in the Middle East, there was wide variation both in the forms of the *hijab* worn and in its use and nonuse by different social classes and groupings. Various forms of *hijab* signified class, regional background, religion, or age. Since 1948 there has been an

ongoing appropriation, transformation, and reinvention of various traditions of clothing and headcovering.[3]

Class transformations and the hegemony of Nasirist modernism in Gaza
in the late 1950s led large numbers of women to dispense with any form of
hijab.[4] Others continued to wear changed versions through to the present.
For instance, the dress and headcovering of older women in Gaza asserts
both their peasant origins and their contemporary status as camp women.
Its primary signification is of a class and group identity rather than a
gendered one. In everyday life camp women wear a black cotton skirt (*da'ir*)
and white or black headshawl (*shasha*). Even the color of the headshawl
denotes if they are from the southern Strip (black) or from the north
(white). These forms of dress were adopted by camp women after 1967,
when the materials for the southern Palestinian peasant dress were no
longer available and women dispensed with their precious embroidered
dresses (*thawb*) for everyday wear. In contrast, Gazan village women, not
wanting to be confused with refugees, wear plain black full-length dresses
cut in the manner of a traditional *thawb*.

Many of these older women opposed imposition of the *hijab* but do not
view their own dress as oppressive. Their generation did not have access to
the socioeconomic structures that entailed the wearing of "modern dress."
Their point of reference remained the older women's culture of the camps
and villages. Their dress has escaped the recent ideologization of the *hijab*
and remains simply an assertion of their membership in their communities.[5]

In the late 1970s the Islamist movement represented by al-Mujamma'
al-Islami sought to impose or, as they saw it, "restore" the *hijab* for women
in Gaza who were not wearing a headcovering—mainly educated, urban,
and petit bourgeois women. The Mujamma' endowed the *hijab* with new
meanings of piety and, implicitly, political affiliation. In order to assert these
new significations, they elaborated new forms of *hijab*. Women affiliated with
the movement started wearing long, plain tailored overcoats they called
shari'a dress, thus making them symbolic forms of adherence to their understanding of the textual tradition of Islam. While supposedly a return to
authentic Islamic tradition, this is an invented tradition in both form and
meaning. Unlike other forms of dress and headcovering mentioned above,
here *hijab* is a fundamentally symbolic form supposed to discipline women's
bodies as part of a larger project of disciplining women's subjectivities. The
political logic represented by *shari'a* dress is the source of its oppressiveness.

INVENTING TRADITION

While *shari'a* dress proliferated in Gaza in the early 1980s, pressure to wear
it remained site-specific—at the workplace, within religious families, or
among students at the Islamic University campus. *Shari'a* dress and the

ideologization of the *hijab* created a new awareness about differences in women's dress, but there remained a social space for women not wearing any form of *hijab*. Only during the intifada was social pressure transformed into an active campaign to impose the *hijab* on all women.

Many commentators assume that the rise of al-Mujamma' al-Islami in Gaza is rooted in the religious nature of Gazan society. Even Gazans themselves often refer to their society as somehow inherently conservative or religious. Yet their religious history is not significantly different from the rest of Palestine. Through the 1950s saint shrines and popular religious festivals were the central forms of religious practice for all but the male urban elite.[6] In Gaza, a version of textual Islam was introduced to large sectors of the population only as part of the curriculum of universal primary education established during the Nasir period. The Nasirist discourse of religiosity promoted the creation of modern Arab nationalist subjectivities. Islam was part of history and a source of Arab identity, but not the basis of a modern social or political order.[7]

The emergence of the Mujamma' as a political force in the 1970s and 1980s was actively encouraged by Israeli occupation authorities, but this cannot completely account for its growth.[8] The movement offered a model of society and social behavior relevant to the problems of the majority of poor Gaza residents. Daily migration into Israel of over half the workforce had profound effects on Gazan society.[9] Drug abuse and alcoholism were perceived as major problems deriving from the experiences of Gazan workers in Israel.

Elements of the left had initially tried, sometimes forcibly, to stop workers from going into Israel, but this only created resentment because they proffered no alternatives. The Mujamma' proposed a practical solution—a return to the moral social code embodied in their interpretation of Islam. They appealed to a common cultural experience and selectively adopted values and meanings from Gazans' everyday lives. This was attractive to many Gazans, even to those who would never join the movement.[10] Those who did join were attracted by the possibility of participating in a political community that claimed to confront the occupation without (until recently) exposing its members to danger—as did belonging to the nationalist groups. Finally, the Mujamma' operated in a context of little religious diversity. Secularism was related to political nationalism, but not understood as a principle for ordering social life.

No one knows how many active supporters the Islamists have in Gaza. Secularists maintain that if a head count were possible, people would be shocked by how few there are. But evident to all is the extent to which, through a mixture of consent and coercion, the Islamists have established their cultural dominance. Their power falls short of hegemony; it has succeeded in putting aspects of secular culture on the defensive without generating its own political legitimacy. As one Popular Front for the Liberation of Palestine (PFLP) activist from Khan Yunis put it, "Their main activities in Gaza are to keep demonstrators away from mosques and to make sure women are covering their heads."

The initial lack of widespread political support for the Mujamma' was due to its poor record in fighting the occupation. Although foreign press reports featured simplistic assertions about the "Islamic nature" of the intifada in Gaza, the nationalist groups (including Islamic Jihad) were at the forefront in mobilizing the population in the first months of the uprising. During the spring of 1988, after heated debate within its ranks, the Mujamma' emerged as Hamas and joined the fray on its own terms.[11] It was the first faction to call for its own strike days distinct from those of the Unified National Leadership; it published a manifesto and soon started calling on women to wear the *hijab*. Graffiti sprang up all over the Strip proclaiming, "Daughter of Islam, observe *shari'a* dress!" In May 1988 religious youths broke into classrooms demanding that schoolgirls wear the *hijab*. During the first year of the intifada, attempting to enforce the wearing of *hijab* was what distinguished Hamas. It did not carry out armed attacks on Israelis until 1989. Subsequently Hamas was banned by the Israelis, but this was almost a year after the popular committees of the intifada were banned.

September 1988 marked the first attempt to deal with the growing pressure on women to wear a headscarf. Male youths attacked girls at the Ahmad Shawqi School in Gaza City for not covering their heads. Other young men and boys caught and interrogated the attackers and concluded that they were lumpen elements being used by the authorities as agents provocateurs. The PFLP in Gaza issued a leaflet describing the incident and warning of Israeli attempts to sow discord. Hamas also issued a local leaflet disassociating itself from the attackers—a recurring reaction of the movement to criticism of its policies. But neither the leaflets nor knowledge of the incident were widely circulated. Activist women in Gaza realized that national action was needed to reverse the unconscious local acceptance of "hijabization" as part of the intifada. The *hijab* "is not an issue for me," explained one woman in the village of 'Abasan. "In my community it's natural to wear it. The problem is when little boys, including my son, feel they have the right to tell me to wear it."

REDEFINITION

The dynamics of the *hijab* campaign are hard to delineate because multiple forces worked simultaneously (though not necessarily jointly) to confront women with demands to wear a headscarf. In Gaza it started with religious youth writing graffiti; subsequently they broke into girls' schools and made threatening speeches. Young boys (eight to twelve), empowered by the intifada, soon joined the campaign. If there were no soldiers to throw stones at, women without headscarves made good targets. Politically unaffiliated youth who felt left out found harassing women a safe way to express "nationalist" sentiment. Simultaneously, soldiers were raiding homes and attacking women; families worried about daughters and wives.

Most problematic for many women in Gaza was that these social pressures accompanied an attempt to nationalize the *hijab*. The original arguments ascribing a religious meaning to the *hijab* were all but swept away by the new intifada signification. The *hijab* was promoted (and to a great extent became understood) as a sign of women's political commitment to the intifada. The most prominent redefinition made wearing a headscarf a sign of respect for the martyrs. By this logic, bareheaded women were considered vain and frivolous or, at worst, anti-nationalist. Another argument was that the headscarf was a form of cultural struggle, an assertion of national heritage. Because these nationalist redefinitions were not completely successful, proponents resorted to arguments based on fear: the *hijab* protects women from soldiers.

Perhaps before the intifada Israeli soldiers were more cautious about attacking women, but casualty statistics demonstrate that soldiers did not discriminate along age or gender lines, and certainly not on the basis of wearing a headscarf. Nevertheless this last argument became a self-fulfilling prophecy; the few women in Gaza who resisted wearing the *hijab* stood out as political activists and became a target for the military. When soldiers attacked and killed women regardless of their dress, *hijab* proponents argued that wearing a headscarf would prevent such incidents from dishonoring the family. Thus, political crimes were transformed into sexual ones.

The final argument was the most honest—wearing a *hijab* will head off attacks by religious youths. At this point it became clear that this "intifada *hijab*" was not about modesty, respect, nationalism, or the imperatives of activism, but about the power of religious groups to impose themselves by attacking secularism and nationalism at their most vulnerable points: issues of women's liberation. Many women cite December 1988 as a watershed of the *hijab* campaign. By then it was a matter of commitment for women not to wear the headscarf. Walking down a street unscarved meant dealing with a chorus of boys shouting "*tahajjubi*" (veil yourself), often followed by a shower of stones. "I was always being harassed when I went outside without [a headscarf]," one woman from Shati camp recounted.

> Once I got into a fight with some youth from Rimal [the wealthiest neighborhood in Gaza] who told me to wear it and that I wasn't modest. I told them they were cowards who spent their time telling women about modesty but never threw a stone at a soldier and never went near a demonstration. I told them that Rimali women wearing *hijab* were much less modest than I am—with

their expensive colored silk long dresses and their faces covered in makeup. They said, "Wear a kilo of makeup, but put on a *mandil* [scarf]."

By the summer of 1989, a number of women who had actively resisted wearing a headscarf started donning one in certain contexts, solely out of fear. They and others who refused to wear the *hijab* understood that the campaign was about the social and political future to which the intifada would lead. "Small things have big consequences in the future," was the analysis of one activist woman from Nasr neighborhood. "I don't wear the *hijab* because I don't want to live in an Islamic state."

A national political response came only in August 1989, after a series of incidents in July brought the issue to a head. First, there were signs that the *hijab* campaign was beginning to spread to the West Bank. For the first time, eggs and verbal abuse were lobbed at bareheaded women in parts of Jerusalem's Old City and in Hebron. This was compounded by a pivotal incident in Gaza City, where two activist women were publicly attacked in a main market although they were wearing headscarves. This was clearly a political attack on the women and their party. Moreover, the incident escalated almost to the level of a mob attack on the women. The instigators were caught and tried by the women activists' popular committee. Their sentence was to apologize to the women's families and to pay a fine of JD 3,000 ($4,500).

THE HIJAB AND THE UNIFIED LEADERSHIP

The next UNLU leaflet (no. 43) finally included a statement on the question of women and the *hijab*: "Let bygones be bygones. All disputes serve the enemy and its collaborators. The UNLU condemns the attacks by radical groups on Palestinian women in Jerusalem, Hebron, and Gaza." A more elaborate statement appeared as an appendix to this leaflet in Gaza:

> In this appendix we would like to raise the issue which has been at the center of many heated debates . . . the issue of women and their role. Woman as we perceive her, besides being a mother, daughter, sister, or wife, is an effective human being and full citizen with all rights and responsibilities. . . .
> We specify the following points:
>
> 1. We are against excessive vanity in personal dress and use of cosmetics during these times. This applies to the same degree for men and women.
> 2. We believe that any dispute outside the purview of the occupation and its various offices should be resolved and settled in a democratic way with any suggestion offered in the course of normal constructive discussion or advice.
> 3. We should value highly the role women have played in our society during these times in achieving our national goals and confronting the occupation and they should not be punished without cause.

4. The phenomenon of harassing women contradicts the traditions and norms of our society as well as our accepted attitudes about women. At the same time it denigrates the patriotism and humanity of each female citizen.

5. Nobody has the right to accost women and girls in the street on the basis of their dress or the absence of a headscarf.

6. The Unified Leadership will chase these hooligans and will stop such immature and unpatriotic actions, especially when it is found that many such hooligans consistently engage in their own suspicious activities.

Soon after, graffiti appeared on the walls in Gaza proclaiming: "Those caught throwing stones at women will be treated as collaborators," and "Women have a great role in the intifada and we must respect them." Leaflet no. 43 was followed by a statement from the Higher Council for Women, a forum of the four women's committees, which also blamed Israeli authorities and collaborators for the attacks on women.

The specific circumstances in Gaza brought to bear both traditional and intifada mechanisms of conflict resolution. Because of the lack of an independent judiciary or police force, most internal disputes in Gaza were handled through *sulha* (mediation) between families by a respected political or religious figure. With the organization of popular committees during the intifada, much of this work has been done by activist youth (*shabab*). The use of the *sulha* in this context has both positive and negative implications for women. The *sulha,* in addition to the UNLU's statement, defined attacks on women as a social and political crime. It was in this sense a political statement about social relations (as well as a financial deterrent). Some women, however, feel that the *sulha* only fed into traditional conceptions of women by involving women's families and treating the issue as a question of honor, and viewing women not as political individuals, but as family property.

The UNLU statement had an almost immediate impact. In a matter of days women seemed to have the power of the intifada on their side. Men who dared to tell a woman to cover her head could be accused of considering themselves greater than the Unified Leadership. The UNLU statement was important in immediately stopping the verbal and physical abuse of women by young men. But it was incapable of reversing the overall effect of the campaign, which had already succeeded in positioning women's dress and behavior as appropriate subjects of political discipline, or as sites for the reproduction of the social and, ultimately, the physical integrity of the intifada.

Many women questioned why it had taken so long for the Unified Leadership to take a stand, and why the Higher Council for Women did not act until after Leaflet no. 43 was issued. The sentiment of women activists was articulated by a woman from Shati Camp: "When the leaflet came out, I wasn't happy. I was angry because it was so late. If they had done it months ago we wouldn't be where we are now. . . . Once you put on the *hijab*, it's very difficult to take it off."

In fact, because the Unified Leadership took so long to act, some women believed that there was tacit support for the *hijab* campaign. "I remember some women in the [women's] committee saying that they wore it because the UNLU didn't condemn it. Therefore they must be for it," explained another woman from Shati Camp.

Why did the Unified Leadership take so long to issue a statement? Activist men told women in Gaza that either the UNLU saw the issue as too divisive or, even worse, as secondary. A number of activist women had a third hypothesis, which motivated them in their refusal to wear the *hijab*. They believed that certain elements within the Unified Leadership, while not supportive of the *hijab* campaign, were interested in forging an alliance with the newly emergent Hamas. They claimed that Fatah, with its poor record on women's rights, its historical links to the Muslim Brothers, and its fear of the left as a mass force was the faction behind this move. Yet leftist and secularist forces did not give priority to combating the *hijab* campaign either. The inability or reluctance of activist men (both of Fatah and the left) indicated the weakness of left and feminist agendas in the West Bank and Gaza. Perhaps simply because men were not the immediate victims of the campaign, they did not fully appreciate its long-term implications.

A reading of Leaflet no. 43 may offer more clues about the delay in addressing the issue and the reluctance of the left and secularist forces to take it up on the ground. The leaflet's main priority is not to roll back the suppression of women but to arrest the potential for disunity caused by attacks on women. Further, instead of active self-criticism, the leaflets of the UNLU and the Higher Council for Women blame the attacks against women on the enemy—the occupation forces and their collaborators. The remarks about traditional social norms are also devoid of self-criticism or responsibility. Both statements claim that the acts "are foreign to our traditions and norms of our society." Finally, both leaflets refer positively to religion in society—explicitly or more generally as religious values. All this bespeaks a defensive and apologetic stance vis-à-vis the Islamist movement, and more specifically toward Hamas.

Placing the *hijab* campaign (at least its more violent aspects) on the shoulders of the occupation forces and their collaborators remains problematic. There was a long tradition of the Israeli General Security Services (GSS) using "modesty" to manipulate women prisoners and their families, especially to force confessions. But neither the UNLU nor the Higher Council for Women acknowledged the extent to which nationalist forces accepted the terms of the *hijab* campaign. Its promulgation by religious groups and the opposition to women's political independence by conservative elements in Palestinian culture were never adequately addressed.

Although leaflet no. 43 dealt a blow to undemocratic processes and validated in words women's right to choose at a critical moment, its title, "A Call for Unity," indicates the absence of self-criticism. Keeping the religious groups in the fray and the national consensus going was deemed more important than confronting sexism and reactionary elements. Ultimately, this victimized not only women but also the left and secular forces.

COLLABORATION AND SOCIAL MORALITY

Subsequent events validated the foresight of the Gaza women who resisted the *hijab* campaign. By 1994 Hamas was the largest political movement after Fatah, and was perceived as the only movement powerful enough to represent an alternative to Fatah's nationalist hegemony—something few nationalists would have believed possible at the outbreak of the intifada.[12] Equally important has been Hamas's effect on the discourses of Palestinian nationalism. It has popularized the notion that its version of social morality is fundamental to Palestinian nationalism and national identity.

Hamas's success in transforming nationalist discourse and practice was based on potentialities provided by the nationalist movement itself. The *hijab* campaign was the turning point in redirecting the focus of the intifada, but it only accelerated a process already under way. By the end of 1988 there was a move away from activism focused solely on confronting the external enemy of the occupation to activism simultaneously focused on cleansing Palestinian society of elements deemed to make it vulnerable to that enemy.

Even before Hamas's rise, the nationalist culture of the intifada contained moralistic edicts such as the closing of restaurants and cinemas, banning wedding parties and other "frivolous" and joyous types of behavior. The UNLU's leaflet condemning the *hijab* campaign expressed this moralism: "We are against excessive vanity in personal dress and use of cosmetics during these times." These sentiments reflected the assessment that Israel had succeeded in dominating the population not only by force but also by promoting materialism and pursuit of the good life. They also contained an implicit critique of those classes that had shunned nationalist resistance to focus on private gain, as well as the power blocs of regional notables and political bosses who had prospered on the patronage systems of Jordan and the PLO. The UNLU's calls for home production of foodstuffs was more about creating a consciousness of hardship and national sacrifice than a realistic call for economic self-sufficiency.

The *hijab* campaign took up the moralism of the discourse of the intifada while quietly subverting it. Moral discourse was mobilized against women. Nationalist correctness shifted from secular puritanism to a discourse of moral rectitude that included modes of behavior loosely associated with religion.

This shift was clearest in the definition and treatment of collaboration. Spontaneous and random attacks on armed collaborators in 1988 by outraged unarmed members of their communities developed, in 1989, into regularized attacks and killings, by armed underground strike forces, against people accused of secretly collaborating with Israeli intelligence forces. Israel's massive redeployment of collaboration as a counterinsurgency measure at the end of 1988 made confronting the phenomenon a strategic priority for the national movement and Hamas.[13] Hamas's broad definition of collaboration led to the arbitrary branding of seemingly innocent individuals as collaborators and also allowed moral policing of society to become part of the intifada. Hamas regarded as collaborators not only those who cooperated with Israeli intelligence but also drug addicts, alcoholics, users of pornography, and those engaging in illicit sexual relations or even social gender mixing—people it accused variously of "ideological," "political," "economic," and "moral" collaboration.[14] With this last definition and its operationalization, Hamas was able to conflate individual behavior and social morality with religio-nationalist order—especially in relation to women's behavior.

Although Hamas does not seem to have attacked economic, ideological, or political collaborators, many Palestinians killed or attacked were found guilty on the basis of immoral behavior. In a case study of the 121 people attacked as collaborators in Nusayrat Refugee Camp in Gaza throughout the intifada, over half were accused of social, moral, and criminal behavior, not of providing information or assistance to the security services.[15] In the same report, seven out of ten women attacked were accused solely of "moral offenses." The report claims that the Fatah Hawks were responsible for the majority of collaborator deaths in West Bank and Gaza, but the critical debates about collaborator killings following the Gulf war were overwhelmingly aimed at Hamas, which was regarded as the main instigator of the phenomenon.[16] The fact that Fatah was responsible for a majority of the killings only confirms that the two were engaged in a turf war, competing on terrain originally marked out by Hamas.[17]

Following the *hijab* campaign and during the period of national obsession with collaboration (1990–92), most Gazans, especially women, lived in a constant state of fear. Questions about any woman could be raised if she acted differently, if she talked to men too openly, if she dressed up a bit, or if she smoked. Everyday interactions between unrelated men and women in Gaza became overdetermined by the context's potential for danger. The dominance of the discourse of morality and its terrifying obverse, accusations of being a collaborator, could be read in the leaflets or newspapers, but even more so in the small interactions of everyday life. In mixed-sex training courses, adult women would separate themselves onto one side of the classroom. In public, women would keep interactions with men to a minimum; laughing or chatting with merchants could be taken as suspect behavior. In some areas of Gaza, a woman who did not have a good reason to leave the house would stay home—so as not to raise the suspicions of neighbors.[18] Schoolgirls, constantly harangued by masked youth who regularly entered classrooms ordering girls not to loiter after school and to beware of schoolmates who might try to organize them into a collaborator network, had to be especially vigilant.

CONSEQUENCES FOR THE WOMEN'S MOVEMENT

Another outcome of the rise of Hamas in Palestine has been the rise of women's resistance to it. If Hamas succeeded to some extent in Islamizing Palestinian national culture, it simultaneously succeeded in bringing parts of the Palestinian women's movement to a new feminist awareness. As many writers have now made clear, the Palestinian women's movement may have been strong on the mobilization of women for nationalism, but it generally preferred not to openly confront women's social oppression.[19]

The national movement's weak response to the *hijab* campaign, as well as the campaign's success, shocked the progressive wing of the women's movement into realizing that ignoring social issues had been extremely shortsighted. It also led some of the leaders of women's committees to reassess their overall political operating mode. Following the *hijab* campaign, a number of women leaders in political factions began to question the traditional strategy of mobilizing women for the national movement to garner points with the various factional leaderships to be cashed in for women's rights after statehood.[20] The slow and weak response to the *hijab* campaign by (male) factional leaderships showed how little commitment they had to women's liberation when it came to *real politik*. Further, it became clear that Hamas was gaining ground by proffering a social agenda in the vacuum left by the national movement, which preferred to evade issues like the role of the family, women's rights, and the construction of social life.

The first evidence of this realization came in December 1990, at a conference in Jerusalem diplomatically entitled "The Intifada and Some Women's Social Issues." It was perhaps the first such event for the various factions and elements of the women's movement, discussing issues like the growing prevalence of early marriage; the oppression of women within the family; the marginalization of women in political decision making; and the imposition of the *hijab* in Gaza.[21] The central but largely unarticulated focus of the conference was the impact of the Islamist movement on everyday life and, ultimately, on the direction of the uprising. Strands of the women's movement have gone on to develop a social agenda for women and to organize programs and activities on social and political issues once considered taboo by the national movement.[22]

THE HIJAB AND THE AUTHORITY

At the two extremes, the women's movement and Hamas defined competing visions of a Palestinian social world. The establishment of the Palestinian National Authority (PNA)—a political body encompassing all the contradictory social groups, political forces, and ideological trends within Fatah both inside and outside Palestine—added a new dynamic in this battle. The arrival of the PNA in Gaza in July 1994 created a general but superficial social openness. Record numbers of Gazans deluged the beaches (off limits to all, but especially for women, throughout much of the intifada). Many women are reclaiming public space. Al-Azhar University is showing record levels of female enrollment, the shopping areas are once again full of women, and women are showing up in record numbers at public cultural events. Three women I interviewed in 1989 who finally succumbed to the *hijab* campaign have, since the Declaration of Principles or the arrival of the PNA, ceased wearing a headscarf. It is no longer strange to see women in Gaza City walking bareheaded.

These reactions can be read as critiques of the social repression promoted by Hamas. They also express society's relief after an oppressive military occupation and a desire to experience some of the fruits of the normalization of everyday life. But this flowering of social openness is not the product of the social hegemony of the Tunis-based Fatah apparatus in Gaza. It expresses Fatah's political hegemony within the PNA, Gazans' celebration of the end of occupation, and the population's assumption that Hamas will not try to directly impose its social will in the presence of the PNA.

The culture of the PNA exhibits all the contradictions of the various social and political forces that have been brought into it. The Authority's dominant cadres in Gaza are from Tunis, and have brought with them the culture of the resistance established in Lebanon, but it seems to have lost much of its popular class component in the Tunis period. This social bloc within the PNA adopts a classic Arab nationalist stance on women's role in nation building: token women figures in the government; wives of the elite as the representatives of national womanhood; and a preference for modernist appearances (i.e., women police, women in the pink collar professions, family restaurants, and clubs). It also exhibits the classic nationalist avoidance of changing the real underpinnings of women's oppression by addressing legislation, or unequal power relations. It has given only a handful of women public roles in the PNA in Gaza (Umm Jihad in charge of Social Welfare and former fighter Fatima Birnawi in charge of the women's police force). Both women have taken public but nonvocal stands against the *hijab*.[23] None of the female bureaucrats from Tunis wear head-scarves and, because it has been so associated with the Hamas, Gazan women have heard it is preferable not to wear one when looking for a government job.

This Tunis-based Fatah culture fits well with the salon culture of Gaza's elite resident families—an important component of their local class base.[24] Much more pivotal to PNA rule, though, are the local Fatah party cadres, especially the activists who led the intifada on the ground. The Authority has been very careful to bring large numbers of them into the military and security apparatus and has taken on almost all of the Fatah Hawks into the Preventive Security Apparatus (PSA), responsible for internal se-curity and intelligence gathering. Unlike the army, the PSA is almost com-pletely made up of local Palestinians and has been given very broad powers while operating in a legal vacuum. It is made up of young men who, on the whole, came of age during the intifada and carry with them all the social and political attitudes dominant over the past few years. Thus, besides arresting (and sometimes torturing) suspected opposition members, they have rounded up people for cases such as drug dealing, alcoholism, and adultery—continuing the tradition of the Fatah Hawks.[25] Ultimately, this suggests that while the Authority nominally adopts the classic Arab nation-alist modernist approach to social and gender relations, on the ground it is still competing with Hamas, using a discourse of social morality.

As of early 1995, the PNA's ability to lead remains hampered by its failure to bring its main opponent, Hamas, under its hegemony. Despite events like the November 18, 1994 massacre of Hamas demonstrators at Gaza's Pal-estine mosque, Fatah clearly envisions a power sharing strategy with Hamas. The women's movement has, through its various activities, been arguing that there is an alternative: strengthen the women's movement and women's agendas in the wider society and Hamas will be weakened. However, while the Authority sometimes gives the women's movement guarded support, for the most part it intends to implement its narrow vision of women's status within confines acceptable to Hamas.[26]

NOTES

Editors' note: This chapter is an update of an article originally written in the winter of 1989 in response to the imposition of the *hijab* on women in Gaza, published in *Middle East Report* no. 164/5.

1. See, for example, Edward Said's statement in "Intifada and Indepen-dence," in Zachary Lockman and Joel Beinin (eds.), *Intifada: The Palestinian Up-rising against Israeli Occupation* (Boston: South End Press, 1989), p. 20: "During the intifada, however, women came to the fore as equal partners in the struggle. They

confronted Israeli (male) troops; they shared in decision making; they were no longer left at home, or given menial tasks, but did what the men did, without fear or complexes."

2. Ze'ev Schiff and Ehud Ya'ari, *Intifada: The Palestinian Uprising, Israel's Third Front* (New York: Simon and Schuster, 1990), p. 118, note that Israeli soldiers were stunned at the presence and militancy of large numbers of women in the mass confrontations that marked the first eight months of the intifada.

3. Of the many studies on Palestinian folk dress, only Shelagh Weir, *Palestinian Costume* (Austin: University of Texas Press, 1989), actually historicizes the different forms of headcovering.

4. 'Isam al-Husayni, from the Gaza branch of the elite Jerusalem family, was the first woman in Gaza to go out without any headcovering as a conscious political act in 1952.

5. This ability to signify community membership is also flexible. Umm Samir Muhanna (born 1942) has worn three entirely different outfits in accordance with her community of residence. As a young refugee girl from the destroyed village of Masmiyya, she wore a simple version of her village of origin's embroidered *thawb*. After marrying and moving to the Gaza village of Shuja'iyya she began wearing the plain black *thawb* of Gaza village women. When she and her husband moved to Shati refugee camp in the mid-1970s, she took up the uniform of the camp women, the *da'ir* and *shasha*.

6. This aspect of Palestinian religiosity has been documented by folklorists, but largely ignored by historians. See the articles of Philip Baldensperger in *Palestine Exploration Fund Quarterly Statement:* "Peasant Folklore in Palestine" (1893): 203–18; "Religion of the Fellahin of Palestine: Answers to Questions" (1893): 307–20; "The Immovable East: Religion, Feasts, Processions" (1920): 161–66. See also Tewfiq Canaan, *Mohammedan Saints and Sanctuaries in Palestine* (Jerusalem: Ariel, 1927). On Gaza, see Salim Mubayyid, *Malamih al-shakhsiyya al-filastiniyya fi amthaliha al-sha'biyya* (Cairo: al-Matba'a al-Misriyya al-'Amma li'l-Kitab, 1990). I deal with the subject more fully in "Between Heaven and Earth: Transformations in Religiosity and Labor among Southern Palestinian Peasant and Refugee Women, 1920–1993," unpublished Ph.D. dissertation, Temple University, Department of Anthropology, May 1994.

7. For example, the introduction to a text used in the religious curriculum of the Gaza secondary schools during the Egyptian administration states: "We want the student to get from the study [of the pre-Islamic and early Islamic literature] an understanding of the great developments that the appearance of Islam brought, changing the life of ignorance [*jahiliyya*], and creating from it a new life. . . . When the student receives the heritage of the old literature, he increases his understanding of Arab society and he fills his identity with his Arabism and is strengthened in his nationalism and in the values and examples built on it." *Al-Adab wa-nusus al-balagha: al-saff al-thani min al-madaris al-thanawiyya* (Cairo: Ministry of Education, 1961), p. 3.

8. Schiff and Ya'ari, *Intifada*, pp. 55–57.

9. For an estimate of the Gaza labor force working in Israel until 1986, see Sara Roy, *The Gaza Strip: A Demographic, Economic, Social, and Legal Survey* (Jerusalem: West Bank Database Project, 1986), p. 32.

10. For a summary of al-Mujamma' social welfarism during the 1970s and early 1980s, see 'Atif 'Idwan, *Al-Shaykh Ahmad Yasin: hayatuh wa-jihaduh* (Gaza: Islamic University, 1991).

11. The Hamas leadership has attempted to rewrite the organization's early nonparticipation in the intifada, claiming that Hamas was the movement which sparked the intifada. See Ziad Abu-Amr, *Islamic Fundamentalism in the West Bank and Gaza* (Bloomington: Indiana University Press, 1994), pp. 59–89.

12. See, for example, Lisa Taraki, "The Islamic Resistance Movement in the Palestinian Uprising," in Lockman and Beinin, *Intifada*, pp. 171–77.

13. On Israel's reorganization of its collaborator networks, see Salih 'Abd al-Jawad and Yizhar Be'er, *Collaborators in the Occupied Territories: Human Rights Abuses and Violations* (Jerusalem: B'Tselem, 1994), p. 163.

14. On Hamas's five categories of collaboration, see ibid., pp. 173–76.

15. Ibid., p. 146.

16. In the summer of 1992 Haydar 'Abd al-Shafi, Faysal Husayni, and others condemned the uncritical killing of collaborators in a debate in the local press. The 'Izz al-Din al-Qassam Brigade of Hamas killed two collaborators on their doorstep in front of the wife and children of a Gaza journalist, Tawfiq Abu Khusa, who actively criticized this practice, as a warning. Ibid., pp. 176–78.

17. Between April 1992 and the end of 1993, Hamas killed more than 150 suspected collaborators, the vast majority of them in Gaza. This stepped-up effort followed the October 1991 Madrid talks and was understood by most observers to be Hamas's attempt to garner popular support in the face of an impending peace agreement which would strengthen Fatah. In response, Fatah Hawks increased their own collaborator-killing activities.

18. A household survey carried out in the summer of 1992 in Gaza and the West Bank found that 56 percent of women surveyed in Gaza and 47 percent in the West Bank claimed they were unable to move freely within their communities. Among young women and unmarried women, 80 percent of fifteen- to nineteen-year-olds claimed their mobility was restricted. See Marianne Heiberg, Geir Ovensen et al., *Palestinian Society in Gaza, West Bank and Arab Jerusalem: A FAFO Survey of Living Conditions* (Oslo: FAFO, 1993), pp. 306–7.

19. Islah Jad, "From Salons to Popular Committees: Palestinian Women, 1919–1989," in Jamal R. Nassar and Roger Heacock (eds.), *Intifada: Palestine at the Crossroads* (New York: Praeger Publishers, 1990), pp. 125–42; Lisa Taraki, "Mass Organizations in the West Bank," in *Readings in Contemporary Palestinian Society 2* (Birzeit: Birzeit University, 1989), pp. 1–32; Joost Hiltermann, *Behind the Intifada: Labor and Women's Movements in the Occupied Territories* (Princeton: Princeton University Press, 1991).

20. This applies to the 'Abd Rabbu wing of the Democratic Front for the Liberation of Palestine (now FIDA, the Palestinian Democratic Union) as well as the former Communist Party (now the Palestine People's Party). The position of the

Popular Front for the Liberation of Palestine women's committee has been contradictory. It sponsored gender actions and events, then embraced the party's alliance with Hamas in the 1994 Bir Zeit student council elections.

21. Women's Studies Committee, *The Intifada and Some Women's Social Issues: A Conference Held in al-Quds al-Sharif/Jerusalem on December 14, 1990* (Jerusalem: Women's Studies Committee/Bisan Center, 1991).

22. Issues addressed recently include violence against women in the home and the oppressiveness of existing legislation for women, especially the laws of personal status. In some committees, the focus has shifted from recruiting women for the nationalist factions to mobilizing them around gender issues using classic feminist consciousness-raising methods. However, there has not been a comprehensive feminist revolution in the Palestinian women's movement; many of the earlier political strategies and activities continue.

23. Umm Jihad set an important symbolic precedent by not wearing a headscarf on the day she and Yasir 'Arafat arrived in Gaza. At the time it was rumored that she was asked to wear a headscarf before addressing the rally in Gaza City but pointedly refused. Fatima Birnawi has made it clear to women police recruits that they cannot wear a headscarf if they want to be part of the force and, according to one recruit, has encouraged them to stop wearing one off duty.

24. Many such women are now being elevated as representatives of modern educated Palestinian womanhood, while Gaza's grassroots women activists of the intifada are being marginalized by the PNA.

25. In one of the most famous incidents, the head of West Bank PSA, Jibril Rajub, ordered a journalist kidnapped from the American Colony Hotel in Jerusalem to question him about charges of adultery.

26. A draft Palestinian Constitution presented by its author from Tunis (Anis al-Qasim) to a conference in Jerusalem in February 1994 made no mention of women's rights—a clear retreat from the 1989 Declaration of Independence. Women's movement leaders fought to have gender equality included in the document. Under the auspices of the General Union of Palestinian Women, women articulated "Principles of Women's Rights" to be incorporated into the constitution and collected thousands of signatures supporting it. This document, ratified by all the factional women's committees, as well as by many of the more conservative women leaders from the charitable societies, calls for full equality between men and women in all spheres of life based on the 1979 United Nations Convention on the Elimination of All Forms of Discrimination against Women. However, when the document was presented at a press conference in Jerusalem in October 1994, Intisar al-Wazir (Umm Jihad) brought a message from President 'Arafat saying that he supported all forms of women's rights as long as they did not contradict Islamic *shari'a*.

18

"Hassiba Ben Bouali, If You Could See Our Algeria": Women and Public Space in Algeria

Susan Slyomovics

On January 2, 1992, Algerian feminists demonstrated against the Islamic Salvation Front (FIS) and its victory in the national elections of December 26, 1991. Their target was the Islamist assault on women's rights and the threat of violence against women. One of their posters addressed a martyred sister, a *mujahida*, killed by the French during the battle of Algiers in 1956–57: "*Hassiba Ben Bouali, Si tu voyais notre Algérie*" (Hassiba Ben Bouali, if you could see our Algeria). At the same time, women marching in Oran waved a similar slogan: "*Hassiba Ben Bouali, Nous ne te trahirons pas*" (Hassiba Ben Bouali, we will not betray you).

In Gillo Pontecorvo's 1967 film, *The Battle of Algiers,* a famous scene shows three Algerian women—one of them represents Ben Bouali—in the act of donning alien European dress in order to pass freely through the French military cordon around the walled Casbah. They enter the French colonial city and leave guns or bombs for Algerian freedom fighters. In the published script, each of the women

> stand[s] in front of a large mirror. [Hassiba] removes the veil from her face. Her glance is hard and intense. Her face is expressionless. The mirror reflects a large part of the room: it is a bedroom.... Every action is performed precisely and carefully. They are like three actresses preparing for the stage. But there is no gaiety; no one is speaking. Only silence emphasizes the detailed rhythm of their transformation. Her blouse and short skirt to her knees ... make-up, lipstick, high-heeled shoes, silk stockings. ...[1]

The camera follows Hassiba as she crosses boundaries: from interior domestic space to the exterior public street, from Arab Casbah to French *nouvelle ville,* from "native" to "colonial" space. The language of the film makes clear that her journey is not only real but highly symbolic, from what Western anthropologists of the Maghrib would call the secretive, cloistered, domestic, female world to its binary opposite, the male and public exterior domain. Domestic space has traditionally defined and reproduced social relations between Algerian men and women; but space outside the home, from which women have been traditionally excluded and in which male ambitions have always been produced and played out, becomes, with Hassiba's journey, the arena not only for a national but also for a gender struggle.

During the Algerian war of independence, women militants often discarded the veil, the traditional North African *haik*, to overcome the spatial segregation that reinforced prevailing values of Algerian men and French society. The absent veil confounded the one unifying perception of what defines the Algerian woman, characterized by Frantz Fanon as "she who hides behind a veil."[2]

Most Algerian women did not follow Hassiba's example; they neither discarded the veil nor placed bombs. Even before the war of independence, during the colonial administration, according to Fanon, the veil became "the bone of contention" in a battle between colonizer and colonized, and the subjects of colonialism "display[ed] a surprising force of inertia." But if women at that time were not able to join in a political discourse still conducted in French by both sides, they were nevertheless visible in their silence. Marnia Lazreg's important work, *The Eloquence of Silence*, describes how Algerian women, primarily Arabophone and illiterate, were structurally marginalized by both colonial and native societies, yet used the weight of their silent physical presence to play an important role in the revolution.[3] Veiled women participated in numerous anti-French marches and strikes, their thoughts and intentions as unknown and as unknowable as their physical appearance—a shocking protrusion of a necessarily private world into the public and political domain.

SPACE AND STATUS

The interplay between society's spatial arrangements and the status of women reveals much about the ideological underpinnings of the Algerian state since independence. The violent deaths of women that are now being reported can be understood as a consequence of a specific policy of National Liberation Front (FLN) rule since independence, namely its emphasis on education and industrialization. This entailed state encouragement of women's presence in two new arenas of public space, the school and the factory, a radical innovation to Muslim traditionalists. In religious terms, women's presence is deemed illegitimate, *haram*. Socially they are perceived as intruders into masculine space, disturbing the equilibrium of a regulated, single-sex, urban milieu.

The short history of working women in Algeria has therefore been a troubled one. Even within factory spaces, the possibility of men and women working together (*mixité*) has been avoided. The interior space of the factory workplace is socially constructed to be the same as the outside world. The daily activities and individual behavior of women workers are shaped by structures that insure men's exercise of power over women. Statistics from Tlemcen's state-run factories show that working outside the home is generally a temporary phase in a woman's life. Most women factory workers are unmarried and from twenty to thirty years old. They work to augment family finances or to prepare financially for their own marriages, and tend to quit after marriage.[4] Thus, for complex historical, economic, and religious reasons, both women and men subscribe to economic and spatial arrangements that reinforce the legitimacy of women's lower status.

The presence and deportment of women in the workplace has continued to be controversial, subject to the ebb and flow of ideological tides. At this moment, the burning issue is the pressure being placed upon women to conform to norms of Islamic dress, and to wear the veil even in indoor workplaces. In Islamist quarters, parallels are often drawn between women in the labor force and the unauthorized presence of women in the street: both in the factory and on the street women are considered to be transgressively visible in exterior space. Women themselves resent this pressure but conform out of fear. "None of us wants to wear the veil," said Fatima B. (a pseudonymous twenty-two-year-old junior manager in a Tlemcen factory), "but fear is stronger than our convictions or our will to be free. Fear is all around us. Our parents, our brothers, are unanimous: 'Wear the veil and stay alive. This will pass.'"[5]

SANCTUARY AND VEIL

In Algeria today, the "veil" under discussion is not the traditional North African *haik* but rather the *hijab*, an article of clothing imported from the Arab East. *Hijab*, a word with many meanings, is now often used as a synonym for modest Islamic dress for women. In Iran and Afghanistan, this may mean a *chador*, a head-to-toe cloak that envelops the female form; in Algeria, it means a headscarf, often worn with a loose gown.

Opposition to the veil is not universal among women who hope to leave traditional constraints behind. In a series of interviews among women students at the University of Algiers, Laetitia Bucaille discovered that Islamist students believe that the *hijab* forces a rearrangement of the male public sphere to make room for the presence of women. It is a badge of religious and political allegiance, but the students also claimed that women who wear the *hijab* escape the male gaze and are therefore exempted from the dominant male group's ability to control social space by means of sexual harassment or sexual objectification of females. It was precisely their protective veiling, these women insisted, that allowed them to escape the traditional female roles of mother and wife in order to pursue professional, educational, and social lives necessarily conducted in public. "I have six brothers and I am the only girl and the youngest," said one student. "Before, everyone used to say: 'Where were you? Where are you going?' Now I am more free, I go to the mosque, even at night during Ramadan. They allow me everything."[6]

In other words, Islamist university women, an elite group, have built on the precedent set by the veiled women of the revolution. Indiscriminate mixing of the sexes in public places is an obstacle to the emergence of women in public space, they insist. Instead, they have articulated for themselves an image of the veiled woman—active in the social order and even on the street—as equivalent to the female body covered and protected within the home. For women to become knowledgeable, they must make their journey from the inside to the outside based on an intellectual sleight of hand that defines the two opposing areas, female interior versus male exterior, as equivalent only if the woman is veiled.

If it is the women of the Islamist movements and not the men who have constructed a new Muslim identity whose core is gender segregation, as Bucaille contends, then a different set of cultural, religious, and ideological justifications of gender segregation has emerged, profoundly altering the relationship between gender stratification and spatial institutions.[7] The views of these Islamist women, however, find little support among the FIS leadership. A FIS leader, 'Ali Ben Hadj, stated in a widely quoted interview in 1989 that

> the natural place of expression for women is the home. If she must go out, there are conditions: not to be near men and that her work is located in an exclusively feminine milieu. In our institutions and universities is it admissible to authorize mixing? It is contrary to Islamic morality. It is necessary to separate girls and boys and consecrate establishments for each sex. . . . In a real Islamic society, the woman is not destined to work and the head of state must provide her with remuneration. In this way, she will not leave her home and consecrate herself to the education of men. The woman is a producer of men, she produces no material goods but this essential thing which is the Muslim.[8]

The spirit of Ben Hadj's statement is congruent with that of the laws enshrined in Algeria's Family Code promulgated by the FLN five years earlier, in 1984.[9] These laws reduced women to the status of minors, subject to the law of father or husband, and presaged the remarkable mixture of nationalism and Islamism (an intellectual FIS-FLN accord) that secularists described much later as le fascisme vert (green fascism). Feminists protested the family code from the very beginning. On March 4, 1985, a group of women rallied in the Casbah of Algiers on the site where Hassiba Ben Bouali had been killed.

SOCIAL ORDER

Since 1991, institutional violence by the state has been matched by Islamist groups committed to the overthrow of the current regime. Emerging armed factions (*al-jama'at al-musallaha*) such as the Groupe Islamique Armé (GIA) and the Mouvement Islamique Armé (MIA) have specifically targeted women. Many women have also died in the violence directed against the intellectual elite (journalists, doctors, professors, writers, or actors), foreign nationals, the police, the military, and government officials.

Women are also assassinated because they are women—working women, unveiled women, and women active in social and political associations, categories that frequently overlap. In March 1994, a FIS/GIA communiqué warned that any woman on the streets without the veil could be assassinated; on March 30, two women students, Raziqa Meloudjemi, eighteen, and Naima Kar 'Ali, nineteen, were killed by gunmen on motorcycles while standing at an Algiers bus station.[10] In May, travel by train was forbidden because men and women shared compartments; shortly afterward, the night train between Bejaia and Algiers was attacked and torched. At the beginning of the 1994 school year, the GIA threatened death to the seven million primary and high school students and their 320,000 teachers unless the norms of Islamic education were followed—the separation of boys and girls, the veiling of women professors and girl students, and the elimination of gymnastics. Earlier, Amnesty International condemned the killing of Katia Bengana, a seventeen-year-old high school student in Blida, shot on February 28 after receiving threats that she would die unless she wore the *hijab*.

Operating as a mirror image to the Islamist violence against women are the activities of a lesser-known vigilante group, the Organization of Free Young Algerians, OJAL (l'Organisation des jeunes Algériens libres), which has ties to the government and claims to represent the secularism of the FLN regime. For them, too, women's spatial boundaries are at issue. They warn women against wearing the *hijab,* and in retaliation for Islamist killings of unveiled women they have killed two veiled women. They have called for reopening public places where women have traditionally congregated, such as beauty salons and public baths, places ordered closed by the Islamists.

Secularist and Islamist groups are attempting to define and promote diametrically opposed positions by using similar strategies. One of these is to control women's access to resources or knowledge by controlling space. To be male in the midst of Algeria's political turmoil means to express a logic of power relations according to which the dominant group, whatever its political ideology, can and must constrain women's movements and actions. What we see unfolding in Algeria is the competition of two very similar demarcations of the spaces that women are permitted to enter or traverse. Secularists allow women a modicum of movement outside the home, especially at beauty salons or baths. These spaces are precisely those not shared by the two sexes. They may encourage female sociability and solidarity that would not be permissible if women never left their homes. Islamists view even so limited a use of public space by women as a threat to their social order. But women are allowed to go to the mosques, interior spaces controlled by the FIS, free of unsupervised and potentially subversive socializing.

Islamist gender segregation extends beyond actual occasions where the sexes might mix in public life; it aims to eliminate even the possibility of such an occurrence. Municipal governments run by the FIS have banned concerts, cinemas, public dancing, wedding ceremonies in hotels, women on the beaches, and women in the municipal cultural centers and recreation halls that they fund and control.

Women in public places, veiled or unveiled, die for the interpretations that secular or religious fanatics attach to their presence and appearance. Their dangerous and circumscribed situation is described in a letter from a friend who teaches at the University of Oran. In practical and symbolic ways, she finds that women have become prisoners in their own homes:

> As for us, we have become accustomed to this situation: here a death announcement, and there, the fear. The daily count of assassinations no longer frightens; we hardly pay any attention. This is, of course, true only on the surface. In reality we have all become anguished, sick and neurotic. Faces are gray, conversations morbid. Laughter has deserted our country. We stay in spite of it all. All this gives us the feeling of being new "moujahidin" and the satisfaction of serving something—even if it means being stupid victims of blind terrorism. We lead a dull life. Work, home, with nothing extra because one must be shut in inside one's home. Even the rare cultural and social events at the university are gone; at least they used to allow us to see each other. As for me, I am like the rest. I take care of my daughters, my job, and my house. My job allows me to hold on. I can escape the problems of Algeria in speaking of the medieval age in Spain. In fact, everything is ruined in Algeria: political life, social life and even family life. Terrorism has installed itself at every level, even in the family unit. We head towards barbarism.

Some women cooperate with the system of stratification out of religious beliefs. "Knowing that I have a message as an educated Muslim woman, I have two choices," Leila, twenty-one, told Bucaille. "The first is to have a family. God created me in order to accomplish a certain mission and one of them is to have a family, have children and transmit this message so that they too could transmit it to others."[11] Others see no alternative and do so out of fear. Still other women struggle against attacks on their rights.

ISLAMIST APPEAL

Hassiba Ben Bouali is one of a long list of women activists and martyrs, *mujahidat* and *shahidat*, who fought for Algerian independence against the French colonial system. There were others: Myriem Ben Miloud, Djamila Bouaza, Djamila Bouhired, Djamila Boupacha, Zohra Driff, Bahia Hocine, Samia Lakhdari, and Zhor Zerari (as well as many women whose anonymous lives and deaths were the subject of Assia Djebar's 1978 documentary, *Nouba des femmes de Chenoua*). They operated clandestinely, often forced to renounce home and family. In a chilling reprise, one of the prominent feminist leaders, Khalida Messaoudi of the Mouvement pour la République (MPR), has gone underground in Algiers, forced to abandon her apartment and her work as a mathematics professor. In a recent interview she announced her readiness to take up arms:

> Unless the MPR to which I belong decides otherwise, for my part, I am ready to take up weapons. Let no one say that I call for civil war. We who kill no one and defend the values of secularism and equality are the victims of violence. Concerning women, what is going on at this moment in Algeria is not a confrontation between a majority and an opposition, but a war between two blueprints for society, one that appeals to the Enlightenment and human rights, the other marking a return to obscurantism and religious fanaticism. The coming of an Islamist state would be the negation of citizenship and Algerian identity.[12]

Like many feminists throughout the Arab world, Messaoudi understands that restrictions imposed in the name of Islam disguise patriarchal structures intent on seizing or maintaining political and military power. "I think I understand why the fundamentalists (*intégristes*) are powerful," she says.

> The FLN had destroyed all the traditionally valued places, the places of the inside (*les lieux de dedans*), but without proposing others: only 4.2 percent of women work in Algeria. The Family Code came and aggravated the situation. The FIS, for those who accept to wear the veil, offers them all "some places outside" (*des lieux dehors*), for example, the mosque. There, they are allowed what even the FLN denies them: a political voice. FIS women's "cells" debate every subject all over Algeria. This way they have the impression of acquiring a certain power and power that interests them.

The FIS has reversed stereotypical value judgments about women's spaces. It has accorded women two things. First, it has assigned a higher status to the feminine knowledge associated with the home and child raising, to the extent that the Islamists have raised even the value of women's home life above the status of women working in sexually segregated workplaces. Second, they have found room for women's study groups, monitored within FIS-controlled mosques. Islamist women can therefore argue that spatial segregation works to women's advantage by allowing them to develop networks and power independently of men.

Messaoudi, when asked what secularists of her movement have to offer women that might counter the appeal of the Islamists, replied that "it is very difficult because we democrats have only in exchange a major transgression to propose: that of the street. The political street, to which one must descend to confront the single party or the religious party; the cultural street, that marks the sexual division of space in the Muslim world."[13] To move women from the female to the male side of what has been defined as the proper place of each is to challenge the FIS's religious notions of how space is divided and delimited; it is, in its view, to commit a sin. To segregate women within the workplace is to insure gender differences in earnings and positions. To restrict women forcibly to the home is to remove women from knowledge, action, and political power.

SOCIAL RESISTANCE

How do we interpret feminists demonstrating in the name of Hassiba Ben Bouali? In the Algerian war for independence, some women rejected both colonial status and the subservient roles traditionally assigned to women in Algerian society—Ben Bouali is only the best known. Most Algerian women played a less assertive role. Nevertheless, their veiled and silent participation in demonstrations and other forms of resistance marked a departure from the traditional confinement of women to the domestic sphere. Education and new social and economic opportunities for women have been part of the new order introduced by the FLN since independence. But these innovations were timid and tentative, and women's limited gains have been subject to continual challenge.

Today, many women in the social and intellectual elite, such as university students, profess fervent Muslim faith but reinterpret Islam's idea of women. It is precisely the protected status symbolized by the veil that encourages them to believe that they will be able to compete in the male public world. They are following in the footsteps of the veiled women of the revolution, not those of Ben Bouali. But these new and supposedly Islamic conceptions of women's roles are not supported by the FIS. More remarkably, the Islamist leadership's attitudes conform to legislation put in place after independence by the FLN. In other words, the factions now struggling for power in Algeria are in fundamental ideological agreement that women's social freedom must be severely restricted.

The FIS victory at the polls and the subsequent coup by the FLN have created an atmosphere in which women have the distinction of being targeted for abuse and even assassination no matter what they do. The threat to women's lives, and to their aspirations for the future, has produced an embryonic underground on the model of women militants in the war of independence. Messaoudi, unlike Ben Bouali, possesses no bombs or weapons. She has frequently called on an international community of democrats and human rights activists to denounce violations directed specifically against Algerian women. Most radical of all, the site of the domicile and domesticity is not where female resistance and subversion are located. According to Messaoudi, the point, as it was before against the French, is to take to the streets against tyranny or face death.

NOTES

1. Piernico Solinas, ed., *The Battle of Algiers,* by Gillo Pontecorvo (New York: Charles Scribner, 1973), pp. 66–67.

2. Frantz Fanon, *A Dying Colonialism* (New York: Grove Press, 1965), p. 36.

3. Marnia Lazreg, *The Eloquence of Silence: Algerian Women in Question* (New York: Routledge, 1994), p. 96. Whatever the power of silence may be, revolutionaries and feminists seem to be ready to turn it in for social equality with men.

4. Rabia Bekkar cites statistics of women workers in a Tlemcen state-run factory: 81 percent single, 8 percent married, and 11 percent widowed or divorced. Rabia Bekkar, "Territoires des femmes à Tlemcen: Pratiques et representations," *Maghreb/Machrek* 144 (1994): 133.

5. *Los Angeles Times,* April 1, 1994.

6. Laetitia Bucaille, "L'engagement islamiste des femmes en Algérie," *Maghreb/Machrek* 144 (1994), p. 111.

7. Ibid., p. 117.

8. Quoted by Elisabeth Schemla, "L'Islam et les femmes," *Le nouvel observateur,* September 22–28, 1994.

9. Ministry of Justice, *Code de la Famille (Qanun al-Usra)* (Algiers: Office des Publications Universitaires, 1986).

10. *New York Times,* March 31, 1994, p. A3.

11. Bucaille, "L'engagement islamiste des femmes en Algérie," p. 111.

12. Khalida Messaoudi, "Le voile, c'est notre étoile jaune," *Le nouvel observateur,* September 22–28, 1994.

13. Ibid.

19

Devices and Desires:
Population Policy and Gender Roles
in the Islamic Republic

Homa Hoodfar

The development of population policy in the Islamic Republic of Iran provides fertile ground for reexamining the widely held assumption that Islamist ideology is the antithesis of modernity and surely incompatible with any form of feminism. Recent strategies that the Islamic Republic has adopted to build a public consensus on the necessity for birth control and family planning indicate the flexibility and adaptability of that ideology in response to political and economic realities.

Family planning decision making is closely associated with women's socioeconomic status in society, and their autonomy and security within conjugal bonds. Women's preference for smaller families is crucial to the success of Iran's population program because the Iranian government, like governments elsewhere, has shifted responsibility for birth control from men to women. Improving women's economic and public involvement, as well as their position within the marriage institution, is crucial to this process, but at the same time fundamentally challenges the gender roles, especially the idea of female domesticity advocated by the regime as a cornerstone of its envisaged Muslim society. How has Iran's government reconciled these two different sets of priorities?

For their part, Iranian women have individually and collectively questioned the prescribed male interpretation of the proper "Islamic" role for women. Islamist women activists have used the ambivalent and contradictory ideological positions of the government to launch their women-centered interpretation of appropriate gender roles. Adopting new and creative interpretations, they have encouraged the government to introduce reforms in the areas of marriage, divorce, and education, and are agitating for more improvement in women's legal and social position.

POPULATION POLICY BEFORE AND AFTER

In 1967, Iran launched its first official population policy, and in 1970 announced the ambitious goal of reducing the population growth rate to 1 percent within twenty years. In 1973, the Pahlavi regime legalized abortion during the first trimester of pregnancy, with permission of the husband. Through a network of family planning clinics, the Ministry of Public Health made contraceptives available. The national women's organization, along with other associations, promoted and distributed contraceptives. Devices and techniques such as the IUD, tubal ligation, and vasectomy were introduced but, given the overall lack of resources, the pill became by default the contraceptive of choice.

There was already considerable demand, particularly among urban middle-income groups dissatisfied with traditional methods. Though there was little effort to extend family planning to the rural population, nationally an estimated 11 percent of women of childbearing age used some form of contraceptive.[1]

Despite considerable improvement in the GNP and per capita income, infant mortality remained very high due to the inequitable distribution of public services. But several changes were introduced to improve women's status both within the family and in the public arena, including efforts to include women in the labor market. The legal age of marriage for women was increased to eighteen, and in 1975 marriage and divorce law was reformed to limit men's arbitrary right to divorce and to enter into polygamous marriages.[2] Although implementation was problematic, the symbolic value of these moves was considerable, and conveyed to women and to the general public that women's rights were officially recognized.

With the establishment of the Islamic regime, the family planning program fell into disarray. The new regime did not formulate an explicit population policy. Many conservative leaders continued to insist that contraceptive devices had been developed by Western powers in order to subjugate oppressed nations and to limit the number of Muslims. The government officially encouraged early and universal marriage and further lowered the minimum age for marriage. Contraceptives became difficult to obtain, as the stock of modern devices, primarily imported, was soon depleted. The side effects of contraceptive pills and IUDs on women's health became a popular subject of discussion, particularly in women's religious gatherings (*sofreh*) where issues of marriage and family are traditionally discussed.[3] Iran's fertility level, not surprisingly, increased immediately after the revolution.

A 1986 national survey estimated Iran's population at over fifty million, which had a sobering impact on the more astute members of the government. The high birthrate and increase in population, together with the depressed economy and massive migration from the war zones to Tehran and other major cities, placed considerable demands on the government. The government of the oppressed, as it portrayed itself, had committed itself ideologically and constitutionally to the provision of basic amenities and equal opportunity in order to move toward a just Islamic society. The leadership was also conscious that Iranian politics is made in the major cities, where shortages and failure to meet basic needs could have severe consequences.

Pressure from more enlightened segments of the religious and political leadership resulted in an explicit pronouncement that the use of pills and other contraceptives which would temporarily stop the creation of a fetus was not *haram* (prohibited). The announcement, justified in theological terms, paved the way for the reformulation of population policies over the next few years. By 1988, the question of overpopulation and its danger, on the national and international scale, had found its way into the political speeches of various leaders. After Ayatollah Khamene'i discussed the necessity of introducing family planning in a Friday sermon, the government issued a national birth control policy, which Ayatollah Khomeini ratified shortly before his death in 1989. A Board of Family Planning, directly under the control of the Minister of Health, started its activities at once.

The population policy of the Islamic Republic differs from the prerevolution program in many important ways. The Islamic Republic has achieved considerable success in convincing the population to accept and practice family planning through a powerful consensus-building campaign and by establishing an effective network to provide affordable and reliable contraceptive means.

BUILDING NATIONAL CONSENSUS

The most outstanding innovation in the Islamic Republic's family planning policy has been the way in which the government has tried to raise general knowledge and understanding of population questions rather than limit its focus to promoting contraceptives. Political and religious leaders frequently address the importance of family planning in nationally televised speeches, and particularly in Friday sermons which publicly define the government's political and ideological lines.[4] The government has also supported research and publication on the question of population and Islamic family planning, including a compilation of medieval writings which demonstrate that family planning has been a concern of Islamic societies long before it was a Western interest.

A number of broad and overlapping themes have emerged.[5] First, the talks raise the question of whether the world can continue to support an ever increasing population, using concrete examples drawn from China, the Philippines, India, Pakistan, Bangladesh, and other developing nations. Another technique examines, in simple and accessible language, the consequences of increased population for domestic food production and dependency, and education and health care costs. By contrast, Western countries, with their low rates of growth and much more balanced population pyramids, can provide education and health care to their peoples and in this manner continue to reinforce their power over the rest of the world. Public discourse phrases it thus: Muslim nations are forced to beg food from North Americans; for reasons such as this the Prophet and other *'ulama'* (religious scholars) allowed Muslims to practice contraception in times of economic hardship. On several occasions our informants argued that family planning is among the most legitimate (*halal*) things a Muslim can do. The claim that Islam is one of the few world religions which has permitted contraception while sanctioning sexual pleasure is sometimes used to show that it is a superior and timeless faith.[6]

Another frequent theme is whether family planning (*tanzim-e-khanevadeh,* or family organization in Persian) is a public issue or a strictly individual family concern. Official speeches stress that in Muslim societies individual decisions have always been taken with much concern for the public interest, while communities have respected individual rights. If Iranians want to build an able, intelligent, educated Muslim nation, official speeches argue, they must find a balance between their individual desires as parents and what society can afford. These arguments are presented with specific comparisons to advanced nations, particularly Japan, which has come to represent a technological ideal to Iranians.

The official discourse asserts that all temporary means of contraception accord with Islamic practice, and backs this opinion with references to various Shi'i and Sunni texts and *fatwas* (religio-legal opinions). Tubal ligation and vasectomy are controversial, as they make an individual *aghim* (unable to bear children). A number of *'ulama',* however, argue that if reversal of the operation is possible, then there is no Islamic barrier. Others claim that a person who already has children cannot be considered *aghim,* but those who do not should not choose these methods. Despite some popular resistance, government-run hospitals perform such operations free of charge. The major complaint is that there are not enough specialists, particularly women, to meet the demand, and consequently there is a long waiting list for the procedures.

Abortion, the most controversial and problematic issue, officially remains illegal unless the pregnancy is judged detrimental to the psychological and physical well-being of the mother. Ironically, Ayatollah Beheshti, an important conservative leader of the revolution, outlined a theological approach which was instrumental in liberalizing the abortion law in 1973. Today, if an illegal abortion takes place during the first hundred and twenty days, before the "ensoulment" of the fetus, the person who performed the abortion has to pay a *dieh* (blood money) to the fetus's lawful heirs, usually the parents. After the time of "ensoulment," abortion is equivalent to murder and punishable by a higher blood price. In practice, medical attestations concerning the woman's health are regularly signed. All our informants, including doctors and nurses, told us that abortion was frequent, and no one had heard of a single case of a doctor being reprimanded.

A further feature of the government's approach emphasizes the effects of numerous pregnancies on the health of mothers and children. Closely spaced births mean that older children do not get the attention they deserve. Moreover, what does motherhood mean if a mother cannot enjoy her children's smiles and watch them blossom?[7] By introducing medical "facts," religious leaders argue that women should only bear children between the ages of twenty and thirty-five.

The government has worked relentlessly to create a broad consensus on family planning at the national level, hosting several widely publicized national and international conferences on population in Tehran. Additionally, there are plans to include population and the history of Islamic family planning in the national curriculum at all levels, and to include information on family planning in adult literacy classes, many of which are held in the local mosques. Although not all these goals have been realized, their existence indicates a comprehensive and sophisticated approach. There are family planning sessions for girls in the last years of high school. There are also segregated sessions for male and female workers in larger industrial establishments. Following Chinese and Indonesian models, many large workplaces include health clinics which provide contraceptives. In rural areas and smaller communities, information and discussion sessions on population and birth control methods are held in "health houses" (local clinics) or in local mosques (usually because there is no clinic or its space is limited).

The government's family planning program demonstrates an understanding of the complex web of variables which influence fertility levels. In an attempt to prevent the kind of criticism directed at the prerevolution family planning program, the Islamic Republic has paid the utmost attention to defining family planning as the prevention of unwanted pregnancies in order to improve families' and society's physical and social health. Several Ministry of Health documents underline the improvement of women's position within family and society as the cornerstone of successful family planning. In the largest health survey in the central province (Tehran), 96.7 percent of women said they agreed with family planning.[8]

THE FAMILY PLANNING NETWORK

Since 1989, when the first population policy of the Islamic Republic was formulated, the Family Planning Board has regenerated itself well beyond its prerevolution capacity in terms of research and public services. Apart from major urban hospitals and clinics, there are "health houses" in rural areas where resident nurses provide family planning services and information along with other services, although the number of centers still falls short of the regime's goals. The 16,654 existing health centers provide for only 63 percent of estimated need, and about 21 percent of rural centers are not yet served.[9]

In major cities, a lively private sector complements the government's efforts, which are directed primarily at low-income citizens. Quantities of contraceptive pills, IUDs, condoms, and several injectable contraceptives have been imported and are distributed either free of charge or at heavily subsidized prices. Vasectomy and tubal ligation are legal and available at major hospitals. Due to a lack of trained personnel, the adoption of the IUD in small communities is more problematic. Much research is directed at identifying varieties of contraceptives with the fewest side effects.

Family planning clients receive routine checkups and advice on contraceptive methods. The majority choose the pill and are provided with a monthly supply of pills or condoms. They are expected to return every month for a checkup and to renew their supply. Ostensibly this procedure is to monitor women's health, but as their supply budget is limited, officials use this strategy to ensure that only those who are committed receive supplies. Transportation and communication problems, however, mean that women cannot always return to the clinic at the appropriate time. Since irregular use decreases reliability, it may be more effective to shift to a two-month supply-and-return approach.

Despite much effort in disseminating information, reliable and efficient use of contraceptives (particularly the pill) has not yet reached its optimum level. One 1991 study covering a thousand urban and a thousand rural households in Tehran province, where the public is assumed to have easier access to information, indicated that over 25 percent of overall participants, including a considerable number of literate women, took the pill either every other night or only before intercourse. Beyond a lack of information, reasons for such behavior varied from hoping to reduce possible side effects to trying to stretch their supply of pills.

Every major study indicates that *azl* (coitus interruptus) is the most common method of contraception, although there is no effort at all by the government to promote it. Both the technical literature and government statistics indicate that men continue to play a prominent role in preventing pregnancies. But today women are the primary target of "family organization" campaigns. The common message is that while family planning should be a joint decision made by a woman and her husband, it is she who should implement the appropriate measures. Information sessions are held for men, but only the female forms of contraceptives are discussed. This suggests that the government holds women, not men, primarily responsible for implementing birth control. The Islamic Republic, despite its own rich Islamic family planning tradition, has chosen to adopt "Western" strategies and goals, with their gender biases.

Iran's family planning campaign demonstrates other contradictions that will affect its success. Despite a concerted attack on individualism in government-produced school manuals, films, soap operas, and radio programs, and the explicit goal of perpetuating a culture of interdependence between family and kin and neighbors and community, population programs are directed particularly at young women. Women's decisions, though, are highly influenced by their network—especially mothers and mothers-in-law. Fear of community disapproval, particularly in small communities, is an important deterrent against contraceptive use. The effectiveness of the family planning program would be enhanced by addressing older women and securing their support. It is ironic that a government which has made the preservation of traditional Iranian Muslim culture and its communal values a paramount goal, has overlooked the importance of women's kin relationships and the central role that older women play in the lives of younger women.

WOMEN'S STATUS

The Islamic Republic's population policy has been successful thus far in trying to reverse the extremely high rate of population growth. Infant mortality and life expectancy, despite the Iran-Iraq war and general state of the economy, have improved considerably. In 1991, the government stated its twenty-year goals as: reducing the total fertility rate to 3.5 children per woman; reducing births to 28 per 1,000; reducing the rate of population growth to 2.2 percent; and increasing the proportion of married women using contraceptives to 44 percent.[10] The success of these policies in the first five years has led some officials to anticipate achieving these goals, particularly a total fertility rate of 3.5, by the year 2001.

The regime is aware that this depends not only on careful planning and implementation but also on the coordination of legal and social change more broadly. To this end, it has emphasized more education for women in particular, improved health, and enhanced social and economic security for all citizens. It has placed great importance on the social and economic integration of women and on the improvement of women's general status both in society and in the family. But the gender roles and female domesticity advocated by the government as the cornerstone of its envisaged Muslim society do not reconcile themselves easily with the improvement of women's position and socioeconomic integration.

In the first phase of revolution, women's status appeared to deteriorate due to the reversal of earlier reforms. Pressure from Islamist women activists and the demands of development have encouraged the government to revise some of its views and adopt a more flexible attitude on gender issues. Both the Islamic Republic and women Islamists have demonstrated considerable creativity in their attempts to modernize their Islamic doctrine. The regime's pragmatic approach, particularly since 1989, has repeatedly linked women's education with the creation of an Islamic society in which discrimination against women does not exist. Ayatollah Khomeini's daughter, who was known to have a very close relationship with her father, has a doctoral degree and is cited as living proof that the supreme leader of the revolution was a strong advocate of female education.

The Islamic Republic has placed great emphasis on reforming the educational system to reflect its ideology, and education has been allocated a generous portion of government expenditures—21.9 percent of the 1989 budget. Although the gap between male and female literacy remains considerable, women's literacy has improved at a much faster rate than during the prerevolutionary era. In 1988, 74 percent of literacy students who had completed their programs were women, a reversal of prerevolution trends.[11] Many universities have reversed early barriers they had placed on women's participation in some disciplines, particularly law and engineering. Although these improvements have sometimes been framed within the Islamic vision of society, officials also indicate a high demand for women health workers and other professionals to respond to the needs of the female population. Medicine, the most prestigious faculty in Iranian universities, has become more open to women, and their admission in different medical fields is now on par with males.

While literacy and schooling rates are improving, the values that the regime propagates through school texts limit the image of women to the domestic arena, with little encouragement for women to look beyond domestic life for fulfillment.[12] While encouraging women to participate in the revolution and support the regime, Iranian religious leaders see domesticity as women's paramount role. This contradictory approach to the public role of women is indicated in various legal documents, including the constitution of the Islamic Republic.[13]

The government has adopted several strategies to reduce women's employment, including the introduction of compulsory *hijab* (veiling), and packages which enable women to retire after only fifteen years of work, or transfer their full salaries to their husbands and resign, or only work part-time.[14] Such programs were ostensibly offered to ease women's lives and allow them to attend to domestic responsibilities. Consequently, women's public sector employment has been decreasing by 2 percent each year. The government's systematic plan to minimize women's employment and reduce their visibility in the bureaucracy has been a major theme of criticism by women Islamists both within and outside the government. Women hold only 3 percent of senior government posts, even though women employed in the public sector are relatively better educated than their male colleagues.[15] Women have not accepted this situation passively and are challenging the government on many fronts.

CONTRADICTORY SIGNALS

Immediately after coming to power, Khomeini and other religious leaders asserted their success over the Pahlavi modernist ideology by annulling the family code which had restricted men's right to polygamous marriages and had given women the right to file for divorce in some circumstances. Temporary marriage, which had been outlawed (although it continued to be practiced among more traditional social groups), was legally sanctioned again. The most dramatic change was the lowering of the legal age of maturity for girls, and therefore of marriage, to nine, and to enshrine this in the constitution.

The pronatalist ideology of the regime viewed marriage as the most important means of eradicating social ills. Not only did marriage and its advantages for society become a frequent subject of official speeches, but the government established the Marriage Foundation to help men and women find spouses within a strict Islamic code, and to provide some financial assistance in setting up new households.[16]

Within several years of the revolution, however, newspapers, magazines, and sometimes even official radio began to carry reports of men who abused their power to divorce at will and to throw their wives into the street after years of marriage, without providing any support beyond the minimum three months' maintenance. Stories also circulated about child marriages and the health risks for the young brides. Senior women activists and women members of parliament raised questions about the meaning of Islamic justice for women. They demanded laws that would obstruct men who were bad Muslims, or whose understanding of Islam was questionable, from causing injustice and misery in the name of Islam.

The result was Khomeini's introduction of a new family law. Although it did not go as far as many Muslim women activists had hoped, it represented one of the most advanced marriage laws in the Middle East (after Tunisia and Turkey) without deviating from any of the major conventional assumptions of Islamic law. Most Muslim schools of law, and certainly Shi'i law, permit women to stipulate conditions in their marriage contract, although in practice it is difficult to discuss these matters at the time of betrothal when everyone proclaims their confidence that the couple will live happily together. Under the new law, the standard marriage contract includes eleven clauses. The two most important are that the first wife has the right of divorce should the husband take a second wife without her consent, and that wealth accumulated during the marriage will be divided equally between the couple in the event of divorce. The burden of negotiation is now upon the groom and his family, should they wish to remove some of the clauses, making it easier for the bride's family to introduce their own conditions, including her right to continue her education or work outside the home.

This partial victory of Muslim women activists has encouraged a new line of public debate and negotiation. Activists have produced women-centered interpretations of Muslim laws, challenging conventional and conservative male-centered interpretations.[17] A recent case in point is the success in winning wages for housework. This legislation protects women who married before the reintroduction of the marriage law, which is not retroactive. Housework wages must now be paid upon divorce, or upon the woman's demand. Women activists argued that Islam does not require women to work in their husband's home, even to the extent that the husband is under obligation to pay his wife for breast-feeding her own child. The controversial law was passed in December 1992, and despite enforcement difficulties, it sends the message that the regime is responsive to women's voices.

These legal gains are not easily put into practice. Men still find "Islamic" excuses to divorce their wives unjustly. Knowing that women have little recourse, men venture into subsequent marriages, rendering their wives economically and psychologically insecure. Islamist women are campaigning to improve laws respecting polygyny, custody of children, and *nushuz* (the right of a husband to divorce his wife without recompense should she leave home against his wishes). Major newspapers and women's magazines debate these issues in an Islamic context, and some religious leaders have been receptive. Observant Muslim women activists have managed to win many concessions from the government, including the establishment of a Council of Women's Affairs which reports directly to the president, a women's legal advisory office in the parliament, and the appointment of women advisors to aid judges in divorce and custody suits (though women cannot be judges themselves). Despite these gains, women still have a long way to go before they will have undone the harm caused by centuries of misinterpretation of Islam.[18]

WOMEN'S OPTIONS

It is within this socioeconomic and legal context that women decide the size of their family. Both marriage and financial insecurity are among the most important factors influencing women as they assess their options. Since women are frequently many years younger than their husbands, most expect to be widows in the second half of their lives; 84 percent of all widowed spouses are women. Women's opportunities for jobs, already typically lower-paying than men's, have decreased since the revolution. Therefore, women hope to have sons who would provide for them. In the process, women will generally have several daughters as well, and thus a larger family than either they want or the government advocates.

Many women point to the contradiction between the government's demand that women have small families and the way women are treated legally and socially. They openly blame legal changes and the government's attitude and ideology toward polygamous and temporary marriages. It is not clear what percentage of men actually have polygamous marriages, as many of these are not registered; all our informants, both male and female, felt that polygamous marriages have increased sharply. Such a perception strongly influences women's childbearing strategies and encourages them to choose larger families in order to consolidate their marriage ties. To bring together women's choice of family size with that envisaged by the government, the regime needs to change its contradictory and ambivalent policies. Reforms that give women the right to divorce if the husband marries a second wife, though ideologically important, are of little practical significance when women's opportunities in the second-marriage market are slim.

Fear of losing one's children, especially when all the ideological slogans and cultural values tell women that their role as mother is the most important element of their lives, is a constant threat. In 65 percent of all divorces that our interviewees knew of and where children were involved, fathers had been granted custody. Unmarried divorced fathers often gave the children to their own mothers or other female relatives to help care for them. The children's mothers are commonly denied visiting rights. The solution to this threat, according to many female informants, was to have many children and make it difficult for mothers-in-law, sisters-in-law, co-wives, or stepmothers to take over their role. Similarly, many women put up with unhappy and sometimes violent marriages just to be with their children. Clearly women are planning their families and using contraceptives, but their assessment of optimal family size does not always correspond to that of the government.

The development of population policy in Iran indicates that, contrary to its image in the West, the Islamic Republic has demonstrated much resilience and adaptability in the face of a rather harsh socioeconomic reality. It has shown a keen awareness that creating an informed public and building a broad consensus is one of the most important elements of success of any development plan, particularly as it touches upon the most intimate and day-to-day aspects of people's lives. Unlike the monarchy, the Islamic regime has popularized the fundamental relevance of the population question to human society.

The most controversial piece of Iran's population policy is the close association between women's socioeconomic position and fertility behavior. While the government has readily promoted women's education, other requirements, such as labor market participation, contradict the state's vision of women's role. This vision and its corresponding legal changes contradict the promise of a just Islamic society for all. The government envisages gender roles that do not correspond with those of Islamist women activists. In their view, much of what is presented is nothing but patriarchy in "Islamic" costume.

The last decade of Iranian debate and discussion on the highly politicized question of women has been characterized by a sharp contrast between this patriarchy and a women-centered interpretation of women's rights in Islam. The image of a pragmatic feminism in Muslim costume can perhaps best capture the gist of much of these debates. The advantage of the new Islamist feminists over more secularized "Western" activists is that they challenge and seek to reform the Islamic doctrine from within rather than advocating a Western model of gender relations. They have already managed to change women's consciousness to distinguish between patriarchal tradition and Islam. Ironically, the "traditionalization" of the marriage institution and the role of women has turned women strongly against tradition.[19] These arguments have made it clear that issues dealing with women's rights and responsibilities affect women's family planning goals. The eagerness to succeed in population policy, and an awareness of the importance of improving women's socioeconomic status in this regard, has introduced a conciliatory and accommodating attitude toward some of the Islamist women's demands. Many conservative religious leaders have adopted some of the women's interpretations. However, given the economic and unemployment pressures, there is little sign that the government will promote women's labor market participation. It also remains to be seen whether the government will redefine marriage legally and socially to make it a more secure social institution for women, and thus encourage a lower fertility rate.

In the end, the lively debates in Iran around the dynamics of the population program and women's rights and responsibilities are further evidence that reproductive choices and strategies, whether the government's or women's, are not decided by Islam but are the product of the political and economic realities of a given society.

NOTES

I thank Carla Makhlouf Obermeyer, Carolyn Makinson, and Patricia Kelly for their insightful comments during the development of this chapter. My special thanks to Azita Roshan who helped collect material and carry out field research. I am also grateful to Joe Stork for his work in collapsing this essay to its present length. The text is adapted from a paper prepared for the Population Council conference on Family, Gender and Population Policy in Cairo, February 1994.

The data presented here are based on an ongoing comprehensive research project on women and law in Iran carried out under the auspices of Women Living under Muslim Laws, an international network of women from Muslim communities, established to promote debate and research for social change in the Muslim world. Fieldwork on reproductive rights and family planning commenced in February 1993, with participant observation and informal interviews in four major public hospitals of Tehran and smaller health centers on the outskirts of Tehran. A core sample of 120 women have been informally interviewed, and 25 nurses, doctors, and hospital managers consulted. Data collected by the research center of the Family Planning Board in the provinces of Tehran and Markazi, and several other works on family planning published in Iran, provide a larger context. Other sources include radio and television programs, major public speeches of political and religious leaders, women's magazines, and national newspapers.

1. Akbar Aghajanian, "Population Change in Iran, 1966–86: A Stalled Demographic Transition?" *Population and Development Review* 17 (1991): 708.

2. The minimum age law was repealed in 1978 under pressure from the religious right and the marriage age for girls reverted to fifteen, though the minimum age was not enforced. See Eliz Sansarian, *The Women's Rights Movement in Iran: Mutiny, Appeasement and Repression from 1900 to Khomeini* (New York: Praeger, 1982), p. 96.

3. I attended two of these gatherings in 1981. Women were warned not to use the pill because it might render them infertile forever; if, because of their infertility, their husbands divorced them, God would not listen to their complaints. For a discussion of the *sofreh*, see Anne Betteridge, "The Controversial Vows of Urban Muslim Women in Iran," in N. A. Falk and R. M. Gross (eds.), *Unspoken Worlds: Women's Religious Lives in Non-Western Cultures* (New York: Harper and Row, 1980).

4. These Friday talks and many other official talks and interviews are also printed in major national print media, including women's magazines.

5. These are usually delivered in the form of questions and answers, the traditional way *'ulama'* deliver their sermons.

6. See, for example, Ayatollah Sane'i in *Zan-e-Ruz* 1329 (1370/1991): 8–12.

7. This theme is frequently discussed by religious leaders and on radio and television programs.

8. The emphasis placed on curing infertility has had a definite impact on the credibility of the program.

9. Hossein Malek Afzali, *Vaziet-e-salamat-e-madaran va kudakan dar jumhuriyyeh islamiyyeh iran* (The health status of mothers and children in the Islamic Republic of Iran) (Tehran: Ministry of Public Health, 1370/1992), pp. 19–20.

10. Ibid., p. 62.

11. Golnar Mehran, "The Creation of the New Muslim Woman: Female Education in the Islamic Republic of Iran," *Convergence* 23 (November 4, 1991): 47.

12. At a recent government reception, Mrs. Shoja'i, advisor on women's affairs to the Home Minister, observed that references to men in school tests are 267 times more frequent than references to women. *Payam-e-Zan* 2, no. 4 (1372/1993): 16–17.

13. Article 28 states, "Every person has the right to pursue the occupation of his or her choice insofar as this is not contradictory to Islam and the public interest or the right of others." *Constitution of the Islamic Republic and Its Amendments* 1368/1990, p. 29. This has been interpreted in the courts and by the public to mean that a husband has the right to stop his wife from being employed outside the home.

14. See Valentine Moghadam, *Modernizing Women: Gender and Social Change in the Middle East* (Boulder, Colo.: Lynne Rienner, 1993).

15. Sharify notes that 18 percent of women in public sector employment have higher education, compared to only 6 percent of men. Feirozeh Sharify, "Mughayat-e-zan dar nizam-e-idariy-e-iran" (Women in the employment structure of Iran), *Zanan* 1, no. 2 (1370/1992): 4–9.

16. The Marriage Foundation existed on a small scale before the revolution, as facilitating marriages was deemed to be *savab* (a good deed). After the revolution it became a social pillar of the Islamic regime, particularly after the war, as it undertook the task of remarrying thousands of young war widows.

17. All six major women's magazines are full of these accounts. National newspapers, radio, and television cover these interpretations, which are sometimes picked up by government officials and even religious leaders.

18. Azam Talaghani, personal communication, January 1993.

19. Carla Makhlouf Obermeyer, personal communication, February 1994.

20

The Women of Sudan's National Islamic Front

Sondra Hale

In 1994, Sudan appears to have carried out one of the most successful of contemporary Islamic revolutions. Yet today's reign of political Islam exhibits a great degree of continuity with Sudan's Islamic past. It is the nature of the Islamic revolution in Sudan, not the fact of its existence, that is now of interest. In 1988, when I conducted most of the research for this essay, Sudanese were still able to debate strategies for democratic change, as well as the advantages and disadvantages of an Islamic state. An air of intellectual and political excitement generated by the 1985 civilian overthrow of Ja'far Nimeiri's dictatorship prevailed. Dozens of newspapers were active, as were radio and television, unions, professional associations, political parties, and the Sudanese Women's Union.

The atmosphere changed abruptly with the military coup in 1989 that brought to power a right-wing Islamist military government, but the nature of debate during the brief democratic era remains of considerable significance for societies where Islam is or may become a factor in the political process. It is a debate with implications for both democracy and gender relations. Discussions of gender relations in Muslim societies often reflect a preoccupation with culture and ideology. In analyzing the relationship of gender and religion, it is important to avoid treating Islam as immutable, singular, undifferentiated, or to oversimplify "Islam's impact on women," as if women are a passive, undifferentiated mass. We need to pay attention to the strategies of resistance, adaptation, and accommodation that women everywhere employ in situations of oppression or subordination.[1] Finally, we need to avoid overemphasizing the theoretical at the expense of giving attention to people's daily lives.[2] A more useful approach analytically distinguishes between patriarchal gender relations within the family and religiously sanctioned patriarchal codes, while sidestepping a simplistic conflation of Islam and cultural nationalism.[3]

Over the past several decades, the Sudanese state has been engaged in a re-creation of religious ideology. Many Sudanese scholars agree that sufi religious orders have historically had a strong claim to represent Islam in the country, but most of the currently politically powerful religious sentiment is of a different kind. Many adherents refer to it as the "New Movement." The nature of identity politics within the framework of rising Islamic sentiment, or Islamism, has had special meaning for women and for the gender divisions of society, such as those prescribed in Sudan's personal status laws.

I approach these issues through an analysis of the National Islamic Front (NIF), a recent revisionist offshoot of the Society of Muslim Brothers (*al-Ikhwan al-Muslimin*)—a revivalist movement that arose in Egypt in the 1930s. The NIF, an integral part of the political forces set in motion during the 1985–89 period, has arguably been the most effective Sudanese political machine in twentieth-century Sudan. A centerpiece of its strategy is to place women and family at the forefront—the former as organizers and socializers, and the latter as the foundation of an "authentic culture."

The "authentic culture" campaign of the NIF posits a cultural nationalism that serves certain class interests. Its framework of cultural legitimacy verges on essentialism. In the name of the ideal woman, morally central to the ideal family, women's behavior is ideologically manipulated by male-dominated religio-political institutions.[4]

NIMEIRI'S STATE AND THE RISE OF ISLAMISM

A combination of sociohistorical processes and conditions underlies the rise of Islamism in Muslim northern Sudan since 1971. These may be summarized as follows:

- Sudan is an Islamic society steeped in other indigenous and often contradictory traditions; the complex sufi-Sunni interaction and the sectarian ethnic identity politics that emanate from this religious history remain active.
- Intersecting with Islamic patriarchal forms are Arab-Nubian-African male-authoritarian customs.
- The modern Sudanese state has had a pluralistic legal system in which *shari'a,* civil, and customary law coexisted.
- Women's rights have been fairly well-developed on paper, but not in practice; there have been active women's organizations and a vibrant non-Islamic women's culture that has endured all types of regimes.

- Since 1972, multinational corporations, nongovernmental organizations, and foreign aid projects (Arab, European, and American) have increasingly dominated Sudan's economy, altering its class structure and changing its gender arrangements; sharp demographic shifts have changed the gender composition of the workforce, especially in the middle class.
- During this last decade, Sudan has experienced an economic crisis of enormous severity.

Despite the historical strength of sectarian politics, northern Sudanese had been relatively relaxed about Islam, and displayed tolerance for diversity. Prior to 1983, civil and customary legal codes were dominant, even though *shari'a* was part of the legal system.[5] Although northern Sudanese women wore a body covering called a *tobe* (*thawb* in standard Arabic) and practiced genital surgeries (both clitoridectomy and infibulation), they were considered to be among the "emancipated" women of the Muslim world, especially after women earned universal suffrage in 1965.[6] The 1973 Permanent Constitution offered women as well as men various civil rights and freedoms, and singled women out for specific gender-related protection.[7]

The rise of Islamism in Sudan relates in part to the dynamics and character of Nimeiri's regime. Nimeiri proclaimed an intent to enforce strict *shari'a* in 1983, and invited Hasan al-Turabi, then leader of Sudan's Muslim Brothers and later the founder of the NIF, into his government. For the first time, the Brothers had a visible power base within the state apparatus. Since then there has been an intensified struggle between secular forces, which see the non-Muslim southern Sudan and women as most severely affected by the implementation of *shari'a*, and cultural nationalist religious forces which see a "pure" and authentic Islam as Sudan's only defense against an invading West and the only answer to Sudan's dismal economic situation.

The specific reasons why Nimeiri launched an intensified Islamization process may have been as much personal as political.[8] We do know that the regime was in trouble. Originating as a left-nationalist coup, it had become steadily conservative, especially after an abortive 1971 *coup d'état* attempt by leftists. A spiraling national debt provoked World Bank and IMF pressure to prune the civil service. Food price hikes caused riots in 1979 and 1982. An increasingly successful insurrection in the south was accompanied by growing political opposition from a coalition of opposition groups, the National Front. A three-month-long judges' strike in 1983 and a doctors' strike early in 1984 led to the declaration of a state of emergency.[9]

The move to Islamize brought Nimeiri some legitimacy in the form of continuity with the Islamic character of Sudanese politics and culture. Another factor was Khartoum's reliance on oil-rich Arab states, namely

Saudi Arabia, and the advantage of co-opting some of the National Front's Islamic themes.[10] In September 1983, Nimeiri passed the notorious "September Laws," declaring Sudan an Islamic republic and proclaiming strict adherence to *shari'a*. The next year or so saw the establishment of "decisive justice courts," the application of harsh *hudud* (Islamic criminal punishments such as amputations), replacement of income tax by *zakat* (an alms tax), and the attempt to "Islamize" banks.

Self-appointed moral guardians harassed women in the streets about their conduct or dress, and Nimeiri himself carried out endless ceremonial "Islamic acts" (e.g., pouring alcohol into the Nile). Poor women initially bore the brunt of the moral guards (e.g., harassment of prostitutes and vendors of local brew). Such treatment offered an ominous hint of things to come for middle-class and professional women. National debates began to focus on whether too many women were being trained in certain professions. The administration of the University of Khartoum, for example, considered quotas in particular fields for women students.

Although Nimeiri was the first head of state to invite the Muslim Brothers into his government, near the end of his regime he arrested Hasan al-Turabi and hundreds of his followers as scapegoats for the failures of his administration. Nimeiri's decision to execute Mahmud Taha, leader of the reformist Republican Brothers, on charges of apostasy, may well have triggered the regime's downfall a few months later. Until prime minister Sadiq al-Mahdi formed a "government of consensus" in the summer of 1988, and invited the National Islamic Front into the official ranks of government, the new regime had simultaneously sought to enlist and to disavow or distance itself from "fundamentalism." But accommodation had its consequences.

WOMEN: THE PUBLIC DEBATES

The spheres of law and labor are two areas where Islamist men and non-Islamist women experience conflicts of interest. In Sudan, women's participation in the formal workforce increased at a slow but steady pace during the years immediately following independence. Initially the state encouraged women's participation. Jobs were available and the government, wanting to appear "modern," geared propaganda toward women's education and work participation. Legal and constitutional provisions seemed to support that tendency.

In recent years, though, women have entered the workforce because Sudan's depressed economy has compelled them to work for wages outside the home. The Islamization process has thrown up very subtle legal obstacles to discourage some areas of work for women, altering the previous trend. The uprising of April 1985 left much of Nimeiri's Islamicization project incomplete. Umma Party leader Sadiq al-Mahdi, prime minister not long after, represented the landowning and commercial ruling class as well as a special Sudanese combination of Sufism and fundamentalism.

The "democratic" interlude between 1985 and 1989 saw a great deal of public debate about personal status provisions in the *shari'a*, and whether they offered enough protection and equality for women. An ambitious paper written by five Sudanese women scholars and professionals, for example, identified a number of elements in *shari'a* personal status laws that were beneficial to women. But for each protection they discerned a societal subversion of the law—that is, a contradiction between ideological prescription and economic necessity. For example, "A girl has the right of consent to a marriage suitor and can get married by court if her guardian did not give his consent; in such case [*sic*] the judge acts as a male-guardian. Yet, it is considered an act of shame for a girl to resort to court."[11] Their project, in this sense, documented the encroaching impact of Islamization on women.

Fatima Mernissi has observed that much of the Muslim world is experiencing a competition between newly urbanized middle- and lower-middle-class men and semiemancipated women from predominantly middle-class urban backgrounds. In her view, the state's use of Islam to accommodate (and at the same time to manipulate) its young (male) followers "makes sense." "Islam speaks about power and self-empowerment," she notes. These are attractive attributes in societies which reluctantly confront "[t]he inescapability of renegotiating new sexual, political, economic, and cultural boundaries, thresholds and limits."[12] Not the least of boundary violations, for Muslim men, is the changing nature of gender arrangements which challenge what Mernissi refers to as "authority thresholds." Women's access to jobs, education, benefits, and political participation allows them to become public people, and thereby a potential threat to an older social order.

In the 1970s, Sudan's government was confiscating most of the economic surplus, and all but the capitalist class fared badly as unemployment rose and salaries could not match inflation.[13] One consequence was an enormous migration of male labor both inside Sudan (rural to urban) but more significantly internationally. At first this did not threaten the prevailing gender ideology because the migrants were working class or minor civil service personnel. But soon intellectuals as well as middle and senior level men were leaving. Many of the better jobs, considered to be the preserve of men, were increasingly being filled by women.[14]

An example of this dynamic, which serves to underscore NIF ideology and strategy, involves the debate over whether too many women are studying medicine. The 1980s saw a dramatic increase in women entering the Faculty of Medicine at the University of Khartoum, at a time when over 80 percent of new male medical graduates were emigrating to Gulf Arab states. Conservatives took the position that women doctors were needed but should be directed into appropriate fields—not including surgery and obstetrics, which just happen to be the most lucrative but are seen as "too physically demanding" for women. Many well-known women doctors with impeccable credentials were subsequently deprived of senior positions in certain fields, while the Ministry of Health attempted to channel women into mother-child clinics, public health, and general medicine.[15] NIF women doctors have organized extensively within the field of general medicine and advocate channeling women into this sphere.

This typifies the "modern" approach of the NIF. It asserts that women should work only if they do not have children and only if their income is needed by the family. Women from working-class families need to work, and *shari'a* makes allowances for them, but there are limits. "Appropriate" jobs should be extensions of women's domestic roles. There is a further set of contradictions, however. Jobs in the informal sector held by lower-class women—for example, vendors of local brew, prostitutes, and some entertainers—are under attack as affronts to Islam. Sweeps of some neighborhoods have closed brothels, beer halls, and the like.

Women are central to the NIF and are among its visible organizers, though the movement is not an emancipatory one for them. Cultural nationalists generally oppose women's emancipation, arguing that it is an imitation of the West and would weaken the family. They romanticize women's role in the domestic sphere, essentializing women as the embodiment of Sudanese culture.

The appeal of Sudanese cultural nationalism, with its Islamic dimension, has now been embraced by the newly educated urban middle class. Islamism as an ideology to some extent reflects commercial class interests. Islamic "fundamentalism," at least as embodied by the Muslim Brothers and the NIF, mainly recruits from the urban professional middle class. In its drive to gain power, the NIF has taken on a "modern" look. Sudan's NIF projects a highly sophisticated articulation of Islam and commerce, especially banking and insurance. Women are important in building the infrastructure of this new class.

ISLAMISTS AND EVERYDAY LIFE

To guard against treating Islam as a monolithic force, and women as an undifferentiated passive mass, it is necessary to examine what Islam and some of its institutions mean for women's daily lives. I asked my respondents what changes they anticipated once *shari'a* was fully implemented. Some of them were professional "experts," while others were nonliterate, working-class women whose lives had been disrupted by the 1983 "September Laws." Others described themselves as "ordinary" housewives, government clerks, and the like.

Their views spanned the political spectrum. Through these interviews and by studying the popular press (very active at the time, with over forty newspapers representing different political groupings), I had access to an active public debate in the summer of 1988 about the potential impact on various groups should Hasan al-Turabi and Sadiq al-Mahdi, under the "Islamic Trend" banner, succeed in implementing *shari'a.*

With the exception of the activist elite women of the NIF, none of the religious women defined women's role as embodying Sudan's culture, or saw Islam as a deus ex machina that would resolve Sudan's crisis. Women did not talk about *shari'a* in any way that revealed an interest in the intricacies of jurisprudence, or in the formation of an Islamic state. For many of those who were observant, Islam was private, personal, and simple. "I am just a Muslim," one woman from the Nuba Mountains said, "but I am not as fanatic as the Muslim Brothers. . . . I'm religious because I pray and that's all."[16]

In fact, although men make a public spectacle of the act, I rarely saw women pray. Except for the NIF activists and sister travelers, I seldom heard women offer proselytizing statements. In short, most women seemed disinterested in the political aspects of religion, and even expressed chagrin that Islam was being used for political purposes.

Most women displayed a low level of participation in organized politico-religious activity. In addition to a history of exclusion from the heart of orthodox religious practice, women's disinterest reflected the extensive time they had to devote to dealing with the implications of the economic crises for their own households. Shortages meant they had to deal with the black market, to locate commodities in short supply or find substitutes. Women of all classes have become urban foragers. At no time in Sudanese history have women's economic networks—rotating credit rings, cooperatives, and the like—been so important and active. For most women, relationship to the state or even to state-endorsed feminism was very indirect.

There were women, of course, who did take an active role in organized activity. For years the secularist Women's Union (a Communist Party affiliate) was a major voice in debates about women, but it had lost a great deal of influence by 1988. The debate on women's rights during the "democratic" interlude was co-opted by the activist women of the Islamist and conservative wings of old sectarian parties—such organizations as the National Women's Front and the women's branches of the Muslim Brothers, the NIF, the Umma Party (led by Sara al-Fadl, Sadiq al-Mahdi's wife), and the Republican Brothers.

By 1988, NIF ideology about ideal roles for women had permeated middle-class urban society. "There are elements in society—mainly women—who are creating a revolution," one liberal professional woman (with a

Ph.D. in public administration) remarked, "and because it is coming from women considered conservative or 'traditional,' it is very confusing to women like me—educated, liberal women."[17]

Of five students interviewed at the University of Khartoum, none was affiliated with the NIF, yet all expressed views regarding women amazingly close to those of the NIF. The most visible Islamist woman activist was Su'ad al-Fatih al-Badawi, one of only two women representatives now in the People's Assembly, both of whom are members of the NIF. In public statements, she took great effort to be forward-looking and open. "We are not opposed to corrections and changes" in current *shari'a* provisions, she said, so long as they do not "take us back to the English laws." Moreover, she declared,

> I do not believe in separatist [gender] roles in the construction of the nation. Men and women complete and perfect each other. . . . It was an obligation for women [to make] the representation of women *authentic* and *real*. . . . Those women who have attained a high level of consciousness which is *progressive* and *untainted* by blind imitation of both the East and the West must not be stingy with their intellectual effort. . . . This era is marked by issues of development which the *enlightened vanguard* must struggle to solve in a fundamental way. [18]

The second woman NIF representative, Hikmat Sid Ahmad, specified that women were responsible for the education of the new generations. In an article and in our interview, she presented a "correct model" for teaching that is the same for home, school, and work. She expressed concern for women gainfully employed as "partners" in national construction. Sid Ahmad believed that only women who *have* to work should do so, and only if they have "appropriate" child care (preferably a close relative). When I pressed the issue, she spoke of a need for Islamic nurseries for working-class women, whose abilities to raise their children in an "Islamic way" were, in the opinion of the NIF, limited. In the interim, she advocated intense proselytizing by NIF women in existing nurseries.[19]

Of the five Islamist women I interviewed, more than once and in different settings, three—well-educated, professional, and upper middle to upper class—gave me the fullest explanation of the ideal Muslim woman. Nagwa Kamal Farid was Sudan's first woman *shari'a* judge, but dissociated herself from public politics; Wisal al-Mahdi was a lawyer, wife of Hasan al-Turabi and sister of Sadiq al-Mahdi, and an NIF activist; and Hikmat Sid Ahmad, mentioned above, was an NIF representative in the government and an Arabic teacher.[20]

In a group interview, Judge Farid was forceful about women's equality under *shari'a*, a woman's responsibility to be "respectable" at all times, and the compelling reasons for remaining at home unless financial need compelled entrance into the workforce. All agreed that *shari'a* permits a woman to work, but conditionally. "There is no NIF program as such to take women out of the workforce," Wisal al-Mahdi asserted. Sid Ahmad added that women are needed in the economy. But they all agreed that women need to raise their children first.

The three also commented on the inherent differences between men and women, especially as related to the *shari'a* provisions that in criminal proceedings two women witnesses are required to offset the testimony of one man. "We know that women are different from men," Sid Ahmad explained,

> Women, by their *nature*, sometimes forget. Sometimes they sympathize with somebody. Perhaps he may be a criminal . . . when one of them [a woman witness] forgets, the other will remind her, and if one of them sympathized with the criminal, the other could correct her. . . . I don't think it is a problem for women to find themselves treated differently in the court . . . because it is *natural* . . . the entire principle [in *shari'a*] is in accord with the way women are *created*, since women are *naturally empathetic*. (emphasis mine)

Al-Mahdi gave an example of a murder trial:

> A woman would be so *excited* that she would not recognize exactly what happened, because after all, a woman is *weaker* than a man and all her *nervous system* is made different . . . women are more *sentimental*, because they are the mothers who breed children. . . . That is why in *shari'a* law we guard against the compassion ['atifiyya] of *womankind*. . . . This does not mean that a woman is less than a man, or that her *mental capacity* is less than a man. It means that her *disposition* is different than [a man's]. We are equal in all rights in Islam. (emphasis mine)

Wisal al-Mahdi maintained that women have a broad range of options under *shari'a*. Differences are spelled out in the law because "we are *women* after all. . . . I am *not* like a man." She went on to say that a woman can be anything or do anything.

All three agreed that men oppress women, that Arabs have a low opinion of women, but they blamed Arab culture and not Islam. They argued that if Arab Sudan were a state with an Islamic legal code fully in place, the oppression of women would end. Arab men try to give a false idea about women's rights under *shari'a*.

> Arab men "are against women," said Wisal al-Mahdi, and that is why *we are much against them*. We know our rights. We know what *shari'a* gives us. We think that *women are better human beings* than they think. . . . *We are standing up for our sex*. We are working in the NIF *to praise women* and to make women have a better status and to tell the world that we are as equal as men and as great as men. (emphasis mine)

To al-Mahdi, there was no distinction between politics and religion, nor between public and private life. Women were active in the NIF because of equal rights under *shari'a,* but also because

> We want Islam to be practiced in everyday life, not just inside the house . . . we don't want it to be only in a corner of the life of the family. We want it to be the *core* of life . . . [for] the whole society and the whole Sudan and the whole Muslim world.

These women's devotion and militant commitment to the NIF were striking. Their contradictory language reflected an internalized view of women as weak, emotional, and sentimental, as having their primary duty in the domestic sphere. These women were actively pursuing, in an Islamist framework, a change in the status of women. Wisal al-Mahdi, at least, should be regarded as a "gender activist."[21] This is not to overlook the fact that these women—the leaders—also have class interests. The state—and political movements related to state formation—recognizes the need to maintain a gender ideology that complements labor needs. Within the NIF itself, contradictions have arisen between the availability of its human resources and the imperatives of organizational strategies. Women are needed in large numbers by the NIF for a variety of political tasks.

In a number of ways, women are the nexus of the NIF.[22] They are among the most active and visible organizers. The strong appeal that the party has for women is reflected in the fact that at the universities over 50 percent of the students were wearing the *hijab* in 1988—many times more than was the case at the beginning of the decade.[23] Women are relied on to socialize the young with Islamic values at such locations as the nursery schools that the NIF is establishing in mosques. This socialization function is also actively carried out in the schools, where the Muslim Brothers have been organizing since the 1950s and where teachers are mainly women. The NIF points to this *public* activity of NIF women in answering the charge that it would return women to the home.

To counter the claim that the tasks women are given are but extensions of their domestic labor, the NIF pointed to the fact that the only two women elected to the People's Assembly during the brief "democratic" era were, after all, NIF representatives. These two, Su'ad al-Fathi and Hikmat Sid Ahmad, had high public profiles. The wives of NIF politicians are known to be active behind the scenes and in public. Wisal al-Mahdi considers herself a powerful force "behind" her husband and an activist in her own right. Her house is segregated into women's and men's quarters, she adheres to the *hijab,* and her lifestyle follows Islamic dictates about the roles of men and women.

CONCLUSION

Sudanese Islamists are attempting to repudiate elements of colonial and postcolonial gender relations while retaining others. Some, with reference to the *shari'a,* interpret men's and women's roles as complementary. Yet the need for state authority over the participation of men and women in the economy, as well as the concern to abrogate Western values, has led to the conflation of particular representations—for example, woman-family and sometimes woman-family-Islamic nation (*umma*). Such expectations often require that a woman earn wages, hold office, drive a car, get an education, and the like.

Islamists have attempted to create a new configuration in the gender division of labor, whereby women are active in the workforce under conditions that fulfill the requirements of the party-state. Islamist women, at least the activists, have been complicit in both these processes. On the basis of Islam, they argue for the possibility, indeed the necessity, of increased gender equality. Identity politics have, for these women, touched not only on aspects of "authentic" Islamic culture but on gender relations as well.

The NIF's need for female participation in the party's program and in the national economy has been accommodated by some ideological reformulation. The various Islamist groups—among which the NIF is the most influential and powerful—continue to condemn the presence of women in working-class or traditional occupations, and to regulate women's access to power and privilege, both private and public. Women will remain the object of concern of Islamization, but this will primarily involve an intensification of the representation of Sudanese women as *ideal Muslim women* in the media, in school curricula, and in family ideology.[24]

In my last exchange with Wisal al-Mahdi, the wife of Hasan al-Turabi, I inquired about the apparent contradictions between Sudan's Permanent Constitution and certain elements of *shari'a* with respect to the status of women, and asked how the NIF planned to resolve them. After pretending not to understand my question for some minutes and conferring with her colleagues, she responded, almost offhandedly, "Oh, we will simply ban the Constitution!" This chilling and arrogant response presaged what was to come. Following the June 1989 right-wing Islamist military coup, the democratically elected People's Assembly was immediately dissolved, the Permanent Constitution suspended, and all political parties, unions, and professional associations declared illegal. Islamic law and governance have been imposed, even on the nearly one-third of the population who are not Muslims. Various rights of due process were suspended or ignored, hundreds have languished in jails, some for many years; executions, torture, and disappearances have been common. Civil servants, including many university faculty, have been sacked. In general, the opposition has been decimated. As part and parcel of these changes, the free movement and association of women have been sharply curtailed and the agenda for women co-opted by the Islamist regime. In November 1991, "the Islamic Fundamentalist military junta decreed . . . that henceforth all Sudanese women will wear long black dresses to their ankles and a black veil covering their head and face . . . those who disobey to be instantly punished by whipping."[25] Although Hasan al-Turabi has claimed that the dress code is not enforced except by "peer pressure," many fear it can be imposed at any time by administrative fiat.

The country is in economic disarray. The capital has become a poverty-ridden, unhealthy, dangerous place. Migrants pour into Greater Khartoum—especially southerners and westerners—only to have their shantytowns demolished and be driven out into the desert. Local militias carry out genocidal attacks on southern and western Sudanese. Thousands are starving.

Al-Turabi has built a reputation as one of the most important Islamist leaders in the world.[26] He himself speaks a great deal about "democracy," the emancipation of women, and human rights within Islam.[27] "The status of women generally in society," al-Turabi states, "is no longer a topical issue . . . we don't bother ourselves a lot about it anymore in the Sudan. . . . In the Islamic movement, I would say that women have played a more important role of late than men."[28]

It is difficult to know what such a "quasi-liberal" view of the role of women in Sudanese society will mean. Certainly it makes oppositional organization more difficult. Al-Turabi has been consistent in arguing that a "pure" Islam is a pan-national movement that can have the effect of emancipating women. To what degree women accept that argument, and to what degree they might be hoodwinked by their culture, remains to be seen.

In 1988, most of my respondents said simply that Nimeiri used *shari'a* in 1983 as a "last resort," and that its implementation had little to do with religion. Perhaps the question posed was not the most illuminating. Instead I might have asked what elements make the Judeo-Christian-Islamic religious tradition useful as political strategies during economic and political crises. Are there social processes by which religions allow a society to realign itself when it seems at a "tilt," when structural changes are moving at a faster pace than cultural understandings? Does Islam lend itself more easily than other religions to such "realignment" strategies? If so, it is necessary to explore further what has been happening in contemporary Sudanese society to have produced this "tilt."

NOTES

An earlier version of this article appeared in *Review of African Political Economy* 54 (1992): 27–41. Fieldwork in Sudan in 1988 was funded by a grant from the UCLA Center for the Study of Women; the Gustave E. von Grunebaum Center for Near Eastern Studies, UCLA; and California State University, Northridge. The author is indebted to the assistance of Sunita Pitamber, Amal Abdel Rahman, William Young, and Sherifa Zuhur.

1. Among those who have critiqued the 1970s and 1980s scholarship on gender and Islam for ahistoricism and/or a lack of class perspective are Nikki R. Keddie, "Problems in the Study of Middle Eastern Women," *International Journal of Middle East Studies* 10 (1979): 225–40; Judith Tucker, "Problems in the Historiography of Women in the Middle East: The Case of Nineteenth Century Egypt," *International Journal of Middle East Studies* 15 (1983): 321–36; and Reza Hammami and Martina Rieker, "Feminist Orientalism and Orientalist Marxism," *New Left Review*, no. 170 (1988): 93–106. This last source calls for the privileging of subaltern voices. More recently, Leila Ahmad has presented her version of the historical roots of the modern debate in *Women and Gender in Islam: Historical Roots of a Modern Debate* (New Haven: Yale University Press, 1992); and Valentine Moghadam has attempted to recast some of the arguments in *Modernizing Women: Gender and Social Change in the Middle East* (Boulder, Colo.: Lynne Rienner, 1993).

2. Sondra Hale, "Gender, Religious Identity, and Political Mobilization in Sudan," in Valentine Moghadam (ed.), *Identity Politics and Women: Cultural Reassertions and Feminisms in International Perspective* (Boulder, Colo.: Westview, 1994), pp. 145–66.

3. Sondra Hale, "The Politics of Gender in the Middle East," in Sandra Morgen (ed.), *Gender and Anthropology* (Washington, D.C.: American Anthropological Association, 1989), pp. 246–67. Deniz Kandiyoti, "Women, Islam and the State: A Comparative Approach," in Juan R. Cole (ed.), *Comparing Muslim Societies: Knowledge and the State in a World Civilization* (Ann Arbor: University of Michigan Press, 1992), pp. 237–38, and passim. See also Aziz al-Azmeh, "Arab Nationalism and Islamism," *Review of Middle East Studies* 4 (1988): 33–51.

4. Elsewhere I suggest that some women's potentially liberatory cultural identity and practices (e.g., the *zar,* a ceremonial gathering of women to exorcise demons from a possessed "sister") may be consciously thwarted by both secular and Islamist interest groups, while other aspects of culture with problematic emancipatory aspects for women are either consciously encouraged (or coerced), viewed with acquiescence, or rationalized. See Sondra Hale, "Transforming Culture or Fostering Second-Hand Consciousness? Women's Front Organizations and Revolutionary Parties—the Sudan Case," in Judith Tucker (ed.), *Women in Arab Society* (Bloomington: University of Indiana Press, 1994), pp. 149–74.

5. Dina Sheikh el-Din Osman relates the process whereby eventually the transitional Constitution was amended and the *Shari'a* Courts Act of 1967 passed, ending the subordination of *shari'a* courts. See Dina Sheikh el-Din Osman, "The Legal

Status of Muslim Women in Sudan," *Journal of Eastern African Research and Development* 15 (1985): 125. For an analysis of Sudan's plural legal system, see, for example, Carolyn Fluehr-Lobban, *Islamic Law and Society in the Sudan* (London: Frank Cass, 1987).

6. The *tobe* is a thin, cotton, full-body wraparound that began as conservative dress, but by the 1970s was worn by many urban women as a form of voluntary national dress (i.e., not a "veil").

7. Osman, "Legal Status of Muslim Women," p. 125.

8. On this point, see Khalid Duran, "The Centrifugal Forces of Religion in Sudanese Politics," *Orient* 26 (1985): 572–600; John Esposito, *Islam and Politics*, rev. 2d ed. (Syracuse: Syracuse University Press, 1987 [1984]), p. 282; and Mansour Khalid, *Nimeiri and the Revolution of Dis-May* (London: KPI, 1985). Mansour Khalid, for some years among Sudan's leading political voices, mercilessly mocks Nimeiri's seeming embrace of Islam.

9. These events have been well chronicled, especially in "Sudan's Revolutionary Spring," *MERIP Reports*, no. 135 (1985); and a special Sudan issue of *Middle East Journal* 44, no. 4 (1990).

10. Esposito, *Islam and Politics*, p. 284.

11. Samira Amin Ahmad et al., "Population Problems, Status of Women and Development," paper for the Third National Population Conference, University of Khartoum, October 10–14, 1987, p. 38.

12. Fatima Mernissi, "Muslim Women and Fundamentalism," *Middle East Report*, no. 153 (July–August 1988): 9.

13. For an analysis of this process, see Medani M. Ahmad, *The Political Economy of Development in the Sudan*, African Seminar Series no. 29, Institute of African and Asian Studies (Khartoum: University of Khartoum, 1987).

14. See Nur al-Tayyib 'Abd al-Qadir, *Al-Mar' al-'amila fi al-sudan* (Khartoum: Department of Labour and Social Security, Division of Research, Information, and Media, 1984); and Samia el-Nagar, "Patterns of Women [*sic*] Participation in the Labour Force in Khartoum," Ph.D. thesis, Department of Sociology, University of Khartoum, 1985. Information also based on interviews in the summer of 1988 with Amal Abu Hasabu, Fawzia Hammour, and Nahid Toubia. See note 15 for information on the Toubia interview.

15. Information based on an interview with Dr. Nahid Toubia, Khartoum, July 22, 1988. Dr. Toubia, Sudan's first woman surgeon, now in exile in New York, took part in the debates and is a former member of the Council of Surgeons and former Head of Pediatric Surgery, Khartoum Hospital. The same debate arose around the increased numbers of women being admitted to the Faculty of Agriculture, University of Khartoum, long an exclusively male bastion. Through Sudan's system of "boxing," students are placed in faculties based on the high school certificate exams; women are often admitted to Agriculture whether or not they request it. Since Sudan is basically an agricultural society, the field is very powerful. Agricultural policy making is probably the most significant in Sudan's economy. Allowing women into the field means gender power sharing in an agricultural society. Part of the debate was captured in *Sudan Now* (October 1979 and January 1980). In one issue,

for example, Omer el-Farouk Hasan Heiba called for the "banning of girls from agricultural education." See "Letters," *Sudan Now* (October 1979). Women, of course, perform a high percentage of agricultural labor.

16. A series of interviews with doctors, nurses, and workers at Abu Anja Hospital in Omdurman were carried out, June 20, 1988. Because of the repressiveness of the current regime, I have not named anyone who is still in the country, whose views were not already written or well-known, or who said anything self-incriminating against *shari'a*, Islam, or particular political parties. The Nuba Mountains are in the west, on the invisible "border" between northern and southern Sudan. Many Nuba are Muslims; some are Christians; and others are of various indigenous religions.

17. Interview in Khartoum, July 14, 1988.

18. Both quotations are from *Al-Sahafa* (Khartoum), May 3, 1986, p. 10 (emphasis mine). Note the appropriation of Marxist and feminist vocabulary.

19. The following statements by Hikmat Sid Ahmad or Wisal al-Mahdi are from an interview at the home of the latter and her husband, Hasan al-Turabi, July 12, 1988. Judge Nagwa Kamal Farid participated in that interview, but was also interviewed alone on July 4, 1988, in Khartoum. Statements are taken from both interviews.

20. The interviews were carried out in the summer of 1988.

21. I borrowed this term from Margot Badran, "Gender Activism: Feminists and Islamists in Egypt," in Moghadam, *Identity Politics and Women,* pp. 202–27. I am trying to avoid both the *imposition* of a "Western" concept, in this case "feminism," as well as the sometimes automatic *exclusion* of Islamic activists from such consideration. That many Islamist women are very active on behalf of women cannot be denied. What name we give to it is a very different matter.

22. Duran, among many other sources, expressed surprise at the significance of women in the NIF. "While it is hardly surprising to have educated women seeking their emancipation through communism, outsiders are at first baffled by the large number of prominent female activists among the ranks of the NIF." Duran, "Centrifugal Forces of Religion," p. 597.

23. Information from a July 17, 1988 interview with University of Khartoum, Anthropology Honors student, Muhammad Osman, who had taken a sample of students for his unpublished paper, "The Social and Political Aspects of the Veil."

24. For the Islamic paradigm as it relates to gender, see Barbara Freyer Stowasser, "Religious Ideology, Women, and the Family: The Islamic Paradigm," in Barbara Freyer Stowasser (ed.), *The Islamic Impulse* (London: Croom Helm, 1987), pp. 262–96.

25. Reported in the *Sudan Democratic Gazette,* no. 19 (December 1991), p. 8. This report on current conditions in Sudan has been gleaned from personal letters, firsthand reports from colleagues, a number of US and European newspapers, as well as *Africa Watch* and *The Nation.*

26. See, for example, Abdelwahab El-Affendi, *Turabi's Revolution: Islam and Power in Sudan* (London: Grey Seal, 1991); Peter Nyot Kok, "Hasan Abdallah al-Turabi," *Orient* 33 (1992): 185–92; Tim Niblock, "Islamic Movements and Sudan's Political Coherence," in Herve Bleuchot, Christian Delmet, and Derek Hopwood (eds.), *Sudan* (Exeter: Ithaca, 1991); Khalid Mubarak, "The Fundamentalists: Theory and

Praxis," A*l-Hayat* (London), June 30, 1992; Alex de Waal, "Turabi's Muslim Brothers: Theocracy in Sudan," *Covert Action*, no. 49 (1994): 13–18, 60–61; and Haydar Ibrahim 'Ali, *Azmat al-islam al-siyyasi fi al-sudan* (Cairo: Centre for Sudanese Studies, 1991), pp. 99–216.

27. See, for example, Arthur L. Lowrie (ed.), *Islam, Democracy and the West: A Round Table with Dr. Hasan Turabi* (Tampa, Fla.: World and Islam Studies Enterprise, monograph no. 1, 1993).

28. Ibid., pp. 46–47.

PART FOUR

The Struggle over Popular Culture

21

Introduction to Part Four

Timothy Mitchell

Popular culture might seem an unusual topic for a book about political Islam. Most contemporary Islamic movements have a strong element of puritanism. Their leaders often advocate an austere and disciplined life and oppose what they see as the immorality not only of Western music, film, or art but also of many local forms of popular dance, poetry, drama, or song.

In practice the relationship between popular culture and new forms of Islamic identity is less simple. A pious, newly veiled Cairo schoolgirl, interviewed on television in the mid-1980s, said she avoided the immorality of the cinema but was an avid fan of the TV serial, "Dallas." She disliked the character J. R. for his illicit affairs but approved of Bobby, whose lifestyle was "close to Islamic behavior."[1] In the same years, according to the chapter by Joan Gross, David McMurray, and Ted Swedenburg on rai music, Cheb Khaled used to open his concerts in Algeria with a song about the Prophet Muhammad before proceeding to sing about women and drink. Islam and popular culture are not necessarily opposed to one another, and mix together in complex ways.

Besides, popular culture means more than just music, television, and folklore. The movements of political Islam generate their own forms of popular art and expression. The 1979 Islamic revolution in Iran produced posters, graffiti, and banners rich in popular images of piety, anti-imperialism, and martyrdom. The markets around major mosques almost anywhere in the world are usually filled with cassette tapes of favorite Qur'an reciters, the recorded sermons of popular preachers, multicolored posters of the holy cities, and assorted religious knickknacks and kitsch.

Popular culture provides images and icons that people draw on to construct their sense of identity and their relationship to others and to the past, often in opposition to the official ideologies of the state. In this wider sense, we should see political Islam itself as a form of popular culture. Islamic movements offer not just cassette tapes and religious posters but new forms of personal identity, new images of self and other, and new versions of the past.

The chapters of this section deal with television serials, popular music, political imagery, and the efforts of subordinate social strata to create meaning and order in urban space. They draw on the experience of two countries in the Arab world, Egypt and Algeria, as well as communities of Algerian and other North African origins in France. A common theme that runs though the articles is the contest between Islamic groups and others over the interpretation of the nation's past.

Egypt and Algeria have different pasts, but the contests over interpretation of their histories are similar. Both countries were occupied by European powers in the nineteenth century. French colonization of Algeria began much earlier and penetrated more deeply than the British occupation of Egypt. One million Algerians lost their lives in the war launched on November 1, 1954, that finally brought Algeria its independence in 1962 under the leadership of the FLN (National Liberation Front). Egypt won its independence in stages through a series of smaller struggles, which the 1952 military coup led by Gamal 'Abd al-Nasir claimed to champion.

Following independence, both the Nasirist state in Egypt and the FLN in Algeria began ambitious programs to develop agriculture and build heavy industry. After initial successes, by the 1970s neither state could maintain the pace of development. Under local and international pressure, both announced a partial "opening" (infitah) of the state-controlled economy to encourage private entrepreneurs and investment. The 1970s oil boom and the availability of migrant jobs abroad (for Egyptians in the Gulf, for Algerians in France) enabled them to postpone more radical reforms, but the collapse of oil prices after 1985 pushed both governments toward political and economic crisis.

This was the context for the reemergence of political Islam and its contestation of the postindependence, state-building projects. Military-based governments in both countries presented themselves as the culmination of the long anticolonial struggle and the guardians of national independence and prosperity. Their one-party states outlawed political opposition, whether Islamist organizations or progressive and secular groups, all of which had played an active part in earlier struggles. In the 1970s, Islamist activists turned neighborhood mosques into centers of mutual aid as the state's own social services failed to keep up with the rapid and unregulated growth of cities.

Some of these groups gathered into more militant organizations, denounced the corruption of regimes whose high officials had created for themselves enclaves of privilege and prosperity, and called for the radical reordering of society. By the end of the 1980s both Egypt and Algeria were in crisis. Growing millions in each country were without jobs or adequate housing, yet neither regime would consider serious remedies, certainly not those that might threaten its own privileges. The United States, France, and other Western governments continued to support these privileged elites, pushing only for measures of financial stabilization that might be attractive to Western investors (who largely stayed away) but would create further shortages of employment and housing.

In Egypt, where the state began to allow a very limited and largely secular opposition in 1976 but no serious criticism of or threat to its power, militant Islamic organizations embarked in the 1990s on a more concerted campaign of violence, carrying out attacks on cabinet ministers, Egyptian Copts (Christians), foreign tourists, and prominent secularists. Highlighting the importance of the cultural dimension to the Islamist struggle, the writer Farag Fuda was assassinated in June 1992, and the novelist Naguib Mahfouz was seriously injured in an assassination attempt in October 1994. The state responded with its own violence—arresting thousands, killing hundreds in armed attacks on suspected militant hideouts, and executing dozens more after summary trials in military courts.

In Algeria, the events of October 1988—a week of strikes and demonstrations bloodily suppressed by the armed forces—compelled the government to make more serious political concessions: freedom of the press, political organization, and open elections. The major Islamic party to emerge, the FIS (Islamic Salvation Front), swept the municipal elections held in June 1990 and dominated the first round of the national legislature elections in December 1991. The following month, to keep the old regime in power, the military seized power in a coup, canceled the elections, and proceeded to clamp down on the Islamic movement.

A violent struggle ensued, in which tens of thousands of lives have been lost, as the military rulers found themselves unable to suppress the Islamist forces. The latter have targeted numerous producers of popular culture including leading rai musicians and the director of the national theater. Secularist journalists, authors, and feminists have also been assassinated. The struggle also spread to France, the chief supporter of the military regime, where many thousands of residents of North African origin found themselves objects of official suspicion and increasing harassment.

The chapters in this section address these political developments from several angles, looking at different dimensions of the struggle over the shared meanings, spaces, and identities of popular culture. "Rai, Rap, and Ramadan Nights," by Joan Gross, David McMurray, and Ted Swedenburg, explores how North African immigrant communities in France have used rai music to create their own identities, neither French nor Arab but a mixture of the two. The difficulty in sustaining these identities is traced through the fate of rai music, as it was first taken over by mainstream French youth culture and then condemned by the Islamic movement in Algeria.

"Dramatic Reversals," by Lila Abu-Lughod, examines how the Islamist movement in Egypt is represented in the country's enormously popular television drama serials. She traces how state-controlled popular programming first excluded the Islamists from its picture of Egyptian society and then in the early 1990s suddenly switched to portraying them as violent or misguided extremists. Although the Islamists have no access of their own to official media, they nevertheless influence television, Abu-Lughod shows, making it conform more closely to the morality they espouse.

"Taking up Space in Tlemcen," an interview with the Algerian sociologist Rabia Bekkar, and Meriem Vergès's "Genesis of a Mobilization," both explore the appeal and power of political Islam among Algerian youth. The town of Tlemcen in northwest Algeria illustrates the local issues of urban decay, unemployment, and gender relations that Islamic activists have sought to address. Vergès examines the broader meaning of the movement to its participants. She argues that the appeal of the FIS is not strictly religious, but lies in its power to translate social issues into political terms. This involves discrediting the official history of modern Algeria as a secular struggle against colonialism and the West and reclaiming a central role for Islam in the construction of the nation. As with Egyptian television serials and rai music among North Africans in France, struggles over personal and national identity represent a response to the contemporary political crisis. The themes and symbols of this struggle are found in the complex interplay of Islam and popular culture.

NOTE

1. See *Middle East Report*, no. 159 (July–August 1989): 8, referring to the 1984 BBC documentary "A Sense of Honor." This issue of *Middle East Report* is devoted to the topic of popular culture and offers a wider introduction to the subject.

22

Rai, Rap, and Ramadan Nights: Franco-Maghribi Cultural Identities

Joan Gross, David McMurray, and Ted Swedenburg

The collapse of the Berlin Wall has forced Western Europe to rethink its identity. In the past its conception of itself as a haven of democracy and civilization depended in part on a contrast to the evils of the Communist bloc. Today there is a revived notion of Europe as "Christendom," in contradistinction to "Islam." This time, unlike the period preceding Columbus's project, the Islam in question is not being held back at the frontier (Spain, the Balkans). New "minority" populations of Muslim background have penetrated Europe's very core. Europeans' anxiety about their identity, and their sense of cultural and economic siege by Muslim immigrants within, has emerged as one of the most contentious issues on the continent.[1]

Juan Goytisolo savagely lampoons this hysteria about "foreigners" in his hilariously provocative novel, *Landscapes after the Battle*. The book opens with the inexplicable appearance of unintelligible scrawls on the walls of the Parisian neighborhood of Le Sentier.[2] At first the natives assume the marks are the secret language of a gang of kids, but then someone spots a man with "kinky black hair" inscribing the mysterious messages. The natives conclude that the scrawls are written in a real alphabet—but backward—and are the handiwork of "those foreigners who, in ever-increasing numbers, were stealthily invading the decrepit buildings abandoned by their former tenants and offering their labor to the well-heeled merchants of Le Sentier." Then one morning a working-class native of Le Sentier drops in at his local bar for a pick-me-up, only to discover that the sign identifying his tavern has been replaced by one written in that incomprehensible script. Wandering through the neighborhood, he is horrified to find that every sign—the Rex cinema's marquee, McDonald's, street signs, the placard on the district mayor's office—has been changed. Even the sign outside the office of the newspaper of "the glorious Party of the working class," *L'Humanité*, is now

Al-Insaniyya. A catastrophic, cacophonous traffic jam has broken out, for neither drivers nor traffic police can decipher the street signs. "Trying to hide his laughter, a swarthy-skinned youngster with kinky hair purveyed his services as guide to whichever helpless soul bid the highest." "[C]olonized by those barbarians!" the unnerved Le Sentier native thinks to himself.

Goytisolo's 1982 send-up of the French *immigrés'* nightmare seems remarkably prescient today. French antipathy is particularly virulent when it comes to the "foreigners" from North Africa who write in that "backward" script. France has never come to terms with its colonial history and its bloody war against the Algerian national liberation struggle, which cost one million Arab lives. From the frenzied reactions of so many white French men and women, one might imagine that colonialism was a generous project, and that the Arabs in France are living the high life with no cause to complain about poverty and racism.

So severe are French apprehensions about the *immigrés* that during the 1989 *"hijab* affair" (when female Franco-Maghribi *lycée* students demanded the right to wear Islamic headscarves), the media successfully welded the signifiers "immigrant," "Muslim fundamentalist," and "invasion," creating the specter of an Islamic France.[3] Then-president François Mitterrand asserted that the country had gone beyond "the threshold of tolerance," and former president Valéry Giscard d'Estaing warned of a foreign "invasion."[4] These opinions of the political elite are widely shared: a 1991 government survey indicated that 71 percent of the French populace think there are too many Arabs in the country, while another 1991 poll showed that over 30 percent of the electorate supported Jean-Marie Le Pen's far-right National Front platform calling for the expulsion of *immigrés.*[5] President Jacques Chirac, then mayor of Paris and leader of the right-wing Rally for the Republic, expressed his sympathy for the decent French working people being driven "understandably crazy" by the "noise and smell" of foreigners.[6]

"Noise and smell"—music and cuisine—are important vehicles through which "foreigners" maintain and construct distinctive identities in France. Probably the most well-known type of "Arab noise" heard in the Franco-Maghribi community is rai music, a genre which began reaching US audiences via alternative radio and nightclubs in the late 1980s and is part of a growing World Music phenomenon.

RAI: FROM BORDELLO TO BANLIEUE

Rai developed in western Algeria during the 1920s, when rural migrants pouring into the growing cities of the west, particularly the permissive port town of Oran, brought their music with them. Rai became a mainstay of Orani nightlife in taverns, brothels, and cabarets, and was also played on festive occasions like weddings. Unlike other Algerian musical forms, rai performances were associated with dancing, usually in mixed-gender settings. Although from the 1930s until the early 1960s rai artists often sang about social issues, including the national liberation struggle, their standard subjects were wine, love, and the problems and pleasures of marginal life. After independence, rai performances were confined primarily to domestic spaces and the demimonde, as a chill descended over public culture with Houari Boumedienne's state-sponsored puritanism. But when president Chadli Benjedid loosened moral constraints in 1979, rai emerged from the shadows and gained national popularity as its sounds, recording techniques, and instrumentation were modernized.[7] When cassette sales of the new "pop" rai took off, producers demanded more risqué lyrics from rai singers, in the belief that the music's marketability depended on its libertine heritage.[8] Cheikha Remitti, for instance, sang:

> Oh my love, to gaze upon you is a sin,
> It's you who makes me break my fast.
> Oh lover, to gaze upon you is a sin,
> It's you who makes me "eat" during Ramadan.

And she chanted: "When he embraces me, he pricks me like a snake," and "People adore God, I adore beer."[9] As the music gained popularity among disaffected Algerian youth, the government attempted to suppress it, banning it from the airwaves and denouncing it as "illiterate" and lacking in "artistic merit."

In France, meanwhile, "pop" rai became one of the chief means of cultural expression for a minority struggling to carve out an identity in a racist environment. Salah Eddine Bariki's 1984 study of radio stations serving Franco-Maghribis in Marseilles (which has the largest concentration of Arabs in France) provides an interesting instance of rai's uses and the hybrid processes of Franco-Maghribi identity formation.[10] The most popular radio programming, he discovered, was during Ramadan nights, the evenings of celebration following daytime fasting during the holy month, when listeners stayed up late and called the stations to request songs, tell jokes, debate politics or religion, or discuss the meaning of Ramadan for North Africans in France. Almost all callers chose to speak *Musulman*, their name for the Arabic spoken in France. Most of the Maghribi radio audience Bariki surveyed admitted to drinking alcohol, few condemned mixed (Muslim-Christian or Muslim-Jewish) marriages, about a third had eaten pork, and less than half fasted during Ramadan. But many made a special effort to buy *halal* meat (slaughtered according to strict Islamic precepts) during the holidays, while a large number claimed they did not drink alcohol for forty days prior to the holy month (a practice invented by immigrants).

The callers described Ramadan nights radio programming as a nostalgic return to an ambience resembling what they had heard of or remembered about Ramadan celebrations in the home country—a time of good food and pleasant relations between parents and children. The evenings of North African entertainment reduced the burden of exile by establishing a mood of community closeness. By far the most common way that listeners reaffirmed their ethnic presence was to call the station to dedicate a song to a relative or friend. And the near-unanimous choice of callers during Ramadan in the early 1980s was the Algerian "King of Rai," Cheb Khaled.

The fact that Arabs of Marseilles looked to Cheb Khaled for comfort and solace during Ramadan underscores the complicated and contradictory nature of North African ethnic identity in France. Ever since his career began in the mid-1970s, Cheb Khaled has cultivated the image of a swaggering, dissolute, and worldly cabaret singer. "When I sing rai," Khaled says, "I talk about things directly; I drink alcohol; I love a woman; I am suffering. I speak to the point. . . . I like Julio Iglesias. . . . But he just sings about women, whereas [I sing] about alcohol, bad luck, and women."[11]

Although these are not the sentiments normally associated with Ramadan observance in Arab-Islamic countries, they are consistent with rai's heritage in Algeria. According to Hocine Benkheira, in Algeria during the mid-1980s Cheb Khaled typically opened his concerts with a song about the Prophet Muhammad, then proceeded to sing about drink and women. The Algerian audience danced whether Khaled's subject was whiskey or the Prophet; no one considered this blasphemous.[12] Such attitudes are congruent with the cultural life in a tolerant country where, despite official puritanism and growing Islamism, mosque attendance remained comparatively low and alcohol was consumed in open view at the numerous taverns of central Algiers and Oran until recently.[13]

In the mid-1980s, rai in France began to break out of strictly "ethnic" space when it gained greater public visibility due to an upsurge of Franco-Arab struggles against racism and the burgeoning Parisian World Music scene. Rai was featured at multicultural concerts sponsored by SOS-Racisme, a multiethnic antiracist organization established in 1985 to counter escalating anti-Arab violence and to channel the militancy of young Franco-Maghribis. The music gained recognition as a token of ethnic identity for militant Beurs (as second-generation Maghribi residents in France were known), as well as winning over a white audience sympathetic to the antiracist struggle. The genre's successes in France were one reason why the Algerian government finally stopped suppressing rai in 1985. The same rai producers who once promoted bawdy lyrics now vigorously cleaned them up to make the music palatable to a wider audience. Some sectors of the state bureaucracy promoted rai as an antidote to a growing Islamist trend.[14] But by 1990, Islamist campaigns against rai caused several of its stars (Cheb

Khaled, Cheb Mami, Chaba Fadela, and Cheb Sahraoui) to relocate in France. Paris became a major rai center, and rai artists began to win an international audience via World Music circuits.

DEFINING FRANCO-MAGHRIBIS

Who is the Franco-Maghribi audience for "Arab noise"? Although French racist discourse lumps all Arabs into a single category, they are in fact a heterogeneous group encompassing Algerians, Moroccans, and Tunisians; Arabs and Berbers; "legal" noncitizen residents, citizens, and "illegals"; and immigrants and their offspring born in France. An estimated 700,000 Algerian "foreigners" (noncitizens), 575,000 Moroccans, and 230,000 Tunisians live in France. Tens of thousands (no one knows for sure) of North Africans reside there without legal permission. Another million French citizens are thought to be of Maghribi origin.[15]

Franco-Maghribis born in France now reject the designation Beurs, preferring "Franco-Algerians," "French Arabs," or "youths originating in North African immigration" (*jeunes issues de l'immigration maghrébine*). The bulk of the Franco-Maghribi population, immigrants and Beurs, reside in multiethnic ghettos—the suburbs, or *banlieues*—ringing French cities. The loci of the "immigrant problem" is in these modernist architectural nightmares, bleak zones of high-rise apartments with minimal public facilities, substandard schooling, and excessive unemployment (70 percent of the children of immigrants in Lyons between the ages of sixteen and twenty-five are unemployed).[16] The *banlieues'* spatial marginalization reflects an economic trend toward an ethnicized labor force and increased dependence on undocumented and "reserve" labor in an era of "flexible specialization."[17]

Franco-Maghribi cultural orientations are also heterogeneous. Moroccan sociologist Adil Jazouli provides a useful map of the various trajectories: the assimilationist, the delinquent, the ethnonationalist, and the hybrid. The assimilationists change their names from Karima to Karine or Boubker to Bob and practice a kind of hyperconformism to French societal norms. This tendency has given rise to organizations like France-Plus, an electoral pressure group pushing for Franco-Maghribi electoral representation on all party tickets (except Le Pen's National Front). In the municipal elections of 1989, France-Plus managed to get 390 Beurs elected, in contrast to only 12 in 1983.[18] France-Plus, which lacks a social base in the *banlieues,* is often seen as representing the interests of the "beurgeoisie."[19] Its chief competitor is SOS-Racisme, which is antiracist but takes assimilationist positions and likewise enjoys little support in the *banlieues.* A media-savvy organization with ties to the Socialist Party, SOS-Racisme's platform of diffuse "multiculturalism" has blunted the distinctly Maghribi thrust of the antiracist struggle.[20]

The second group—the delinquents—are young Franco-Maghribis from the *banlieues* who seem incapable of fashioning coherent identities, who feel trapped between two distinct cultural poles, neither of which can accommodate them. Denied decent educations or regular employment, they are best known for their random acts of violence and petty criminality.[21] The third segment, the militant ethnonationalists, affirm allegiance to an Arab or Berber sociocultural universe premised on an eventual return to the homeland. In the meantime they seek to create an autonomous and separate social space, while having minimal contact with (white) French. Also included in this category are the militant Islamists. The hybrids are young Franco-Maghribis who embrace cultural diversity and attempt to fashion a positive, syncretic, minority identity out of their "in-betweenness." Their slogan is "*le droit à l'ambiguité.*"[22] This group attempts to forge a new identity, fusing elements from French and Arab culture.

North African music offers important channels of public communication for each of these marginalized groups who have few formal institutional channels at their command. Rai has been a means of articulating desires to belong to a collectivity within France that shares a tolerant Arab-Islamic ethnonational identity. Moreover, rai mobilizes a cultural sensibility that is simultaneously Arab, modern, and socially progressive. The secular character of rai lyrics and performances reflects a general trend toward secularization of Franco-Maghribi sociocultural life. Religion has become another form of ethnic identification, like holidays, cuisine, language, and music. By some estimates, only 5 percent of the "potential" Islamic population are actually practicing Muslims, although Islamic practices like Ramadan are widely, if rather idiosyncratically, observed.[23] Rai singers like Cheb Khaled articulate the younger generation's rebellion against the constraining mores of the older generation and the Islamists: "I am against Islamic fundamentalists. Young people want to progress. Even now, I can't smoke in front of my father, not even a cigarette. Young people who want to speak with a girl or live with her can't talk about it with their parents. In rai music, people can express themselves. We break taboos. That's why fundamentalists don't like what we're doing."[24]

FROM RAI TO RAP

Recently, rai in France has followed various tracks. The "beurgeoisie" and their white liberal and Socialist allies tend to sponsor Arab music concerts and festivals to celebrate the "authentic" culture or folklore of "the people." Such strategies disguise the fact that the "beurgeoisie" lacks a social base in the *banlieues.* Among the Franco-Maghribi masses, rai today is primarily the music of choice for recent immigrants and older Beurs. Rai performers who tour the communities mainly play to modest audiences at local dance halls and weddings.

The signal exception is Cheb Khaled, who after years of performing rai for adoring Franco-Maghribi audiences, has begun to "cross over" into the French pop scene. His album, *Khaled* (Barclay), featured an impressive range and mélange of styles, from "folk" and "pop" rai to funk beats, reggae riddims, flamenco stylings, and Stephane Grappelli-flavored violin. During the spring of 1992, Khaled's hit single "Didi" was "heating up all the dance floors" in France.[25] The "Didi" video, shot in rapid-fire MTV style, blends images of Moorish wood screens, Sufi dancing, and the latest hip-hop moves. Khaled's new crossover commercial appeal is demonstrated by the fact that "Didi" made the Top 10 in the call-in vote for "Hip Hip Hourah," M6-TV's music video program, in May 1992.

While Khaled invades the mainstream and other rai artists work the local immigré circuit, it is rap that has emerged as the musical expression of the new generation of Franco-Maghribi youth. They regard "Arab" music like rai (or Kabyle and other Algerian genres) as an important, if somewhat dated, part of their minority heritage, while increasingly viewing rap as the key vehicle for articulating their complex identity. Rap offers a means of expression in French, which minority youth inflect with hip street argot, *frankaoui*, and African-Americanisms. Rap's stance vis-à-vis white French society is aggressively confrontational and allows *banlieue* French youth to feel connected with oppositional "Black" culture throughout the world. But *rappeurs* and *rappeuses* have not turned their backs on Arab heritage: Malek Sultan, the Algerian member of I AM, France's most famous rap group, chants in "Do the Rai Thing": "Cheb Khaled . . . C'est le Public Enemy Arabe."[26]

The rap/hip-hop/graffiti culture of the *banlieues* is also increasingly associated in French racist discourse with criminality—gangs, drugs, welfare scrounging, and the violence thought to inhere in immigrant culture. The right-wing press suggests that the big (immigrant) drug dealers of Marseilles are using profits from heroin sales to finance "certain Arab movements in France."[27] The Socialist establishment tries to co-opt rap. "*[L]e rap, le graff* [graffiti]; I believe in this generation," claims culture minister Jack Lang, who invited rappers to perform at a prime minister's garden party for National Assembly members.[28] But it is unlikely that commercial success or attempts to mainstream will soon tone down the messages of rappers like MC Solaar: "*Ce monde est caca, pipi, cacapipi-taliste.*"[29]

Both rap and rai are vehicles through which Franco-Maghribis identify simultaneously with French and Arab cultures and resist French ethnocentrism and Algerian conservatism. Yet the pressures from both sides often seem overwhelming. Memories of French racist violence, colonial and postcolonial, remain vivid: for instance, the three hundred Algerian immigrants killed in Paris in October 1961. Protesters carried the photo of Habib Grimzi, an Algerian who died after being tossed from a speeding train by French soldiers in November 1983, at the head of the hundred thousand-strong December 1983 march on Paris. The racist violence, moreover, has increased. The position of Franco-Maghribis was particularly vulnerable during the Gulf war, when French newspaper headlines howled about "The Arab Threat in France" and "Arab Terrorism in France," and Giscard d'Estaing's former interior minister, Michel Poniatowski, suggested the mass expulsion of immigrants.[30] A poll in *Le Figaro* taken during the war showed that 70 percent of all French "Muslims" (i.e., Arabs) feared they would become targets of terrorist attacks, and more than half felt that the war could lead France to deport Muslim immigrants.[31]

Meanwhile, hybrid cultural forms have been under attack in Algeria, where conservative forces consider music like rai not merely "noise" but "illicit" and "immoral." In March 1991, the Algerian Islamist party, the Front Islamique du Salut (Islamic Salvation Front, or FIS) mounted a vigorous campaign against the public performance of music (rai and other genres) during Ramadan. On March 21, 1991, fourteen persons were injured in Algiers when young Islamists, attempting to torch a performance hall and stop a concert, clashed with police. A few days later, crowds led by FIS militants threw bottles and stones at another concert audience, injuring several fans. An antirai plank was a central part of FIS's electoral platform in December 1991.[32] More recently, Cheb Hasni, a favorite among our informants in France, was murdered on September 29, 1994, after militant Islamist leaders called for a death sentence for singers they considered vulgar. Several thousand people joined his funeral procession in downtown Oran. This incident followed on the heels of the kidnapping of anti-Islamist Berber singer, Lounes Matoub. Franco-Maghribi writer Mohamed Kacimi attended a Friday prayer service in late 1990 at an Algiers mosque in which FIS second-in-command 'Ali Ben Hadj delivered the following speech: "As for the secularists, pseudo-democrats, atheists, feminists and francophones, and other evil-doers [*suppôts de Satan*], the day when we gain power we'll put boats at their disposal which will take them to their motherland, France." The crowd at the mosque, Kacimi reports, was entranced. Given such hostility to hybridity in France and Algeria, where, he wondered, should the Franco-Maghribis go?[33]

EL HARBA WAYN?

Kacimi's question recalls Cheb Khaled's celebrated song of alienated fury "El Harba Wayn?" (To flee but where?), taken up as an anthem by Algerian youths during the violent urban insurgencies of October 1988 which resulted in some five hundred deaths.[34] The song goes:

> Where has youth gone?
> Where are the brave ones?
> The rich gorge themselves,
> The poor work themselves to death,
> The Islamic charlatans show their true face.
> So what's the solution? We'll check it out.
> You can always cry or complain
> Or escape . . . but where?
> The good times are gone,
> With their celebrations and prosperity.
> Baraka has fled
> And selfishness destroyed solidarity . . .
> Where in this organized chaos
> Are the men of yesteryear
> And the proud women?
> Youth no longer answers,
> This life is nothing to smile about.
> Let's stop saying: everything's all right . . .
> Gold has turned into worthless lead
> Whose cover stifles all understanding . . .
> There's only flight . . . but where?

Rai is one line of flight, a cultural border zone of syncretism and creative interminglings of French and Arab. At once "ethnic" and French, rai is a front in a wider cultural struggle that "despite racist opposition" is recasting French national identity, performing a kind of genetic mutation of French culture. While the "beurgeoisie" enters the political structures, the cultural arena is full of dynamic examples of popular Franco-Maghribi practices of "interculturation" which problematize dominant Eurocentric notions of what it means to be French.[35] Khaled has hit the pop charts with music that combines the Maghribi drumbeats of the *derbouka* with African-American funk. Dazibao, an acid-rock band, sings in Arabic and performs with a smoke machine. Jimmy Oihid croons in blues and jazz-funk styles, and his concerts include a song for the Palestinians. Carte de Séjour ("residence card"), a band of Franco-Maghribi rockers, sing in French and Arabic and play guitar riffs tinged with subtle arabesques. Rappers like I AM and Human Spirit mix reggae, Nigerian highlife, African-American beats, and Arab melodic strains. Amina, France's most famous pop musician of North African (Tunisian) origin, was the nation's representative at the 1991 Eurovision contest (a decidedly mainstream affair). She sings cabaret ballads and disco-funk in French and Arabic, backed by Euro-French, West African, North African, and Israeli musicians. "I will continue preaching for the mixture of cultures," Amina proclaims. "The more hybridization we have, the less we'll hear about claims to [a pure] culture."[36]

Maybe one day the "decent" people in France will be those who listen avidly to the sounds of Cheb Khaled or I AM's Malek Sultan, and who consider the speeches of Le Pen and Chirac to be obnoxious "noise." Maybe one day its natives will decipher the graffiti, and learn that L'Humanité and Al-Insaniyya are synonyms.

NOTES

1. David Morley and Kevin Robins, "No Place Like Heimat. Images of Home-(land) in European Culture," New Formations, no. 12 (1990): 1–21.

2. Juan Goytisolo, Landscapes after the Battle, translated by Helen Lane (New York: Seaver Books, 1987 [first Spanish edition, 1982]).

3. André Koulberg, L'Affaire du voile islamique: Comment perdre une bataille symbolique (Marseilles: Fentre Sur Cour, 1991), p. 34, shows that in the media onslaught the fact that 48 percent of French Muslims opposed wearing the hijab was ignored..

4. Alan Riding, New York Times, May 27, 1990; Paul-Marie de la Gorce, "Chirac joue du tam-tam," Jeune Afrique (July 3–9, 1991): 30; Daniel Singer, "Le Pen's Pals—Blood and Soil," The Nation (December 23, 1991): 814.

5. The government survey also found that 24 percent think there are too many Jews in France (Le Monde, March 22, 1991). For the second poll, see Alan Riding, "Europe's Growing Debate over Whom to Let Inside," New York Times, December 1, 1991. A March 1992 report by the National Consultative Commission on the Rights of Man found that nearly half of the French expressed open antipathy toward North Africans, while 40 percent claimed to dislike the Beurs. See Féedrigot Olivier, Minute-La France (April 8–14, 1992): 15.

6. William Drozdiak, Washington Post, July 12, 1991; Stuart Hall, "Europe's Other Self," Marxism Today (August 1991), p. 18.

7. See David McMurray and Ted Swedenburg, "Rai Tide Rising," Middle East Report, no. 169 (March-April 1991): 39–42; Marie Virolle-Souibès, "Le rai entre résistance et récupération," Revue d'études du monde musulman et méditerranéen 51 (1989): 51–52.

8. Virolle-Souibès, "Le rai entre résistance et récupération," p. 59.

9. Marie Virolle-Souibès, "Le ray, côté femmes: Entre alchimie de la douleur et spleen sans idéal, quelques fragments de discours hédonique," Peuples méditerranéens 44/45 (1988): 208, 211, 214.

10. Salah Eddine Bariki, "Identité religieuse, identité culturelle en situation immigrée," in Jean-Robert Henry et al., Nouveaux enjeux culturels au Maghreb (Paris: Éditions du CNRS, 1986), pp. 427–45.

11. Banning Eyre, "A King in Exile: The Royal Rai of Cheb Khaled," Option 39 (July–August 1991): 44; Jean-François Bizot, "Sex and Soul in the Maghreb," The Face 98 (May–June 1988): 88–89.

12. Hocine Benkheira, "De la musique avant toute chose: Remarques sur le rai," Peuples méditerranéens 35/36 (1986): 176.

13. Arun Kapil, "Algeria's Elections Show Islamist Strength," *Middle East Report*, no. 166 (September–October 1990): 36.

14. Among those involved in the cleanup was Rachid Baba, producer of one of the most acclaimed rai releases marketed in the United States, *Rai Rebels*. See Virolle-Souibès, "Le rai entre résistance et récupération," p. 60; Benkheira, "De la musique avant toute chose," p. 177.

15. Pierre Lanier, *Les nouveaux visages de l'immigration* (Lyon: Chronique Sociale, 1991), pp. 16–17. An indication of the number of "illegal" residents in France is the fact that 131,000 came forward to claim citizenship when an amnesty for undocumented residents was proclaimed in 1981. Ibid., p. 14.

16. Some Beurs are French citizens, some are foreigners, and others binationals. Algerian children born in France after January 1, 1963 automatically received French citizenship, while those born before this date remain Algerian citizens. See Azouz Begag, "The 'Beurs,' Children of North-African Immigrants in France: The Issue of Integration," *Journal of Ethnic Studies* 18, no. 1 (1990): 4, 6.

17. Sami Naïr, *Le regard des vainquers: Les enjeux français de l'immigration* (Paris: Bernard Grasset, 1992), pp. 39–46.

18. Begag, "The 'Beurs,'" p. 9.

19. Farid Aïchoune, "Une mouvance en questions," *Qantara* 3 (April–June 1992): 15.

20. Adil Jazouli, *Les années banlieues* (Paris: Éditions du Seuil, 1992); Farid Aïchoune, *Nés en banlieue* (Paris: Éditions Ramsay, 1991).

21. Majid's gang in Mehdi Charef's *Tea in the Harem* (London: Serpent's Tail, 1989) is reminiscent of this tendency. This group provides the media with suspects whenever violence erupts in the *banlieues*. For instance, Patricia Tourancheau's report on the March 1991 Sartrouville riots (*Libération*, March 30–31, 1991, p. 19); and Paul Moreira on the November 1990 Vaulx-en-Velin riots (*Le Monde Diplomatique*, December 1990, pp. 4–5).

22. Adil Jazouli, *La nouvelle génération de l'immigration maghrébine: Essai d'analyse sociologique* (Paris: Centre d'Information et d'Études sur les Migrations, 1982), p. 27.

23. Jazouli, *Les années banlieues*, pp. 133–34; Daniel Singer, "In the Heart of Le Pen Country," *The Nation*, June 18, 1988, p. 861; William Safran, "Islamization in Western Europe: Political Consequences and Historical Parallels," *Annals of the American Academy of Political and Social Science* 485 (May 1986): 104.

24. Eyre, "A King in Exile," p. 45.

25. Dominique Guillerm, *Max*, May 1992, p. 21. The album was produced by noted producers Don Was (of Was Not Was) and Michael Brooks of 4AD Records.

26. See Rabah Mézouane, "Le rap, complainte des maudits," *Le Monde Diplomatique*, December 1990, pp. 4–5; Nicole Leibowitz, "Attali: 'Le rap remplace le bal,'" *Le Nouvel Observateur* 1441 (June 18, 1992), p. 20; Georges Lapassade, "Qu'est-ce que le hip-hop?" *Hommes et migrations*, October 1991, pp. 31–34.

27. Arnaud Folch, "Petit glossaire de la chasse aux vilains racistes," *Minute-La France*, April 8, 1992, pp. 17–21.

28. Alan Riding, *New York Times*, February 6, 1992; Barry James, *International Herald Tribune*, July 4, 1991.

29. Bernard Zakri and Pascal Azoulay, "Pour le métissage," *Actuel,* February 1991, p. 26.

30. Rabha Attaf, "Écoutez: comment ferons-nous la paix?" *Actuel,* February 1991, p. 55. On racist violence in the 1980s, see Jazouli, *Les années banlieues;* and Aïchoune, *Nés en banlieue.*

31. Howard LaFranchi, *Christian Science Monitor,* January 31, 1991. For a vivid account of the North African experience in France during the Gulf war, see Tahar Ben Jelloun, "I Am an Arab, I Am Suspect," *The Nation,* April 15, 1991, pp. 402–4.

32. Foreign Broadcast Information Service, *Near East and South Asia Daily Reports,* March 27, 1991, p. 5; Doug Ireland, *Village Voice,* January 14, 1992, p. 8.

33. Attaf, "Écoutez," p. 55.

34. Miriam Rosen, "On Rai," *Artforum,* September 1990, p. 23. Baraka is the spiritual power said to inhere in *sharifs,* the descendants of the Prophet Muhammad. This translation is adapted from Steve Arra's on the liner notes to Cheb Khaled's release, *Fuir mais où?*

35. Kobena Mercer, "Black Hair/Style Politics," *New Formations,* no. 3 (1987): 33–54.

36. Attaf, "Écoutez," p. 52.

23

Dramatic Reversals:
Political Islam and Egyptian Television

Lila Abu-Lughod

Walk the streets of Cairo or village lanes in Egypt any early evening and you will see the flicker of television screens and hear the dialogue and music of the current serial (*musalsal*). Read the newspapers and you will find articles and cartoons that can only be understood if you have been following these televised dramas. The serials, each usually composed of fifteen episodes aired on consecutive days, seem to set the very rhythms of national life. Extensive access to television and limited broadcast hours and channels mean that the audience will likely include a majority of Egyptians.

If the serials produce a national community, and television in Egypt, as in many Third World countries, is state-controlled, how does the entertainment provided to these large audiences articulate with national politics and policies? Although debates and talk shows airing political views take up some broadcast time on Egyptian television, much more popular, and thus perhaps more influential, are the melodramatic serials. Meant to entertain, they are by no means free of political messages. Who controls these messages and who is excluded? Do the powerful Islamist groups also influence television drama?

Writing after the June 1992 assassination of Egyptian human rights activist Farag Fuda, Karim Alrawi noted that the decision to assassinate Fuda was taken after a debate in February at the Cairo Book Fair between secularists and supporters of the Muslim Brotherhood, a debate that was filmed but never broadcast. He attributes the failure to broadcast to "the influence of the Islamic lobby on the state-controlled media." He notes that neither the Islamic university, al-Azhar, nor the Muslim Brotherhood condemned the assassination. "Instead," he writes, "they have criticized the government for allowing secular writers access to the media."[1] Alrawi's concern mirrors the widespread sentiment that access to and control over the media, especially television, is a crucial political question in Egypt.

I will argue that a look at key serials of the late 1980s and early 1990s reveals that although the writers and producers of the most sophisticated of the Egyptian serials have a certain independence from the government (reflected in the social criticism characteristic of their productions), they nevertheless participate in a shared discourse about nationhood and citizenship. This consensus is most directly presented in the changing treatment of the place of religion, one of the most pressing political contests in Egypt today.

Questions about the place of Islam are at the center of Egyptian public life. Armed attacks and periodic government crackdowns on Islamist groups alternate with attempts at co-optation and accommodation. Signs of a self-consciously Islamic cultural identity are growing. The contest is sharply drawn, and is reflected and managed in the mass media, especially television, in subtle ways. In the late 1980s Mamduh al-Laythi, director of the sector of the Union of Television and Radio responsible for the production of films and serials, confirmed that it was a concern of television producers, and said that subject matter has to change with viewers' concerns. Among the problems facing people in the 1990s, he listed the housing shortage, family planning, drug addiction, and religious extremism.

ISLAM AND PUBLIC CULTURE IN THE 1980s

The dynamic between the secular television producers and the forces of "religious extremism" has played itself out in the popular serials in different ways in the 1980s and the 1990s. With one important exception (the controversial "Hilmiyya Nights" to be discussed below), the serials of the 1980s maintained a noticeable silence on the Islamist movements and deliberately ignored the alternative vision these movements offer of Islam's place in Egypt's future—for specific political reasons. This changed dramatically in the 1990s when a policy of using media to combat "terrorism" was put into place.

As exemplary of the attitudes of the 1980s we can consider the work of Muhammad Fadil, arguably Egypt's foremost television director, and productions by Usama Anwar 'Ukasha, a thoughtful writer dedicated to providing high quality television fare. Their collaboration resulted in two programs in the 1980s that were immensely popular and also generated intense debate in the press and at public meetings around the country. Both works can be seen as critical commentaries on contemporary Egypt, skillfully embedded in an entertaining mix of melodrama and comedy. One serial, "The White Flag," was aired in 1989 after several years of trouble with the censors; a second, "The Journey of Mr. Abu al-'Ala al-Bishri" and subtitled "A Comedy about People and the Morals of These Times," was broadcast several years earlier.

The protagonists of both serials are dignified, highly moral men in their late fifties or early sixties who have spent their lives in public service, one as an ambassador in Europe and the other as an irrigation inspector in provincial Egypt. Both are well educated and cultured. The ambassador returns to Alexandria after a long stint abroad; the engineer returns to a Cairo he has not visited for years. Both find a changed Egypt, and are forced to confront the contemporary forces of corruption threatening Egyptian society.

In "The White Flag," the educated man of taste, with an appreciation for his national heritage, art, books, and Tchaikovsky, is pulled into a war with a crass (if ultimately irresistible) nouveau riche real estate developer. Aided by her unscrupulous lawyer, some misguided thugs, and a host of bribed public officials and newspaper editors, this very determined woman tries to force him to sell his historic seafront villa in Alexandria so she can put up apartment buildings on the site. In "The Journey of Mr. Abu al-'Ala," the earnest man goes to Cairo to try to sort out his relatives—all embroiled in family and financial difficulties. He suddenly comes into some wealth and is then ruined by the schemes of everyone around him scrambling for his money. He, too, encounters corrupt officials, dishonest lawyers, greedy businessmen, people who have bought their way into professions through bribes and cheating or who now use their skills for selfish ends. As one character puts it, "They are all running, running after money. No one stops to catch his breath or ask himself where he is going or what he is doing."

"The Journey of Mr. Abu al-'Ala" also treats the problem of the corrosion of family values. Older brothers abdicate family responsibilities, mothers fail to discipline their children, wives argue with their husbands, children do not respect their parents. "Where is the family spirit that binds you together?" the protagonist complains to his relatives. "Where is the respect of young for old and the compassion of the older for the younger? Where is the mother's concern for her children? Where is the children's fear of their mother? Where is it all?"

The serials, directed by Fadil and written by 'Ukasha, are more clever, subtle, and complex than the works produced by most other television professionals. But they differ little in their catalog of social ills. Other serials of the 1980s show individuals and families struggling against bureaucratic red tape, the near impossibility of getting anything done without connections and/or bribes, the housing crisis, and high prices. The tough circumstances of an expensive world are always depicted as tempting the younger generation to compromise their values and disrespect their parents. They seek degrading, unrespectable, or even illegal work (such as waiting on tables, acting, or drug dealing) or they try to marry for money.

The serials, in other words, are often about the struggles of good, decent people and families striving to remain so in trying times.

What may be unique about these two popular serials is that they personify morality and immorality not by the contrast between tradition and modernity or local versus Western but between two social classes. One class consists of those who took advantage of the economic liberalization and "opening" that Anwar al-Sadat initiated in the 1970s. These people are portrayed in the serials as fat cats who drive around in the latest model Mercedes while others cannot afford to marry, and who wear fancy suits and sit in glass and steel office buildings, dealing in construction, taking and offering bribes, and embezzling while others are unemployed. The young people of this class are spoiled and self-centered, dazzled by money and glamour, trying to become movie stars, pop singers, and boutique owners.

The other class consists of educated professionals—not just irrigation engineers and diplomats, but lawyers, architects, doctors, medical students, university students, philosophy teachers, school principals, responsible journalists, serious artists, and translators. Some have risen from the bottom of society through education; others have been comfortable all their lives. The qualities they share are honesty and concern for others and for society.

No opposition is set up between Westernization and an authentic indigenous identity, however defined. Both classes are presented as having appropriated much that could be considered modern and Western; the difference is in what they have incorporated into their lives. The nouveau riche villains have borrowed foreign cars, pop music, English words they do not know how to use, gaudy telephones, and garish wallpaper. The protagonists have taken as Egyptian values literacy and an appreciation for art and heritage. Mr. Abu al-'Ala's library contains books by Aristotle, Taha Husayn, and Voltaire. The villa in "The White Flag," full of art treasures like Chinese vases, was also the site of meetings of the early Egyptian nationalists.

What is startling in these works, in the context of the current situation in Egypt, is the absence of religion as a source of morality and the avoidance of overt signs of Muslim piety and identity in the protagonists. Silence on the Islamist movement as a modern alternative is broken only to mock. The villainess of "The White Flag" wears clothes that are a travesty of the new Islamic modest dress that has become a fashionable sign of piety. Her head is wrapped "modestly" in a turban and she carries the title (*hagga*) of someone who has been on the pilgrimage to Mecca. But her turbans are of gold lamé sometimes further graced by brightly colored pompons. Her speech is crude. The gaudy plaque of religious calligraphy that decorates her office is overshadowed by a huge television set and a photograph of herself smoking a water pipe. Nothing in her behavior suggests genuine piety.

EXCLUSIONS

The everyday forms of piety that are so much a part of life in Egypt were occasionally reflected in the popular serials: older characters or simple peasants are sometimes shown praying or using religious phrases. Except in the fourth installment of "Hilmiyya Nights," however, one never saw the young in the cities asserting an Islamic identity in the serials of the 1980s. The obscuring of this crucial group can be tracked through dress. There is a stark contrast between what the fashionably outfitted bareheaded actresses wear in the serials and what real urban women, educated and semieducated women on the streets, in schools, in health clinics, and in offices (including those of the Union of Television and Radio itself) are more often than not wearing—the *hijab* (headscarf) and full-length modest Islamic dresses.

This is not to say that religious programming on television did not exist; there was an increasing amount of it in the 1980s. But it was generally kept segregated from the more popular shows, especially the serials. Qur'an recitations open and close the television day; the call to prayer interrupts programming; there are numerous religious discussions and programs; the Friday mosque prayers are televised; there are even religious television serials—didactic and stilted historical costume dramas about the early days of Islam, always in the classical Arabic that few people fully understand and fewer speak.

A look at who is involved in television gives some indication of why this segregation occurred. Television was introduced to Egypt in 1960 under Gamal 'Abd al-Nasir and used, along with radio, as an instrument of national development and political mobilization. This ideology of mass communication in the service of national development persists for some, like the director whose serials I have been describing. He diagnoses the problem of citizens of this "developing nation" as "cultural illiteracy," and sees television drama as the best instrument for eliminating such illiteracy.

Many urban intellectuals within the television industry, people like Fadil and 'Ukasha who came of age during the Nasir period, see their vision of modernity and progress under threat today from both the newly wealthy and the religious groups. Their serials uphold the secular national institutions of the postcolonial state, promote the ideals of informed citizenship, and deplore what they view as abuses of basically good institutions like the law, government, education, and the family. Although somewhat controversial, the social criticism they offer remains within the bounds of the familiar paradigms of the official political parties.

Not so for the Islamists. They speak directly to the same corruption and consumerism the serials deplore. In their meetings, pamphlets, magazines, and Friday sermons in the thousands of private mosques for which the

Ministry of Religious Endowments cannot provide preachers, they offer an alternative path to modernity—a path that rejects the West and the secular nationalist vision that derives from it, as well as those Egyptians who have associated themselves with the West. This alternative vision has widespread appeal in part because it seems to offer people a moral way to deal with the times.

What Fadil, 'Ukasha, and other television professionals appeared to be contesting in excluding the Islamist vision from the serials during this period, was not the value of religious faith and piety but the place where Muslim discourse was relevant. The segregation of religious and popular programming produces a sense of the separation of spheres, declaring the *irrelevance* of religion in the public domain of political development, economic progress, and social responsibility. The same television professionals who refuse or are unable to portray the appeal of the Islamist vision, or who criticize it openly, may be personally pious. But they carefully construct boundaries rejected by the Muslim activist groups.

If the back page of *Al-I'tisam,* the magazine of the Muslim Brothers, is any indication, these groups resent this exclusion and are quick to condemn television. For example, articles published in 1989 as open letters to Safwat al-Sharif, the Minister of Information, criticized female television announcers for the impious display of their beauty, faulted a serial for falsifying history by erasing the role of the Islamic forces in Palestine and by glorifying 'Abd al-Nasir and his notorious intelligence service, and denounced the scandalous behavior of a number of major actors and actresses recently arrested for drug trafficking. One article hyperbolically described the mass media in contemporary Egypt as "a humiliated slave girl in the palace of the sultan who needs a protracted war of liberation in order to become her own mistress." Television was commended for airing one program that would be counted as a "good deed"—a religious program on the beautiful names of God—but the programmers were criticized for scheduling it so late at night that "only those suffering from insomnia watch it."

The magazine was even critical of the voice of official Islam in Egypt, Shaykh Jad al-Haqq, rector of al-Azhar University. A junior faculty member at a provincial university took him to task for remaining silent about Egypt's participation in the Miss Universe pageant. He noted sarcastically that even after shamelessly exposing her body in a bikini in front of the world media, the Egyptian beauty did not win.

In a *fatwa* (legal opinion) on the arts published in 1988, Shaykh Jad al-Haqq had stated that "Islam does not forbid entertainment or enjoyment."[2] To be permitted, though, the themes should follow the principles of Islam and its instructions; styles of performance should not stimulate any lustful desires; performances should not be in venues where instinctual desires will be stimulated or which are associated with alcohol or drugs.

Unlike critics in *Al-I'tisam*, he noted that "acting can be used as a tool to educate society by discussing issues that are threatening to the harmony of a successful society."

This judgment would condone the work of the socially conscious television drama producers I have been describing. Here, as in many other arenas, the position of the highest official in the religious establishment in Egypt did not challenge the government, insofar as television represents the position of the government that controls it.

NOSTALGIC FOR 'ABD AL-NASIR

Since some of the best directors can and do fund most of their productions through independent financing, the state television bureaucracy has at its disposal only the power of censorship, together with the preemptive self-censorship that accompanies it. In recent years, an even more powerful force for self-censorship has been the economic necessity of selling programs to the conservative, wealthy Arab nations of the Gulf.

Unlike many other serials, the works of Fadil and 'Ukasha are often controversial because they are so critical of social conditions in Egypt and, by implication, of government policy. Fadil has always been known and respected for this political criticism. His first serial, "Cairo and the People," aired after Egypt's defeat in the 1967 war, focused on cases of corruption and the abandonment of national ideals in the Nasir period. Written by two judges, some of the stories were inspired by court cases. As Nur al-Sharif, the famous film actor who got his start on this show, explained, "The serial harshly criticized the defects and mistakes that led to the defeat and what followed." When asked whether Fadil, the director, was supporting or attacking government policy in that series, he replied, "'Cairo and the People' was not opposed to the political theory of the time; it was against the weaknesses and errors in the way the theory was being applied."

With the significant shifts in government policy pursued by Nasir's successors al-Sadat and Mubarak, Fadil and 'Ukasha seem to have become even more critical. Their productions now nostalgically invoke the period of socialist ideals and nationalist vision through charged symbols of the Nasirist era, like the great singer Umm Kulthum or the Aswan High Dam. In fact, an upsurge of interest in the Nasir period is noticeable in a number of the popular serials aired during the last few years. "Hilmiyya Nights," an extremely popular serial written by 'Ukasha and shown during the month of Ramadan for each of five years beginning in the late 1980s, is an epic of modern Egyptian history that follows the rich and poor families of Hilmiyya, a popular quarter in Cairo, from the days of King Faruq to the present. Its positive depiction of 'Abd al-Nasir and the period before Sadat was controversial. In 1990, for example, every major periodical carried stories and editorials condemning or defending the serial.

This revival of interest in Nasir's day was surely related to growing disaffection with the social and economic changes brought on by al-Sadat's *infitah* (economic opening) and what may have been a popular rethinking of the peace treaty with Israel that accompanied this policy. Even more relevant was an extraordinarily popular serial called "Ra'fat al-Haggan," whose first two series were shown during Ramadan in 1989 and 1990. Based on a book by Salih Mursi, it claimed to tell the true story of an Egyptian spy successfully planted in Israel for twenty years, beginning in the 1950s. The hero is a handsome James Bond character, except that he is a chain-smoker and works at a low-tech level—placing pieces of string over his door to detect break-ins and writing in invisible ink. He is backed by a team of dedicated and patriotic Egyptian intelligence officers. Unlike most Egyptian television serials, this was a political rather than a family drama. It offered, however, only the simple message of identity politics, which guaranteed its appeal to a wide constituency.

The opening scene set the terms. Shown writhing in pain, the protagonist is dying of cancer in his home in Germany. He confesses to his German wife: "I'm not an Israeli, I'm an Egyptian. I'm not a Jew, I'm a Muslim." His widow then goes to Egypt in search of the truth about her husband. The rest of the serial unfolds the story of his life, through flashbacks accompanying the narrative his handler recounts to her.

What matters in this opening scene, and another in the same episode, is that our hero, although initially a small-time crook, is a patriotic Egyptian who has sacrificed himself for his country. His cleverness in outwitting the Israelis, his irresistible attractiveness to a bevy of beautiful Israeli women (played by some glamorous Egyptian actresses), and the triumph of the Egyptian intelligence service are meant to inspire national pride. Any political message besides this general love of country is noticeably absent. There is nothing to indicate the tenor of Egypt's internal politics at the time, although one hears some of 'Abd al-Nasir's emotional radio broadcasts about the 1956 war. More intriguing, neither the politics nor history of the Palestine conflict are presented, even though the hero is living in Israel.

The serial, perhaps inadvertently, conveyed a double message. Although its primary purpose was to promote national pride and identity, an effect produced by reviving memories of the Nasir period during which Israel was unequivocally the adversary on which heroic Egyptians should spy, it also seemed to normalize the traffic with Israel that al-Sadat had initiated. Israelis were portrayed as sometimes corrupt (the men) and immoral (the women all fall in love with Ra'fat, even when they are married), but generally normal and, in the case of women, quite attractive people. The roles were played by familiar and well-liked Egyptian actors. Our hero regularly greeted his new friends with *shalom* and *mazal tov;* his use of these terms taught them to children and adults all over Egypt. As one cartoon in the magazine *Ruz al-Yusuf* suggested, the serial also filled people's heads with a host of previously unfamiliar names like Charlie, David, Yakov, Cohen, Levy, and so forth. Significantly, the censors found little to criticize in the script and only minor changes were required by the Egyptian intelligence.

Concerning Islam, the most fascinating aspect of the serial is the way it asserts that Islam is an essential part of our hero's Egyptian identity even though he is not living a religious life. In Israel he is regularly shown drinking wine over meals and gambling (to obtain secrets); moreover, since he is passing himself off in Israel as an Egyptian Jew, he even attends temple. Yet two moving scenes proclaim his Muslim identity. The first occurs right after Ra'fat's death. His body has been prepared for burial and lies in a casket. The Egyptian intelligence officer who has taken special charge of him cannot bear the thought that he will have a Jewish burial and that no Egyptians will attend to honor him. So he flies to Europe and, disguised as a rabbi, manages to get into the house while everyone is away. As he stands before the casket he slips off his shoes, as one would do to pray in a mosque, and pulls out from his breast pocket a copy of the Qur'an. With tears in his eyes, he recites over the corpse of the hero the proper verses for praying over the dead.

We will see this officer cry in another episode as well, the one in which, late one night, he first discovers the file of Agent 313 and thus the existence of Ra'fat in Israel. Although others in the intelligence service have lost faith in Ra'fat because he is not sending worthwhile information, this young officer in training is moved by what he finds when he looks through the file; he decides to take responsibility for the young spy. When he opens the folder, he finds an envelope marked, "To be opened after my death." It begins, and we hear Ra'fat's voice repeating after him, "In the Name of God the Merciful the Compassionate. Truly we are God's and to Him we return." This is our hero's will, to be executed, he says, if he does not return alive to the land of his beloved Egypt. In a broken voice, with mournful music playing in the background, Ra'fat goes through, one by one, the sums to be given to each of the members of his family, even those brothers who mistreated him after the death of his father. He ends, by now practically sobbing, with the Muslim profession of faith: "Thus I will have cleared myself of all guilt in front of God, after I sacrificed everything in the service of the cherished homeland. God is Great, and for the glory of Egypt, I testify that there is no god but God and that Muhammad is His prophet."

The protagonist has, in this document, neatly linked Egyptian patriotism with Islamic identity. The serial thus asserted that those in the more militant Islamic movements today—and by implication perhaps their brethren jailed during the Nasir era—had no grounds for accusing their secular government of being less than fully identified with Islam. This program could thus be seen as part of a struggle to reappropriate Islamic identity for secular nationalists, a struggle in which the state-controlled mass media, as in much else, are instrumental.

CONFRONTATIONS OF THE 1990s

Beginning in 1991 violent confrontations between members of Islamic militant groups and government forces became disturbingly regular. Although many ordinary people disapproved of the violent tactics of the Islamic groups, especially when innocent bystanders were hurt, they were not particularly sympathetic to the government. The perception that the government was unable to solve Egypt's problems combined with concern over the harsh measures taken against Islamists, including mass roundups of "extremists" and then executions, to keep them cynical about the regime.

At the same time, in a related development, the 1990s marked a shift in media treatments of the Islamists. Still mostly excluded from producing for television, they were no longer to be ignored. Most striking was the fact that the silence on them in the popular serials was broken. Instead of struggling with censors just to be allowed to depict a mosque scene as part of his chronicle of the 1970s, as he had in 1990 for Part 3 of his celebrated serial "Hilmiyya Nights," 'Ukasha in Part 4 actually included a subplot organized around a "religious extremist."

Not surprisingly, the modernist nationalist serial did not present its religious extremist in a positive light. He was of problematic parentage, the son of a good character who had been seduced into a second (secret) marriage. The father died when the boy was an infant. Then his mother abandoned him. He was raised by his father's first wife and his aunt. Under the influence of an Islamic group he turned from a sweet little boy into an irritable and abusive young man who insulted his stepmother for working outside the home and intimidated another young woman for not wearing the *hijab*. He became more deeply involved with his group at the mosque and eventually disappeared. When he reappeared, it was as a fugitive banging on his stepmother's door and begging her to hide him. He had, he confessed, killed someone while robbing a jewelry store. His leaders had convinced him that it was fine to rob in the name of Islam for their cause, but he had not intended the murder.

Although an unpleasant character, the serial nevertheless portrayed him with some sympathy—as part of a generation that had gone astray because it found itself in a corrupt society with no ideals, in a country with no national spirit and no mission or role models for its youth. In the end this young man realized he had gone wrong. He realized his stepmother loved him. And he turned himself in to the police.

The negative depiction of an extremist no doubt met with the approval of the censors, who try to keep productions in line with government interests, but the real target of "Hilmiyya Nights'" critique was, like other serious productions of the 1980s discussed above, the corruption of entrepreneurs in post-Nasir Egypt.

Serials produced after "Hilmiyya Nights" and since the intensification of violence have been less subtle and more confrontational toward the "extremists." Their goal seems to be to discredit Islamists by showing them to be not only misguided but hypocrites or agents of foreign powers. "Hilmiyya Nights" had again led the way in its portrayal of an old rogue who emerged from prison sporting beard and white robes, a repentant born-again Muslim. A former informer to the British, drug smuggler, and currency dealer, this fat swindler's pious affectations were shown to mask, and actually enable, new forms of unscrupulous business practice (luring people into investment scams) and shameless personal desires (trying to use his wealth to "buy" himself a young attractive wife).

The more blatant attempts to discredit the Islamists followed a year or so later in serials like "Antar's Stable," in which the same comic actor played the role of a religious leader who gathered around him a group of young men seeking answers and a new society. Unbeknownst to them, he was working for someone linked to the Israelis.

Meanwhile, Egypt's long-standing Minister of Information, Safwat al-Sharif, began making pronouncements about the crucial importance of using the media to confront "terrorism." This was the same official to whom the critical open letters cited above from Al-I'tisam, the magazine of the Muslim Brothers, had been addressed. In April 1993 he himself became the target of "terrorism." He was shot at in what was assumed to be an assassination attempt. He escaped with only a hand injury but then began to appear frequently at news conferences, on television, and in photographs— with his prominently bandaged hand—calling with redoubled energy for the use of media to confront terrorism. Articles began to appear in the press about dramatic serials in various stages of production that had religious extremism as their theme. They described scripts waiting to be produced or to clear the censors. They reported on productions in progress ("on their way to viewers of the small screen," as they say) that were having difficulty recruiting actors and actresses willing to play the parts. One of these serials ("Hala and Darwish") was described in the headlines as the first to speak directly to terrorism.

I argued above that in the 1980s the strategy of secularist television producers was to insist that Islam was a matter of personal faith, not a solution to Egypt's problems or a guide to its political future. In the serials of the 1990s a new strategy seems to be at work. In the major release shown during the month of Ramadan in 1994 called "The Family," the narrative technique is to pit good, proper, official understandings of Islam against the misreadings and misinterpretations of uneducated Islamic extremists. The serial is organized around dialogues about the correct interpretation of Islam between a reasonable school headmaster and a religious militant of lower-class origins.

The portrayal of middle- and even upper-class Egyptians as measured, tolerant, and patriotic in contrast to confused lower-class militants manipulated by cynical leaders was echoed in a major film released in the same year produced by and starring Egypt's most famous comic actor, 'Adil Imam.[3] In a 1992 film called "Terrorism and Kebab" he had already begun to poke fun at the Islamists by showing a pious bureaucrat using his religious observances to avoid working in his job. The new film, entitled "The Terrorist," went much further in attacking the militants. It drew fire from many such groups and was banned in Jordan. Even supporters of the government's media campaign against terrorism criticized its lack of subtlety. A character modeled on the assassinated secularist Farag Fuda, mentioned in the opening of this chapter, delivers most of the didactic speeches about the true Islam.

Given the general support for piety, arguments are now rarely couched in fully secularist language. In his 1993 interviews, the Minister of Information had defensively asserted that combating terrorism was a way of defending true religion. He noted that media should use the weapons of democracy and freedom but he also stressed that above all it should use the weapon of belief in God in pursuing its true mission. Like the television director Muhammad Fadil quoted above, he described the mission as the elimination of all kinds of illiteracy—cultural, vocational, and, he added specifically, religious.

CONCLUSION

Although excluded from official media production and, at least since the 1990s, depicted negatively in the popular evening serials, the Islamists may nevertheless be influencing television in Egypt, not only by encouraging it to broadcast more religious programming (relatively uncontroversial and actually helpful in allowing the state and its media to appropriate religious correctness for itself), but also in making dramatic programs more socially conservative. It is obvious to everyone that the plots of current serials avoid the kinds of moral and sexual dilemmas that animated Egyptian films of previous eras.

Another small sign of the changes may be read into the following news-paper item. In June 1993, after a particularly grisly incident in which a bomb set in a crowded poor neighborhood killed some schoolgirls, a small article headlined "By Orders of the Minister . . . Wearing Makeup is Forbidden" reported something intriguing.[4] Minister of Information Safwat al-Sharif had given instructions that television announcers were to wear subdued makeup and to refrain from wearing brightly colored or flashy clothing. This, he informed the television staff, was to show the broadcasters' sym-pathy for the families of the victims of terrorism. He also announced that the subjects discussed on television programs during the coming months should be in keeping with "the mood of the Egyptian street."

It is difficult to interpret the minister's motives. Was the reason he gave genuine? Was this directive part of the campaign to ally state media and the people against the Islamists? Or could it also be read as a capitulation to the Islamists by attempting to reform television so that it would not be such a target of their hostility? Since wearing somber clothes and no makeup is indeed one of the ways women mourn in Egypt, this call to tone down the attractive announcers' appearances could well have been a form of con-dolence for the families and a tactic to convince viewers of the sympathy of state television.

But it is also true that the extravagant clothing and excessive makeup of these female television announcers had been denounced specifically in the religious press, where these women were vilified as provocative agents of temptation, just as the "shameful" dancing in television advertisements had been attacked as corrupting of social mores. If Safwat al-Sharif could enforce this new dress code for announcers, just as he had felt compelled to publicly announce his opposition to advertisements that were offensive to families, this would be a small move toward accommodating the kinds of values that make the Islamist program, in its moderate aspects, appealing to so many people in Egypt.

NOTES

A segment of this chapter was adapted from "Finding a Place for Islam: Egyptian Television and the National Interest," *Public Culture* 5 (3): 493–513, and based on research in Egypt supported by a grant from the ACLS/SSRC Joint Committee for the Near and Middle East and by an NEH fellowship from the American Research Center in Egypt. The final sections were written after further research in Egypt in 1993, supported by a Presidential Fellowship from New York University. I am grateful to Kamal Abdel Malik, Maha Mahfouz Abdel-Rahman, and Timothy Mitch-ell for helpful references and comments. I bear sole responsibility for the views expressed.

1. Karim Alrawi, *Guardian*, June 23, 1992, p. 19.

2. Shaykh Jad al-Haqq, *Al-Azhar,* July 5, 1988.

3. For a good discussion of the film, see Joel Beinin, "Terrorism, Class and Democracy in Egypt," *Middle East Report,* no. 190 (September–October 1994): 28–29.

4. *Al-Wafd,* June 16, 1993, p. 12.

24

Taking up Space in Tlemcen: The Islamist Occupation of Urban Algeria

Rabia Bekkar, interview with Hannah Davis Taïeb

Rabia Bekkar, an urban sociologist who has spent more than twelve years doing research in Tlemcen, Algeria, works at the Institut Parisienne de Recherche: Architecture Urbanistique et Société. She first came into contact with the Islamist movement in the form of neighborhood charitable associations. When the Islamic Salvation Front (FIS) became a legal entity in 1989, these associations became the support network of the new party. Bekkar was in Tlemcen during the 1990 municipal election campaign that led to the victory of the FIS, and when she returned in 1991 she met with newly elected FIS officials. Although the FIS is now banned and its leaders imprisoned, Algerian Islamic activism remains a significant phenomenon. Rabia Bekkar's observations provide a rare local perspective on the Islamist movement. Hannah Davis interviewed Bekkar in Paris in April 1992.

．　．　．　．　．

Can you describe Tlemcen?

Tlemcen is a city of 170,000, in Northern Algeria, not far from the border with Morocco. It lies against a mountain, part of it on the mountainside, and part of it on the plain. Looking down on the city from above, you can see that it's fragmented, with ensembles of urban fabric that are completely different.

Tlemcen has a *madina*, an old city. Around it is the colonial city with wide avenues, beautiful villas. On the periphery of the city is an expanse of housing projects. One of these, Sidi Said, is where I'm now doing my research. Then there's a part of the city that is self-constructed, juridically "illicit," which clings to the slope of the mountain. The people squatted on the land, and built their own houses in this enormous quarter. I did my

doctoral research in Boudghène, the largest of the self-constructed neighborhoods, with over 30,000 inhabitants.

Does each of these quarters have a particular population?
The only place in which there is a mixing of social strata is in the *madina*,
which mainly consists of working-class people but includes some who are
more well-to-do. The villas are occupied by the traditional bourgeoisie,
which is rather strong in Tlemcen, and also by the new bourgeoisie, including high state functionaries. The housing projects are mainly inhabited by the middle strata, including technicians, engineers, doctors,
and so on.

What about the self-constructed neighborhoods, like Boudghène?
Boudghène is inhabited by three kinds of people. There are old immigrants from the Sahara, nomads who lost their land. There are people who
left the *madina* when it became crowded due to the rural exodus. And there
are the rejects of the city. People with no place to live, no way to get into
the circle of housing allocation.
It is not entirely true to say that this quarter is inhabited by the most
disadvantaged. The first generation is largely made up of laborers, construction workers, the unemployed, but these families had children who
sometimes succeeded. They became teachers, functionaries.

What are the problems facing the people of Tlemcen?
More or less the same as in the rest of Algeria. There is an enormous
backlog in housing construction. At the same time, the rate of population
growth is among the highest in the world. In the villas, you might find only
two people living in an enormous home. But in the *madina,* you find twelve,
fifteen, twenty people in one room.
The other problem is unemployment, in spite of a very strong industrial
sector in Tlemcen—several large electronics and textiles factories and other
smaller industries. Tlemcen is in what used to be an agricultural region, and
since the beginning of the rural exodus people have been arriving from the
countryside, trying to find work.
Unemployment essentially affects youth. The factories gave jobs to the
first generation after independence. But these people will not retire to-
morrow. So there is saturation, without the creation of new jobs.

*The crowding at home—fifteen people in a room—must put pressure on public
space.*
This depends on whether you're talking about boys or girls. The girl is
educated to be turned toward the interior. But the boy, from the earliest

age, is pushed outside. By the time they reach adolescence, young men think of their life as taking place entirely outside. Public space, it's theirs.

What is there for them to do?

There are youth centers, and cultural centers built as part of the FLN [National Liberation Front] programs. But these places are so institutionalized. The young people feel suffocated; they can't relax. There have been a few attempts to create mixed tea salons. You find places with signs reading, "second floor for families." Around the university there are a few cafés that will admit young women as well as men, but in the center of the city there is no mixed café. It's unthinkable.

So there is no space where men and women can meet in a relaxed way?

Women can circulate in the city, on the same sidewalk as the men. But meeting, exchange—this does not exist in public space. Tlemcen is a superb city with a magnificent pine forest, but a woman cannot go walking there with a man without being stopped and having her papers checked—by virtue of no law, because there is none. Working women go out in the street, but it's really a passage. You have to be very courageous to go places and do things and at the same time tolerate the comments, insults, obscenities, shoving, sometimes even abuse. Where's the relaxation?

And women who don't work?

They can go out. There's just an entire framework controlling access to the outside—the veil; the accompaniment (your little brother, big brother, sister, mother); the "authorizations" and pretexts such as "I'm going to my aunt's" or "I'm going to the bath house."

There are certain places where women can go that are legitimate—the bath house, family visits, the doctor, the saint's tomb, the cemetery. And there are places that are legitimated by economic or social necessity—school, work. But one day a husband might say: "All right, now you stop working. We're married, you stay at home now."

Are public spaces the domain of men?

Young men call themselves *hittistes*—those who hold up the walls. When you walk through the city, there are entire quarters full of them: settled in, leaning back against the walls. The impression is of some kind of event, as though something is happening or is about to happen. Once I asked my brother what he does when he spends the day outside. He told me he goes to his regular café, meets his friends, drinks a cup of coffee. He leaves the café and takes a stroll in the city. He returns to the café, drinks a cup of coffee with other friends, then he walks until noon.

So you can see the vacuum, the emptiness, the readiness for any force at all that could attract them.

The Islamist movement apparently managed to harness some of this energy. How did this happen?

The first thing that happened was the emergence of many so-called "charitable" neighborhood associations in vulnerable quarters like Boudghène—places where there are chronic problems.

Before the Islamists emerged, the mosque served as a kind of community headquarters, rather like the village council. The mosque was active, but in a social rather than a political sense. Neighborhood conflicts and disputes were resolved; a family with economic problems could get help.

In the self-constructed quarters there is an enormous amount of mutual aid. It starts with the construction of a house—the whole neighborhood helps. This network of mutual aid laid the groundwork for these associations. In Boudghène, the first thing the association did was work on building and embellishing the mosque. They financed this by collecting funds door-to-door.

What kind of people were active in these associations?

University students, unemployed people, and former delinquents. These were the three groups in Sidi Said and in Boudghène. The members were entirely from the quarter, the office was in the quarter, the leader was from the quarter. The central organization came afterward. There was a progression: from the mosque regulating social conflicts, to a semiorganized system of neighborhood committees, to a national organization after the legal incorporation of the FIS in 1989. The local groups were easy to pull in. All the FIS had to do was to incorporate them politically, ideologically. They were already doing the work. Before 1989 there was already this base.

So after they fixed up the mosque, what next?

Their work expanded after the FIS won the municipal elections of 1990. In Sidi Said, for example, the associations began to clean up the housing project. You have to imagine what it's like in these neighborhoods. It's desolate. You go out, you come back with fifteen kilos of mud on your shoes. Public space is abandoned. The Islamist groups started planting trees and rose bushes, creating a green space. They painted stores, facades of buildings. They marked out a soccer field, put up the goal posts, and cleaned the field every day. In these housing projects household garbage is just thrown outside where children play. Through the municipality, they brought in big garbage bins with lids. A truck comes, empties the bin, and takes away the garbage.

In Sidi Said there was a university student on the neighborhood committee. Whenever he saw a child about to destroy a plant, or whatever, he went over and said to him, "No, that's a plant. It lives like a human being. God doesn't want you to hurt it." They sensitized children to the plants, but in relationship to religion.

How did things change at the mosque itself?
Before the elections the Islamists occupied only the mosques in the peripheral quarters of the city. These were really just prayer rooms turned into mosques. The main mosques are under the state. The *imam* is named by the state, and the weekly sermon is sent in by the Ministry of Religious Affairs. The Islamists didn't try to occupy the large mosques. But in the peripheral quarters, the mosque, its upkeep and embellishment, was financed by contribution. There, people made the mosque, with contributions and shared work. It was *their* space. And the Islamists quickly put in one of their own *imams*.

The imam *in the peripheral quarters wasn't named by the state?*
Well, like any other shortage—food shortage, housing shortage—there was an "*imam* shortage." The state couldn't keep up with urban growth, and with the proliferation of mosques, they couldn't find enough people to appoint as *imams*. So the Islamists occupied that space. After the municipal elections, they spread out into all the mosques.

In June 1990, I happened to go to the City Hall to see the FIS mayor. In came the technical director: the mayor had asked him for a map with all the mosques marked on it in red. The technical director said, "Why point out the mosques, we have other urban problems!" And the mayor said, "I want first to know which quarters have mosques, how many mosques there are, and where they're situated." It was the key for them!

As for children, there were more and more young people, preschool kids of five or six years old, going to Qur'an school in the mosque.

Was this new?
The state couldn't put a Qur'an teacher everywhere. The Islamists found volunteer teachers who gave free courses. So more and more parents, while they prayed, had their children in Qur'an school. You can't imagine how happy the mothers were to find a place they could leave their children instead of having them play in the mud. There are no kindergartens, no child-care centers. Parents also liked the idea that their children were learning something before they started school. Of course, in the minds of the Islamists, it was good that children start to learn the Qur'an rather than watch Mickey Mouse on TV.

What about adolescents?

At certain hours, the Qur'an school becomes a kind of tutoring center for junior and high school students. The Islamists asked university students and high school teachers from the neighborhood to give courses in math, physics, languages—any subject—for pupils with problems. In these quarters, one of the major problems is failure in school. Free tutoring was great.

Did the teachers and university students do this out of religious conviction?

Most of them were Islamists, but not all. In Sidi Said, I met young people who had practically nothing to do with the Islamist movement, but were either giving courses or taking courses, not out of ideological conviction. Others found themselves swept up in the movement.

The Islamists had an implicit project of trying to find activities for unemployed young people and delinquents. This included not only volunteer activities but projects that allowed them to make a little money. They set up a system of small shops, like newspaper kiosks, where they could sell newspapers, fruits and vegetables, groceries, perfume.

How did they do this?

In Sidi Said, there had been a site under construction for a "farmer's market." It was part of an FLN state project for neighborhood renovation. Then the FIS took over the municipality, and they took over this space. The platform had been built, the foundations already laid. But the Islamists built little shops, and gave them to unemployed people. Of course, on the list were young people judged potentially favorable to the Islamist movement.

Symbolically, the Islamists occupied an empty space. These foundations had been built years ago but the supermarket never appeared. Then, in a very short period of time, they created shops, and commerce started: a concrete fact in public space, seen by the whole housing project.

Did they try to give a religious resonance to this project?

The opening ceremonies were held at the mosque, even though the municipality was running the project. They took great care that the ceremony was religious even if the project was secular. This took place in 1990—three months after the municipal election. When I left in 1991, people were still talking about it.

How did the FIS manage to finance these projects? Did FIS municipalities get money like other city governments?

It seemed that the FLN had a strategy of reducing municipal budgets: "We'll cut the budget, things'll get even worse and the people who elected the FIS at the municipal level will see that they've done nothing." But the charitable associations stepped in and bailed out the FIS. At the municipal level, the FIS couldn't yet run things. They didn't have the means and they were inexperienced. But the charitable associations were in place; they had already done consciousness-raising in their neighborhoods. They made sure everyone knew that the FIS hadn't been given the budget to run a city.

The charitable associations and the FIS were separate groups?

In a given neighborhood you would find what was known as a "family" of FIS militants which was the base organization of the FIS. These groups operated alongside the charitable associations, which were larger, more open, and included FIS militants as well as other local people. It was the FIS militants who ran for municipal office. The associations supported the FIS candidates.

How did the municipality get money to function?

As a municipal government the FIS couldn't receive any money officially from a private source or a foreign government. But the charitable associations could. There were several levels of funding. Locally, the associations continued door-to-door fund-raising. The commercial bourgeoisie was a very important contributor. In Tlemcen there are mosques and charitable sites (shelters) that are entirely maintained by the local bourgeoisie. There were the *affairistes*—entrepreneurs who wanted to get rich quick. The FLN had blocked them with various laws controlling import-export, resale, and speculation. There were the big industrialists who also felt suffocated by the regulation of commerce and investment. All these groups supported the FIS because the FIS had promised to suppress taxes and deregulate production. There was also external financing, from Saudi Arabia in particular. The FIS wasn't worried about money.

They always seemed to have money to carry out their projects. For example, in Tlemcen there used to be a colonial square in the middle of town. A part of the *madina* had been destroyed and a rectangular plaza installed, with the great mosque on one side, the city hall on the other, the *madina* to one side, and across from it the colonial city. This square was cut in two by a roadway. The FLN municipality destroyed the road to create one big square with the traffic going around the outside. In the middle they built a monument: a rock with fountains. Outside Tlemcen there used to be waterfalls that are now dried up because of a dam. Maybe the rock was supposed to ease the nostalgia of the Tlemcenians for these waterfalls.

The FIS came and said, "What's this? It's no good! The space was better before!" In two days, they took out the rock and the fountains, rebuilt the road, put it all back the way it was before, but fixed up. How could a municipality with budget problems do this so quickly? They called on people to volunteer. But also there were two big private companies with modern equipment that did the work. One can deduce that the companies supported the FIS, since they did it for free.

I'm struck by your description of the efficacy of the FIS.

In meeting these young people, one *is* struck by their great discipline and by the organization of their local cells. At the same time, as a woman, as a democrat, I find it terrifying that an institution this well organized can do so much. In the electoral campaign, we saw this same efficiency and mobilization. They were everywhere.

How do you explain that enthusiasm?

Islamists came onto a completely empty field. You had a society that was morose, mired in a kind of lassitude, where people were completely burned-out, in despair—and they suggested something.

In the electoral campaign, the FIS brought up questions of honesty, of justice. The FLN had a program: housing, work, education. But the FIS said: we won't promise you anything. We'll have a state where we apply Islam, where honesty and justice will reign. And if there's no corruption, there'll be money. If there's justice, there'll be an equitable distribution of housing, and so on. It's a moral contract, not an electoral program.

There was another important element. The FIS touched on the issues which are the most sensitive: concerns about women, about the degeneration of moral values. On their side were upright women, as guardians of moral order. They were cleaning up public space. On the other side were bars, alcohol, urban degradation.

Did the moral hegemony of the FIS work for women as well as for men?

What is paradoxical, among many other paradoxes, is that the party narrowed enormously the space of liberty for women—restricting speech, returning to a very strict system of surveillance of women. Yet, at the same time, you saw militant women, including university women, who worked extremely hard for the charitable associations and for the electoral campaign. How to explain this? Most women didn't have that much liberty to lose. When they left the house they were subjected not only to family and social pressure but also to the obscenity of the street.

Then the Islamists asked them—or, in some cases, imposed on them—the wearing of the *hijab.* There was some imposition, say from a father or husband who says, "You can't work if you don't wear this." But there was also consent by women. A woman putting on the *hijab* puts on virtue, respect, and freedom of movement. Wearing the *hijab,* she can go out and not have to submit to insults. From the point of view of relaxed access to public space, it's important.

What has happened in Tlemcen since the rupture in the electoral process in December 1991?

I was in Tlemcen the day after the forced resignation of President Chadli Benjedid. We had the impression that political life had stopped for a moment. The next day, I went out to Sidi Said to see what people were saying, how people experienced the end of the electoral process. There was consternation. Many people had forgotten about the army, about the possibility of intervention. There had been the feeling that a breath of liberty was coming, and then—it collapsed.

There was incredible restraint on the part of the Islamists, which was much more important than what happened afterward: the coup d'état, military takeover, and then the punishing of the FIS.

Police and soldiers kept a close watch on the associations and the mosques. They tried to push them to extremism. Then there was violence, imprisonment. This is all classic.

Now, the FIS is legally out of commission. There is a new party called the Islamic Solidarity Front—the acronym is still FIS. But its activity is under close surveillance.

The FIS discourse made it clear that they weren't going to be democratic. But to stop the process by nondemocratic methods gave the FIS the ideological and moral claim to say, "The FLN just doesn't want to let go of its power, its privilege."

Before the multiparty system was instituted and the FIS became a party in 1989, all their activities took place clandestinely. In 1989, an Islamist Party emerged from underground. Now, they're being pushed again into clandestinity but their activities have not stopped.

25

Genesis of a Mobilization:
The Young Activists
of Algeria's Islamic Salvation Front

Meriem Vergès

In 1989, the single-party regime in Algeria began a process of legalizing multiple political parties. One of these was the Islamic Salvation Front (FIS). The National Liberation Front (FLN) officially accepted a party speaking in the name of Islam, with the avowed objective of establishing an Islamic republic. The success of the FIS in the municipal and regional elections of June 1990 and in the first round of national legislative elections in December 1991 furthered the rupture with the single-party system.[1]

This victory was interpreted by Algerian and international observers in several ways. Some regarded it as a rejection of Western values imported by colonialism, and a return of religion to reappropriate modernity.[2] Others emphasized the continuity embedded in the role of the FIS, comparing its religious and populist discourse to that of the Association of 'Ulama', the Party of the Algerian People (PPA), and the Movement for the Triumph of Democratic Liberties (MTLD), all of which had been subsumed in the FLN.[3] A third tendency looked for an explanation in the socioeconomic trends of exclusion and frustration motivating the activist cadre of the new movement.[4]

These analyses focus on the structural origins of conflict but ignore the question of how this conflict is perceived by the mobilized activists. The development of collective action depends not only on social and structural tensions but also on the significance that actors attribute to them. Central to this is the persuasive appeal of protest movements through which mobilization projects construct an ideology. I interviewed many youth of the Casbah of Algiers in an effort to understand how and why the FIS appeals to them. I propose to reexamine here the elements with which the FIS movement has constructed an interpretive order and an organizing principle for expressing existing demands in ways that resonate with the dominant belief system.

The FIS is not a religious movement, strictly speaking. Rooted in the social discontent that has been expressed in urban violence since 1985, the FIS gives political form to an emergent social movement. In contrast to the Islamic Society Movement (Hamas), and the Movement of the Islamic Renaissance (MNI), which have a weak electoral base,[5] the FIS is the primary beneficiary of networks organized around mosques established since the early 1980s by the Islamist movement. It uses religious rhetoric to translate social discontent into political terms. FIS leaders strategically use language evoking the Algerian war of national liberation and the activists' representations of the postindependence single-party regime.

To understand the dynamics of the FIS and the representations and heterogeneous practices with which it is inscribed, we must deconstruct the object termed "Islamist mobilization." The politically strategic under-thirty population comprises 70 percent of Algerians. As the field of action of the militant Islamists, socially marginalized urban youth at risk constitute the base of support of the FIS in Algeria, in particular downwardly mobile students and the unemployed, who together comprise a sort of lumpen proletariat. They have, in addition, a common memory of the Algerian war of liberation that diverges from the official history, the basis of the political legitimacy of the Algerian state.

THE STRUCTURE OF POLITICAL OPPORTUNITIES

The logic determining individuals' engagement and participation in the FIS is primarily a function of preexisting affiliations. Socialized by preachers or self-proclaimed *imams,* most of the activists are the product of networks organized around the *jami'* (the district mosque) or the *masjid* (prayer room) of colleges or universities established by the Islamist movement working in society "from below" since the late 1970s. Neighbors of the same quarter or students of the same cohort are fundamental in motivating involvement and constitute the networks of movements. But the activists mobilized by the FIS are not a spontaneous generation that appeared on the national stage instantaneously in September 1989. They emerged from a particular history of Islamist organization.

In March 1989, Islamist activists regrouped in the League of Islamic Preaching (*Rabitat al-Da'wa*) of Shaikh Ahmad Sahnun. Its objective was to federate Algeria's different Islamist tendencies. Some of them joined the FIS, which was publicly established at the Ben Badis mosque in Algiers. The FIS was the result of an unusual agglomeration of several more or less formal groupings. One was the *salafi* (retraditionalizing) movement, formed largely by "neofundamentalist" preachers inspired by either the Egyptian Muslim Brothers or the Saudi Wahhabis. Another tendency was the Algerianists, composed of francophone academic graduates in the sciences under the intellectual influence of Malek Bennabi, an engineer and author of many works on the conditions of the rebirth of the Muslim world.[6] Thus the FIS unites a diffuse network of groups and circuits of solidarity and constitutes them politically as an organized collective actor.[7]

The Islamist current, a tendency before it developed into a movement and organized in parties, can be traced back to the early part of this century. As in most Muslim countries, Algeria's Islamic movement combined religious renewal, moral reform, and nationalism, exemplified by the Association of 'Ulama' led by 'Abd al-Hamid Ben Badis. It fought assimilation by defending the Arabic language and the Muslim religion. In the same interwar period, the North African Star (ENA), formed of militant emigrant workers demanding the independence of the Maghrib, turned toward Arabo-Islamism under the influence of the Lebanese *amir,* Shakib Arslan. The successors of the ENA—the Party of the Algerian People (PPA) and the Movement for the Triumph of Democratic Liberties (MTLD)—maintained an Arabo-Muslim orientation of Algerian nationalism that was confirmed by the ideology of the FLN. This orientation defined identity based on religious adherence as the cement of national unity.[8]

After independence in 1962, the representatives of this current first mobilized around the issue of the status of religious teaching. The Islamic Values Association (*al-Qiyam al-Islamiyya*) was formed in 1964 around Hashimi Tijani, and spoke in the name of restoring Islam's authentic values. It proclaimed the superiority of Islamic values over those of socialism and national-populism, and demanded full application of the *shari'a.* After several confrontations, the regime banned and dissolved the Islamic Values Association in March 1970, thereafter claiming to monopolize the religious arena itself.

The agrarian policies of the government of Houari Boumedienne in the early 1970s provoked a new rupture between the regime and the religious current. While the students mobilized by the FLN and the Party of the Socialist Vanguard (the former Communist Party) explained to the peasants the benefits of the nationalizations inspired by the "agrarian revolution," the *'ulama'* and the first neoreformist nuclei campaigned against the attacks on private property guaranteed and protected by Islam. Shaikh 'Abd al-'Aziz Sultani, a former member of the Association of 'Ulama', published a virulent critique of Boumedienne's "socialist" option. Entitled *Mazdakism Is the Origin of Socialism,* it is considered the first manifesto of the Islamist movement in Algeria.[9] The Muslim Brothers (known locally as the *khwanjiyya*), then a minority in the university, retired to the mosques, where they developed a parallel Islam. Eventually an alliance developed between landowners dispossessed by the "agrarian revolution" and the religious current, and the landowners helped finance the construction of hundreds of mosques and religious activities with a charitable character.[10]

In 1978, the first organized Islamist opposition took the form of study groups in the "free" mosques not subject to the control of the Ministry of Religion. In 1982, they mobilized during the strike of Arabophone students in the University of Algiers that culminated in violent clashes. In 1984, on the occasion of the funeral of Shaikh 'Abd al-Latif Sultani, they regrouped around the question of the law of personal status. Mustafa Bouyali, a former FLN militant, returned underground to lead an armed Islamist opposition group until he was killed in a clash with the army in February 1987.[11]

The youth organization of the FLN, the National Union of Algerian Youth (UNJA), created in 1975, failed to incorporate activist youth.[12] This, along with the inadequate number of cultural institutions (youth centers, theaters, cinemas), encouraged the rise of the mosque as an alternative space of socialization, first in poor quarters and then in some high schools and universities. During this period, mosques played a fundamental role in motivating, involving, and constituting the networks of the movement. The mosque became the principal space of communication. Beyond strictly religious activities, "things that matter," such as domestic or emotional problems, were discussed. In this setting, the preacher occupied a central position.

Coming from a pious milieu, the underprivileged youth I interviewed prayed and fasted during Ramadan in their childhood, even if some abandoned these practices in adolescence. Whatever type of family they came from, this religious socialization was apparently effective. Thus, the mosque became a central locale of association with a restructured mission in the early 1980s. The self-proclaimed *imams* provided youth with revalorizing myths, and reconstructed a Muslim identity which gave individuals a sense of place in society.

Preaching solidarity and social cohesion, the "brothers" provided various services which helped to alleviate the inadequacies of the state. Charitable networks were organized around targeted categories: collection of donations for the needy, visits to the sick in hospitals, assistance in arranging funerals. Such activities were indispensable in enabling groups with limited economic resources to function collectively. Recreational activities—soccer games, hikes, group camping trips outside Algiers—multiplied the occasions for gatherings of the faithful. Activists eventually reorganized life in the quarters to the smallest detail. They took charge of road repairs, cleaned apartment buildings, and collected the garbage. As in Egypt, the "brothers" provided tutoring for university students. All these activities offered Islamist solutions to the inadequacies of the public sector in the

realms of redistribution and socialization, and encouraged the crystallization of new subjectivities. The youth I interviewed asserted that they had
found their "real brothers" in the mosque. Their individual lives were
enhanced by a subjective confidence in religious education as an alternative to the disintegration of their identities.

THE EVENTS OF OCTOBER 1988

A social movement can only emerge if it encounters favorable political
opportunities. The contexts in which protest movements are defined influence their chances of success. The emergence of the FIS on the national
stage in 1988 is linked to the "events of October," which were the result
of a complex political and economic process.

As Abdelkader Djeghloul notes, 1986 marked a rupture in the economic
and social evolution of Algeria. The collapse of the international price of
oil deprived the country of half of its export income, inducing a severe crisis.
While economic reforms, begun in the early 1980s, had not yet brought
about an appreciable increase in private investment, liberalization and
privatization of agricultural markets had produced a significant rise in the
price of vegetables, fruits, and meat.[13] Landless peasants, seasonal construction workers, unskilled production workers, and the unemployed were
the main victims of this disengagement of the welfare state.

The activist youth of the slum quarters of the capital were well placed to
contest the dramatic growth of inequality. The slogans these youth chanted
during international soccer games attended by top government officials
expressed their preoccupation: "A room, a kitchen is better than the castle
of Halima" [president Benjedid's wife], they proclaimed; or "For us, only
Artane" [an anti–Parkinson's disease drug popular with the poor]; or "Al-
zetla [cannabis] or exile."

The PAGS (Parti Avant-Garde Socialiste) and above all the old guard
inside the FLN, who maintained positions of socialist orthodoxy, opposed
the economic reform. On October 2, 1988, the conflict between the reformist and antireformist tendencies in the FLN escalated when the General
Union of Algerian Workers (UGTA), the FLN trade union federation, called
strikes in the industrial suburb of Algiers. This detonated the riots of
October 1988.

Youth destroyed cars and shop windows in the Bab el-Oued quarter of the
capital on the evening of October 4. The next day, the main downtown
commercial artery and the Riyad al-Fath shopping complex, a symbol of
luxury consumerism built as a memorial to the martyrs on the occasion of
the twentieth anniversary of independence, were trashed. The government
declared a state of siege on October 6, but the troubles spread to the main

towns of the country. On October 7, following Friday prayers, about seven thousand worshipers marched from the Belcourt quarter and First of May Square in Algiers. When the security forces intervened, 'Ali Ben Hadj, the young preacher of the al-Sunna mosque in Bab el-Oued and later a founding member of the FIS, called for "an assembly of the faithful of Algiers."[14] Although criticized publicly by Shaikh Ahmad Sahnun, a march of twenty thousand people took place in Bab el-Oued on October 10, leading to the deaths of some thirty participants in clashes with the army.

At that time, Benjedid received a delegation of Islamist leaders composed of 'Ali Ben Hadj, Ahmad Sahnun, and Mahfoud Nahnah (a leader of Hamas, who began his career as an opponent of the Boumedienne regime), who conveyed a list of grievances. That evening, using the crisis to dismiss antireformist figures in the FLN and the army, Benjedid announced a referendum for November 3. The president proposed to modify the constitution of 1976 by inscribing the principle of government accountability to the Popular National Assembly.

The amendments were approved by 92.27 percent of the voters, with over 83 percent participating. A new constitution was adopted by a second referendum on February 23, 1989, opening the way to a multiparty state, authorizing associations "with a political character" and guaranteeing trade union freedom and the right to strike. Instead of convening a Constituent Assembly to draw up a new constitution, the regime preferred the procedure of a referendum, which permitted it both to short-circuit and keep in place the Assembly elected under the aegis of the FLN. In this way the regime succeeded in negotiating an opening of the political system without putting into question its hold on power, at least not immediately.

After the events of October, a protest movement of "democrats" formed to defend the victims of repression and torture, who came primarily from poorer quarters. Journalists, university faculty, artists, trade unionists, and other groupings established political committees, one of which was the Association of Former Mujahidat (women independence fighters). Together they formed the National Committee Against Torture and organized a march to Bab Ezzouar, an Algiers suburb, on October 24, demanding serious reform of the political system, an end to single-party rule, and guaranteed democratic liberties. They were joined by other informal groups as well as established political forces like the Hocine Aït Ahmed's Front of Socialist Forces (FFS) and the PAGS.

While Islamists and democrats alike criticized the government, the Islamists, unlike the democrats, had at their disposal significant popular networks organized around mosques. Though they were not the initiators of the events of October 1988, the leaders of the Islamist opposition were its main beneficiaries.

CONQUEST OF PUBLIC SPACE

Strengthened by recognition from the highest authorities of the state as a result of the meeting with Benjedid on October 10, the dean of Algerian preachers, Ahmad Sahnun, created *Rabitat al-Da'wa*—a nonpolitical organization of various Islamist tendencies with the objective of "defending Islam"—in March 1989. Very quickly dissension appeared among the leadership. This led to an initiative to constitute an Islamist mass organization, the Islamic Salvation Front or FIS, around 'Ali Ben Hadj on March 10, 1989. Undoubtedly for reasons of personal rivalry, some Islamist leaders, like Mahfoud Nahnah and 'Abd Allah Djaballah, leader of the preachers of Constantine and the eastern part of the country, refused to participate. Consequently, 'Abassi Madani, an academic, a former militant of both the FLN and of the Islamic Values Association and, like many Islamist preachers, a former prisoner of the Benjedid regime, was designated the leader of the young party in September 1989. The birth in 1990 of Hamas, and of the Movement of the Islamic Renaissance, led respectively by Mahfoud Nahnah and 'Abd Allah Djaballah, posed no threat to the leading position of the FIS, which claimed three million adherents, and which is in fact the only mass party on the national stage.

The eruption of the FIS onto the political field foregrounded a singular strategy of investment in public space. The FIS occupied the street and transformed that space into a privileged arena for the diffusion of its message. This was first expressed by the prominence of certain images and sounds: Islamic dress (the *qamis* [caftan] and *hijab* and the loudspeakers used for the call to prayer. The overflow into the street during mass Friday prayers was a visible expression of large-scale mobilization. The youths of the various Algiers districts and the towns of the countryside poured out to listen to the most famous preachers: 'Ali Ben Hadj at the al-Sunna mosque in the Bab el-Oued quarter, Shaikh al-Aïd at Fath al-Islam in the Triolet quarter, 'Abd al-Malik in the Colonne quarter, Shaykh Sahnun at Chevalley, Kamil Nur at the Kabul mosque in Belcourt, and Guemazi at al-Taqwa mosque. The big FIS marches reinforced the presence of its militants in the city. We may note in particular the demonstration of January 18, 1991, at the start of the Gulf war, when 'Ali Ben Hadj, dressed in military garb, led a demonstration to the doors of the Ministry of Defense to demand that training camps be opened for volunteers to enlist on the side of Iraq, and the mass meeting organized on June 4, 1991, at Algiers's July 5th Stadium. The mass strike of May–June 1991 marked the ultimate stage of this process. In April 1991, following the 1990 municipal elections, the Popular National Assembly approved an electoral redistricting law that overrepresented the south of the country, where the FIS had less support. On May 23, 'Abassi Madani called for a general strike. On May 24–25, 1991, several thousand

FIS militants occupied two of the main squares of Algiers—Martyrs' Square and First of May Square—where they prayed, cooked, and stayed up or slept.[15] Algiers began to look like a bivouac. The protest gathered momentum and assumed the character of a movement of civil disobedience. The strike ended in a bloody clash with the security forces on the night of June 3–4.

The ability of the FIS to adapt tactically was confirmed by its external relations. In presenting itself publicly, the FIS attracted substantial international media coverage. The mosque played a fundamental role in internal information and communication among the militants. Likewise, the support of businessmen contributed to the organization of the movement. The superior material resources of the FIS were evident in the mass transportation at the disposal of the militants during public demonstrations.

Beyond institutional constraints, the heterogeneous practices of the mobilized youth contributed to modifying the stance of the organization in 1990, for instance. Some FIS leaders had quickly denounced Iraq's invasion of Kuwait, but the infatuation of much of the population with Saddam Husayn led the FIS to condemn publicly the intervention of Western troops "in the holy places of Islam." During the strike of May–June 1991, the FIS leadership abstained from publicly denying the rumor circulating about the strikers' "convivial consumption of cannabis after the evening prayer." This permissiveness on the question of psychotropic drugs is significant. Indeed, there is an unstable group among the mobilized youth who alternate between cannabis and the mosque.[16] In Algeria, using and dealing drugs is not only common, but appears to be integrated into social life.

The occupation of public space encouraged the identification with peer groups extending beyond local space, reinforcing larger solidarities and blurring identifications with a particular quarter. The electoral results of the FIS in the Casbah of Algiers expressed this new phenomenon. Candidates of the FIS from outside the district beat FLN and independent candidates native to the district. Thus, 'Ali, thirty-three years old, a shopkeeper, and 'Aziz, twenty-four years old, a white collar worker, presented themselves to voters as "Muslim Algerians." Regional origin or district of residence seem to have declined in significance.

SOCIAL CONSTRUCTION OF PROTEST

Mobilization does not depend entirely on the accumulation of human and organizational capacity, but develops from the capacity of a group to formulate and adopt mobilizing interpretative frameworks.[17] The meaning of collective action is not located in external factors, but constructed by the actors in the course of the interactive process of mobilization. The interpretative framework that governs the situation is implicit; those mobilized do not think of it as such, but they operate inside this framework. It must, of course, be shared publicly by the participants in order to be collectively adopted. This is the work of long-term organization.

The adoption of a conception of injustice is one element of the process by which a group mobilizes.[18] A sense of injustice permits a group to formulate a mobilizing framework that encourages disobedience and participation in conflict, a framework that replaces the previously dominant interpretative order legitimizing the status quo and encouraging submission to the authorities. Mobilization is not a direct consequence of dissatisfaction, but requires a social elaboration of that which is unjust, illegitimate, or unacceptable, an elaboration closely bound up with previously accepted representations and categorizations.

Exclusion from school and unemployment in Algeria have left large numbers of youth in the street. These marginalized youth and déclassé students, socialized by the mosque since the beginning of the 1980s and mobilized by the FIS since 1989, consider themselves victims of social injustice, and the object of *hugra* (humiliation, contempt) by the regime. Surviving in a drab world without cohesion and without a future, they regard themselves as cursed (*kukra*). They live in slums and devastated residential blocks of the capital, where structural deterioration seems to reinforce and illustrate the deterioration of social relations. They hang around the overcrowded streets of the capital, resorting to "small jobs" in periods of unemployment and filling up their days, augmenting their meager resources by petty larceny or small-scale drug dealing. They are professional *hittistes*.[19]

Even high school graduates do not escape the *kukra*. As a result of the demographic explosion of the 1970s, young adults face a relative scarcity of work and housing.[20] Single by necessity more than choice, they know that marriage is beyond their means. Urban housing, a precondition to marriage, constitutes one of the major failures of the social policy of the former regime.[21] Thus many youth in the twenty-five to thirty age-group find themselves in an indefinite status of prolonged childhood. Entry into adult life as defined by basic changes in status—beginning a working life, leaving one's parents, and marriage—appears very precarious.

Engagement in collective action has also encouraged a cognitive liberation—a sudden sense of revelation, a new understanding of events and social conditions.[22] The concessions granted by the regime convinced the mobilized activists of the effectiveness of protest and persuaded them that solutions could only be obtained through mobilization. The leaders played a critical role in generating and diffusing this understanding. By identifying social problems, by redefining the situation in religious language and then translating it into political terms, the leadership of the FIS decoded reality in ways the mobilized youth found persuasive.

A study of the *khutba* (sermon) of 'Ali Ben Hadj on November 12, 1989, following the earthquake at Tipasa west of Algiers, is an exemplary illustration of the process of imposing an interpretative framework. He built his speech on rhetoric already in place, establishing his own definition of problems and relevant solutions. The preacher integrated several structurally separate problems by linking them ideologically. He clarified and developed an existing interpretative framework by insisting on religious values. He interpreted the earthquake as a punishment by God, a warning to "the society of vice." He mesmerized the audience with details of moral corruption and permissiveness, and the disasters that these entail for families and children. The urgency of moral awareness, as he presented it, justified his invectives against the impious enemy and the solutions afforded by Islam. By designating the entire political regime as the cause of injustice, Ben Hadj implied that its disappearance would automatically lead to the reign of justice inherent in Islam. Appealing to the faith of his audience and to the image of the Algerian war of liberation, he called for "a battle for Islam" that would continue "the *jihad* of 1954." "The grave-digger regime of national independence" had betrayed the martyrs sacrificed for Islam and social justice. Himself the son of a martyr, Ben Hadj did not delegitimize the Algerian war of liberation. Rather, he discredited the nationalist commitment of Rabah Bitat, then president of the National Assembly and a hero of the nationalist struggle.

The FLN's ideology linked patriotism with demands for social justice: "to fight for independence was to fight for justice."[23] By reclaiming some of the principles of equity derived both from the Algerian revolution and Islam, FIS activists affirm the injustice of present conditions. Like the earlier generation of FLN militants, they hold the regime to account on the question of social justice, posed in terms of distributive justice. Their principal demand is to obtain the legitimate expectations which they now see as guaranteed by Islam: a job and housing in order to establish a family. They denounce the unequal and unjust character of the distribution of economic resources by a state which represents only "a corrupt minority." They do not impute the responsibility for their misfortune to a personally shameful history, but to a political regime accused of diverting the national wealth and violating Islamic ethics.

A key determinant of the relative success of the FIS's interpretive framework is the degree of resonance, measured by its congruence with the dominant belief systems of potential adherents.[24] In effect, the domestic socialization of the protagonists had already implanted notions of the FLN regime as the "gravedigger" of independence. This symbolic capital is part of the terrain on which the crisis of legitimacy of the state has developed.

In Algeria, the national liberation struggle is celebrated as the founding act of a nation. The absence of an academic memory—the various history-writing seminars of the war of liberation organized by the FLN between 1982 and 1984 resulted in failure—which might confront the memories of the actors, has favored the crystallization of diverse memories and representations. The subtle dialectics of forgetting and remembering favor the capacity of the makers of local histories to pass off *their* history as *the* history. The FLN regime forged a totalizing representation of society, translated into an official, anonymous history which perceives "only one hero, the people" and occludes the conflicts and divisions of the national movement.

Today, the identification of two types of memories has allowed for the fragmentation of cognitive space, contested by descendants of the "Messalists" and the "grassroots militants" of the FLN, subdivided into various regional groups.[25] The followers of Messali Hadj knew the segmented universe of the colonial world; their sons know an Algeria split in two. The fathers resided in the "Arab quarter," and the sons survive in a condemned quarter. For the elders, the European district was inaccessible. For the offspring, it is the luxurious "club des Pins" complex in which they cannot dream of residing. Postindependence Algeria barely resembles what the FLN militants dreamed of twenty years ago. For them the revolution has been "diverted."

In this way, the state is perceived as a political entity that confiscated independence by reappropriating for itself the historic role of the "real people" to establish its power. Placed in the position of a contestant, the state cannot function as the regulator of social conflicts. The generation of independence regards the regime as illegitimate, formed of "officers of the French army" or the "army of the frontiers," placed in a situation of exteriority. This explains the noticeable absence of the FIS at the independence ceremonies of November 1, 1989. This refusal to participate in marking the launching of the revolutionary war does not question the founding date, but the official memorial.

CONCLUSION

By exploring competing memories of the Algerian war, I have questioned the usual dichotomy between the FIS and the FLN. The young activists of the FIS claim descent from the "deceived heroes" of 1954. Support for the FLN in the 1950s and the FIS in the 1980s rests on similar foundations: an identity defined by religious belief, an organic representation of society, and the demand for social justice.

Moving from heroic struggle to managing the country, the FLN inherited a society with a deeply damaged social structure. The FLN was not able to reconstruct social relations. The FIS, by inserting itself into this troubled structure, was able to represent a large group of atomized individuals. The conflict between the FLN and the FIS should not be analyzed in terms of a rupture, which evokes a transformation of beliefs or a revolution in value systems, but in terms of continuity.

Translated from the French by Joel Beinin.

NOTES

1. The FIS obtained 4,332,472 votes (54.25 percent of the votes cast and 33.73 percent of the registered voters) in the municipal elections and 3,260,222 votes (47.27 percent of the votes cast and 24.59 percent of the registered voters) in the first round of the legislative elections. This gave it control of a majority of municipalities and 188 deputies in the legislature, as opposed to 16 for the FLN. See J. Fontaine, "Les élections législatives algériennes," *Monde Arabe: Maghreb/Machrek,* no. 135 (January–March 1992): 155.

2. F. Burgat, "Les mutations d'un islam pluriel," *Le Monde Diplomatique,* June 1993.

3. L. Addi, "De la permanence du populisme algérien," *Peuples Méditerranéens,* no. 52–53 (July–December 1990); M. Harbi, "Aux racines historiques de la crise," *Le Monde Diplomatique, Manière de voir,* no. 24 (1994); B. Stora, *Histoire de l'Algérie depuis l'indépendance* (Paris: La Découverte, 1994).

4. A. Rouadjia, *Les frères et la mosquée: Enquête sur le mouvement islamiste en Algérie* (Paris: Karthala, 1990).

5. In the first round of the 1991 legislative elections Hamas received 368,697 votes (5.35 percent of the vote and 2.78 percent of the registered voters) and the MNI received only 150,093 votes (2.18 percent of the votes and 1.13 percent of the registered voters). See Fontaine, "Les élections législatives algériennes."

6. Séverine Labat, "Islamismes et Islamistes en Algérie: Un nouveau militantisme," in Gilles Kepel (ed.), *Exils et royaumes: Les appartenances au monde arabo-musulman aujourd'hui* (Paris: FNSP, 1994), pp. 42–67.

7. In an interview, FIS leader 'Abbasi Madani explained, "It is a front because it confronts, and because it has a large array of actions and domains; it is the front of all the sectors of the Algerian people across its vast territory. It is open to a variety of tendencies and ideas who achieve, across their richness and diversity, a coherent unity." *Parcours maghrébin,* March 26, 1990.

8. The FLN understood Islam not only as culture but as the foundation of society and public unity, regulating both the public and the private. See Monique Gadant, *Islam et nationalisme en Algérie d'après "El Moudjahid" organe centrale du FLN de 1956 à 1962* (Paris: L'Harmattan, 1988).

9. Mazdak led a fifth-century Iranian religious movement with an egalitarian ideology in opposition to the dominant Mazdeism.

10. According to Aïssa Khelladi, *Les islamistes algériens face au pouvoir* (Algiers: Alfa, 1992), the number of mosques grew from 2,000 in 1962 to 11,221 in 1992.

11. On the historical evolution of the Islamist movement, see M. Al-Ahnaf, B. Botiveau, F. Frégosi, *L'Algérie par ses islamistes* (Paris: Karthala, 1991); F. Burgat,

"Le potentiel islamiste," *Encyclopaedia Universalis,* vol. 1, pp. 789–90; idem, *L'Is-lamisme au Maghreb, la voix du sud* (Paris: Karthala, 1988); Rouadjia, *Les frères et la mosquée.*

12. Following its fourth session, the National Council of the UNJA reported that "The current weakness of our organization is due in large measure to its loss of credibility." *Révolution Africaine,* January 7, 1988.

13. Abdelkader Djeghloul, "Limites et crises de l'indépendantisme algérien," *Encyclopaedia Universalis,* vol. 1, p. 784.

14. Ben Hadj (b. 1956) had been a militant in the Islamic movement close to Mustafa Bouyali's group in the 1970s. In 1983 he was arrested, and in 1985 the state security court condemned him to death before he was pardoned by president Chadli Benjedid.

15. Smaïl Hadj 'Ali, "Ville et violences à travers la grève du FIS, L'occupation de la ville d'Alger (mai–juin 1991)," *Les Cahiers du C.E.R.E.S.* (Tunis), November 1991.

16. See Meriem Vergès, "La Casbah d'Alger, Chronique de survie dans un quartier sursis," in Kepel, *Exils et royaumes,* pp. 69–88.

17. Erving Goffman, *Les cadres de l'expérience* (Paris: Minuit, 1991).

18. W. Gamson, "Le legs de Goffman à la sociologie politique," *Politique,* no. 3–4 (1988): 71–80.

19. An untranslatable Arabo-French mélange meaning young Algerians who lean their backs on walls and whose "job" is to "hold up the walls," in the popular derisive phrase. See my interview with an Algiers "hittiste" in *Middle East Report,* no. 192 (January–February 1995): 14–17.

20. Philippe Fargues, "Demographic Explosion or Social Upheaval?" in Ghassan Salamé (ed.), *Democracy without Democrats? The Renewal of Politics in the Muslim World* (London: I.B. Tauris, 1994), pp. 156–79; idem, "From Demographic Explosion to Social Rupture," *Middle East Report,* no. 190 (September–October 1994): 6–10.

21. At the end of the second four-year plan in 1987 the housing deficit was estimated at more than two million units. Consequently, the average number of occupants in units of one to three rooms (of which two-thirds were two-room units) was seven to eight persons. See Pierre-Robert Baduel, "L'écrasant problème du logement urbain," in Camille and Yves Lacoste (eds.), *L'état du Maghreb* (Paris: La Découverte, 1991), p. 186.

22. See D. MacAdam, *Political Process and the Development of Black Insurgency, 1930–1970* (Chicago: University of Chicago Press, 1982).

23. Gadant, *Islam et nationalisme en Algérie d'après "El Moudjahid,"* p. 119.

24. See D. Snow and R. Benford, "Ideology, Frame Resonance and Participant Mobilization," in B. Klandermans, H. Kriesi, and S. Tarrow (eds.), *From Structure to Action: Comparing Social Movements across Cultures* (Greenwich, Conn.: JAI, 1988), pp. 197–218.

25. The FLN was constituted by the unification of various political currents operating in Algerian society except for the supporters of Messali Hadj, founder of the ENA, then the PPA- MTLD, who formed the Algerian National Movement in December 1954. The rivalry with the FLN for exclusive representation of the Algerian people took the form of a civil war and in May 1957 culminated in the

massacre of three hundred villagers of Melouza suspected of being Messalists. On the history of Algerian nationalism, see M. Harbi, *Le FLN, mirage et réalité* (Paris: Jeune Afrique, 1980); idem, *Les archives de la Révolution Algérienne* (Paris: Jeune Afrique, 1981); idem, *La guerre commence en Algérie* (Paris: Complexe, 1984); and B. Storra, *Les sources du nationalisme algérien* (Paris: L'Harmattan, 1988); idem, *La gangrène et l'oubli, La mémoire de la guerre d'Algérie* (Paris: La Découverte, 1992).

Movements and Personalities

26

Introduction to Part Five

Joost Hiltermann

At the end of a brief visit to al-Najah University in the West Bank town of Nablus in the summer of 1994, I was approached by a young student as I was about to pass through the gate. He had the beginnings of a beard curling around his chin and appeared a little nervous, but was perfectly courteous, if not deferential. He asked if I had a moment to spare. He wanted to know what I, a foreigner, thought of the university, of Nablus, of the Israeli occupation, of Palestine. We talked for a little while. Then he thanked me for my time, wished me a pleasant stay, and went on his way.

The short encounter threw me back some ten years earlier, to 1984–85 when I first arrived in the West Bank to conduct field research for my dissertation on popular mobilization.[1] On many of my visits to al-Najah and other universities in the West Bank, students would come up to me with similar questions, often to test my positions on Palestinian nationalism, or just out of curiosity. They were activists in one or another of the factions of the PLO—not always clean shaven perhaps, but almost invariably without beards. Across a decade, the experience thus remained markedly similar, with the crucial difference that in 1994 the Palestinian nationalist who came up to me belonged to the Islamic Resistance Movement (Hamas) and sprinkled his nationalist oratory with the vocabulary of religion.

The two rival movements themselves—secular Palestinian nationalism and political Islam—do have a lot in common, even if the participants have often been loath to recognize this. This should not be surprising. As several of the essays in this section show, both movements were born in the turbulence and disenchantment of the late 1960s: the shattering Arab defeat in the 1967 war and the fervor of student protest across the globe.

It was in 1968 that Yasir ‘Arafat managed to seize control of the PLO from its stolid, discredited pro-Nasirist leadership, while the same uprising in

France that gave us Danny the Red also gave the Tunisian Islamist leader Rashid al-Ghannoushi his start—even if their motivations were not the same and they went off in radically different directions.

Both movements formed essentially in opposition to the Arab regimes that had come to power in the 1950s under the banners of Arab nationalism and socialism, and both employed similar mobilizational strategies. Both found fertile ground first in the schools and universities, then moved into the wider arena of institutions, associations, social clubs, trade unions, and other organizations of civil society, including the mosques in the case of the Islamists. The Palestinian nationalist movement in the West Bank, for example, was born in voluntary work projects organized by teachers at local schools and at al-Najah and Birzeit universities in the early 1970s. The young activists graduated to the trade unions, women's organizations, and underground factions of the PLO in the late 1970s and early 1980s, taking over the day-to-day management of mass protest against the Israeli occupation once the intifada broke out in late 1987.

The Islamists likewise had their start in the schools. As Hamid al-Nayfar points out, students were radicalized once they entered the universities and encountered the discourse of student politics, then heavily dominated by left- and right-wing ideologies. Mimicking their leftist rivals' methods, they became a force to reckon with, in some instances even gaining power. The Gama'at Islamiyya (Islamic Groups) in Egypt, for example, took control of the student union at Minya University in 1977–78. In the 1970s and 1980s, the Islamists built a vast web of charitable associations and religious institutions, providing social services in urban neighborhoods where municipalities—or, in the case of Gaza, the Israeli military government—would not reach.

Both movements, Palestinian nationalism and political Islam, were curbed in their organizational efforts by constraints imposed by the state. The PLO was outlawed in the Occupied Territories; local activists accused of membership disappeared behind bars for months or years, reemerging as leaders of a movement that rapidly gained respect at the level of the street. The Islamists, though originally tolerated and even encouraged by the regimes (including Israel) that saw in them a useful tool in defeating left-wing challenges to their repressive rule, found refuge in the welter of religious establishments whose politics remained muted in favor of vigorous pursuit of a social agenda that did not directly threaten state power.

As their political opposition was manifested, their leadership was subject to arrest or worse. Al-Ghannoushi in Tunisia and Tal'at Fu'ad Qasim in Egypt both spent many years behind prison walls. In Lebanon, the charismatic leader of the Movement of the Dispossessed, Imam Musa al-Sadr, was kidnapped and disappeared in 1978. In the 1980s, Israeli forces in Lebanon kidnapped or assassinated a number of leaders of Hizb Allah (as they had murdered PLO leaders in Beirut in the 1970s).

Finally, both movements adopted a strong anti-imperialist tone, pointing an accusing finger at foreign influences as the root cause for all the ills besetting their societies. The same Arab nationalist regimes that had sprung from the anticolonial struggles now found themselves accused of being pawns of the Western powers. What Palestinian nationalism and political Islam offered was to counter this old enemy with a new vigor and a new language. Palestinian nationalists pointed at the strategic alliance between the United States and Israel as evidence of continuing imperialist designs on the Middle East. The Islamists have concurred, adding the charge of moral laxity due to Western cultural penetration through television, discotheques, pop music, and the latest fashions in Paris and New York.

It is easy to stretch the comparison too far. The Islamist movement has largely replaced a fading Arab nationalism in the 1990s. The various "branches" of the Islamist movement show intriguing variations across Arab societies, suggesting perhaps that they are not branches as much as parallel movements bearing the same name. Salim Nasr shows how profound social and economic changes in Lebanese society in the 1950s and 1960s gave rise to a powerful political movement of Shi'a that, in the 1970s and 1980s, strove to reform Lebanon's confessional system by nonviolent means while undertaking guerrilla actions against Israeli forces occupying the south. The Movement of the Oppressed, later the Amal militia, advanced a social program, identifying local factors—exploitative government, discrimination, and inequality—as its main targets. Interestingly, and contrary to the situation in Gaza, Egypt, or Algeria, the fact that even Amal's more radical successor, Hizb Allah, did not seriously pursue a cultural agenda (introduction of *shari'a,* imposition of "Islamic dress," etc.) suggests the relative power of Lebanon's urban, rather Westernized, "culture," which has, for example, permitted young women to wear the latest fashion in short dresses even in the heart of Bir al-'Abd, the neighborhood in southern Beirut where Hizb Allah has its political headquarters (as I observed in the fall of 1991).

In Tunisia, too, the Islamist thrust has had its unique features (e.g., its decision to work through the trade unions), and its leaders have set themselves expressly apart from their ideological forebears in Egypt and Saudi Arabia whose ideas, they argued, simply bore no relationship to the problems and needs of Tunisian society. Shaikh Hamid al-Nayfar has even referred to a "Tunisian Islam" (a term that recalls, again in an interesting comparison, the postcolonial era with its multiple paths to socialism) to mark his frustration with the writings and pronouncements of a Sayyid Qutb or a Hasan al-Banna. There are also plenty of parallels between the Tunisian

Islamists and movements elsewhere in the Arab world. For example, Rashid al-Ghannoushi claims that he does not reject modernity but merely seeks to "Islamize" it.[2] If Islamist leaders in other parts of the realm have not always spoken similarly, they have at least tended to play by the same rules.

In Egypt, Tal'at Fu'ad Qasim explains with chilling candor his motivations for establishing the military wing of al-Gama'at al-Islamiyya and his justification for killing tourists (many tourist activities, he claims, are forbidden from a religious viewpoint and an "abomination" as a source of "all manner of depravities"). On the flip side of the coin, Nasr Hamid Abu Zayd argues with great courage for a democratic Egypt that will accommodate Islamists and secularists alike, including persons like himself with "radical" ideas about the crucial role of the interpreter in reading texts like the Qur'an, and a historicist understanding of how interpretive authority is established.

In occupied Palestine, we have witnessed the ascendance of an Islamist movement that is profoundly nationalist in its outlook. Bassam Jarrar makes clear that the collapse of the PLO, its political rival, would not be in the interest of the Islamists, and he stresses that Hamas is prepared to participate in the electoral process at the level of municipalities and associations. Rather than striving for political control over the Palestinian quasi state, Hamas, as Graham Usher shows, is content to remold Palestinian society in its image by pushing a cultural agenda that would reform the curriculum and strengthen the application of *shari'a*. Here again is an interesting parallel: Graham Usher argues that much like Fatah, which opened its doors to Palestinians of all ideological stripes as long as they accepted the leadership of Fatah's founding fathers, Hamas operates as a broad alliance that requires consensus in its decision making.

Today's Islamist movements appear to be virtual replicas of the earlier nationalist movements, but for the fact that the narrative has become religious. The moment the PLO joined the political process, it created a space for Hamas to represent the nationalist fervor and militancy that it had formerly embodied. Hamas foot soldiers are precisely the young men and women who would have joined Fatah a decade ago. Even within the Islamist movement this generational pattern holds true; just as 'Arafat's young Fatah revolutionaries took over the PLO from its stodgy, traditionalist founders in 1968, so today younger, more radical activists are taking Hamas out of the hands of the more conservative Muslim Brothers that spawned it, and turning it into a potent weapon against the Israeli military occupation. In Lebanon, the struggle against the Israeli occupation became a vehicle for Hizb Allah to largely replace Amal in the 1980s, as Amal joined the political process and became virtually indistinguishable from the other political parties. Today, Hizb Allah has also begun to transform itself into a political party.

In the context of enduring deep social and political inequalities in the Middle East and the Western economic interests which reinforce them, the question is not, will the Islamists be able to deliver on their promise to provide a new dawn? Rather we should ask, what resistance to the Islamist agenda is being articulated in the schools of the Middle East today? Which fresh ideological outlook is being primed to take on the seemingly intractable problems of the region?

NOTES

1. Published as Joost R. Hiltermann, *Behind the Intifada: Labor and Women's Movements in the Occupied Territories* (Princeton: Princeton University Press, 1991).

2. See Linda G. Jones, "Portrait of Rashid al-Ghannoushi," *Middle East Report*, no. 153 (July–August 1988): 21.

27

What Does the Gama'a Islamiyya Want?

Tal'at Fu'ad Qasim, interview with Hisham Mubarak

Tal'at Fu'ad Qasim got his start in the 1970s, when al-Gama'a al-Islamiyya (the Islamic Group)[1] took control of many student organizations in the Egyptian universities. He led the student union in Minya, a hotbed of the Islamist movement, and later was a founding member of the *majlis al-shura* (governing council) of the organization at large. Shaikh 'Umar 'Abd al-Rahman later became head of the *majlis*.

In 1981, the Gama'a *majlis* recruited an artillery officer, Khalid al-Islambuli, to carry out its decision to assassinate president Anwar al-Sadat. Qasim, who was al-Islambuli's superior within the Gama'a, had been arrested two weeks before the assassination and incarcerated in Tura Prison, but security forces failed to uncover the assassination plot. In the subsequent trials Qasim was sentenced to seven years, and was actually incarcerated for eight before escaping and making his way, via Sudan, to Peshawar, Pakistan, and the ranks of the Afghan *mujahidin* (fighters against the pro-Soviet regime in Kabul).

In Peshawar, in 1990, he began publishing *Al-Murabitun* (The holy fighters), the first magazine of the Gama'a. He was also involved in setting up a *mahkama shari'iyya* (Islamic court), which passed death "sentences" on various Egyptian officials and secularist personalities in Egypt. It was this court which issued the order resulting in the death of Farag Fuda. *Al-Murabitun* published rationales for Fuda's assassination and for the Gama'a's decision to target tourists.

Over the next four years, Qasim traveled between Peshawar and Afghanistan, where militants were trained for armed operations in Egypt. In 1989, Qasim became *na'ib al-amir* (deputy chief) of al-Gama'a al-Islamiyya. Following the arrest of Shaikh 'Abd al-Rahman, he became the Gama'a leader. Egypt put pressure on Pakistan to extradite Qasim after an Egyptian court sentenced him to death in the case of the "Afghanis." He then fled to Copenhagen, where he was granted political asylum. We spoke with him there in November 1993.

. . . . .

How was al-Gama'a al-Islamiyya formed? How did it evolve from the 1970s to the organization of today?

It began in the mid-1970s with nine people in Minya reading the works of Ibn Taymiyya, Abu al-'Ala al-Mawdudi, Sayyid Qutb, Sayyid Sabiq, and others. [Ibn Taymiyya was a medieval Hanbali jurist widely regarded as the source of much contemporary Islamist thinking. The other names listed here are leading figures of the modern Islamist movement.] A group began in Asyut around the same time. The Minya group pressured the school administration to segregate girls and boys, to halt classes at prayer times, and to establish mosques. This activism then spread to neighborhoods and surrounding villages. The group worked to change the *munkar* (that which is forbidden), and after some destruction of property they got a law passed banning alcohol. It was after this that these activists formed al-Gama'a al-Islamiyya, a real organization. In Minya University in 1977–78 they took over the student union.

When did the Gama'a move from being an evangelical organization to one devoted to confronting the state?

Religion requires not just personal "conversion." We began by spreading our message, but our goal has always been the establishment of an Islamic state.

What was the state's response?

The confrontation with the state began in earnest in 1978, with the arrest of some members after protests against Camp David. Soon afterward protests against al-Sadat's offer of asylum to the Shah of Iran led to the murder of some of our members by security forces.

Some say that al-Gama'a al-Islamiyya was supported by the Egyptian state to fight the left.

Propaganda. Like the claim about Shaikh 'Abd al-Rahman working with the CIA. In fact, al-Gama'a al-Islamiyya was the only organization to confront the state. Many members suffered as a consequence.

How did you meet 'Umar 'Abd al-Rahman?

Muhammad 'Abd al-Majid, a disaffected Muslim Brother, introduced 'Abd al-Rahman to audiences around 1978. We got to know him then.

What was Shaikh 'Umar's influence on the founding of al-Gama'a al-Islamiyya?

His only influence was as a *shari'a* professor at al-Azhar. We youth did not have his knowledge.

Why and when was the military wing of al-Gama'a established?

In 1987, after the establishment of the first *majlis al-shura* which included Karim Zuhdi, 'Isam Dirbala, Najih Ibrahim, Salah Hashim, 'Usama Hafiz, 'Asim 'Abd al-Majid, Sabri al-Banna, 'Ali al-Sharif, Hamdi 'Abd al-Rahman, Rifa'i Taha, and myself. The idea was first suggested by 'Isam Dirbala in my house during a meeting of the *majlis,* in response to violent attacks by the state. We supported the idea because "the only way to express yourself in this world is through force, the only language that is understood."

What was your evaluation of the Muslim Brothers?

After we started al-Gama'a al-Islamiyya, al-Sadat released a number of Muslim Brothers from jail to clamp down on us in Cairo. When they tried to take on our people, we developed our critical orientation toward the Muslim Brothers.

Were there differences within al-Gama'a al-Islamiyya over this orientation?

In late 1978, several Gama'a leaders, including the leader of the Gama'a, Muhyi al-Din Ahmad, were arrested in the *sa'id* [Upper Egypt]. Some Muslim Brother lawyers came to the defense of these leaders. Muhyi al-Din was too poor to afford a lawyer, so the Muslim Brother lawyers agreed to defend him in exchange for his joining the Muslim Brothers. This was the first proposition by the Muslim Brothers to the Gama'a. After that, leaders of the Muslim Brothers held a meeting at 'Ayn Shams University. They invited us to this meeting. The Gama'a was represented by three of its leaders, Muhyi al-Din, Abu al-'Ila Madi, and myself from al-Minya University and by Najih Ibrahim and 'Usama Hafiz from Asyut. The Muslim Brother leaders who attended that meeting included Mustafa Mashur and Salah Abu Isma'il. They asked us frankly if we would join the Brothers. We refused because of the differences in our agenda. But they succeeded in influencing some Gama'a leaders, the most prominent being Muhyi al-Din and Abu al-'Ila Madi from the *sa'id;* 'Isam al-'Ariyan, Hilmi al-Jazzar, and 'Abd al-Mun'im Abu al-Futuh from Cairo; and Ahmad 'Umar and al-Za'farafi from Alexandria University. These agreed to follow the Muslim Brother leaders and they split from the Gama'a.

Did they become the youth organization of the Brothers in the universities?

That's correct. But they kept moving under the banner of the Gama'a even though they had split from it. They wanted to profit from the reputation of the Gama'a among students. They stopped doing this, however, after the events of 1981 due to the torture they endured at the hands of the security forces.

What was the effect of this split?

There were conflicts with the Muslim Brothers in the *sa'id* but no conflicts took place in Cairo because 'Isam al-'Ariyan, Hilmi al-Jazzar, and 'Abd al-Mun'im Abu al-Futuh had a strong base among the students there and they faced no competition. We continued our work in the *sa'id* and we started in 1978 to hold meetings in al-Rahman Mosque in Asyut every Monday. Our differences with the Brothers began to emerge at this point. The majority of youth would go to al-Rahman Mosque and the minority to the Brothers' mosque.

You said you studied the writings of Sayyid Qutb. He was a leader of the Muslim Brothers.

There are two points here. One is our relation to the ideas of Qutb; the other is the extent to which Qutb's ideas are those of the Brothers. Qutb has influenced all those interested in *jihad* (holy struggle) throughout the Islamic world. At the time there were many interpretations (*turuq*) and we were in need of direction. This Sayyid Qutb's teachings provided. The Muslim Brothers today have abandoned the ideas of Sayyid Qutb.

But two years ago there was a declaration by 'Abud al-Zumr [head of the Jihad organization] calling for an Islamic Front between the Muslim Brothers and al-Gama'a al-Islamiyya.

We published this statement in *Al-Murabitun*. We have defined general areas where we can cooperate with other Islamic groups. But neither 'Abud al-Zumr's statement nor what we wrote in *Al-Murabitun* intended cooperation with the Muslim Brothers. Our disagreements with the Brothers prevent cooperation. We think that multiplicity and variety are useful as long as the Islamic state has not yet come about.

When and how did you escape from prison to Peshawar?

I spent seven years in prison. Then I was under house arrest, was rearrested and spent another year of imprisonment, interrogation, and torture. In 1989 I was able to escape in the course of all the transporting from court to prison to central prison.

How did you get to Sudan?

I was aided by people later involved in the attempt on the life of the minister of interior and the assassination of the speaker of Parliament. I was almost caught at the airport on my way to Sudan. I spent twelve days in Sudan before going to Pakistan, where I met Afghan Islamic leaders and the brother of Khalid al-Islambuli.

Some say there was a discussion between you and Egyptian security officials after you were released from prison in 1988.

There was no such discussion. General Sa'id Thabit, an important official from the state security forces, called upon me while I was under house arrest in October 1988, following my release from prison. He told me it was necessary to stop the violence undertaken by the Gama'a in the *sa'id*, at 'Ayn Shams, and in other regions. I specified our conditions: first, releasing Gama'a prisoners, including those who had not yet been sentenced; second, lifting the ban on our propagandizing and rescinding the order to close our mosques; and third, ending state torture and the taking of hostages.

Of course, these conditions were not met, and the security around my house intensified. After my escape and rearrest in 1989, I was visited by the same man who demanded again that we end the violence, especially around 'Ayn Shams, where there had been a notable escalation in Gama'a activities against the police. I repeated our conditions and he his refusal. There was no dialogue and there will be none.

But there was a mediation council which included 'ulama', and as a result Minister of Interior 'Abd al-Halim Musa—who was a participant—was forced to resign.

We issued a communiqué denying this. There will be no dialogue until one side is victorious over the other, or the Islamic regime is established.

Does this mean al-Gama'a rejects any dialogue that could stop the escalation of violence?

We will only entertain discussions with the state security officials and intellectuals of the state (*mashayikh amn al-dawla wa-'ulama' al-sultan*) in order to clear our name in the face of lies propagated by the state. After coming to power perhaps we will enter into a dialogue with the leaders about how they can leave the country.

Some have said 'Abud al-Zumr was part of the dialogue.

There was no dialogue, and 'Abud al-Zumr himself denied it.

Another report claimed that Safwat 'Abd al-Ghani [a lawyer who has defended Islamists] had a part in the mediation council, and that he there confirmed the existence of a dialogue.

First, there were changes in the statement of Safwat 'Abd al-Ghani. No one speaks for the Gama'a except myself, and I have only spoken to deny the existence of the mediation council.

What of talk of contacts between the Gama'a and the American embassy?

The same. There have been no such discussions at any level. The Americans approached us and we rejected them.

How did the Americans approach you?

Right after my first release, I met with three foreigners. One of them was an American journalist who asked human rights questions and what Gama'a members had faced in prison.

Were there other attempts?

The American journalist tried again and I refused. I had asked to see his report from our first meeting.

What about the American embassy?

After my rearrest in 1989, the political attaché at the American embassy tried to contact me through the same lawyer who arranged the original meeting with the journalists. I asked him what the attaché wanted. He said the attaché could assist in my release and wanted to get to know me personally. He said he wanted to affirm that America was not the Great Satan, and to stress that American assistance does not aid the Egyptian government in clamping down on the Gama'a.

Of course, I refused. We consider the United States the main enemy and do not distinguish between the United States and Israel, or among Mubarak, Clinton, and Rabin. We will never meet with them, ever.

How about discussions between the Gama'a and the Jihad organization?

There is no such organization led by 'Abud al-Zumr. He is part of the *majlis al-shura* of the Gama'a, and has created no rival organization.

In 1984, 'Abud al-Zumr released a statement opposing the leadership of the Gama'a in the sa'id. *He entitled it "Invalidity of Rule by the Blind."*

Indeed, there was a debate over Shaikh 'Abd al-Rahman's leadership, instigated by 'Abud al-Zumr, who asked for a *fatwa* (legal opinion) supporting his leadership. Since he joined the Gama'a, he has been on the *majlis al-shura* and has always been a militant for the sake of God. We are proud of his presence among us.

It came out in a court case that there is a Peshawar-based organization, led by Dr. Ayman al-Zawahiri, called Gama'at al-Jihad, with 'Abud al-Zumr as one of its principals.

The question of 'Abud al-Zumr I have already dealt with. As for Gama'at al-Jihad, this is an organization with which we have no relations. We met in prison after the events of 1981, but we have no relations with them. There was no unity to begin with, so no question of a split.

What was the role of this organization in the events of 1981 and the assassination of al-Sadat?

Gama'at al-Jihad had no role in the assassination of al-Sadat or the events in Asyut; al-Gama'a al-Islamiyya was responsible. Jihad was simply caught up in the arrest campaign in 1981, and we met in prison. They are brothers and have exerted efforts in this sacred struggle. But they had no role in the events of 1981.

When you met with al-Zawahiri in prison you must have learned about the creation of this organization and its development.

According to al-Zawahiri, they started in the 1960s with eighteen and ended in 1981 with just three. During the arrest and torture campaign, security forces discovered several secret groups, and included them in our case. They got short sentences. Some went to Afghanistan and some to Saudi Arabia. Al-Zawahiri went to Peshawar, where I met him in 1985. Al-Zawahiri started working among the Arabs and came to know a rich Saudi, 'Usama bin Ladin, who helped create a base for those who wanted to help the Afghan struggle. From that point, they began to call themselves Gama'at al-Jihad.

Did Gama'at al-Jihad dominate activities in Peshawar? Where was al-Gama'a al-Islamiyya?

With the arrival of the leadership of al-Gama'a al-Islamiyya in Peshawar in the mid-1980s, people began to hear more about us, especially because of the events of 1981. From that time on, the Gama'a had a strong presence not only in Peshawar but on the battlefield throughout Afghanistan.

Ayman al-Zawahiri's group focuses on military activities. Is this a reason for the division between your groups?

I think they discovered that military activities alone would not suffice to attract new members. One must be involved in ideas and the propagation of new ideas in order to attract new adherents.

Is there still the matter of the "rule of the blind"?

Yes. The book they published on the conditions of *khilafa* (caliphate) is weak. Shaikh 'Abd al-Rahman has not asked to be the *khalifa* (caliph), because [the institution] does not exist yet. As for leadership of the organization, Shaikh 'Abd al-Rahman has the qualifications for leadership (*imara*) of the struggle. In any case, we put forth a long rebuttal to al-Zawahiri's book, which we did not publish because we want to keep the discussion at this level.

What about reports of a union between your two groups?

There are many efforts in this direction. What I can say is that we have bridged many gaps.

Why the violence against tourists?

First, many tourist activities are forbidden, so this source of income for the state is forbidden. Striking at such an important source of income will be a major blow against the state. It does not cost us much to strike at this sector.

Second, tourism in its present form is an abomination: it is a means by which prostitution and AIDS are spread by Jewish women tourists, and it is a source of all manner of depravities, not to mention being a means of collecting information on the Islamic movement. For these reasons we believe tourism is an abomination that must be destroyed. And it is one of our strategies for destroying the government.

Why do innocent tourists have to be killed?

There are tourists who are innocent. That is why we declared tourism, not tourists, our target. We have tried to warn tourists not to come to Egypt. Otherwise they open themselves to danger.

There are countries without tourism which still suffer from AIDS and drugs. AIDS and drugs are not a result of tourism.

The Egyptian people did not know drugs. Tourism is not the only reason, but it is the main reason for the spread of AIDS, drugs, and spying.

For the sake of argument, let's accept that tourism is a source of abomination. Why did you decide to strike at tourism only in 1992, even though you were based in the sa'id, *which is a center of tourism in Egypt? You have been active since the 1970s.*

Tourism [as such] is not forbidden in Islam. But people come to the *sa'id* even though they know of the danger. There must be other reasons why they continue to come.

You mentioned that industry and agriculture—institutions of exploitation, you said—are your next targets. When will this start?

It depends on government hostility toward us.

What are the Islamically sanctioned reasons for striking at government industry and agriculture?

We will strike at these institutions without bloodshed as much as possible, and our military units will undertake those activities when the time is right.

The Gama'a has suffered a lot from attacking tourism. Many members have been imprisoned, and the organization has lost influence in some areas. Did the Gama'a make a mistake in striking at tourism?

The real fight has not yet started. You will find in the newspapers accounts that say 99 percent of the Gama'a is in prison. The police and the press do not know our true strength.

The security forces have been able to diminish your activities.

The Gama'a exists in eighteen provinces, including tens of centers and hundreds of villages. Up to now the state has not won one battle in any of the thirteen centers, just in the province of Asyut. And the government suffers from grave economic and political crises. For every member killed, twenty join. Contrary to what some think, the power of the Gama'a is on the rise. We are doing God's work and it is a duty to keep up the struggle. The rest is up to God.

I disagree. There is no Gama'a presence in Imbaba, 'Ayn Shams, Qina, Aswan, and Damietta. Your military wing has suffered many losses. Drafting forces from Afghanistan is a last resort.

You are wrong. Our activities are still strong in these provinces. Our proselytizing continues and we are using new means of communicating and strengthening our ties with the people.

There are reports of splits in the Gama'a's ranks, and that this is why the provinces of Minya and Suhag have been quiet.

There are no splits in the Gama'a. The reasons for relative quiet in some areas are two: first, the government cannot open fronts all over the country, so they have not attacked us in certain areas. Second, it is in our interest—at this stage—to keep certain provinces quiet.

What are the main axes of the Gama'a's work now?

First, we are making ongoing preparations for a military coup. The security forces don't know about these because they are preoccupied with skirmishes in the *sa'id*. Second, we are working in the area of mass mobilization. When the Islamic revolution happens there will be mass support to head off foreign intervention. Our commando units have acquired important experience over many years. The absence of such operations does not mean activity has stopped. The state does not know anything about these operations because of our cell formation.

I think you are exaggerating. What is the evidence for the existence of military units?

In 1981, the security forces had no idea of the existence of the military unit. The lack of arrests now by the security forces is no indication that our military units do not exist. In the Jihad case many government military persons were involved.

Those military who were arrested were of low rank and had no influence inside the military.

I disagree. The lower ranks are critical. This is the lesson of history.

Some say the recent increase in Gama‘a activities is a function of the Gama‘a's illusion that it has as much power as the state.

We have no illusions. The Gama‘a is not just a movement of protest or limited opposition but an alternative to the regime, to the state. No other political forces will survive. There will be only al-Gama‘a al-Islamiyya.

The role of the Gama‘a members from Afghanistan in the acts of violence committed in Egypt has drawn a lot of attention. What prompted you to go to Afghanistan to begin with?

From the beginning we have aimed at preserving our presence in Egypt, and focused on spreading our activities within the country. After the events and arrests of 1981 we suffered from a loss of leadership. In 1984, when the first imprisoned activists were released, we reignited our activities and regained our following. As we expanded beyond Minya and Asyut into the Delta and Cairo, particularly ‘Ayn Shams and Giza, the security forces started to clamp down hard on our young activists again. We refused to compromise, so they launched a campaign of liquidation against us. It was at that point that the idea of protecting those youths by sending them to Afghanistan came up.

Why Afghanistan?

For different reasons, the most important being the need for military training.

What groups facilitated your travel to Afghanistan?

No governments. Afghan nationals involved in al-Da‘wa ila Jihad (Call to Holy Struggle), which had reached its peak in the mid-1980s, facilitated our travel and accommodations in Peshawar.

Did al-Gama‘a participate in the fighting in Afghanistan? How was it at the start?

The martyrs ‘Adli Yusuf, ‘Abd al-Fattah, Abu al-Yusr, and Muhammad Shawqi al-Islambuli, the brother of Khalid al-Islambuli, went to Afghanistan in the mid-1980s. ‘Adli Yusuf established the military camp there in 1989. After gaining military experience these men began to participate more and more with the Afghan fighters.

How did the Afghan experience influence al-Gama‘a intellectually and practically?

Intellectually, there was no influence. All had been influenced by the events of 1981 and after. Practically, militarily, in intelligence gathering, and in the spread of our message, we learned a lot. The leadership of al-Gama‘a delivered the *khutba* (sermon) at the time of ‘Id al-Fitr (end of Ramadan holiday) in Peshawar. We started to publish *Al-Murabitun* in

Peshawar, which was distributed throughout the Islamic world and printed in Algeria and Indonesia, and the bulletin *'Ajil,* which presented news on our activities to the whole world, including Egypt (by fax), in addition to the distribution of cassettes and documentary videos.

News reports say the Americans helped the Afghan resistance. Did you receive American support too?

The Americans had two goals: first, to weaken the Soviet Union, and second, to create a fifth column within the Afghan resistance which would be friendly to them after the victory over the Soviets. We, the Arabs, warned the Afghans of these strategies. We never received any aid from the Americans. They are our enemies.

How did you publish Al-Murabitun?

The first issue came out in February 1990. The cover story, with a picture of a gun, was entitled "Terror is a Means to Confront God's Enemies." Our aim was to familiarize people with our ideology. We were shocked by its sudden success. Soon it was being distributed throughout the Arab world, first legally and then secretly. After publishing articles critical of the Gulf states, particularly Saudi Arabia, pressure was brought to bear to stop publication. There were twenty-seven issues altogether. Its publication will continue with a new issue under a new name, *Al-Ard* (The land).

What is the situation of al-Gama'a in Pakistan, which is under Egyptian pressure to hand over Gama'a militants to them?

There are many areas not totally under government control. In those areas tribes have control and we are safe from Egyptian, American, and Saudi intelligence.

What about Afghanistan?

Because of the terrain in Afghanistan and because of our warm relations with Afghan parties and tribes we are protected from the Egyptians.

There have been reports of Gama'a activities in northern Afghanistan, near the border with Tajikistan.

We are present there to assist the Tajiks against the communists in Tajikistan and to provide reserves for the Gama'a units in Qanuz.

Where are your military camps and what happens in them? Where do your militants go after training?

The location and activities of our camps is not a topic for discussion. As for where our militants go after training: some go to fronts under the control of al-Gama'a where there are other Arab fighters, and some to fronts under the control of Afghan forces with which we have good ties. Some forces about whom we don't want anything known go to areas under the complete control of al-Gama'a.

The Afghan war has ended. What are these elements doing in Afghanistan now?
Some have died in battle, and some have gone to northern Afghanistan. Others are being kept in Afghanistan to be sent, when the time is ripe, to Egypt. Some have already been sent and are under the leadership of military units.

You say you have areas under the control of al-Gama'a. So why did you leave Peshawar for Denmark?
I am not a military man, and those areas are only for military operations. Since I am in charge of information, I was in Peshawar, where our media activities were centered. But since last year I have been banned from there. If I went inside Afghanistan I would have to end my activities because the country suffers from devastation.

What pressured you to leave Peshawar?
The pressure began after I wrote a number of articles criticizing the Saudi family for preventing pilgrims from countries that support Iraq from going on the *hajj* (pilgrimage). The Saudis demanded that charity groups in Afghanistan stop supporting the Gama'a. They asked Nawaz al-Sharif, the Pakistani president, to hand me over to the Egyptian authorities. Shaikh 'Abd Rabb al-Ra's al-Sayyaf, president of the Islamic Union of Afghanistan, put me under his protection. I found my activities hampered in Afghanistan. So, after receiving an invitation from Denmark, I sought political asylum there and got it.

Haven't the Egyptians succeeded in hampering your activities?
The center of our activities has always been the *sa'id*. Since pressure was brought to bear on us in Peshawar we have moved to Europe, where we are very active. Modern means of communication make it easier for us to be in touch with Egypt, and probably new means of activity here we have yet to discover.

Translated from the Arabic by Souhail Shadoud and Steve Tamari.

NOTES

Editors' note: This interview is part of a research project on political Islam in Egypt, the results of which will be published in Arabic (Cairo: al-Mahrusa Press).

In September 1995, Tal'at Fu'ad Qasim was arrested in Croatia, and subsequently "disappeared." Both the US and Egyptian governments disclaim responsibility and knowledge of his whereabouts.

1. Al-Gama'a al-Islamiyya (the Islamic Group) should not be confused with al-Gama'at al-Islamiyya (Islamic Groups), the common term for all the diverse Islamic associations.

28

"Silencing Is at the Heart of My Case"

Nasr Hamid Abu Zayd, interview with Elliott Colla and Ayman Bakr

In March 1993, a Cairo University committee voted to deny Professor Nasr Hamid Abu Zayd tenure on the grounds that he was an apostate and a heretic, launching a public debate in Egypt about the power of religious institutions managed by and serving the state, intellectual terrorism, and the absence of protection for critical thought. Coming less than a year after Farag Fuda's assassination, and in the midst of general anxiety about where the social and ideological tensions at work in Egyptian society are leading, Abu Zayd's case crystallized the struggles between Islamism and secularism, Egyptian critical thought and Western cultural imperialism, and most importantly, the struggle between the Egyptian state's ideological institutions and free thought. In a work that appeared shortly before the tenure case, Abu Zayd argued that the rhetoric of the "moderates" of the official state religious institutions (al-Azhar, Dar al-'Ulum) and that of the "extremists" of the political-religious opposition (the Muslim Brothers, al-Gama'at al-Islamiyya [the Islamic Groups], Jihad) differs more in style than in content.[1] This claim was sadly proven true. Many of the more prominent opponents of his promotion came from among the ranks of the so-called moderates.

The decision of the promotions committee was based only on the negative assessment of Abu Zayd's work by Professor 'Abd al-Sabur Shahin. It was attacked by all Abu Zayd's colleagues in the Arabic Language and Literature Department and also later by one of the committee's members, Mahmud Mikki, who retracted his original support for the committee's negative decision. Over the next few months, scores of articles and at least one book were published both in support of and against Abu Zayd's work.[2] Readership of his work has soared since the first days of his case, but most Egyptians have come to know him more as a symbol—positive or negative—

than a Muslim intellectual, for, as he has stated repeatedly, he considers himself neither an apostate nor a heretic, but rather a thinker who produces work that is faithful to Islam.[3]

Not only was there a massive campaign on the part of the Islamist writers attacking his work, but a group of seven lawyers, with the support of the Muslim Brotherhood, initiated a case to divorce him from his wife, Ibtihal Yunis, on the grounds that her status as a Muslim woman was in danger because of her marriage to Abu Zayd.[4] The court ruled that the issue was outside its jurisdiction and that those bringing the case had no legal standing in the matter. Subsequently, a *fatwa* (legal opinion) was issued against Abu Zayd, and he has continued to receive threats against his life. In June 1994, Abu Zayd received the Freedom of Expression award from the Egyptian Organization for Human Rights. He continues to teach and write, and in 1995 accepted an invitation to teach in the Netherlands.

This interview took place at Abu Zayd's Cairo home on May 25, 1993.

.   .   .   .   .

Could you tell us what you intend to accomplish through your work in the Egyptian academy?

The Arabic Department at Cairo University needed someone in the department to specialize in Qur'anic and *hadith* studies. I was thinking of pursuing literary criticism, not religious studies. I didn't have any objections to working on this, but I did know that the last graduate student in the department working on this topic was dismissed on account of his dissertation: he wanted to study stories in the Qur'an from a literary-critical perspective.

And what happened?

It caused a huge uproar, just like the one we have on our hands now. He was expelled from the university. There was something within me that didn't completely object to working on this topic, but I made one request: If the department was going to compel me to specialize in this field, they should at least allow me the freedom to decide under whom I would work. I chose Professor 'Abd al-'Aziz al-Ahwani.

My first thesis focused on *Mu'tazili* concepts of figurative speech in the Qur'an.[5] This began my acquaintance with the Arab religious tradition, and led me to a number of conclusions which have since been at the forefront of my work. One is that interpretation of religious texts in the Qur'an has been an integral part of the cognitive framework in Arabo-Islamic consciousness. Any intellectual concept had to find its legitimacy by virtue of not contradicting the Qur'an. The ideas of the *Mu'tazila*, philosophical ideas with social and political implications, had to be legitimized by returning to the Qur'an. Hermeneutics, I mean the interpretation of the Qur'an, emerged as one of the fundamental scholarly tasks of the *Mu'tazila*. Moreover, interpretation was not just used by the *Mu'tazila* but by all the different groups. Even in the divisions of the Qur'an into what are called "clear" and "unintelligible" passages, you see that the different schools of thought vary. Any verse which the *Mu'tazila* held to be "clear" and thus not in need of interpretive reading, when looked at by any other school might be deemed "vague" and in need of interpretation. Qur'anic interpretation was one of the tools used in intellectual, social, and political struggles. If an idea did "contradict" the text of the Qur'an, there was no choice but to resort to interpretation.

I became preoccupied with the idea that interpretation of Qur'anic texts was, within Arab culture, the base upon which any idea had to be founded. At that time, during the 1970s, al-Sadat's regime released Muslim Brothers from prison to offset the left in the universities and outside. The Brothers began to organize and the Gama'at Islamiyya began to be active. Al-Sadat's speeches were fertile ground for me, because they showed how the matter of interpretation isn't just connected to classical Arab culture. I was raised in the 1960s. The common understanding was about the Islam of social justice, the Islam of the underclass that defended human rights and spoke out against exploitation. With the change in the regime's political tendencies, a different kind of Islam came into being. For instance, with regard to the Arab-Israeli conflict, it used to be that Islam was the religion of *jihad* against the occupying Zionist enemy, then Islam became the religion of peace.

Living through this transformation in political, social, and religious discourses, I realized that religious texts from the past are interpreted according to present-day concerns and pressures. I began to wonder whether or not religious texts were open enough to accept these different types of interpretation. I became influenced by the science of interpretation and Western hermeneutics, and the role of the interpreter, the commentator, in reading texts and making them understood.

This inquiry is designed to uncover the ideology which the discourse serves, and the extent of the authority which a given interpretation might offer to the text. My project crystallized and widened—should I only look at religious discourse, or should I consider the kinds of political discourse filled with interpretations as well, not only the official political discourse but also nationalist and Marxist discourses?

You attempt to distinguish the original religious text from its various interpretations, and from its use in contemporary discourse.

The text has an existence independent of interpretation and commentary. It has a history and historical context. The reader, whether a medieval

Mu'tazilite or a modern one, whether a secularist, Marxist, or modern-day *salafi* [neotraditionalist] more often than not undervalues the original context for the benefit of his or her interpretation.[6] Once the context is done away with, the text is left hanging in midair, and one can pin any meaning onto it.

I like separating the text and the reader. There should be a cognitive distance between the text and the reader. The reader must become absorbed in the text in order to produce a reading, but this doesn't cancel out either the text's historical context or the reader's.

The role of commentators seems invisible.

There was a belief that whatever the commentator said about the text was really only a restatement of what the text said—"what the text really wanted to say." Many of those who find fault with my work have cited the opinions of commentators—as if the opinion of this or that commentator is the measure to which we have to submit ourselves.

Why did some commentators acquire a holy status?

This holy status was given by others. The commentators in the early generations of Islam knew fully that their interpretations or grasps of the text of the Qur'an might not have completely agreed with the original. The expression that's used at the end of any opinion—"God the Almighty is more knowing"—was a very important expression that's since become a cliché. But in its first uses it meant that if ever two commentators would disagree over interpretation, the validity of any one [human] interpretation could not be final.

What is the current state of intellectual freedom in Egypt?

In the field of literary culture, there has been a strong attack by the Islamists on what's called modernity, attacking Arab intellectuals interested in modernism as being Orientalists, collaborators with Zionism or imperialism. There has been a fight going on, but not with the same degree of vehemence and viciousness as in studies of tradition or religious thought.

This fight has made the point clear to everyone that the types of discourse which are "closed" are those which, when you transform them into politics, are undemocratic. All of us defend democracy, but we place an implicit condition: that it not increase the power of anyone else. A lot has been said about the blood that might flow if the Islamists were to come to power, and therefore we should get rid of democracy before the Islamists do. That's part of the structure of closed thinking—that "we" know the truth and give ourselves the authority to predict and preempt the future. There was no democracy in Algeria, and Algeria has paid in blood for its absence. If the mechanisms of the political system bring one's opponent to victory, one does not stop resisting. Conceding victory doesn't mean surrendering. We are mixing two issues here: what it means to concede others their rights, and what it means to surrender. The struggle for advancement won't ever be decided in the Arab world until it tries Islam—the Islam which the Islamists have in mind. Of course I'm scared. If they come to power, I'll be left out in the cold. No doubt about it. But my fears about my own personal safety should not outweigh my fears about the future of the *umma* [Islamic community]. Defending our opponents, the Islamists, as intellectuals is like defending ourselves as individuals. I don't mean to defend their interests, but I can't support freedom and say "except the Islamists." Some will tell you that when the Islamists talk about freedom, they mean freedom only for themselves. That's true. But that doesn't mean we should make the same mistake.

When we talk about freedom, we unleash a number of problems. I'll give you an example. When our society moved from nationalist economics to open-door capitalism we had to carry the burden of all sorts of corruption. We bore the brunt of it in order to get out of the economic crisis. Now we're in a social crisis, and greater freedom is the way out. It will create all sorts of problems. Who shoulders the burdens of economic crises? The people do. Who will bear the brunt of the social crisis? The regimes will. Now there is economic freedom, but there is no intellectual, or political, or social freedom. The ruling elites do not understand that freeing up the economy can only succeed when it is accompanied by intellectual, social, and political freedom.

There does seem to be some intellectual freedom, but there is a prohibition on putting those ideas into practice.

It's been said that, "Nasr Hamid Abu Zayd's books don't amount to anything. Let him say whatever he wants." That's essentially correct. But look at the upshot: he's free to say whatever he wants outside the university, which means he's deprived of freedom in the one place where freedom of thought is absolutely necessary. Write all the books you want, say all the heresies you want, but there is a danger if you teach. Students might debate with you. You're free, but prevented from ever trying to transform your ideas into any sort of power.

Didn't we see the same thing sixty years ago with Taha Husayn?

Taha was accused of apostasy by people from outside the university, and the university defended him. In my case, I was accused of apostasy inside the university, and some people from outside are defending me. Taha

Husayn was never called a *kafir* (unbeliever). What's most telling is how the conception of apostasy has now been transplanted into the university.

Then what was the accomplishment of the nahda *[the nineteenth- and early twentieth-century Arab renaissance]? Why does it seem we're back where we started?*

The *nahda* was an intellectual project marginally tacked onto Muhammad 'Ali's political project [constructing a centralized and militarily powerful Egyptian state]. It wasn't an independent intellectual project—it was largely dependent upon the regime's political needs. When Rifa' al-Tahtawi came into conflict with the program, he was sent off to the Sudan and the colleges were closed down. Mustafa 'Abd al-Raziq was interested in Western technological achievements, but he wasn't willing to contest the cultural legacies of Arab society. Muhammad 'Abduh's project was to articulate an Islam that could assimilate the accomplishments of European culture. A large part of the *nahda*'s indecision was the result of its subservience to the larger political project.

The second thing we could say about the *nahda* is that it dealt with problems which were forced upon Arab culture from outside by Europe. The questions were raised at them, not by them. When someone else is posing the questions, you have to take up a defensive response—your cultural tradition is transformed into a shield. Because of this, the tradition was deprived of real critiques and subjected to superficial ones.

Part of your case relates to criticisms you have made of the official religious establishment and those Islamic scholars who worked in Islamic banking schemes.

The personal part of it was maybe what drove them initially. But what has sustained them is a general struggle between the Islamists within the regime and those whom the Islamists consider to be secularists. The Islamists regard all the Marxists, socialists, enlightenment thinkers, the intellectuals from the Nasirist period, as the same: they are all people unsympathetic to the Islamist political tendency.

Some of the attacks on you have come from the Gama'at Islamiyya, but the more serious attack is from the moderates, those religious scholars or thinkers who work within the official state institutions.

Everyone's been saying that the problem is religious extremism. The moderates put themselves forward to the regime as representatives of the type of Islam with which the state should and must deal. The state may wake up to this mistake sooner or later. There are [also] people within the regime who have defended me, people writing in the government media.

Is there a secular, "enlightened" tendency, and an "Islamic" wing of the government?
Is the government really committed to being a secular state—for instance, committed
to protecting the rights of Christian Egyptians to the same degree as it protects the rights
of Muslims?

You've put your finger on the problem. The part of the government which has to keep up its relations with the West is the "enlightened" wing. The Arab regimes need the Muslim Brothers in order to situate themselves where the West wants them vis-à-vis the oil states. The oil is under the control of states whose regimes are reactionary in all senses—religiously backward, xenophobic, and tribal. And it's in America's interests that no genuinely democratic states are set up. After 1967 and the peace with Israel, Egypt lost its political power in the region. Then Egypt lost its economic power after it was transformed into a labor-exporting society for these Gulf states. The government is forced to deal with the "moderate" Islamists so it can bargain with the Gulf states.

Why does the government need an enlightened tendency at all?

The United States has no problem dealing with the Muslim Brothers. If the regime has to choose between the two tendencies, if one of them has to go . . . it will be the secularists. Our own history of colonialism prevented any real enlightenment from taking place. When the government's *Muwajaha* [Confrontation] series published Farah Antun's book, they took out the part in which Antun calls for a secular state. None of the contemporary secularists use the word "secularism." They talk about civil society. But we know that number one on the program of civil society is secularism.

Of the regime's two tendencies, the secularist one is weaker. I think perhaps—I have to say perhaps—there will be an alliance between the state and the Islamists. The greater fear would be that this sort of alliance will happen by means of bloodshed. Sometimes politics sanctions killings. I wasn't able to get that through to Farag Fuda.

Silencing is at the heart of my case. Expelling someone from the university is a way of silencing him. Taking someone away from his specialization is a way of silencing him. Killing someone is a way of silencing him. They need to get rid of some people.

What is the role of the Egyptian intellectual now?

The role of an intellectual is to produce concepts. I continue to fight. If they take me out of my specialization, I'll continue to teach. It's not the subject you teach, but the method you use to teach.

Translated from the Arabic by Elliott Colla.

NOTES

1. Nasr Hamid Abu Zayd, *Naqd al-khitab al-dini* (Cairo: Dar al-Sina, 1992).

2. *Al-Qahira* (April 1993) and *Adab wa-naqd* (May 1993) dedicated entire issues to Abu Zayd's promotion case. For overviews, see Faruq 'Abd al-Qadir, "Takfir al-asatidha fi jami'at al-qahira," *Ruz al-Yusuf,* April 4, 1993; and Lutfi al-Khuli, "Cairo University and Academic Freedom," *Al-Ahram Weekly,* April 8–14, 1993.

3. A partial list of his books should give some indication of the breadth of his thinking: *Falsafat al-ta'wil* (The philosophy of interpretation); *Mafhum al-nass: dirasa fi 'ulum al-qur'an* (The concept of the text: a study in the Qur'anic sciences); *Al-Imam al-shafi'i wa-ta'sis al-iydiyulujiyya al-wasitiyya* (Imam al-Shafi'i and the founding of medieval ideology); *Al-Ittijah al-'aqli fi al-tafsir* (The rationalist tendency in Qur'anic commentary).

4. Ibtihal Yunis, "Hatk al-'arad," *Al-Katiba* (May 1994), recounts her experience of being publicly subjected to Islamist scrutiny.

5. The *Mu'tazila* were a theological school dating from the ninth century who advocated a rationalist orientation within Islam.

6. The *salafiyya* is a modern Islamic revivalist tendency which calls for restoring the practices of Muhammad and the first generation of Muslims. *Salafis* legitimate their project by portraying it as the continuity of "tradition." Abu Zayd uses the word critically to denote the claim to derive legitimacy from a supposed nondeviance from tradition.

29

The Islamist Movement
and the Palestinian Authority

Bassam Jarrar, interview with Graham Usher

Bassam Jarrar, a leading Islamist thinker in the occupied territories, is a teacher of Islamic studies at UNRWA's Teacher Training Center in Ramallah in the West Bank and a member of the Board of Trustees of the Union of Islamic Scholars. He was among the 415 Palestinians expelled by Israel in December 1992 for alleged membership in the Islamic Resistance Movement, Hamas (Harakat al-Muqawama al-Islamiyya).

There have been two prevailing views on the role of Hamas in the period after the PLO-Israeli Declaration of Principles (DOP). For some, it is in the vanguard of a "rejectionist" Palestinian bloc bent on wrecking the DOP. Others believe the renewed political legitimacy and economic sustenance autonomy will supposedly confer on the PLO will marginalize groups like Hamas and Islamic Jihad.

One would do better to listen to what Islamist leaders are actually saying, and to analyze events on the ground. Since Oslo, Hamas representatives have repeatedly said that they do not want conflict with the nascent Palestinian authority, but their peace will come with a price—namely, influence on the social and cultural fronts via the schools, mosques, and law.

This interview was conducted in March 1994. Since then, events have demonstrated that Palestinian Islamists are fully cognizant of the new realities raised by self-rule, and of the politics it augurs. In April, Hamas offered a "cease-fire with the occupation" if Israel withdrew to its 1967 borders, dismantled all settlements, and permitted international observers to be stationed along the Green Line. One week later, Hamas's and Fatah's military wings in Gaza signed a pact outlawing all violence between them and placing a moratorium on the vexing issue of collaborator killings. And in May, leading Hamas figures let it be known that they were considering the idea of an "Islamist political party" and that the "resistance to occupation" need not be by "armed struggle alone," but also by "words, opinions, and unifying the people."

People in Gaza regard these moves as extremely important, not just because they imply Hamas's de facto recognition of Israel, but equally because they suggest Hamas's metamorphosis from a sociomilitary movement into the loyal political opposition of the new Palestinian polity.

What Hamas will want in return for this compromise is currently the subject of a fierce debate within Palestinian Islamism. Bassam Jarrar, an informed and significant voice in that movement, here spells out some key aspects of Palestinian political struggle in the new era.

. . . . .

How would you characterize the Islamists' attitude toward the interim period of Palestinian self-rule, particularly their relations with the new Palestinian authority? You said recently that because the Islamist movement will form the "main opposition" to self-rule, "this will lead to interaction with the transitional authority." What do you mean?

Although the Islamic movement rejects the Declaration of Principles [DOP], it has no interest in defeating it by force. It views its role as one of trying to convince Palestinians of the agreement's shortcomings, and of dealing with its negative aspects on both the Arab and Islamic levels. But it does not seek confrontation with the transitional authority, because confrontations will not promote these objectives.

Dialogue, however, depends ultimately on the attitude of the authority. If elections for the Palestinian municipalities and professional associations are held in a democratic way, then this will promote a rapprochement between the opposition and the authority. If the opposition is denied its democratic rights, there will be tension.

Similarly, in the field of education, if the new school authorities try to falsify certain aspects of Palestinian history, there will be conflicts. Islamists want a curriculum that is based on Arab and Islamic civilization, not one that is adulterated by foreign influences. I am talking here of the cultural curriculum rather than the scientific curriculum. If, on the other hand, the authorities take cognizance of these concerns, then again, there is room for reconciliation.

Finally, there is the issue of personal status [family] law. This is particularly important for Islamists because in most Arab countries this is explicitly based on *shari'a* law. It is not necessary for me here to say what I think the personal status law should be. This is a matter for the Palestinian *'ulama'*. But if the authorities deal with the law in a subjective way, this could lead to violations of the *shari'a* and so to infringements of our human rights as Muslims. We are not against innovation [*ijtihad*] in law, but we cannot compromise on rights that are guaranteed by the *shari'a*.

If there were cooperation over issues like these, wouldn't the Islamists be participating in self-rule?

No. There is a distinction between the Islamists' attitude toward the transitional authority and its attitude toward the peace process. "Interaction" refers to the relationships that the Islamists want to obtain among the Palestinian groups during the transitional period. Let me repeat: they have no interest in fighting the Palestinian authority. They do, however, have an interest in fighting the Israeli occupation. Were, say, the Islamists to stand in the self-rule election, this distinction would be lost and would create confusion among their supporters.

First, from the Islamists' point of view, participation in self-rule gives legitimacy to the peace process. Suppose the Islamists won the election. They would then be in the position of negotiating with the Israelis on the basis of the Oslo accords. They would have to recognize the legitimacy of the agreement even though they reject it! For this reason the Islamists distinguish between elections for the municipalities and associations, etc., where they would participate, and elections for the autonomy born of the DOP, where they wouldn't.

Second, and especially after [the massacre in] Hebron, the Islamists believe that the present atmosphere in the occupied territories is hardly conducive to democracy. Palestinians thus feel obliged to participate in the autonomy for the negative reason of wanting to be rid of this atmosphere. They are like a man in a tunnel: he is given a "choice" to leave the tunnel or wait for the train to kill him. Of course, he will leave, but this is hardly independence.

Third, should the Islamists participate in self-rule elections, then naturally their supporters would vote for them. In effect 90 percent of Palestinians in the occupied territories would then become involved in the autonomy in some way, lending the DOP a credibility it otherwise would not have.

I still don't see how the Islamists can wield legislative influence without participation in the self-rule institutions. It is not going to be professional associations or the municipalities that will draw up school curricula or law. . . .

But the transitional authority will have to take cognizance of what the associations and municipalities are saying—if, that is, it wants to build an atmosphere of genuine national consensus during the interim period.

Under what conditions would the Islamist movement, and particularly Hamas, agree to a cessation of the armed struggle against Israel? For example, last October, Hamas's spiritual guide, Shaikh Ahmad Yasin, is reported to have said that if Israel withdraws to the 1967 borders, then Hamas would be prepared to declare a cease-fire with it.

Yes, he did say that. But remember, for Hamas the 1967 borders are no more legitimate than the "borders" of Gaza and Jericho, so it would be a cease-fire and not peace, and certainly not a recognition of Israel. In my opinion, to speculate now about what would be the possible conditions of an armistice with Israel is futile. In any case, the only possible cease-fire would be one declared unilaterally by the Islamists. It certainly won't arise out of negotiations with the Israelis. The Islamic movement refuses, and has always refused, to be hemmed in by conditions dictated by the enemy. It will cease the armed struggle when it sees it to be in its best interest to do so. In other words, it will take the initiative.

The same logic applies to the Islamic movement's relations with the transitional authority or the PLO. While they don't seek conflict with the authority, this doesn't mean that the PLO has the right to lay down conditions about, say, Hamas's military operations against the occupation. This is a decision solely for Hamas.

Now for sure, the main bone of contention between the Islamists and the PLO is likely to be this issue of armed struggle during the transitional period. And if, for instance, Hamas launched an attack against settlers or soldiers in Ramallah or Gaza during the autonomy, this would undoubtedly cause problems for the PLO leadership. But what if Hamas were to hit targets in Tel Aviv or at the Israeli embassy in Cairo? What has the PLO to do with the protection of Tel Aviv or Cairo?

Does the Islamist movement want to reform the PLO or does it want to stand as a political alternative to it?

The Islamic movement is very concerned about the current state of the PLO. For example, after Oslo, some Palestinian factions sought the disintegration of the PLO. The Islamists, however, insisted on the preservation of the PLO. The PLO has a long history of struggle and therefore of legitimacy in Palestinian eyes, and there is currently no real alternative to it. Thus it would not be in the Palestinian interest—including the interest of Palestinian Islamists—to have it fall apart.

The Islamic movement's position is quite clear: it wants a national dialogue between all national and Islamic forces based on democratic reform of the PLO and its decision-making structures. If, however, the PLO disintegrates because of the catastrophic political decisions its leadership has made—specifically, its acceptance of Oslo—then this is the result of those decisions. The blame cannot be laid at the door of the Islamists. But if it does disintegrate, this does not mean that there is a political vacuum. The Islamic movement is there because it exists independently of the PLO and is an integral part of Palestinian political culture.

30

What Kind of Nation?
The Rise of Hamas
in the Occupied Territories

Graham Usher

In December 1992, the 'Izz al-Din al-Qassam Brigade—the military wing of the Palestinian Islamic Resistance Movement, Hamas (Harakat al-Muqawama al-Islamiyya)—launched a series of guerrilla actions in the West Bank and Gaza that claimed the lives of six Israeli soldiers in as many days. The spectacular military success of these operations—and the fear they aroused in Israeli society—prompted the Rabin government to expel summarily 415 alleged "Islamic fundamentalists" to the hills of South Lebanon, inaugurating the worst period of Israeli repression in the occupied territories since the outbreak of the intifada in 1987 and arguably since Israel's occupation in 1967.[1]

Hamas's actions impressed on Israeli government and people alike the urgency of extracting themselves from the "quagmire" of Gaza—in Rabin's words, of "getting Gaza out of Tel Aviv." The solution, cultivated in secret Israeli-PLO negotiations during the course of 1993, was Israel's proposal to partially withdraw from Gaza and the West Bank town of Jericho as a prelude to a full-fledged peace agreement. This remedy underpinned the Israeli-PLO Declaration of Principles (DOP) signed in Washington nine months later, in September.

If Hamas had done nothing else, these military operations and their dramatic political consequences would have ensured it at least a footnote in the annals of the Palestinian-Israeli conflict. Hamas, however, is more than a military formation. Its modern political Islam challenges both Israel and PLO nationalism.

CULTURALIST POLITICS

Hamas first appeared publicly in February 1988 as "a wing of the Muslim Brothers in Palestine."[2] Under the stewardship of its "spiritual guide,"

Shaikh Ahmad Yasin, a specifically Palestinian Muslim Brothers emerged in the occupied territories in the 1970s as a culturalist and social movement whose primary goal was the "founding of the Islamic personality."[3] Politically, the movement abstained from all forms of antioccupation activity, giving priority instead to cultural struggle against the PLO's "atheist" commitment to secular nationalism.

Lubricated by Saudi money, the Muslim Brothers built, especially in Gaza, an impressive social infrastructure, controlling 40 percent of Gaza's mosques by 1986. Hamas also controlled Gaza's single Islamic University—with seven thousand students, then the largest in the territories.[4] These advances were facilitated not only by the internal crises that rocked the PLO after its 1982 military defeat in Lebanon, but also by the Israeli occupation authorities, who viewed the rise of political Islam as a useful tool for fomenting dissension within Palestinian nationalism. "We extend some financial aid to Islamic groups via mosques and religious schools," acknowledged the former Israeli military governor of Gaza, General Yitzhak Segev, "in order to help create a force that would stand against the leftist forces which support the PLO."[5]

When the intifada erupted, the Muslim Brothers confronted a dilemma: either forgo its de facto accommodation with the occupation or lose the Palestinian street. After initial doubts about the durability of the uprising, it resolved the dilemma through the formation of Hamas, an Islamist formation dedicated to national liberation.

In August 1988, the Muslim Brothers published the Covenant of the Islamic Resistance Movement, which spells out "who Hamas is and what it represents." Essentially a political manifesto—it mirrors the PLO's founding National Charter—the Covenant blends a socially puritanical version of Islam, an accommodation to PLO nationalism, and a rehash of Eurocentric anti-Semitism. Thus, territorial nationalism—once adjured by the Muslim Brothers as "idolatry"—is now "a function of religious belief," while the distinction made by the PLO between anti-Zionism and anti-Semitism is so obscured that the Jews are held responsible not just for Israel and the "murder of the prophets" but also for "the second world war" and "the League of Nations."[6] The legacy of the pre-intifada social agenda persists with a swipe at "secularism as completely contradictory to religious ideology."

Hamas pledged "unity with our PLO brothers" during the uprising's early years, but on the street it made a point of organizing independently of the Unified National Leadership of the Uprising (UNLU)—issuing its own leaflets, establishing its own calendar of strike days, and refusing to acknowledge the sole representative status of the PLO.[7] It continued its largely culturalist thrust, imbuing the uprising with an Islamist flavor rather than making a political or military contribution. Its principal activity in this early period was a social offensive against all manifestations of "un-Islamic behavior," especially in Gaza where women were forced to wear a head-scarf as a sign of both modesty and nationalist rectitude.[8] The UNLU responded with a defensive, apologetic stance to this campaign, which cost it dearly among the crucial constituencies of women, youth, and Christian Palestinians.[9]

Despite the vitriol of its propaganda against Jews as the "sons of apes and swine," Hamas's relations with the occupation authorities was essentially quietist. The Israeli army (IDF) never interfered "with Hamas strike days." Israeli Defense Minister Yitzhak Rabin went so far as to meet such prominent Islamists as Mahmud Zahar and Ibrahim Yazuri for "talks" in the summer of 1988.[10] Only in the fall of 1989, after discovering that Hamas was behind the kidnap and killing of two Israeli soldiers, did the Israeli army finally declare the movement illegal[11]—nearly two years after the outbreak of the intifada, and one year after Israel banned all PLO/UNLU-backed popular committees. Until then, the Israelis stubbornly assumed that the Islamists' social conservatism was equivalent to political conservatism.[12]

POLITICAL CULTURE

By the end of the 1980s, Hamas became an integral part of the Palestinian scene, regularly polling second only to 'Arafat's Fatah movement in professional and student elections across the territories. In the initial phase of the intifada Hamas did not so much oppose the PLO politically as ignore its existence.[13] It was well on the way to becoming a counterhegemonic force when two events led Hamas to challenge the PLO's claim as the sole legitimate representative of the Palestinian people, thereby transforming Islamism from a culturalist politics to an alternative political culture for the liberation of Palestine. The first was the Palestine National Council's decision in 1988 to recognize Israel within its pre-1967 borders and formally endorse a "two state" solution. This Hamas deemed a sacrilege. As its Covenant states, "Palestine, from the river to the sea, is a holy trust afforded to Muslims by God." The second was the PLO's October 1991 decision to participate in the US-brokered peace plan following the Gulf war.[14] "We will confront the [Madrid] conference," railed Hamas leader, Ibrahim Ghusha, "and we will do that by escalating the uprising in the occupied territories."[15]

Hamas vowed "a full return to the military option" and demanded "40 to 50 percent representation on all PLO bodies"—a demand that invited, and received, rejection. The PLO accused Hamas of "being the plaything of Israel and the US and of intending to replace the PLO as leader of the Palestinian movement."[16] The period of tenuous unity between Palestine's nationalist and Islamist wings, that by and large had held during the uprising, was over. The Israelis fanned the flames by choosing this time to arrest several hundred Hamas supporters and by sentencing Yasin to life imprisonment for his alleged involvement in Islamist-inspired "terrorism."[17]

In late 1991, openly defying the PLO leadership, Hamas mounted a series of ominously popular actions, shutting down Gaza with three consecutive days of strikes and exposing the frail nationalist consensus behind the Madrid formula. Subsequent events, marked by rising popular frustration at the lack of progress at the negotiating table and, on the ground, by factional tension and tit-for-tat strikes that turned the intifada into the personal property of rival bands of masked men, only confirmed this frailty. The degeneration reached its nadir in July 1992 when street battles in Gaza between Fatah and Hamas supporters left over a hundred injured and three dead.

The prevailing political wisdom at the time held that because of the "July clashes" Hamas lost the street; when it came to the crunch, Palestinians remained nationalist first and Islamist second.[18] This was true, but only in part. Hamas moved into open confrontation with Fatah not only because of the growing unpopularity of Madrid, but also because of the election of a Labor government in June 1992, whose pledge to "make peace with the Palestinians within nine months" threatened to undercut the "rejectionist" basis of its support.

Hamas's belated turn to full-fledged armed struggle in December 1992 may have been based less on any strategic vision for the intifada than an attempt to rescue its credibility among a Palestinian public increasingly weary of the sacrifices entailed by the uprising as well as of such "negative phenomena" as the rising toll of "collaborator" killings and a stifling social puritanism.[19] Having failed to wrest legitimacy from Fatah on the street, Hamas tried to appropriate its nationalist legacy of armed struggle against Israel and, by upping the military ante, stymie Rabin's plans for a quick fix on Palestinian autonomy.

In the months before the signing of the Declaration of Principles, Hamas could regard the intifada as a period of sustained activism in which it had made considerable inroads into the PLO's hegemony on the social, political, and military fronts. For the first time in the occupied territories, Palestinian nationalism was faced with an indigenous, authentic, and mass opposition completely outside the sway of the PLO. In the aftermath of the December 1992 expulsions, opinion polls showed that 16.6 percent of Palestinians in Gaza and 10.5 percent in the West Bank held that "the Islamic movement rather than the PLO represented them."[20] Like other radical Islamist currents in the Middle East, Hamas had become a barometer of political discontent, nurtured in this case by a divided national leadership and by an immobilizing Madrid formula that stubbornly stood in the way of peace.

AFTER OSLO

With the signing of the Declaration of Principles, or Oslo accords, in September 1993, many contend that Hamas's days as a counterhegemonic force were numbered. Not only had the peace agreement restored the PLO's standing, but more importantly, international funds pledged to underwrite the deal would replenish the PLO's empty coffers and so lubricate the networks of support and patronage through which legitimacy could again be consolidated.

Nonetheless, since Oslo Hamas has established itself as the single largest political opposition in Palestinian society through well-calibrated tactics of guerrilla warfare, political alliances, and a pragmatic social agenda. Hamas's goal has become not so much to destroy self-rule as to pursue flexibly a long-held strategy to assert an Islamist culture for Palestinian society.

In 1989, following the PLO's formal recognition of Israel, former IDF General Aharon Yariv paid a backhanded compliment to two decades of Palestinian armed struggle. The PLO, he said, "understand[s] that the aim of any military operation is political, and that the success of such operations should be measured in political terms."[21] A like logic drove Hamas military policy after Oslo. The aim was less to scuttle the Declaration of Principles than to stall the pace of its implementation. The longer the delay, the Islamists figured, the greater the PLO's loss of support and legitimacy.

Actions such as Hamas's ambush in December 1993 of Lt. Col. Meir Mintz, coordinator of the IDF's undercover units in Gaza, or the killing of General Security Service operative, No'am Cohen, by one of his own informers in the West Bank in February 1994, not only generated huge political kudos on the Palestinian street; they succeeded in putting the fear of death into the Israeli military establishment. On the Mintz assassination, IDF sources whined that, in terms of professionalism, Fatah "had achieved nothing remotely resembling it during the 26 years [*sic*] of its existence."[22]

The military targets were Israeli, but Hamas's political sights were fixed firmly on the PLO leadership, particularly 'Arafat. No Palestinian leader could possibly condemn the killing of a Mintz or a Cohen. A similar logic obtained with Hamas's actions after the Hebron massacre in February 1994, especially its revived penchant for hitting Israeli civilians inside the Green Line.[23] In April 1994, a West Bank Palestinian rammed a car full of explosives into a crowded bus station in the Israeli town of 'Afula, killing eight and wounding forty others. A Hamas statement issued after this "revenge" for Hebron, said that ending the attacks was "conditional on Israeli settlers quickly leaving the West Bank and Gaza"—a sentiment which polls showed 88 percent of Palestinians in the territories shared.

Domestic Israeli opinion compelled a gesture from the Israeli leadership after every Hamas outrage, usually in the form of a rote demand that 'Arafat curb "fundamentalist terror." The problem for Rabin was that he knew that 'Arafat was ultimately powerless to stop Hamas. His Palestinian Authority (PA) with its "strong police force" had yet to be installed. More to the point, such impotence was written into the Oslo agreement, which states categorically that Israel retains responsibility for the "external security" of the "autonomous areas"—that is, for Israel and the Israelis. Hamas knew this too. "If Hamas launched an attack against Israelis in Gaza during the autonomy, this would undoubtedly cause problems for the PLO leadership," said one leading Islamist. "But what if Hamas were to hit Israelis in Tel Aviv? What has the PLO to do with the protection of Tel Aviv?"[24]

Rabin was thus repeatedly pushed into using collective sanctions against Palestinians, which politically strengthened Hamas rejectionism at the expense of the PLO's awkward conciliation. Israel closed off the West Bank and Gaza, rounded up hundreds of "Hamas suspects" and launched massive punitive raids against Palestinian communities to dredge out and usually execute "Muslim extremists." Each successive crackdown chipped away at the PLO leader's support in the territories and also at Rabin's own conviction that "only 'Arafat" could make self-rule work.[25]

As Dani Rubinstein wrote, after Oslo "Hamas's terrorist activities contain two main political messages. The first—to 'Arafat and the PLO—is do not dare ignore us; the second—to the state of Israel—is that negotiations with the PLO do not constitute the final word and that Hamas must also be taken into account."[26]

GUN AND OLIVE BRANCH

If Hamas military policy since Oslo has been a considered series of spectacular strikes designed to pack the maximum political punch, it has demonstrated similar foresight in handling its relations with the PLO, and especially Fatah. However rejectionist its public face against the Declaration of Principles, Hamas's stance toward other PLO factions has been essentially conciliatory, signaling that the Islamists are fully cognizant of the new political realities inaugurated by self-rule.

In January 1994, Hamas announced its formal enlistment in the Palestinian Forces Alliance (PFA), a Damascus-based coalition of ten Palestinian organizations opposed to the Declaration of Principles, including the PLO's Popular and Democratic Fronts. Hamas's participation in this nationalist-Islamist bloc was completely instrumental. It worked with the PLO rejectionists when it was in its interest to do so, such as the elections to the Bir Zeit University Student Council in November 1993. There, for the first time in twenty years, a Fatah-led coalition lost out to an anti-Oslo bloc. But Hamas abandoned the Fronts when it perceived no political need for them. In the Engineers' Association elections in Gaza in February 1994, Hamas aligned itself only with Islamic Jihad, scoring a tie with pro-Oslo nationalists. Both Bir Zeit and the Engineers had been historical bastions of Fatah.

Participation in the PFA allowed Hamas to drop some of the more offensive (and unpopular) features of its social agenda in the name of Palestinian unity. In the months after Oslo Hamas visibly relaxed its strictures against "un-Islamic behavior," such as unveiled Palestinian women in public or families going to the beach "at a time of national suffering and martyrdom," in favor of a more pragmatic and permissive attitude. It was a great irony that in their desire to avoid "giving 'Arafat cover," the PLO's Marxist factions had given cover to the Islamists, ideologically their greatest foe.

Most Palestinians in the territories feared that the Declaration of Principles would lead to civil strife between Fatah and Hamas. A deft mix of clear political direction and discipline by both leaderships kept this nightmare scenario largely at bay. In September 1993, PLO and Hamas prisoners signed a pact banning violence to resolve political disagreements over Oslo. Apart from a few street skirmishes, this line of coexistence was implemented, even regarding potentially explosive issues such as the fate of collaborators and the role of the Palestinian police. Hamas repeatedly warned the PLO in its negotiations with Israel not to amnesty collaborators in exchange for promises to release Palestinian prisoners. Yasin stated that as long as the Palestinian Authority "settles accounts with the criminals," Hamas would "not intervene in those affairs."[27]

Similarly with the police, in October 1993, after two Hamas guerrillas, dressed as Israelis, ambushed two IDF reservists near a Gaza settlement, Hamas released a video promising peace with the Palestinian police "unless they raise their guns against us." On the eve of the police's entry into Gaza and Jericho, even this vaguely adversarial tone was moderated to the point of fraternity. "We welcome the Palestinian security forces as brothers," said Yazuri in May 1994.[28]

This new conciliation accompanied Hamas's shifting perceptions of the centrality of the PLO to Palestinian politics. Palestinian Islamism had emerged largely as a reaction to the PLO's secular nationalism. But after Oslo, Islamists were at pains to stress the patriotic credentials of their opposition. "It would not be in the Palestinian interest to have the PLO fall apart" over the Declaration of Principles, said Islamist intellectual Bassam Jarrar. 'Abd al-'Aziz Rantisi, a Gaza leader of Hamas, mused that Hamas sought not the "downfall of the PLO" but rather that its "structure and shape be redefined on a democratic basis."[29]

THE BALLOT BOX

From the moment 'Arafat shook Rabin's hand, most Islamists understood that the Declaration of Principles was politically irreversible. "We can't stand up and say to people we want the occupation to stay. That would be irrational," said Islamist journalist Khalid Amayreh.[30] The issue for Hamas was: What would self-rule comprise?

The formal PLO opposition line out of Damascus was to have no truck with "any elections or bodies to be established in compliance with the Gaza-Jericho accord." But in October 1993, Yasin reportedly said that Hamas would take part in the Palestinian Authority elections "because it wanted to have influence on the daily lives of Palestinians in the occupied territories."[31]

In the year after Oslo, Hamas's position on the Palestinian Authority elections shifted between these two poles, suggesting a rigorous debate within the movement. Many Hamas supporters viewed any participation in self-rule as lending the Declaration of Principles "a credibility it does not have." Others pointed to the electoral successes Islamists scored after Oslo, not just at Bir Zeit and in Gaza, but in an array of professional and student associations across the occupied territories.[32] Participating in the self-rule elections, they argued, would almost certainly not lead to the defeat of the PLO, but they would be the strongest opposition party. The PLO would have to accommodate the political and social leverage this would give Hamas in the territories.

When the Palestinian Authority was installed in July 1994, Hamas publicly adopted a compromise between these pragmatic and rejectionist tendencies, most clearly articulated by Bassam Jarrar and Hamas Gaza spokesperson, Mahmud Zahar. Both stated that while Hamas would not initially participate in elections "born of the Declaration of Principles," it would stand for institutions of "Palestinian public interest" such as municipalities and the professional bodies. Other Islamists have suggested that their eventual participation in the Palestinian Authority is conditional on the extent of the independent legislative powers the Authority enjoys. Either posture suggests a nonantagonistic, almost "loyal" oppositional role in self-rule.

A NEW POLITICS

In April 1994, a month before the ten thousand-strong Palestinian police force rolled into Gaza and Jericho, Fatah and Hamas military wings in Gaza signed a nonbelligerence accord promising a moratorium on collaborator killings, an end to all "defamatory campaigns" between them, and the reduction of separately called strike days "to lighten the economic burden of our people."[33] While Palestinians in the territories breathed a collective sigh of relief, news of the pact sent Israeli leaders (to borrow Rabin's parlance) "spinning like propellers." Rabin was enraged that the liaison had made no mention of Hamas's armed attacks, let alone any commitment to end them. "It is out of the question," he thundered, "that the PLO should even think of achieving cooperation" with Hamas "on the basis of attacking Israelis."[34]

However, the Israeli government itself had previously flown numerous trial balloons to entice Hamas to join the autonomy. Shortly after the Fatah-Hamas pact was announced, IDF Commander Doron Almog met with Hamas leader Muhsin Abu 'Ata to discuss the Israeli-PLO agreement and the new PLO-Hamas modus vivendi. At about the same time, Foreign Minster Shimon Peres floated the idea that his government would "sit down with Hamas" and release its prisoners if it renounced violence and started "down the road to negotiations."[35] For PLO activists in the territories, this meant Hamas had accepted the Declaration of Principles as a fact and was about to participate in the new politics it augured.

SOCIAL BASE

The bulk of Hamas's support in the territories is drawn from socially conservative sectors for whom the ideology of "secular nationalism" remains an apology for the rank materialism, corruption, and moral permissiveness of the region's ruling regimes (as well as the PLO). Such strata formerly embraced the Muslim Brothers' cultural orientation. For them, the chief attraction of Islamism is its austere moral code, stressing pious conduct and application of Islamic values and law to all social spheres. Thus, for Islamist religious figures such as Shaikh Jamal Salim, the "red lines" governing Hamas's role in the autonomy are not the incendiary political questions of Israeli settlements and Jerusalem, but "freedom of expression in the mosques and the right to speak about the religious point of view not only in religion but in politics, social values, economics, etc."[36]

The "red line," then, demarcates the Islamists' insistence on a total separation between the territories' existing *shari'a* courts, which adjudicate personal status such as marriage and divorce, and the Palestinian Authority's new Ministry of Justice, which (it is assumed) will employ positive law. For Hamas, the preservation and consolidation of *shari'a* rule over personal status, which is key to the social reproduction of the patriarchal Palestinian family as the basic unit of Palestinian society, is perhaps the greatest potential prize of self-rule.[37] It ensures, says Bassam Jarrar, "the guarantee of Palestinians' human rights as Muslims."[38]

These demands now have to be accommodated to more overtly nationalist slogans. With its turn to armed national struggle in the intifada, Hamas succeeded in attracting increasing numbers of younger, more militant elements of Palestinian society.[39] For these generations, Islam means not just the mosque and *shari'a,* but also liberation from Israeli occupation. For them Hamas's message is exemplified less by the sage wisdom of figures like Yasin than by the exemplary military actions of Islamic Jihad and Hizb Allah, the daring (and often successful) operations of the 'Izz al-Din al-Qassam Brigade, and the heroic martyrdom of fighters like 'Imad 'Akl.[40]

This suggests a transformation of nationalist ideology, imbuing it with a religious tone of "spiritual and community release" that secularism is felt to lack.[41] If Hamas had to accommodate nationalism because of the intifada, it did so by reinventing an Islamist tradition that is now regarded, especially among those generations politically forged by the intifada, as an integral part of Palestinian national identity.[42]

Whether this mix of social conservatism and radical nationalism can be contained within one movement is the dilemma Hamas now faces. Unlike most of the smaller PLO factions,[43] but very much like Fatah, Hamas operates as a broad alliance whose line is determined by consensus. On the eve of the Palestinian Authority's entry into Gaza and Jericho, the consensus was revised in an "important official statement" issued by the head of Hamas's Political Department, Musa Abu Marzuq. Hamas, he said, would offer a truce (*hudna*) with the occupation if Israel withdrew to its 1967 borders, disarmed all settlers as a prelude to dismantling all settlements, released Palestinian prisoners, and permitted elections to a "sovereign" body that would represent all Palestinians and possess the authority to "define Palestinian self-determination" (including the legislative power to repeal or at least modify the Declaration of Principles).[44]

Israel, of course, rejects these conditions. Hamas sought not only to highlight the deficiencies of the Declaration of Principles, whose text guarantees none of these points, but chiefly to rally centrist Palestinian opinion. Hamas references to "1967 borders" and "settlements" suggested a de facto recognition of Israel, and so placed it in the mainstream of contemporary Palestinian nationalism.[45]

While Hamas's more militant cadres murmured against Abu Marzuq's statement, moderates like Khalid Amayreh intimated that the new line returned Hamas to its "ideological fundamentals by placing more emphasis on its bedrock theme—Islam is the solution—and less on its ultimate religio-political objective, the complete liberation of Palestine and the establishment of an Islamic state."[46] In this scenario, according to a leading Islamist in April 1994,

> The Islamic tendency has reached the conclusion that it is no longer possible to halt the [Declaration of Principles] negotiations, since the US, which rules our region, is pushing towards [their] completion. But the negotiations with Israel must grant the Palestinians minimal rights, such as the 1967 borders, and at this time they will be satisfied with that. The continuation of the solution of the Palestinian problem will be in the hands of future generations.[47]

Another leading Hamas figure said that for mainstream Islamism in the occupied territories there is now "only one taboo, and that is the recognition of Israel . . . anything else is permissible."[48]

If Hamas wants to return to its "ideological fundamentals," it will have to establish a working relationship with the Palestinian Authority. But no rapprochement will be feasible—none that would survive the long reach of Israel's (and now the Palestinian Authority's) security forces—without the Islamists' commitment to end the armed struggle, at least in the areas under Palestinian autonomy. Figures like Jarrar say only that "Hamas will cease military operations when it sees it to be in its best interest to do so."[49] The debate hinges on the timing of "best interest." The moderates say it should be now, to foreclose any "fratricidal" conflict with the Palestinian Authority. The rejectionists say it should be on realization of Israel's military withdrawal from the West Bank and Gaza.

In October 1994, in response to a crackdown on Hamas supporters by both Israel and the Palestinian Authority, the 'Izz al-Din al-Qassam Brigade unleashed the worst onslaught on Israeli civilian and military targets of its five-year history. Three separate operations—a random gun attack in West Jerusalem, the kidnap and killing of an Israeli soldier near Ramallah, and a bomb planted on a bus in downtown Tel Aviv—left twenty-five Israelis dead and over fifty injured. The demands that accompanied these actions were nationalist rather than Islamist: that Israel immediately release two hundred Palestinian prisoners, including Shaikh Yasin; and that the Palestinian Authority cease supplying "information . . . on our *mujahidin* . . . to the Zionist intelligence and occupation authorities."[50]

The Palestinian Authority arrested over three hundred Hamas activists in Gaza after the kidnapping of Nahshon Waxman, but it is too early to say what long-term impact the massive military escalation will have on Hamas's posture vis-à-vis Israel or its relations with the Palestinian Authority. It is already apparent that the 'Izz al-Din al-Qassam organization's revamped militarism has stretched the Islamist consensus to the breaking point. In the wake of the Tel Aviv bombing, Amayreh said that the action "would be detrimental to Hamas and its popularity" and that "some people identified with Hamas will distance themselves from the perpetrators."[51] A Hamas leader in Gaza, Shaikh Ahmad Bahar, however, justified the operations as "legitimate . . . as long as the occupation continues."[52]

One solution to Hamas's political dilemma—currently under intense discussion in Islamist circles—is the formation of an Islamist political party for the changed circumstances of autonomy. This would be affiliated to Hamas and would enjoy the same quasi-independent relations with it as Hamas originally had with the Muslim Brothers. While the party would focus on promulgating "Islamic values," Hamas's military arm would be kept in reserve, to pursue, in Mahmud Zahar's words, its "own independent policy and strategy."[53]

As another Hamas leader, Isma'il Haniyya, implies, even this "independence" would have to be "rationalized." "I think the movement will carry out military operations only in response to blatant Israeli aggression against our people, and the scale of the attacks will be determined by the level of popular support for such a strategy," Haniyya said. "A political party is crucial for dealing with the new situation" if Hamas is to cope with the dual challenge of "resisting the occupation, but avoiding a showdown with the Palestinian Authority."[54]

CONCLUSION

Hamas's metamorphosis into a loyal opposition may ensure its political survival and also provide a genuinely independent opposition, which the PLO sorely needs if it is to pull through what is increasingly being recognized as its midnight hour.[55] This will come at a price, probably in terms of augmented Islamist influence in the legal and cultural spheres of Palestinian civil society.[56] The alternative—continuation of Hamas as a military organization—is liable to provoke, at best, an extremely authoritarian form of self-government or, at worst, civil war. Ultimately, though, the prospect of an emergent Islamist political culture in the occupied territories carries many risks for the Palestinian national struggle.

Like other variants of political Islam, Hamas represents an apparent conundrum. On the one hand, it is a modernist political movement, deploying mass modes of mobilization and social organization to propagate its ideology, and garnering for itself a deserved reputation for financial probity and community service, often in contrast to the PLO's institutions. On the other hand, its interpretation of Islam meets none of the political, social, and economic challenges thrown up by the struggle for self-determination and risks establishing a version of Palestinian national identity that it is antidemocratic, sectarian, and racist. This vision may ultimately corrode the foundations of contemporary Palestinian nationalism.

Palestinians' support for Hamas is not the result of their mass turn to faith, but the fruit of two interrelated crises of PLO nationalist ideology and practice.[57] One is a political crisis of representation, aggravated by an increasingly unaccountable, autocratic, and inadequate national leadership. The other is an ideological crisis over the social agenda and content of any future Palestinian polity. It is not, as Hamas's ubiquitous slogans would have it, that "peace with Jews is blasphemy" or that "Islam is the solution." Such sentiments have popular, and populist, resonance because they beg the cardinal, yet unanswered, questions: What kind of peace? And if not an Islamic nation, then what kind of nation?

As long as Palestinian nationalists—left and right alike—avoid these issues, movements like Hamas will flourish.

NOTES

1. Between February and May 1993, 67 Palestinians were killed and 1,522 injured in the Gaza Strip alone, including 29 in May, making it the bloodiest month of the uprising. For an account of the unprecedented scale of Israeli repression, see Graham Usher, "Why Gaza Says Yes, Mostly," *Race & Class* 35, no. 3 (January–March 1994): 68–73.

2. Islamists claim that Hamas was founded on December 8, 1987, the very eve of the uprising. The first leaflet signed by the Islamic Resistance Movement, however, was issued on February 11, 1988. See Jean-François Legrain, "The Islamic Movement and the Intifada," in Jamal R. Nassar and Roger Heacock (eds.), *Intifada: Palestine at the Crossroads* (New York: Praeger, 1991), pp. 175–89.

3. Before the Israeli occupation of 1967, the Muslim Brothers in Gaza were a branch of the Egyptian Muslim Brothers and in the West Bank of the Jordanian Muslim Brothers. Yasin's innovation was to form a branch that operated exclusively in the occupied territories, though with organizational and financial links with the Jordanian "Brothers." See Ziad Abu Amr, *Islamic Fundamentalism in the West Bank and Gaza* (Bloomington: Indiana University Press, 1994), pp. 10–22.

4. Ibid., pp. 15–17.

5. Yitzhak Segev, as quoted in "A Special Report on Religious Fundamentalism" (Damascus: Palestine Studies Centre, August 1988).

6. The sacrilegious nature of any commitment to territorial nationalism was eloquently expressed by a West Bank Muslim Brother, Sabri Abu Diab, in the early 1980s: "The land . . . is either a land of atheism or of Islam; there is no such thing as Arab, Palestinian, or Jewish land. . . . Land cannot be considered holy, because holiness is only characteristic of Allah, so how can we sanctify and even worship a very small geographical area [e.g., Palestine] rather than Allah, as the so-called nationalists do?" 'Abd al-Qadir Yasin, *Harakat al-muqawama al-islamiyya fi filastin (Hamas)* (Cairo: Dar Sina', 1990), p. 32.

7. "The PLO," commented Hamas leader Khalil Kuka acidly in 1988, "is the sole legitimate representative of its constituent organizations." See Ze'ev Schiff and Ehud Ya'ari, *Intifada: The Palestinian Uprising—Israel's Third Front* (New York: Simon Schuster, 1990), p. 235.

8. A popular wall slogan of the time read, "Hamas considers the unveiled to be collaborators of a kind."

9. See Rema Hammami's chapter in this volume.

10. Schiff and Ya'ari, *Intifada,* p. 235.

11. This was the first acknowledged operation by Hamas's military wing, the 'Izz al-Din al-Qassam Brigade. Israel's outlawing of Hamas also led to the arrest of Shaikh Ahmad Yasin, who until then had been unmolested by Israel's security forces during the uprising. He had even appeared on Israeli TV. See Lisa Taraki, "The Islamic Resistance Movement in the Palestinian Uprising," in Zachary Lockman and Joel Beinin (eds.), *Intifada: The Palestinian Uprising against Israeli Occupation* (Boston: South End Press, 1989), pp. 171–77.

12. The Israeli occupation authorities misread Islamism as a "traditional" social structure rather than an "ideological" (i.e., nationalist-modernist) one. See Rema Hammami and Islah Jad, "Women and Fundamentalist Movements," in *News from Within*, October–November 1992.

13. "The PLO is never directly attacked by the IRM [Hamas]; never quoted, it does not exist." Legrain, "The Islamic Movement and the Intifada," p. 181.

14. Hamas was not alone in this view, but its public defiance of the PLO leadership aggravated dissension in the PLO.

15. Graham Usher, "The Rise of Political Islam in the Occupied Territories," *Middle East International,* June 25, 1993.

16. Quoted in Jean-François Legrain, "A Defining Moment: Palestinian Islamic Fundamentalism," in James Piscatori (ed.), *Islamic Fundamentalism and the Gulf Crisis* (Chicago: University of Chicago Press, 1991), pp. 70–88.

17. The specific charge was Yasin's involvement in the 1989 kidnapping and assassination of two Israeli soldiers.

18. "I am certain that the Islamic Movement is interested in not having any conflicts with Fatah. I'll go even further than that, to say that . . . the Islamic Movement will lose in [any] confrontation," said Hamas Gaza leader 'Abd al-'Aziz Rantisi immediately after the July clashes. Interview with author.

19. For a critique of this crisis of the intifada, see Ghazi Abu Jiab, "The Killing of Collaborators," and "Reflections on the Present State of the Intifada: Achievements and Failures," reprinted in *News from Within* 8, no. 7 (July 1992): 10–11.

20. Jerusalem Media and Communication Centre opinion poll, January 1993.

21. Quoted in Andrew Gowers and Tony Walker, *Arafat: The Biography* (London: Virgin, 1994), p. 129.

22. Israel Shahak, "Hamas and Arafat: The Balance of Power," *Middle East International,* February 4, 1994.

23. "Revived" because Hamas's first attacks on civilian targets came after the al-Aqsa mosque massacre in Jerusalem in 1990, when eighteen Palestinians were shot dead by the IDF. This "war of the knives" consisted of random stabbings by isolated individuals. The "suicide missions" after the Hebron massacre, however, were more planned, professional, and deadly.

24. See Graham Usher, "The PLO Opposition: Rebels without a Constituency," *Middle East International,* October 7, 1994.

25. See Ehud Ya'ari, "Can Arafat Govern?" *Jerusalem Report,* January 13, 1994.

26. Dani Rubinstein, *Ha-Aretz,* December 21, 1993.

27. Yizhar Be'er and Saleh Abdel-Jawad, *Collaborators in the Occupied Territories: Human Rights Abuses and Violations* (Jerusalem: B'tselem, 1994), pp. 219–28.

28. Ibrahim Yazuri, as quoted in *Al-Nahar,* May 18, 1994.

29. Graham Usher, "Hamas' Shifting Fortunes," *Middle East International,* September 24, 1993.

30. Ibid.

31. Shaikh Ahmad Yasin, as quoted in *Al-Wasat,* Nov. 1, 1993.

32. See my interview with Bassam Jarrar in this volume.

33. Joint Statement, Fatah Hawks and 'Izz al Din al-Qassam Brigade in Gaza, April 23, 1994; quoted in Graham Usher, "Why Fatah and Hamas Have Struck a Deal," *Middle East International,* April 29, 1994.

34. Yitzhak Rabin, as quoted by Jon Emmanuel, *Jerusalem Post,* April 24, 1994.

35. Graham Usher, "Seeking a Place at the Table of Self Rule," *New Statesman/ Society,* June 10, 1994.

36. Graham Usher, "Women, Islam and the Law in Palestinian Society," *Middle East International,* September 23, 1994.

37. Hammami and Jad, "Women and Fundamentalist Movements."

38. See my interview with Jarrar in this volume.

39. A recent survey of social attitudes among Palestinians in the occupied territories thus reveals a consistently more religious consciousness on the part of women aged fifteen to nineteen than women aged twenty to twenty-nine. See Marianne Heiberg and Geir Øvensen (eds.), *Palestinian Society: A Survey of Living Conditions* (Oslo: FAFO, 1993).

40. 'Imad 'Akl was a leader of the 'Izz al-Din al-Qassam Brigade in Gaza killed by the Israeli army in November 1993. He had been wanted for three years and the army alleged he was responsible for killing eleven Israelis and collaborators. His assassination led to widespread protests throughout the Gaza Strip.

41. The phrase is Amira Hass's. See her "What If an Israeli Jew I Knew Had Been in Hadera?" *Ha-Aretz,* April 26, 1994.

42. On Hamas as an "invented tradition," see Rema Hammami's essay in this volume. On the general concept, see Eric Hobsbawm and Terence Ranger (eds.), *The Invention of Tradition* (Cambridge: Cambridge University Press, 1983).

43. The Marxist factions in the PLO (PFLP, DFLP, Fida, and People's—formerly Communist—Party) are organized on broadly democratic centralist lines. Fatah is "organized" around a system of *dakakin* ("shops") or groups based on one or more local leaders. The ultimate source of authority lies less in the decision-making structures of the organization than in the political and economic dispensations of the single leader ('Arafat).

44. For the Islamists *hudna* cannot be translated as peace, since peace assumes recognition of the enemy. It is a truce until power relations once more favor the forces of Islam. The truce may last for months, years, or even centuries.

45. If anything, it bows to nationalist orthodoxy, particularly the "theory of stages" formulated by the PLO in the 1970s, in which a "national authority" would be established on any area of liberated territory as a prelude to the recovery of all of Palestine.

46. Khalid Amayreh, "Hamas Debates Its Next Move," *Middle East International,* May 27, 1994.

47. Yossi Torfstein, "Despite the Sword," *Ha-Aretz,* April 26, 1994.

48. Amayreh, "Hamas Debates Its Next Move."

49. See my interview with Jarrar in this volume.

50. "Self-Rule Intelligence Assisted Zionists to Reach Place of the Mujahedeen," Hamas Palestine Information Office, October 16, 1994.

51. Khalid Amayreh, as quoted in *Jerusalem Post,* October 29, 1994.

52. Graham Usher, "Hamas after the Tel Aviv Bombing," *Middle East International,* November 4, 1994.

53. Interview with the author, October 1994.

54. Lamis Andoni, "Palestinian Islamist Group Signals Shift in Strategy," *Christian Science Monitor,* September 13, 1994.

55. As the Palestinian secularist George Giacaman said in this regard: "The opposition will be unable to stay alive except under a Palestinian Authority that guarantees freedom of association and political activity, defends civil liberties, allows public decision making and governs by rule of law instead of the random will of an individual or party. The pillar of Palestinian civil society is going to be the presence of opposition parties." George Giacaman, "The Role of the Opposition in the Coming Stage," *Al-Quds,* January 14, 1994.

56. See Usher, "Women, Islam and the Law in Palestinian Society."

57. Jamil Hilal, "PLO Institutions: The Challenge Ahead," *Journal of Palestine Studies* 23, no. 1 (autumn 1993): 46–60.

31

Roots of the Shiʻi Movement
in Lebanon

Salim Nasr

Many saw the Shiʻi revolt in west Beirut and its southern suburbs in February 1984 as the sudden and unexpected mass uprising of a rapidly expanding social group in the midst of a tumultuous religious revivalism. But the February uprising was a significant social movement with roots in the profound social transformation of the Shiʻi community over the course of thirty years, from Lebanese independence at the end of World War II to the beginning of the civil war in 1975.

The Shiʻi movement first emerged in spectacular fashion under the leadership of the charismatic Imam Musa al-Sadr in the winter of 1974. From the outlying regions in the south and the northeast to the gates of Beirut, Imam al-Sadr's movement signified the transformation of the Shiʻa into a major new actor on the social and political scene. It represented the movement of the Shiʻa toward Beirut and toward the center of Lebanese political life. On February 6, 1984, the Shiʻa rose in revolt in the heart of the capital, affirming that they were a force that would have to be included in any new arrangement of the Lebanese political system.

THE SHIFT TO BEIRUT

In the late 1940s, nearly 85 percent of the Lebanese Shiʻa were concentrated in two "heartlands," one in the south, in the area known as Jabal ʻAmil, and the other in the northeast region of Baʻalbek-Hermel. They were a homogeneous and rural people. No more than 10 percent of the entire community lived in cities. The vast majority of the Shiʻi peasantry lived on meager plots with poor soil and very limited water resources. They practiced subsistence dry farming (primarily grains, olive trees, and vineyards in the south, grains and some orchards in Baʻalbek). Only tobacco production, well suited to the dry plateaus of southern Lebanon and grown as a cash crop, had expanded since the 1930s. But in 1948, tobacco was still a minor crop, planted in only 3 percent of the cultivated area of the south and involving some three to four thousand farmers.

In the Hermel area, the main form of property ownership was collectively owned (*musha'*) land, more often a grazing area than a well-defined holding. In the Ba'albek area, very large private estates existed alongside fields collectively owned by villages. The breakup of large tracts of land into smaller, private holdings had been under way since the 1930s, but peasant small holdings were still insignificant except near the towns and larger villages of Jabal 'Amil. The peasants gradually increased their access to the land through contract planting and buying the property of bankrupt feudal lords with savings from wage labor in the countryside and towns, and as time went on a prosperous middle peasantry emerged. But the distribution of property remained very unequal. Large estates still accounted for three-fourths of the best land in the Shi'i countryside.

Although very few Shi'a lived in the cities, a number of important small towns grew up in the Shi'i areas during the period between the two world wars. This was primarily on account of the caravan routes between northern Syria, southern Syria, Palestine, and the Lebanese coast. Fairs and markets were held in such towns as Tyre, Bint Jbail, Nabatiyya, Jwayya, Khiyam, and Ba'albek, where people concluded business deals and exchanged various regional agricultural products. Related cottage industries developed in this commercial atmosphere—shoemaking in Bint Jbail and pottery in Rashayya al-Fakhar, for example.

In spite of these changes, the Shi'i community had not yet experienced the social disruption, peasant revolts, or rapid expansion of export farming that had already transformed the Maronite area of Mount Lebanon as it was integrated into the world capitalist economy. In 1948, Shi'a constituted only 3.5 percent of the population of Beirut. The Shi'i community was socially, economically, and even culturally peripheral (68.9 percent illiteracy as compared with 31.5 percent among Maronites in 1943). It was equally peripheral to the Lebanese political system that had developed under the French mandate and was consolidated with independence. The intercommunal National Pact of 1943 was essentially a division of power between the Maronite and Sunni political elites.

From the 1920s to the mid-1950s, Shi'i political representation was practically monopolized by six prominent landowning families—the As'ads, the Zayns, and the 'Usayrans in southern Lebanon, and the Hamadas, the Haydars, and the Husaynis in Ba'albek and Bint Jbail. This elite was divided into quarreling rival factions. They were constantly shifting between alliance with and opposition to the central power in Beirut. The Shi'i community, representing less than a fifth of the population, was an insignificant force in Lebanese society and politics at the end of the 1950s.

During the following quarter of a century, this situation changed radically. Export agriculture expanded rapidly. Banking and commercial networks based in Beirut, Sidon, and Zahle spread throughout the Shi'i rural areas. This completely restructured traditional social and productive relations. Sharecropping practically disappeared (down to only 5 percent of agricultural workers by 1970). Food production greatly diminished (only 15 percent of food consumed was locally grown by 1970–75). Farmers increasingly specialized in two branches of export agriculture: nearly two-thirds of the value of agricultural production was concentrated in the cultivation of fruit trees and poultry farming. The number of agricultural wage earners increased and included non-Lebanese labor. Above all, the peasantry was in a state of permanent and deepening crisis, indebted to and exploited by merchants, moneylenders, small local banks, and suppliers of machinery, fertilizer, and pesticides. The development of certain industrial crops such as tobacco and sugar beets was blocked by powerful commercial cartels like the cigarette and sugar importers who had great influence on government policy. Thousands of sharecroppers and poor Shi'i peasant families were uprooted by indebtedness and bankruptcy, and forced to sell their property and move to the miserable suburbs of Beirut in search of work and better living conditions. More than 40 percent of the rural population had migrated by 1975. In the south, migration was above 60 percent.

A second process was the gradual integration of the outlying Shi'i regions under the control of the Lebanese state administration and the dominant Beirut-based commercial and financial interests. This began with independence but accelerated during the 1960s.

A third process was also at work: migration to other countries. Under the French mandate, the migration was mainly to West Africa, and primarily affected villages and market towns like Nabatiyya, Bint Jbail, Tyre, and Jwayya. During the 1950s and 1960s, emigration was increasingly oriented to the Arab oil-producing countries (especially Kuwait and Libya) and affected many more villages. The social effects of emigration on the Shi'i community were considerable. Local power relations in the villages shifted. Traditional notables and religious families lost ground in favor of wealthy returning migrants who purchased land and orchards, established new commercial networks, and carved out their own spheres of social influence. A new Shi'i bourgeoisie emerged. As newcomers, they could not compete directly with the Sunni and Christian bourgeoisie, so had to seek their fortune in relatively secondary sectors: real estate development, citrus crop cultivation, leisure activities, and trade with Africa. In the early 1970s, this Shi'i bourgeoisie began to expand its activities. Shi'i overseas capital now entered the banks, industries, and large business concerns. Finally, a new Shi'i elite emerged, including religious figures, politicians, and financiers.

EVE OF THE CIVIL WAR

By 1974, the Shi'a had ceased to be a largely rural community, situated on poor lands in marginal areas. Now they were nearly two-thirds (63 percent) urban, and more than 45 percent of these urban dwellers were concentrated in Beirut and its suburbs. The Shi'a were now split into two groups, one at the center and the other at the periphery of the Lebanese system, though the ties between them remained very close.

A high birth rate and an improvement in sanitary conditions in the countryside speeded up the Shi'i exodus to the metropolis. In 1948, the Shi'a numbered 225,000, or 18.2 percent of the population. They were the largest community after the Maronites and the Sunnis. By 1975 they had grown to an estimated 750,000, nearly 30 percent of the population and perhaps the largest community in the country. Not long before they had been largely illiterate, confined to a declining agriculture, and dominated by a small traditional elite of large landowners and a reactionary clergy. Now, their class structure had changed significantly, with a new migrant bourgeoisie, a layer of middle-level salaried workers in the cities, an industrial proletariat in the suburbs of Beirut, and a community of migrant workers in the Arab oil-producing countries.

The Shi'a now had an active and radicalized intelligentsia, an ambitious and enterprising counterelite, and other new strata with new demands. They began to challenge the rules of the game and to question the distribution of power and resources in the Lebanese system. In this context, the movement of Imam al-Sadr was born in the early 1970s, an expression of the demographic Shi'i and socioeconomic shift from the periphery toward the city-state of Beirut.

The movement was called different names: the Movement of Imam Musa al-Sadr, the Movement of the Dispossessed (Harakat al-Mahrumin), the Movement for the Rights of the Shi'i, or, more simply, "the Shi'i Movement." Whatever the name, it was a mass movement in the Lebanese Shi'i community, guided and inspired by its spiritual head and charismatic leader, Imam Musa al-Sadr.

During the years before the outbreak of civil war in 1975, the movement attempted to satisfy its social and political demands through various forms of mobilization, pressure, and action. This had a powerful effect on the sectarian balance and the functioning of the political system and the state administration. It was a popular movement with a strong rural base in the major outlying towns, and among the clans of Ba'albek and the uprooted migrants in the suburbs of Beirut. Stimulated by the sermons and the

energetic personality of Imam al-Sadr himself, it was essentially a spontaneous popular upsurge defined by religion and its social base. Its main
constituents were the dispossessed urban migrants, the poverty-ridden peasantry, the growing petit bourgeoisie whose advancement was blocked, and
the new bourgeoisie which was excluded from the political system.

The movement used moral and religious language, and themes based on
the Shi'i tradition of protest. As a movement of "moral" rebirth and community reorganization, it was clearly a reaction to the breakdown of rural
Lebanon and the crisis of the new migrants in the cities. It was also a political
movement of self-defense against increasing Israeli attacks, and a means of
pressuring the state to take action.

The movement was largely autonomous, and began to develop its own
character in the summer of 1973. Yet it was also part of the general mobilization and intercommunal conflict in Lebanon during the 1970s. As
such, it often took part in larger actions with the Lebanese left and the
Palestinian resistance movement. Links with the Palestinian resistance were
initially quite strong. In 1975, the Palestinians began to provide training
bases, instructors, and arms to the movement's military organization, Amal.
There was a strong political and religious affinity between the Lebanese Shi'i
movement and the Iranian opposition to the Shah led by Ayatollah
Khomeini.

The movement grew at a fairly steady pace over several years. Occasionally
there were periods of intense activity, such as mass rallies, religious celebrations, political actions, sit-ins, strikes, and the observation of national
solidarity days. Such major events occurred practically every month during
1974 and 1975.

It is difficult to pinpoint the birth of the Shi'i movement, but two dates
in particular stand out. On May 22, 1969, Imam Musa al-Sadr was elected
to head the Supreme Shi'i Council (SSC) which had been created by the
Lebanese parliament and charged with administering the religious affairs
of the Shi'i community. The second date, June 6, 1973, was that of the
special joint session of the *shari'a* committee and the executive committee
of the SSC, which drafted a memorandum to the Lebanese government
presenting a list of sixteen demands and setting a deadline of four months.
Thirteen Shi'i ministers and members of parliament threatened to resign
or call for a vote of no confidence if the demands were not met. The first
date marks the emergence of a new political initiative and the beginning
of mobilization within the Shi'i community. This was followed by a period
of incubation, during which strategy was formulated and the movement
was strengthened internally. The second date marks the moment of takeoff
for the movement, which now entered a period of expanded organization
and intensified collective action that went on throughout 1973, 1974, and
1975.

GOALS AND OPPONENTS

The name of the movement stabilized as Harakat al-Mahrumin in 1974. The leaders did not want to come out then as an explicitly sectarian group within the Lebanese system. They deliberately left the constituency of the movement ambiguous: at times it was the Shi'i; at other times it was all the dispossessed or citizens deprived of their rights. There was a strong consciousness of belonging to the Shi'i community, with its history, traditions, and culture, its historical oppression and its secular struggle. But the movement laid claim to a wider mission: to save Lebanon from social crisis, from the incompetence of the government and from the "monopolists" who were enemies of the people.

As a movement for the emancipation of oppressed people, how did it perceive its adversaries? The internal enemy was defined in general terms: the monopolists, the exploiters, the privileged few, the "modern tyrants," the "government of despots," the "complacent and incompetent officials," the "government that exploits the people." Nowhere, neither in speeches and publications nor in slogans, banners, and chants at demonstrations, was there a clear and precise social definition of the adversary, even when there was a very specific class conflict at issue, such as the movement of tobacco growers or that of fishermen from Sidon and the coast. There were strong moral overtones in the picture of the enemy, seen as the "money lover," "sucking the blood of the people," and using "infernal methods such as war, fanaticism, and racial discrimination" to maintain domination. The external enemy, Israel, was identified as evil, criminal, coveting the land of the south and the water of Lebanon, and likened to Yazid, the caliph who murdered Husayn, one of the most venerated of the Shi'i *imams*.

The movement most often defined the enemy as a group, very rarely as a system. When it spoke of a system, it always referred to the Lebanese confessional system, guilty of discriminating against its citizens and standing in the way of their development. There was virtually no reference to class relations. The relationship to the adversary was above all one of domination and exploitation. The favorite targets of attack were the political centers, primarily the Lebanese political class and, secondarily, the state of Israel. There were no attacks against the centers of economic power as such. The adversary was almost defined by conduct, rarely by interests.

The main purpose of the movement was to defend a community in crisis—the crisis of rural breakdown, of Israeli attacks, of mass rural exodus, and of proletarianization. The movement also sought to achieve "equality" with other communities within the Lebanese confessional system, including a share in the administration, the national budget, and the economy.

Two themes of the movement's discourse stand out. The first is the relationship of the community with the state and the resulting distribution of wealth. This was often discussed in terms of the unfair allocation of government posts and civil service jobs, as well as discriminatory economic and social policies (not enough development projects or irrigation schemes, limits on tobacco production, and so forth). There were also the extreme backwardness and poverty of most Shi'i areas and the monopoly of a minority over political power. The second main theme of the movement was the relationship of the Shi'i community to the Arab-Israeli conflict. There were constant references to the Israeli attacks which concentrated on south Lebanon, the need for a national defense, and the right and duty of popular self-defense.

The movement saw change as working to the detriment of the Shi'a, contributing to their social marginalization, their exclusion from power, and the historical backwardness of the Shi'i hinterland. The goal was to remove the barriers, particularly at the level of state employment, development policy, and the confessional and regional allocation of funds. The Lebanese ruling class and the confessional system stood in the way of advancement for the Shi'i community—and the dispossessed in general— and jeopardized the future of the country itself.

The movement emphasized economic development as a means of bringing south Lebanon and the Ba'albek region up to the level of the rest of the country. Detailed lists of projects were proposed, stressing irrigation schemes (dams, irrigation networks, reservoirs) and infrastructure (schools, hospitals, roads). The movement's view of economic development was narrowly conceived. It was short-term and regionally limited. Furthermore, the movement saw economic development in terms of distribution, not production. It demanded a truly proportionate share, seeing the state alone as responsible for economic development and backwardness.

The movement's political program included:

- A gradual reform of the confessional system, to begin by eliminating the confessional distribution of civil service posts except at the highest executive and legislative levels.
- A chamber of religions to be created alongside the chamber of deputies (parliament). This body would strike a balance between the sects and arbitrate among them. It would meet for one month each year to take up cases of discrimination and "correct the unequal opportunities" available to citizens in their "democratic competition."
- A change in the electoral law to "allow for a better representation of the political aspirations of the Lebanese public." The proposed system was a proportional one, which would clearly give the Shi'a a greater voice.
- Overall improvement in the quality and morality of political life. "The movement was not established to take power or win portfolios or seats in parliament," Imam al-Sadr said in late 1974. "Our purpose is to

reform the political climate, not to elect politicians. We are struggling against corruption and voter intimidation, but it is not our role to influence the voter's choice."

Social goals seem to have been most important for the movement: to challenge the monopoly of privilege, to achieve a fairer distribution of wealth, to struggle against confessional and regional inequality. Next came political goals: to increase the national role of the Shi'a and their political and religious leadership, and to force the state to adopt a serious national defense policy. Economic and cultural goals seem to have been less important.

MOBILIZATION AND POLITICAL ACTION

All observers agree that the movement of Imam al-Sadr mobilized very broad social support within the Shi'i community. He formed a multiclass bloc whose goal was to bring together all parts of Shi'i society. The movement gradually affected a social and political realignment within the Shi'i community itself. As of early 1975, before the movement gained hegemony, the community was structured politically into three main components:

- Followers of traditional leaders, such as large landowners, heads of clans, and traditional clergy. These constituencies comprised tenant farmers, part of the small peasantry, minor officials, and the subproletariat.
- Followers of al-Sadr's Movement of the Dispossessed, who included new agrarian and commercial "emigrant" bourgeoisie, small artisans and merchants, the crisis-wracked small peasantry, the new intellectual elite (professional and civil servants), young office workers, teachers, and new migrants to the cities (working class and low-level salaried workers in the administration and the service sector).
- Followers of the Marxist and the Ba'thist left, who included some of the new intelligentsia (professors, lawyers, journalists, teachers), pauperized peasants, and agricultural and industrial workers.

The movement of Imam al-Sadr gained predominance only gradually. It continued to have groups to its right and left, whose supporters were drawn from different social strata and who only recognized its primacy around the spring of 1975. Demonstrations and rallies are one indicator of the relative strength of the three groups. The movement regularly drew between seventy and a hundred thousand people to mass rallies in 1974. These were enormous and unprecedented in Lebanon. By comparison the left drew between twenty and thirty thousand (nearly half of whom were Shi'a), while the traditional Shi'i notable Kamal As'ad was able to bring out only between five and ten thousand.

There was only one by-election during this period, held in December 1974 in the southern town of Nabatiyya, but it served as an important test of strength. The candidate backed by Imam al-Sadr received twenty thousand votes, compared with seven thousand for the one backed by As'ad and five thousand for the two candidates fielded by the left.

The third indicator is perhaps the most telling. The executive committee of the Supreme Shi'i Council was chosen by an electorate of twelve hundred council members of the liberal professions, academics, union presidents, and the like. In the May 1975 elections for twelve seats on the committee, the left-wing parties won five seats and al-Sadr's candidates won five. The two remaining were on the left but personally very close to the Imam.

By 1975, then, the movement of Imam al-Sadr was the most significant grouping at the base, with a level of mass support higher than 80 percent. It also held a clear majority of the Shi'i "electorate," but only equaled the various left-wing parties among the intelligentsia, the bureaucracy, and the newer Shi'i middle class.

The leftist Shi'i intelligentsia, activists in the progressive parties, adopted restraint toward the movement of the Imam during 1973 and 1974, while al-Sadr openly fought the traditional Shi'i leadership led by Kamal As'ad, then speaker of parliament and leader of a bloc of nine Shi'i deputies. Eventually, in early 1975, the growing popularity of the movement forced As'ad's resignation. The movement also won the allegiance of secondary traditional notables and a more cooperative stance on the part of the Shi'i left, whose willingness to "work from within" led to the successful election of seven of their candidates in May 1975 to the Supreme Shi'i Council. Five or six years after its emergence, then, the movement of Imam al-Sadr had finally succeeded in giving the Shi'i community a strong and united political leadership.

RELIGIOUS SYMBOLISM

The movement mobilized the Shi'i community in the midst of a general ideological crisis. The traditional authority of the state and the *zu'ama'* (traditional leaders) was collapsing with the spread of Ba'thism, communism, and Nasirism. The traditional concept of religion was losing ground to the liberal ideology of the urban marketplace.

Symbolically, the movement represented a struggle against many old ways. It was opposed to the alienation of the Shi'i masses and to traditional relations between peasants and rural leaders. It was also opposed to the relationship between the masses and the central government, to the traditionally conceived status of the Shi'a and their place in Lebanese history, to traditional religion as instilled by the dominant ideology, and to the image of the movement itself as purveyed by government propaganda.

The movement drew heavily on the Shi'i religious heritage, with its symbolism, its rituals, its values, and its heroes. Shi'i ideology had always been principally an Islamic ideology of social protest. The movement attempted to reinterpret these symbols, to give a contemporary meaning to the rituals, and to draw out their implications for the current struggle. It used religious symbolism to legitimize political action. As al-Sadr said at the time of the SSC elections in early 1975, "[W]e began our movement in this way because we believe in God and we know that the believer who is unconcerned with the fate of the dispossessed is an unbeliever and a liar."

Religious symbolism provided a direct translation of social struggles into a religious code, giving followers a frame of reference. "I invite all southerners to demand their rights because anyone who doesn't speak up for his rights is a mute devil," said the Imam in late 1984. "The price of tobacco hasn't risen in twelve years. Everything else has gone up while the price of tobacco remains the same, as though it were alms distributed to the poor. They ask us to pay our taxes, and the money goes to the monopolists and their accomplices. We've paid our dues, but do we have security? Is the state concerned?"

The movement used religious symbolism to evoke the collective memory of the community—the Shi'i history of repeated revolts against the Umayyads, the 'Abbasids, the Mamluks, the Ottomans, and the French. The history is symbolized by the life of Imam Husayn, hero of the Shi'i community, whose tragic story is reenacted every year during the festival of 'Ashura. There are frequent commemorations of other important historical figures as well. The movement usually held mass rallies on such occasions; al-Sadr always began by recalling the event and the person being commemorated and drawing a lesson for the current struggle.

Imam al-Sadr often invoked the thoughts and actions of the Shi'i founders to underline the fundamental virtues of the movement. As he said in an 'Ashura sermon in early 1974, "Imam Husayn explained the motivation for his action in two sentences: justice does not prevail and injustice is forbidden. I ask you, if he were among us today and saw not only that justice does not prevail, but that justice is scorned, what would he do?" A month later he called on Shi'i traditions again in a defense against critics: "'Ali, the prince of believers, was called an atheist and condemned from the pulpit for eighty years. The judge of Kufa accused Husayn, son of 'Ali, of having gone too far, saying my duty is to be content to defend the faith. Faith is not what props up your thrones, O rulers!"

The use of religious symbolism implied a cult of the charismatic leader. There were many signs of this during the critical years of 1974–75. Al-Sadr's portrait was pasted on walls of towns and villages, and carried by demonstrators. One of the slogans most often chanted at mass rallies was, "Our blood and our souls are yours, Imam." Al-Sadr sought to create a feeling of oneness between himself and the masses, walking barefooted among the crowd and letting himself be touched and kissed. Reportedly, during a mass meeting in Tyre, his robe was torn and his turban was completely blackened from having been touched by so many hands. In all his speeches he sought to identify himself with the ideal *imam*, the spiritual guide, the just man, the perfect Muslim. He often compared himself to the Shi'i founding fathers, the Prophet's cousin 'Ali and his son Husayn.

Al-Sadr presided over reconciliation ceremonies between feuding Shi'i clans and extended families, encouraging them to overcome traditional local conflicts for the sake of larger group solidarity. He spent numerous religious and civil holidays in southern border villages presiding over religious ceremonies while the local hierarchy usually traveled to the capital to celebrate. He also engaged in symbolic resistance. In February 1975 he prayed in the mosque of Kafr Shuba, a border village that had been half destroyed by Israeli artillery and bombs and abandoned by its inhabitants. Through the media, he called on the villagers, and on all southerners, to return and defend themselves. In late June 1975, he began a hunger strike in a Beirut mosque to protest the civil war. His action triggered a series of protests throughout the Shi'i regions, including dozens of local demonstrations and strikes and the occupation of a number of government offices.

The ideology of the movement was clearly controlled by the leadership, and in particular by Imam al-Sadr himself. His themes, slogans, images, and even his style were easily recognizable in the pamphlets and communiqués of the Supreme Shi'i Council and the Movement of the Dispossessed, on banners, wall posters, and in the conversation of movement participants.

VIOLENCE AND SOCIAL CHANGE

The movement had two policies on the use of violence as a means to bring about change. It officially rejected violence directed toward the internal adversary, advocating pressure tactics and nonviolent actions, including mass rallies, strikes, and demonstrations instead. On the other hand, it encouraged and actively planned violence against the external adversary (Israel). Faced with what it considered to be an abdication by the state, and paralysis of the army by the political class, the movement called for popular self-defense and created its own military organization, training camps, and cadres.

In fact, movement followers did use certain forms of violence against local adversaries, including armed demonstrations and roadblocks. Armed men occupied and sometimes sacked police stations, as in Marj 'Ayun in February 1975 to protest the lack of defense for the border villages, and in

Ba'albek in June 1975 in support of al-Sadr's hunger strike. Many movement followers probably participated in the first clashes of the civil war in late May 1975 in the southern Beirut suburb of Shiyah.

The movement's attitude toward Israel was basically defensive, while its attitude toward the internal adversary and social change was clearly offensive. "They will never bring the south to its knees," said al-Sadr at 'Ashura in 1975. "They cannot humiliate Husayn's people, who would have been proud to stand with him a thousand years ago. . . . No one can kill a people. If we stand up to them, even if it means suicide, there will be others after us who will stand up. The reign of Israel will disappear like the reign of the Umayyads."

Earlier, at a 1974 mass rally in Tyre, he said, "It is our duty to form a Lebanese resistance before we're expelled from our land. . . . Even if the government fails to perform its duty, it is still the people's duty to defend themselves. . . . Anyone who doesn't know how to handle a weapon is straying from the teaching of our Imams 'Ali and Husayn."

The offensive nature of the movement's internal strategy is suggested in the text of the Pact of the Movement of the Dispossessed (1975):

> Our movement is the movement of all the dispossessed. It lives their suffering and shares their grievances. It studies the solutions and sets to work immediately to put them into effect. . . . Our movement is the movement of every Lebanese who is deprived in the present and worried about the future. It is the Lebanese movement toward a better future. If the ruling class won't discharge its duty, we will build the future by ourselves. We want to save the country from those who are plundering it and leading it to its destruction.

There were several stages in the movement's use of action, and a gradual shift away from political pressure tactics to the creation of a military organization. From June 1973 to February 1974, there were street demonstrations, letters, petitions, and institutional pressures. Between February and November 1974, negotiations were broken off and there were armed mass rallies, strikes, and threats of civil disobedience. December 1974 saw the first participation of the movement in the legislative by-elections. From January to May 1975 there was a return to petitions, demonstrations, and institutional pressures. From May to July 1975 there were general strikes and hunger strikes, roadblocks, and the official birth of the military arm, Amal. Tactical flexibility and the needs of the movement resulted in a variety of forms and combinations of political action.

The movement alternated between periods when the emphasis was on the spontaneity of the mass movement and the charisma of its leader, and periods when it tried to consolidate its gains by developing the organization and training cadres. Mass activities had a highly charged atmosphere: thousands of voices chanting slogans, the shrill cries of women, the jostling to touch Imam al-Sadr and receive his *baraka* (blessing), extended ovations, shooting in the air to welcome the Imam or merely to punctuate his speech. Sometimes there were deliberate attempts to heighten the emotional level, for al-Sadr was capable of inflaming the crowds by his speech. "Collective vows" were taken by tens of thousands of people repeating after the Imam. For big events like general strikes or the Imam's hunger strike, the *muezzins* called out the people (similar to sounding the tocsin in Christian villages). Yet the primary characteristic of the movement remained the spontaneity of mass actions, which often went far beyond the plans of the organizers.

BACK TO BEIRUT

The end of the first phase of the Lebanese civil war (December 1975) was also the end of the first phase of the movement. In 1976 the Palestinians and the Syrian army became directly and openly involved, and the Lebanese army and state collapsed. Henceforth, the nature of the Lebanese conflict would be quite different. The new phase saw the disappearance or trans-formation of the communal movements of the early 1970s. The Shi'i move-ment would reemerge in different form, beginning in 1977–78, to play a major role in the struggle. Behind the success of the movement of Imam al-Sadr through this first phase were several important principles:

- To form the broadest possible front, including Shi'a of all classes and all manner of political opinion, excluding only those who excluded them-selves or who played the game of the ruling political power (e.g., Kamal al-As'ad).
- To present a minimal platform, with specific demands that could be met in the short or medium term and vague general principles for the long term.
- To alternate between mobilization and negotiation, drawing on the change in the balance of power brought on by mobilization.
- To mollify Christian sectarian movements by maintaining a commitment to Lebanon as a political entity, and by appearing as a division within Muslim ranks.
- To mollify Sunni sectarian movements by appearing to reinforce the position of Lebanese political Islam vis-à-vis the state, which Sunnis saw as representing the historical hegemony of the Maronite upper class.

The guiding principle for the movement's tactics can be very clearly defined: always concentrate on the main enemy and the main contradiction. Never completely burn your bridges and always retain the possibility of reopening negotiations at any time. Take part in all efforts at mediation in order to expose the fundamentally bad faith of the adversary. Always distinguish between the Lebanese army (ready to defend the country) and the authority responsible for the lack of adequate national defense. Never directly or explicitly attack individuals, even if they are adversaries, so as to leave open the possibility of dissociating them from the group designated as the adversary. Never take irreversible positions except on a few basic questions, such as the defense of southern Lebanon and the rights of the community. Never make the first move in attacking or explicitly criticizing either the left or the right, and rarely respond to criticism by these forces.

The movement seemed to turn its back on Beirut. It held tumultuous meetings and armed demonstrations in the provinces far from the capital, in traditional Shi'i strongholds such as Tyre and Ba'albek. Given the monopoly of the capital in Lebanese political life, the movement deliberately looked to the areas excluded by the growth of the Beirut city-state. Threats and plans to hold an armed rally in the capital were never carried out. The movement in Beirut in this first phase limited itself to sermons delivered behind closed doors, meetings of intellectuals and students, political negotiations, and contacts with other groups.

The movement's attitude toward the city was ambiguous—threatening it from without, appeasing it from within. Only once did the movement demonstrate its power to affect the center, when al-Sadr held a three-day hunger strike in June 1975 to protest the fighting in Beirut. His strike took place in the heart of the city, inside the mosque of 'Amiliyya College, one of the oldest institutions in one of the oldest Shi'i neighborhoods. It sparked off a series of actions, some of them violent, in the provinces; support groups and delegations from Shi'i areas all over the country converged peacefully to a central location in the capital.

The movement was transitional, en route toward the city, present in the city, but not of the city. Its top leadership reflected this. It comprised seventeen men, evenly distributed in terms of their profession: six from Beirut (three lawyers, two high officials, one police officer), six from the suburbs (three clergy, two professors, one journalist), and five from the provinces (two bank employees, one clergyman, one professor, and one clan chieftain). More than two-thirds of the leadership lived in greater Beirut, yet none of the old Shi'i families long resident in the capital was represented. Ten years later, in 1984, this new leadership would gain access to the government when Nabih Berri became minister of justice and Husayn Husayni became speaker in parliament.

The urban question had only a minor place in the original program of the movement. Of the seventeen points included in the final demands of February 1974, only two dealt with the city. The movement saw its role as pressuring the city to do justice to the countryside and redress "unequal development." By 1984, the "question of the southern suburbs," along with the Israeli occupation of southern Lebanon, had become a major focus of the movement's program. The Shi'i movement had fully arrived in Beirut and on the national scene.

Translated from the French by Diane James.

NOTE

This chapter was written and originally published while the author was a researcher at the Centre d'Études et de Recherches sur le Moyen-Orient Contemporain in Beirut.

32

"How Can a Muslim Live in This Era?"

Shaikh Hamid al-Nayfar, interview with François Burgat

What is the meaning of the name of your magazine, 15/21?

The basis of our project is to ask how one can be simultaneously a Muslim and live in this era—how to be a Muslim today. Fifteen stands for the fifteenth century of the *hijra*, the beginning of the Islamic community. Twenty-one signifies the fact that we are living now on the edge of the twenty-first century, with all the problems that poses for the world community.

Can you recall the route which led you into religious thought and then political action?

The end of the 1960s in Tunisia saw some fundamental changes. The departure of the Ben Salah government in 1970 marked the end of the socialist period, particularly the experience of the [agricultural] cooperatives. The change was very abrupt. Ben Salah was put on trial. Young people saw that the very same government could strike a leftist pose and then switch to right-wing economic policies. Many were completely disoriented. We realized that this was proof that there was no fundamental policy orientation.

Who joined the Islamist movement?

They were neither leftists nor rightists. They were uprooted. There was no longer any ideology that they could connect with. A search for identity became characteristic of this period.

To this Tunisian problem, you have to add what was occurring in France. I was living in Paris in May 1968. The question there was: "Where is the West going?" I discovered that we shared the same type of intellectual angst. It wasn't only a Tunisian or Arab problem.

The third thing that helps explain the emergence of the Islamist movement in Tunisia is the defeat in the 1967 Six-Day War. This represented a failure of the nationalist-Arab factor.

How did things fall into place in the Islamist movement?
A number of intellectuals, including Rashid al-Ghannoushi, began meeting together. Al-Ghannoushi was in Paris at the same time I was. Before that we had been together in Damascus. Immediately the question of religion was posed. None of those programs, which for so long had seemed to offer certain solutions, could provide the answer—neither Arab nationalism nor Tunisian nationalism nor the West.

Had religion always played a significant role?
I'm from a very conservative family that was active in the University of Zaytuna. Religion and religious studies have always had an important place in my family.

So you never distanced yourself from religion?
Well, I was like everybody else. I didn't practice at all. Religion was part of the past, it was no longer current.

Why did you decide to organize yourselves into something besides informal meetings?
At that time there was the Qur'anic Preservation Society (QPS), set up by the ministry of religion. We began to congregate there. There was also Jama'at al-Da'wa (the Preaching Association), a group that used to visit us every year from Pakistan. Soon Tunisians also joined their group. Jama'at al-Da'wa people travel around the world preaching a return to Islam, to religious practice. We were influenced by their simplicity, a way of life that seemed old-fashioned in Tunisia.

Jama'at al-Da'wa was apolitical; it spread the "good news" and beseeched people to return to the straight path. There was a more intellectual tendency in the cadre of the QPS. They wanted to organize conferences and meetings.

We functioned like that until 1973. Those years now seem to me ones of groping. But we were certain of one thing—that the religious aspect had become essential. By contrast, the political aspect was still very vague. No one agreed with the government, of course, but neither did anyone have a well-thought-out plan of political action.

How was this vacillation resolved?
First, we came in contact with a Mr. Benslama, who was educated at Zaytuna. He had ideas that were a bit old-fashioned, of course, but he was very nice. Everyone readily agreed to relaunch the magazine, *Al-Ma'rifa*, which had published one issue in 1962.

The second new element was al-Sadat's release of the Muslim Brothers in Egypt. The Brothers resumed their literary production. Even before this, publications from Egypt had been very important. The shaikhs of Zaytuna were disappearing one by one, until we didn't have any more. Zaytuna University was completely closed. So the Egyptians encouraged us to engage more directly in political action as well as in underground planning.

What kind of ideological formation did you and Rashid al-Ghannoushi bring back from Syria?

I believe it was in Syria that al-Ghannoushi had his first contact with the Brothers. At the end of the 1960s the Islamist tendency was very weak, so upon returning from Damascus our political formation was still rather sketchy.

So it was from the reservoir of Muslim Brothers' thought that the future Islamic Tendency Movement (ITM) took its principal ideological references, strategies, and tactics?

Yes. We read about how the Brothers in Egypt established their first cells. We lived in a country that was quite different from Egypt. The Tunisian government didn't concern itself much with the mosques. We could therefore meet very easily, outside the usual Friday sermon. We also organized in the high schools. We held meetings during recess and lectured the students.

The government ignored you, but you considered yourselves essentially as political opponents?

We were tacitly against the government, but our ideology and plan of action weren't clear. We were against all Western forms of society, but we did not know what alternative society we should propose.

Things became clearer when our first high school students entered the university. There they came into contact with people from the left and the extreme right. This confrontation between traditional Islamic thought and the thought and modes of action of leftist groups radicalized our group. I believe it was at that moment that the political profile of the ITM was formed. The Islamist students couldn't escape the university methods: political protest, meetings, graffiti, political "analyses."

Imperialism—before no one ever spoke of imperialism. Only when we came in contact with leftist elements did we discover that there was a history of foreign intervention in the lives of underdeveloped countries.

Did the movement then become more structured?

Not really. A bureau wasn't established until 1981. But by that time I had already left the movement. In 1977 there was what we called a "central nexus" which, under the direction of al-Ghannoushi, planned activities, decided what was to be done in this or that mosque.

Why did your attitude toward the organization change?

Well, after 1975 I traveled to Egypt, where I met a number of religious personalities, especially among the Muslim Brothers, many well-known personalities who wrote in the newspapers and journals. In the end it turned out to be a deception.

You mean that their doctrine seemed insufficient to you?

Precisely. Let's take the example of Muhammad Qutb, whom I met in 1974 in Saudi Arabia. I explained to him that I was editor-in-chief of a magazine called *Al-Ma'rifa*. He shouted at me, "You are the agents of Bourguiba!" I realized that this man knew nothing about what was happening in Tunisia. He undoubtedly wrote very well. I read everything he published. But regarding the reality of the Arab countries, or at least Tunisia, he knew nothing whatsoever.

The second disillusion I had was with 'Abd al-'Alim 'Uways, who was reputed to be the political theoretician of the Muslim Brothers and a specialist in the political history of the Muslim world. I asked him what the Brothers sanctioned in matters of curriculum and scholarly reform. He referred me to a text by Hasan al-Banna, who had died in 1949. We were then in 1974! The problems had changed.

I came to realize that the Brothers of Egypt corresponded more to legend than anything else. What they called their methodology slowly appeared to me to be totally obsolete and could only lead to disaster. They spoke of three million members and sympathizers. I asked myself how a movement of such importance could have been broken up in a couple of months by 'Abd al-Nasir—broken up not only physically, but ideologically! This organization hadn't been capable of creating an ideological movement that could survive repression. A brotherhood of four thousand members depending on three million sympathizers—and in a few months they were imprisoned as if one was herding a flock of sheep. Obviously something had gone wrong. Besides, what they wrote was too general. This disillusionment gave me another way of seeing.

You somehow reclaimed your independence of thought?

Yes, but the problem was that our magazine, *Al-Ma'rifa*, was essentially that type of literature. I began to distance myself from the people there. Still, the movement spread and the audience for that type of literature grew.

With the radicalization going on inside the university and with what was happening at the trade union headquarters, you couldn't take time to reorient yourself. We perceived the danger from the left to be imminent.

If I put myself in al-Ghannoushi's shoes, I understand that it was quite difficult to make any changes during that period. But I couldn't continue. I felt we needed to create something Tunisian. I began to apply a notion that was completely taboo during that period: "Tunisian Islam."

We also fought against what I called "the new sufism," which ignored the uniqueness of each Arab country and only addressed Islam as a whole. For me, to emphasize solely the spiritual side of Islam is a form of sufism. Our project cannot have a real impact on our societies as long as we do not understand the workings of those societies, their recent history, their problems.

And on this basis you broke with what became the ITM?

At the end of some articles that I wrote for *Al-Ma'rifa* I pointedly attacked Hasan al-Banna. I wrote that this man was certainly a brave man, a militant, but he had not understood the ropes and he was dead. D-e-a-d. To die physically is not important, but when one leads a movement that is dismantled with surprising ease after one is gone, that proves that the ideology was not in step with the real problems of society. We should not reemploy that strategy. We should study him, understand why all al-Banna's work went up in smoke. That's what I wrote.

Since I was editor-in-chief of the magazine, I brought the text to the printer. Later, when I had the issue in hand, I noticed that the entire paragraph where I discussed Hasan al-Banna had been deleted. The director of the magazine had cut it out without even consulting me.

I requested that a statement be published in the next issue and it did appear. Then I withdrew. I remained alone for almost a year. "He's someone whose faith is weak," they insinuated. "He no longer believes in certain things." But at that time, I have to say that they were hardly concerned with those problems. Not as long as the meetings and sermons were successful. And the Iranian revolution was about to occur and give the movement greater significance.

That's another important date in the history of this movement, right?

Absolutely. But I remember that at first the leadership of the ITM kept their distance. Rashid al-Ghannoushi thought that it was above all a Shi'i revolution. After seeing the magnitude of the revolution, the participation of the entire Iranian population, it was no longer possible to remain neutral. So they threw themselves onto the side of the Iranian revolution, especially in the magazines *Al-Ma'rifa* and *Al-Mujtama'*. In its last issue, *Al-Mujtama'* published a huge picture of Khomeini on the cover. It was from that moment on that the authorities started to become alarmed. They arrested al-Ghannoushi for a few days and seized internal documents of the movement. I had met with Rashid al-Ghannoushi months before his arrest. I said that now that they were involved in this political business they could never turn back. He told me he didn't think he was risking more than six months in prison—if the government had the guts to put them on trial. They truly believed they were too strong for the government to dare to try. But all those people who followed them in the mosques did not constitute a real base.

A movement can only be important if it fulfills two conditions—first, if it has structures and associations involved with various social classes and represents a definite social phenomenon, not marginal, frustrated people. Otherwise it's some kind of crowd. The second condition is that the movement provide a plan that society can identify with. A plan must have a well-developed social profile, and that is something that the ITM has never had.

For you, the ITM stepped into political action much too soon, without the necessary theoretical reflection on which to base its activities?

It's true. Theoretical reflection and reflection on reality. But they couldn't engage in this reflection as long as they believed that everything that took place between 1881 and 1956, and even between 1956 and the emergence of the Islamist movement—the Bourguiba project of modernization and all that—amounted to nothing, just a historical parentheses.

Translated from the French by Linda G. Jones.

CONTRIBUTORS

Lila Abu-Lughod teaches anthropology at New York University. Her most recent book is *Writing Women's Worlds: Bedouin Stories* (University of California Press, 1993).

Nasr Hamid Abu Zayd teaches Arabic literature at Cairo University. He was interviewed by *Elliott Colla,* a doctoral student in comparative literature at the University of California, Berkeley, and *Ayman Bakr,* a recent graduate of Cairo University's Department of Arabic Language and Literature.

Joel Beinin teaches history and directs the Program in Modern Thought and Literature at Stanford University. He is an editor of *Middle East Report.*

Rabia Bekkar is an urban sociologist at the Institut Parisien de Récherche: Architecture Urbanistique et Société. She has been researching Tlemcen for more than fifteen years. She was interviewed by *Hannah Davis Taïeb,* co-editor of the Paris-based journal *Mediterraneans/Méditerranéennes.*

Sheila Carapico teaches political science at Richmond University and is an editor of *Middle East Report.*

Alexander Flores is coordinator of the postgraduate program for Middle Eastern studies at the University of Erlangen, Germany.

Joan Gross teaches anthropology at Oregon State University.

Sondra Hale teaches anthropology and women's studies at the University of California at Los Angeles.

Rema Hammami teaches in the Women's Studies Program at Bir Zeit University and is a contributing editor of *Middle East Report.*

Barbara Harlow teaches English and postcolonial literature at the University of Texas and is an editor of *Middle East Report.*

Joost Hiltermann is an editor of *Middle East Report.*

Homa Hoodfar teaches anthropology at Concordia University, Montreal. Her chapter is adapted from a paper prepared for the Population Council conference on Family, Gender and Population Policy in Cairo, February 1994.

Bassam Jarrar teaches Islamic Studies at the UNRWA Teacher Training Center in Ramallah.

Suad Joseph teaches anthropology at the University of California at Davis and is an editor of *Middle East Report.*

Deniz Kandiyoti is senior lecturer in the Social Sciences Division of Richmond College, London, and the editor of *Women, Islam and the State* (Temple University Press, 1991).

Assaf Kfoury is a Lebanese journalist and researcher.

Gudrun Krämer is Professor of Islamic Studies at Bonn University, Germany, and the author of *Egypt under Mubarak: Identity and National Interest* (in German).

Ronnie Margulies lives in London and co-edits a monthly newsletter on Turkey.

David McMurray teaches anthropology at Oregon State University.

Khalid Medani is a doctoral student in the Department of Political Science at the University of California, Berkeley.

Timothy Mitchell teaches political science at New York University and is a contributing editor of *Middle East Report.*

Salim Nasr is the director of the Ford Foundation's office in Cairo.

Shaikh Hamid al-Nayfar (generally rendered Enneifer in the French press) is a leading figure in Tunisia's Islamist movement. He was interviewed by *François Burgat*, a researcher at the Centre de Recherches et d'Etudes sur les Sociétés Méditerranéennes.

Karen Pfeifer teaches economics at Smith College and is a contributing editor of *Middle East Report*. Research for her chapter was assisted by a grant from the Joint Committee on the Near and Middle East of the Social Science Research Council and the American Council of Learned Societies with funds provided by the National Endowment for the Humanities and the Ford Foundation.

Tal'at Fu'ad Qasim is a spokesperson for the Egyptian Gama'a Islamiyya. He was interviewed by *Hisham Mubarak,* former director of the Egyptian Organization for Human Rights and currently director of the Center for Human Rights Legal Aid in Cairo.

Yahya Sadowski is a senior fellow at the Brookings Institution in Washington, D.C., an editor of *Middle East Report,* and author of *Political Vegetables? Businessman and Bureaucrat in the Development of Egyptian Agriculture* (Brookings, 1991).

Susan Slyomovics teaches comparative literature at Brown University and is an editor of *Middle East Report.*

Joe Stork is a founder of the Middle East Research and Information Project and was Editor of *Middle East Report* for its first twenty-five years.

Ted Swedenburg teaches anthropology at the American University in Cairo and is the author of *Memories of Revolt: The 1936–1939 Rebellion and the Palestinian National Past* (University of Minnesota Press, 1996).

Graham Usher is a journalist working in occupied Palestine and the author of *Palestine in Crisis: The Struggle for Peace and Political Independence after Oslo* (Pluto Press, 1995).

Meriem Vergès lives in Paris and is completing a doctoral thesis on the urban transformations of contemporary Algeria.

Robert Vitalis teaches government and international relations at Clark University and is an editor of *Middle East Report.*

Carrie Rosefsky Wickham is assistant professor of political science at Emory University. She researches the dynamics of political opposition in authoritarian regimes, and her doctoral dissertation examines the causes and consequences of Islamic mobilization in Egypt.

Ergin Yıldızoğlu lives in London and co-edits a monthly newsletter on Turkey.

Sami Zubaida teaches sociology at Birkbeck College, University of London, and is a contributing editor of *Middle East Report.*

INDEX

Text: 10/12 Baskerville
Display: Baskerville
Composition: Braun-Brumfield
Printing and binding: Braun-Brumfield